MODERN WARFARE IN SPAIN

RELATED TITLES FROM POTOMAC BOOKS

Franco: Soldier, Commander, Dictator
by Geoffrey Jensen

MODERN WARFARE IN SPAIN

AMERICAN MILITARY OBSERVATIONS ON THE SPANISH CIVIL WAR, 1936–1939

JAMES W. CORTADA

Potomac Books
Washington, D.C.

Library of Congress Cataloging-in-Publication Data
Modern warfare in Spain : American military observations on the Spanish Civil War, 1936–1939 / James W. Cortada.
    p. cm.
Collection of dispatches by US Army and Navy officers, primarily written by Stephen O. Fuqua.
  Includes bibliographical references and index.
  ISBN 978-1-59797-556-8 (hardcover)
  ISBN 978-1-61234-101-9 (electronic edition)
  1. Spain—History—Civil War, 1936–1939—Campaigns—Sources. 2.
Spain—History—Civil War, 1936–1939—Diplomatic history—Sources. 3.
Fuqua, Stephen Ogden, 1874–1943. I. Cortada, James W. II. Fuqua, Stephen Ogden, 1874–1943. III. Title: American military observations on the Spanish Civil War, 1936–1939.
  DP269.M29 2011
  946.081'4—dc23
                                                  2011023381

Printed in the United States of America on acid-free paper that meets the American National Standards Institute Z39-48 Standard.

Potomac Books
22841 Quicksilver Drive
Dulles, Virginia 20166

First Edition

10 9 8 7 6 5 4 3 2 1

To colonel, professor, friend
Raymond Proctor

CONTENTS

MAPS

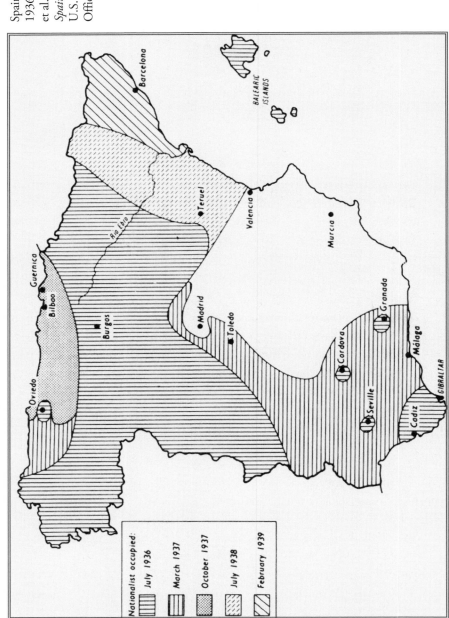

Spain, Spanish Civil War, 1936–39. [Eugene K. Keefe et al., *Area Handbook for Spain* (Washington, D.C.: U.S. Government Printing Office, 1976).]

PREFACE

"This war, which lasted for 989 days, has been one of the longest, bloodiest, costliest and most brutal internecine struggles of modern history."

Lt. Col. Henry B. Cheadle, USA,
American Military Attaché,
April 3, 1939

This book presents a selection of military reports prepared by American Army and Navy officers observing the Spanish Civil War of 1936–39. This event in modern European history, as the epigraph above (written by an eyewitness) describes, proved central to the history of modern Spain. The body of material reproduced here represents one of the most important new collections of non-Spanish contemporary military papers on the civil war to appear in recent years. These reports (both those published in this book and those not selected for inclusion) constitute a massive, thorough, and relatively accurate history of the military aspects of this important twentieth-century European conflict. Put in blunter terms, the collection of American military dispatches is the most comprehensive, professionally precise documentation on the military aspects of the war available in English. The only comparable collection of materials are Spanish military records themselves and a number of books published during the 1970s and 1980s by the Servicio Histórico Militar that was based in part on archival materials. What makes this book so significant is its broad coverage. Career officers, most with experience in other wars (especially World War I), commented on campaigns, leadership, command, matériel, personnel, discipline, equipment, weapons, personalities, effects on civilians, and geography, always with analysis written by professional military observers for military audiences. As a collection, it nearly outstrips all other military memoirs and commentaries written at the time of the conflict. In short, it constitutes a de facto military history of the most important European war to take place between World Wars I and II.

Readers interested in general modern military tactics and technology of the interwar period will also find this collection of papers a major new addition to the literature. First, the documents provide definitive evidence that all the major European and American military establishments considered the Spanish Civil War the single most significant military event since the end of World War I. This realization, which became unequivocal after the important Battle of Madrid in November 1936, drew the attention of military analysts like no other war prior to World War II and since the American Civil War of the 1860s. They clearly and quickly recognized that it was a proving ground for new equipment and tactics, particularly the role of aircraft and aerial bombardment, and the use of tanks—two classes of technologies experiencing rapid innovation in the 1930s. Second, for those keen on measuring the effectiveness of a wide range of military organizations and practices, this conflict unearthed a great deal about the role, activities, and thinking of Spanish, Russian, German, Italian, French, and to a lesser extent, proletarian/militia-like units, and adds to our understanding of the intentions of Great Britain, France, Germany, Italy, the Soviet Union, the United States, and Portugal. If one were searching for a "smoking gun" for the significance to armies in the Western world energizing contemporary interest in this conflict, these papers provide it. War Departments on both sides of the Atlantic stationed observers on the ground who reported frequently and in considerable detail the results of personal observations and interviews with the combatants themselves. As a collection, these reports provide evidence of the intensity of interest displayed by military communities in many countries and make clear to historians the breadth of this interest. In fact, these papers offer much insight into all manner of military affairs relevant to many nations, not only to events in Spain.

In reading these documents it becomes quite clear that by December 1936—a mere five months after the outbreak of the civil war—it seemed every military attaché in Europe was attempting to study the conflict and report on its results in detail to their respective War Departments. In the case of the Americans, for example, dispatches came regularly into Washington, D.C., written by Army and Navy officers stationed in Spain, Germany, Britain, and France. Their superiors in various military agencies, initially within the military intelligence communities (e.g., G-2) and later at senior military levels, wanted even more information than they were receiving and sometimes chastised officers in Spain for not reporting more rapidly on major battles. Many of the documents published in this book circulated widely within military communities in and outside the United States. Findings were rapidly transferred to training programs, such as those for mid-career and senior U.S. Army officers at Fort Leavenworth, Kansas, by late 1937. The same occurred at the U.S. Military Academy at West Point, New York, and at British, French, and German training centers.

Already aware that Europe might be headed toward a future conflict, in the 1930s officers demonstrated a growing sense of urgency and anxiety to learn about the effectiveness of everything military, from bullets and food to tactics, strategies, and rapidly transforming technologies. Lessons were quickly drawn and applied. For instance, the French modified the design of their tanks based on information about how Russian tanks performed in Spain in the early months of the war. The Germans and Soviets were already transforming their military aircraft when the war began; they now applied lessons learned to that effort as well.

But the greatest lessons these reports teach us concern twentieth-century Spanish history and most specifically the Spanish Civil War. We are approaching the seventy-fifth anniversary of the start of this conflict, and it appears that interest in the war has hardly waned over the decades. In Spain alone, the volume of publications that appear annually has actually gone up since 1996, reflecting an impressive revival of interest in the war. Yet each year since the start of the conflict there has been a continuous flow of publications; the best we can guess is that there are now more than 60,000 titles, and I personally believe that number may be low. With archival collections now widely available to historians in Spain and around the world, one can expect to see a continuing flow of new publications far into the future, mimicking what occurred with the American Civil War of the mid-nineteenth century and, of course, with the two world wars of the twentieth.

Military history of the Spanish Civil War, while always voluminous, matured as historians began writing more thorough histories of battles in the 1980s and biographies in the 1990s and, most recently, integrating these into synthetic histories of the war as a whole. In short, we have a qualitatively better understanding of military events today than we did even in 1996. Even now, the dispatches published in this book add a rich layer of detail to that body of knowledge, and most important, it occurs in three fundamental ways: First, they provide a level of detail of the activities in battles and campaigns not normally discussed by historians, such as the configuration of trenches, specific features of ammunition, and even

of small arms. Second, the mundane—important to military officers and not necessarily to historians—gets its due, such as the kind of underwear worn by members of the International Brigades (blue wool). Third, we are exposed to a level of
military analysis of strategy and implications of political and military events that
could only be provided by a professional soldier and, in the case of these American
reports, by some officers far more senior than the normal mid-career professionals
who usually serve as military attachés—a theme we will have more to say about
later on, as it is a unique feature of this collection of papers. Additionally, these
observers provide discussions of things readers would expect to see: descriptions of
people, life in such cities as Madrid and Valencia, and a considerable amount of
discussion about trains and roads in Spain in the 1930s. Interviews with soldiers,
officers, and high-ranking political leaders bring us closer to the lifestyles and re-
alities of the participants of the war, augmenting a continuously growing body of
such publications, most notably memoirs, that appeared in the years following the
death of Gen. Francisco Franco in the mid-1970s.

HOW THE REPORTS ARE ORGANIZED

The materials are organized in essentially chronological order as they were written,
with some bunching up in quantity around short periods of time, often reflecting
a spike in activity in Spain, such as the occurrence of a major battle or a rise in
interest in some topic, as occurred at the end of 1936 with aerial military tactics,
strategies, and technologies. There were periodic increases in the number of publications as interest in the International Brigades and militias rose, particularly with
respect to the latter when they were very disorganized and undisciplined (1936)
and later when they had hardened into tough combat veterans (1938). Com-
mentary about the International Brigades is continuous, and despite the numerous publications about them that have appeared over the past half-century, these
dispatches offer new and important details, including summaries and assessments
of interviews with specific members of these units and their commanders, by an
American officer with considerable personal command experience.

    This collection includes reports from multiple individuals. American mili-
tary attachés, like their counterparts in other countries, were career officers. Invariably they were captain-grade to full colonels, which ensured the proper technical
background and experience to judge the particulars of war. Many were graduates
of West Point and had combat experience, acquired mainly during World War I
but sometimes going as far back as the Spanish-American War. Thus, multiple
views from a cadre of skilled observers, all adhering to a common reporting format

(specified by the U.S. War Department), provides a diverse yet thorough view of an important chapter in modern military history.

The body of material from which these reports were drawn consists of several collections. The most important one, and from which I drew the most for this book, concerned military operations in Spain. The most unique accounts are the dispatches of the military attaché Col. Stephen O. Fuqua, about whom I have more to say later. He would customarily produce a narrative of recent military events on about a two-week schedule, and these reports were the core of his contribution. These documents were supplemented with other dispatches describing his visits to military fronts and armies. He also wrote on specific topics, usually at the request of the War Department, on myriad themes ranging from strategy, military organization, combined use of infantry and tanks, logistics, and command leadership. He had more junior staff highly experienced in aircraft to discuss aerial technologies, events, and strategies. He was amazed and appalled at the sloppy organization and discipline of the Republican militias and, in the early months, of the International Brigades, although his views of both changed over time. He found the Nationalists to be a more professionally managed military machine, highly respected the Russian and German contingents, and found much to fault among the Italian forces, particularly as a result of their poor performance in executing the Battle of Guadalajara. War Department officials wanted to know about aerial tactics in considerable detail and about the effectiveness of various weapons and the dynamics of infantry and tanks fighting together. Morale was a popular topic as well. Officials in Washington, D.C., seemed to have an insatiable appetite for information comparing the aircraft and weapons systems from various countries. Many of the reports coming out of the military community focused on comparisons between specific aircraft and weapons. On average, between Fuqua and others working with him, the U.S. War Department would receive a dispatch of some sort every two to three days and almost daily a telegraph transmitted through the U.S. State Department, either from the American Embassy in Valencia or from other diplomatic posts, usually in France.[1]

Other files tapped for this book include reports from other embassies in Europe written by officers and sent to the U.S. War Department to round out the picture of military events in Spain. These include reports originating from attachés in London, Paris, Berlin, Moscow, and Italy, all similar to the materials generated by Americans in Spain. The intelligence division within the War Department received and analyzed the material, summarizing its content for the most senior military and civilian officials in the department. Whenever a major event was going on in Spain, summary reports, such as details of major battles, would go to the chief of staff.

The files include many drawn or typed maps of campaigns, battles, and military positions. On rare occasions the observers included photographs in their reports. Maps are very important to soldiers, and those in Spain in the 1930s were no exception. Fuqua in particular proved very precise in describing exactly on which roads various battle lines were, distances between military units, and the condition of the roads. An informative illustration of that focus was his description of the roads at the Battle of Guadalajara, which in part, once understood, makes much clearer why the disaster for the Italians proved so great. Fuqua relied largely on Michelin road maps published in the prewar period to orient himself and his readers on specific positions. I consulted a Michelin road map from the period to validate the spelling of names of villages and roads, and it was clear to me that it was the source of many of his precise descriptions of locations. He found commercially available maps quite accurate in comparison to those he obtained from the Spanish War Ministry, some of which he sent on to the War Department. His choice of civilian maps proved fortuitous, as Michelin's were some of the best available in Europe in the 1930s. And they were relatively current, an important feature with respect to Spain because many new roads had been built, upgraded, or otherwise changed in the 1920s and early 1930s.

Not included in this book is an equally voluminous collection of papers concerning economic and political activities in Spain. Most of these were written by American diplomats, with many of the files dating back to the 1880s, but they were rarely written by military observers. These are of value for understanding Spanish economic history but have hardly been examined by historians.

The papers reproduced here are clustered together into chapters that approximate traditional historical divisions commonly applied to the military phases of the war. That structure should help historians who might be interested in a particular period of the war, while the index provides thematic and factual pointers that cut across chapters. Thus, one chapter is devoted predominantly to the fighting around Madrid in the fall of 1936, while another focuses on the conquest of Catalonia and the collapse of the Central Zone and Madrid in 1939. It was customary at the time for documents prepared in Washington to begin with the date but no city, while reports written in the field cited the city where written, a report number, and the date following the signature. I have moved the city, document number, and date to the start of each document to make it easier for the reader to know when and where it was written. Not all reports were reprinted, although when published, they were usually published in full. When I chose to omit content from a report, I indicated it with an editorial note. Very few attachments are reproduced, since they did not add materially to our appreciation of the events described. Often they were hand-drawn maps, copies of local publications, and newspaper clippings. While many technical discussions about weapons, for instance, are presented from the period 1936–37, fewer are reprinted from the second half of the war because they add little to the story, often reconfirming information learned earlier, either from the same writer or another observer. However, reports on weapons systems used in Spain continued to come into the War Department from around Europe after the end of the Spanish Civil War in April 1939, and they do not end until the start of World War II in September of that year.

I left grammar and sentence construction as originally written, although I silently corrected the rare typographical or spelling error. All names of people and places were checked for accuracy of spelling. When a person's last name only was presented by a writer I tried, where possible, to include in brackets his first name the first time he is mentioned in the book. Sometimes I had to guess at a name because while Fuqua, in particular, was a meticulous writer and observer, he could have used newer typewriter ribbons, as some pages were not very legible. If he signed a document, I did not include his name at the end of the document to save space, so the reader can safely rely on the fact that a document without a name was written by Fuqua. With all other documents, I included the name of the author at the end of the report.

All of this leads to the larger question of what was included in this book. The fundamental criterion for inclusion was whether a document added to our knowledge about military aspects of the civil war. With a growing number of monographs and a few general military histories of the conflict available to historians (mainly in Spanish) and interested readers, we did not need to duplicate those materials. However, it should be noted that one could write a very complete and accurate military history of the civil war just relying on the unpublished records of the U.S. military community, because they are that thorough, accurate, and useful. The combined mass of material hovers at about four thousand pages, or perhaps a bit more, as I am not confident I found everything, such as lecture notes from West Point. From the body of War Department and attaché records, I organized about 2,000 pages, then reduced that to about 850 typed pages of text. I then sought out the help of two experts on the Spanish Civil War—Professors Raymond Proctor and Stanley Payne—to help me whittle the collection down further, this time to select only the best of the material as defined as valuable to historians, casting aside material that, while providing new facts and insights, just would have made this book too long. My objectives were to produce a book that provided important new insights about this war, told a good story, read well, and reflected the nature of the material available in the files, all of which are located at the U.S. National Archives and Records Administration in Washington, D.C. For the researcher writing about the military history of Spain of the 1930s, that individual should still consult the original files, as they are vast.

Most of these documents compose a file entitled "Correspondence of the Military Intelligence Division." Many can also be found on twelve reels of microfilm prepared by the archives covering the period 1918–41. Officially, these papers are part of RG 165, Records of the War Department General and Special Staffs. Copies of some reports can also be found in the U.S. Embassy files that make up the formal diplomatic records of the State Department for the period, also housed at the U.S. National Archives and organized by country. The military papers in this book remained classified "restricted" until the early 1980s, when some were declassified and turned over to the archives by the Department of Defense. The bulk of the material, however, was not declassified until 1986 and was not made available until 1988. I began working with these documents in 1990.

Biographical information about the authors of these papers is not included in that set of records and thus had to be uncovered from other varied sources, such as personnel records of the U.S. Department of Defense. In the case of Colonel Fuqua, I reached out to his family.

WHAT THE REPORTS TEACH US

The first thing that seems so obvious is the reports offer such a large volume of details on so many aspects of the civil war. The volume and their content suggest that the interest in the civil war held by military authorities in Europe and in the United States exceeded what historians might otherwise have thought. The requests for information on the conflict, as documented in the form of letters from various levels of the military establishment, indicate that the topic caught the attention of a wide range of officials, from battalion to corps commanders, from the various military schools and colleges within the U.S. Army, and from other government agencies, all testimony to this interest. The daily telegrams sent by the military attaché made the rounds of high government circles (most of which were located in the same building, today the executive branch offices located next to the White House, and at the U.S. Navy Department). Periodically, various military personnel stated that the Spanish Civil War was the most significant land war since World War I.

The material is particularly rich about events and circumstances on the Republican side because the military observers were part of the diplomatic staff that represented the United States to the Republic. The United States did not have diplomatic relations with Franco's side until after the conclusion of the civil war. Viewed through the trained eyes of military experts, normally quite unbiased in their views toward the two warring sides, we are given specific details in particular about Republican military units. Often they are compared to practices widely understood in French, British, and American armies of the period, or of World War I. That kind of perspective made it possible to compare, for instance, the use of trenches and trench warfare tactics in this conflict versus those of World War I. The relative contribution of various types of military organizations (divisions, battalions, corps, regular army, legionnaires, militia, and International Brigades) were discussed in more organized detail than is available in the memoir literature or in many military histories. The Americans were amazed at the variety of military organizations and modes of operation on the Republican side, and they were not shy about discussing that plethora of organizations. In many ways these discussions surpass even Spanish accounts, often written by participants with obvious biases. While the material on the Nationalist armies is far less voluminous when compared to that on the Republicans, it teaches us a great deal more about Franco's military strategy and talents than is available from many biographies of key leaders, almost all of which were written by civilians (often reporters) or panegyric biographers. Franco emerges from these American documents as a brilliant military leader, capable of making mistakes but also of recovering well, blending political and military requirements into plans that worked.

Republican senior officers are often presented in a more favorable light than historians have generally done, but below the rank of colonel, Fuqua and his colleagues were harsh critics of the sloppiness, poor training, lack of discipline, and weak command and control they found in various Republican forces. In short, the reports point out that the better-run and better-equipped armies usually won. What is impressive, however, is how much matériel the Republicans had, correcting an impression built up over a half century by pro-Republican writers that the Republic was starved for ammunition and weapons. When the Republicans were overrun in each major campaign (with the exception of Guadalajara), the Nationalists acquired massive quantities of weapons and supplies, reflecting virtually every form of weapon and matériel in use in Europe (and even American supplies) available in the world, some of it dating back to the Boer War and the Spanish-American War.

The Americans obviously had more access to the Republican military than to the Nationalists. In the case of Fuqua, the Spanish War Ministry had granted him a pass that would allow him to cross all lines and called on senior military officials to pay attention to him. In part, this was because of his diligence in cultivating access and sources and because of his distinguished military career prior to coming to Spain. He was able to meet soldiers and talk frequently with officers in the field and with military officials in the Spanish War Ministry, including its top leadership. Some of his reports are memorable because of his access, such as his account of the American volunteers serving on the Republican side. The same access existed for others who would serve under his authority at the embassy during the war. American military observers in other countries always had more access to the Germans, some of whom had served in Spain on the Nationalist side, providing additional primary data on Nationalist activities.

Those who read these military papers will learn more about why particular military activities took place, such as orders of battle for an offensive. In fact, the analysis for why things were done and their military consequences are probably explained with greater clarity in these pages in general than by just consulting most any other source. Even published military histories often are not as clear. One would find it difficult to underestimate the value of the analysis of these reports. Yet, curiously, the papers provide very little biographical data, other than passing comments on the appearance and personalities of military figures, with the possible exception of the American commands of the Lincoln and Washington Battalions. On the other hand, we are provided with a considerable amount of detail about the daily living conditions and activities of soldiers and officers on both sides and within types of units, such as militia versus regular army, International Brigades versus artillery, and so forth. Naval activities in the war proved minor and probably accounts for the paucity of material on the subject in these dispatches. Nonetheless, naval engagements, weaponry, and command and control functions are described.

Since the observers often were called upon to make judgments about fast-moving events, it is impressive how sound they were frequently in light of what we know today. Fuqua, for example, usually a cautious reporter of events and reluctant to predict outcomes, carefully described options and scenarios and why one versus another might be adopted and, when he voted, proved invariably correct. Descriptions of activities, such as battles in progress, were overwhelmingly accurate when compared to what historians learned long after the events. In large part this accuracy stemmed from his impulse to obtain verifiable facts before presenting events as actual occurrences. The absolutely best case in this book is his continuous treatment of the Battle of Guadalajara and to a similar extent his accounts of the Belchite campaign. One must admire the remarkable accuracy of the information he presented when viewed over the span of nearly seventy-five years. A few errors here and there can be forgiven. For example, we are led to believe that about 1.5 million Spaniards died in this war; historians continued to overstate the number of casualties for decades yet gradually lowered the number over many years to today's consensus that casualties were probably closer to half that number. In the scheme of things, it is a minor issue for the historian wishing to use these American papers, because what it says is how available information was and, through the eyes of a trained military professional, how one could size up accurately a fast-moving situation like a battle or campaign, or sense how some event might turn out given the nature of the military forces and institutions in play at any moment. The Americans typically reported correctly the numerical size of the various forces on both sides. Land battles fought with between 50,000 and 150,000 soldiers on either side were impressive by any standard, but they also presented difficulties for those reporting because of the possibilities of not including all the military units in a count. The attention to detail displayed by the American military accounted for much of the high accuracy in their data; they even would report how many rounds of ammunition were spent, the number and weight of bombs dropped, and examined artillery logs to count how many shells were used. Getting accurate figures on the number of casualties for either side always proved challenging, however. Official data was obfuscated with propaganda, leading officials to minimize their own losses and to exaggerate those of the enemy. So the American data was not always as informative on these matters, although these officers knew what was going on and took pains to explain when their views on any matter deviated from what propaganda or the press (Spanish, American, and European) reported. That attention to explaining differences is quite useful.

We know who won the war, but that fact does not take away from the excitement and anticipation of the narrative. We read about campaigns as they are unfolding, not fully certain how they will turn out until the next dispatch or telegram. By presenting the material in roughly the order in which it was written and sent to Washington, D.C., it is possible to sense the anticipation that must have existed in military circles on both sides of the Atlantic when, for example, a major campaign was under way and a battle was raging. It also becomes obvious that military attachés in other countries attempted to "get in on the act" of reporting on the most central military event of the period. In some cases, particularly with the attaché in London, the most trivial of information on the conflict was not too minor to deny sending to Washington, touting these as more important than they often were. Cohorts in Paris, also eager to be part of the focus on Spain, however, sent back more useful, if different, analyses that relied effectively on substantive French perspectives. As one would reasonably expect, the French military establishment spent an extraordinary amount of time and energy tracking Spanish events and participating in the deployment of some matériel and various participants in the conflict. The American Embassy in Paris did an effective job of tracking many of these activities and reporting on French-acquired data and perspectives.

SPECIAL ROLE OF COL. STEPHEN O. FUQUA

In addition to the value of these papers, made possible by the sheer volume of material and information they provided, was the special role played by the various American military attachés in Spain, a fortuitous circumstance for both the U.S. War Department and now for historians of the conflict. These individuals, then as now, were career officers, usually from the mid-career ranks and drawn from the army and navy. The ranks usually varied from lieutenants to full colonels, with most in the range of majors and lieutenant colonels, which ensured the proper technical background and experience needed to judge the particulars of war and a broad range of military affairs, while establishing relations with the military establishment in their assigned countries. In the 1930s many of the army attachés were graduates of West Point, the naval officers from the U.S. Naval Academy at Annapolis, Maryland. Those of the 1920s and 1930s often also had combat experience gained during World War I. Thus, multiple views gained from a cadre of skilled observers, all adhering to common reporting practices, provided the American government, and later historians, an uncommon yet thorough view of a very important chapter in modern military history.

Military historians of the civil war were blessed by a coincidence of circumstances and talents that made it possible to have what must in hindsight appear as an ideal observer of the conflict operating in Spain. Throughout the war, the central military reporter for the U.S. government was Stephen O. Fuqua, who brought to the assignment nearly forty years of experience, ranging from combat in three wars to senior military staff assignments. His skills were further enhanced by the fact that he came to Spain in 1933 and thus established his lines of communications in the Spanish military community well before the start of the conflict. By living in Spain for several years before 1936, he gained a great deal of situational awareness of the politics and culture of the country in its run-up to war. That this background proved effective became obvious as he was able to report quickly and authoritatively about the rebellion literally from its earliest hours.

Fuqua was born in Baton Rouge, Louisiana, on Christmas Day 1874, the youngest of eleven children of a Confederate Army colonel who died in early 1875. His eldest brother and mother raised him. Stephen (called Steve by his friends) entered West Point in 1893 but left after one year, completing his studies at Louisiana State University. On July 8, 1898, he was mustered into the Second U.S. Volunteer Infantry as a captain and served in the Spanish-American War in Cuba. In addition to combat in Cuba, he fought in the Philippines in 1901. In that same year he received a commission as second lieutenant in the regular army. In the years before World War I he served twice again in the Philippines (1905 and 1908) and in various posts in the United States. At the start of World War I he held the temporary rank of major, having spent the previous years in assignments involving infantry and taken courses at the Infantry and Cavalry School (Fort Leavenworth, Kansas) and at the Staff College. He went to France in World War I as assistant and acting chief of staff, Twenty-eighth Infantry Division; participated in the Aisne-Marne, Somme, St. Mihiel, and Meuse-Argonne offensives; and became chief of staff, First Division, during its march into Germany.

After the war Colonel Fuqua held a number of assignments, including the chief of staff responsible for intelligence activities for the Third Corps. In 1929 he was appointed chief of infantry at the rank of major general, serving in that capacity for four years (as prescribed by law). Instead of retiring, as would have been the custom after such an assignment, he wanted to continue serving and thus was assigned to Madrid as the military attaché, reverting to his previous rank to his chief of infantry assignment, or colonel. He served in his new capacity in Spain until his mandatory retirement at age sixty-four in late 1938. However, he remained in Spain as a civilian helping his replacement report on the war. Therefore, his coverage of the civil war remained uninterrupted.

In July 1939, some three months after the cessation of hostilities, Fuqua returned to the United States with his daughter and wife (who had lived in Biarritz, France, during the civil war). His son, also named Stephen O. Fuqua, had graduated from West Point in 1933 and went on to a distinguished career that culminated with the rank of brigadier general. His father, whom we should refer to as General Fuqua, since it was the custom to address an officer by the highest rank he attained, became *Newsweek* magazine's military adviser at the outbreak of World War II, in part because of his reporting reputation gained in Spain, and he wrote a weekly column for the magazine until his death from a heart attack on May 11, 1943. During his military career, the senior Fuqua was recognized for his accomplishments with the Distinguished Service Medal, the Cross of the French Legion of Honor (Chevalier), and the French Croix de Guerre.

Thus, he brought to the Spanish period an enormous range of experience, particularly at many levels of infantry and command, which he applied to his judgment of affairs in the civil war. His various assignments with military intelligence organizations ensured that he knew what to focus on and how to present findings to the War Department. He proved to be a thorough, well-organized individual, known to his friends early in his career as "System Steve." He demonstrated objectivity and was a true product of the military system. Short, slightly stocky, even looking like a Spaniard, he commanded the respect of Spanish officers who also knew of his prior military record. He was allowed more access to Republican forces, for example, than any other nation's military attachés, so much so, as demonstrated by the historical record, that others came to him for information.

The American ambassador to Spain Claude G. Bowers thought of him as precise and meticulous. The Associated Press's American journalist in Spain, who had arrived there at about the same time as Fuqua and left the same year, H. Edward Knoblaugh, knew him well and left us a description in his account of the civil war. He wrote that Fuqua was "beloved by Spaniards and Americans alike for his fearlessness and cool-headedness, his energy and organization ability, and his Louisiana chivalry."[2] In the waning days of the civil war, as the time came to consider evacuating Americans, Knoblaugh commented that "although Secretary Eric Wendelin was acting chargé, it was Col. Fuqua's seasoned experience as a veteran of many wars which was principally responsible for the smooth running of the embassy during those nerve-wracking days before it was officially closed."[3] He commented further, "His military judgment, coupled with an utter indifference to danger in almost daily trips to the front, has enabled the American War Department to receive more reliable, first-hand information on the war than many other governments having military representatives on the scene."[4]

Fuqua personally admired the military forces of the Nationalists more than those of the Republicans, primarily because Franco and his generals were better military leaders and had developed a superior army to that of the Republic. He reported on as many aspects of both sides as he could, although the preponderance of material about the Republicans is obvious. While Fuqua had cultivated a circle of military officers he talked to regularly, he also read communiqués from both sides, reported on radio broadcasts from each, and visited every major front of the war. On two occasions he got so close that he was fired upon by National-ist soldiers who thought he was a Republican. Although not fluent in Spanish, he acquired enough skill and had access to U.S. Embassy personnel to ensure that his Spanish documents were translated in a timely and accurate fashion. During the civil war itself, he drafted personally some two thousand pages of typed mate-rial and sent at least an equal amount of additional documents back to Washing-ton, D.C.

Because aviation quickly became an obvious technology that would require detailed investigation, he had an Army Air Corps captain sent to Spain to work for him. Townsend E. Griffiss (1900–42), a 1922 graduate of West Point, spent his entire career flying, except for the period he served in Spain. Captain Griffiss came to Spain in the fall of 1936 and served as an assistant military attaché un-til July 1938, when he transferred to Paris to assume the same responsibilities. While in Spain he wrote very detailed descriptions of all aircraft and bombs used and about their tactics and strategy, and he collected details on every significant and many hundreds of minor aerial military events. His reports alone could fill a book. Lieutenant Colonel Griffiss had the unfortunate distinction of being the first American airman to die in the line of duty in Europe during World War II, when the Royal Air Force shot him down on February 15, 1942, thinking his was an enemy aircraft.

Fuqua's replacement as military attaché was Henry Barlow Cheadle. Born on May 1, 1891, in Cannon Falls, Minnesota, he graduated from West Point in 1913. He, too, grew up in infantry, serving in Gen. John J. "Blackjack" Pershing's Mexi-can campaign in 1914 and in France during World War I. During the 1920s he was an infantry battalion commander and also served in the Military Intelligence Division. In October 1938, at the rank of lieutenant colonel, he became assis-tant military attaché in Budapest, then subsequently Fuqua's replacement. During World War II he held various infantry assignments and served in North Africa and Europe. He was the first American regimental commander made a general officer in World War II on the field. Considered a highly trained and skilled military offi-cer, Cheadle retired a few years after World War II and died on December 16, 1959.

While the documents presented in this book are important, they represent only a fraction of a large body of materials that cover modern warfare in Spain.

ACKNOWLEDGMENTS

What might on the surface appear to be a relatively easy project to execute—just copy interesting papers essentially already in the correct order—turned out to require the help of many people over twenty years. The biggest debt of gratitude goes to the late Gen. Stephen O. Fuqua Jr., who encouraged me, provided biographical material on his father, and made photographs of him available for this project. He made our military attaché far more human than the historical record might have suggested. John Taylor at the Military Branch, National Archives, introduced me to the documents and taught me how to find information in various U.S. military records. The staff at the Center for Military History, part of the U.S. Defense Department, made available to me official biographies of the key military observers. In particular, Hannah M. Zeidlke proved responsive and effective. The Still Picture Branch at the National Archives helped with illustrations.

But more than simply collecting and publishing a large collection of material was the real issue of determining which material to include in the book, and for that I turned for help to two historians. The late professor Raymond Proctor, who taught Spanish history at the University of Idaho, was of particular help. First, before becoming an academic, he had been a career officer in the U.S. Air Force and had served in Spain in the 1950s, and thus he knew what military attachés did for a living. He was familiar with the tactics and weapons of the civil war period, having served as a pilot during World War II and later befriending many Spanish Army and Air Force officers. Second, he had the experience of a historian, complete with a PhD in European history, and had written two major books on Spanish military history of the 1930s and 1940s. His history of the Condor Legion led him to learn more about the military aspects of the Spanish Civil War than most historians knew; in short, he was the perfect blend of the practitioner and scholar. He critiqued the material in this book, conducted research into possible Spanish military sources on the American observers, and most important, helped me understand the accuracy and significance of this material.

The second historian who helped was Professor Stanley G. Payne of the University of Wisconsin. Considered the dean of historians of modern Spanish history, he used his considerable knowledge of the Spanish Civil War, gained through decades of research, to help me select those documents that contributed most to my understanding of both the military and general history of this war. His aid was essential at that stage where I wanted to move from an 890-page collection of material to a manuscript that needed to be half that size. Additionally, Professor Payne gave me sound advice on how the material should be organized and what should be discussed in the introductions for each chapter. In short, as with Professor Proctor, I owe him a deep debt of gratitude for his wisdom, support, and time.

The fact that this project took a long time had nothing to do with those who helped me; all were prompt. Other projects kept intruding over the years, forcing me to set this one aside and work on it piecemeal. If nothing else, it is a small piece of evidence that if one perseveres long enough, eventually a book can be completed. Meanwhile, interest in the military history of the civil war grew, along with the broader attraction of all aspects of this important conflict. As we approach the seventy-fifth anniversary of the start of this conflict, I continue to be amazed and delighted at how interest in the topic remains vibrant and, for many people, a passionate theme in modern history.

Finally, I want to acknowledge the good work of my publisher, Potomac Books, Inc., and in particular Elizabeth Sherburn Demers, who demonstrated so much interest and faith in the project. Additionally, my hat goes off to the production team for designing and putting together all the pieces that went into making this book.

I also owe a deep debt of gratitude to Professor Joan Maria Thomàs, of the Universitat Rovira i Virgili, for his detailed advice and help.

SELECTED CHRONOLOGY

of Military Events of the Spanish Civil War,
1936–39

The purpose of this chronology is to help the reader keep in
mind various events as they read the military dispatches.[1]

1936

February–July	Civil and political unrest erupts in various parts of Spain
July 17	Military garrison in Morocco rises against the Republic
July 18	General Franco issues manifesto justifying the rebellion
July 30	Nationalists occupy Seville
August 12	First members of the International Brigades arrive in Barcelona
September	Republican army lays siege to the Alcazar and Nationalist forces in Toledo but is repulsed
November	Fighting in and around Madrid intensifies as Nationalists seek to occupy the city

1937

January 13	Nationalists begin campaign against Malaga
February 7	Malaga falls to the Nationalists
February	Jarama campaign begins
February 28	Battle of Jarama ends; Abraham Lincoln Brigades is in its first combat
March	Battle of Guadalajara ends
April 20	Nationalists invade Basque territory
April 26	Town of Guernica bombed by German aircraft working for the Nationalists
May 8	Uprising in Barcelona quelled

May 29	German cruiser *Deutschland* attacked by Republican aircraft, triggering international incident
June 19	Nationalists occupy Bilbao
July 6	Republican offensive at Brunete commences
July 26	Battle of Brunete ends with Republican offensive stopped by Nationalists
August 22	Republicans begin offensive in Aragon
September 6	Republicans capture Belchite
October 19–21	Nationalists complete occupation of Gijon and Aviles in Asturias
October 31	Republican government moves from Valencia to Barcelona
December 15	Republicans begin Teruel offensive to block Nationalist advance on Madrid
December 24	Nationalist counteroffensive at Teruel begins

1938

February 22	Nationalists reoccupy Teruel
April 15	Nationalists reach the Mediterranean Sea, splitting Republican zones
July 25	Republicans launch what came to be known as the Second Battle of Ebro, which becomes the largest military campaign of the war
November 16	Battle of Ebro ends with Nationalists regaining territory initially lost to the Republicans in July
December 23	Nationalists begin their final invasion of Catalonia

1939

January 22	Nationalist troops penetrate Barcelona
January 26	Nationalist forces occupy Barcelona
February 10	Nationalists declare that they control all of Catalonia
March 5	National Defense Council created to negotiate peace with Nationalists
March 7	Communists rebel in Madrid against National Defense Council
March 28	Nationalists occupy Madrid
March 29	Nationalists occupy Cuenca, Ciudad Real, Jaen, and Albacete
March 30	Valencia and Alicante surrender to the Nationalists
March 31	Other Republican-held territories surrender to the Nationalists
April 1	Franco announces, "The war has ended." The United States recognizes the Nationalist government

1

Start of the Rebellion
(July–September 1936)

"The main forces of the opposing sides are now at grips with each other and operations of a decisive nature and of real military interest may be expected."

Col. F. N. Lincoln,
September 14, 1936[1]

While military officers in Europe and in the United States watched the buildup of military affairs in Europe in the 1930s, almost all were caught by surprise at the outbreak of the Spanish Civil War in July 1936, despite prior eruptions of civil unrest in the country in the early 1930s and growing despondency on the part of the Spanish officer class with how the Second Republic was treating it. Nonetheless, when war broke out, as often is the case at the start of civil wars in other countries, for various reasons expectations were that this one might end quickly. However, what Col. Stephen O. Fuqua's earliest reports of the situation make abundantly clear is how quickly the civil war became a complex, massive operation all over Spain. To use an engineering phrase, it quickly gained a lot of moving parts. Fighting erupted in northern Spain, along the Catalan coast to the east, and, of course, extensively to the south of Madrid. The focal point was, however, Madrid. For the rebels it was the prize, much for the same reasons that in the American Civil War, Richmond became the objective of Union armies. While the fighting around Madrid quickly settled into a stalemate that lasted for the entire war, it was not clear that it would be the situation in the early months of the war. The dramatic siege of the Alcazar at Toledo, a city south of Madrid and on the main road from southern Spain to the capital city, quickly caught Fuqua's attention, as it did for other contemporaries and historians of the civil war over the past seven decades.

The reports presented in this chapter demonstrate several things. First, Fuqua was able to extend his reporting to cover all the major military initiatives that seemed to pop up almost overnight all over the nation, scaling up his coverage at the same speed with which events unfolded. This task was not easy, since he was situated in Madrid, within Republican military lines, and had no access to rebel army officers with whom to discuss events. He had to rely on the increasingly suspicious local press, which rapidly became the mouthpiece for the Republic and assorted leftist political parties and cliques. He listened to various radio programs coming from both sides and acquired rebel propaganda and information when possible. The result is a remarkably accurate account of the earliest days of the fighting, when chaos and confusion became a normal state of affairs. Second, he lays out in many of these reports the military rationale and significance of individual activities that might otherwise seem mundane, such as the reason for an army to want to take control of one small village here and another there. These explanations are the main strength of his reporting for the entire war, and thus the dispatches that follow are important to set up the various circumstances that would play out over the next several years.

A third feature of Fuqua's reports concerns his descriptions of activities not normally discussed by historians. An important example is his brief description of the various military factories making armaments in Spain. Normally, historians have focused on the matériel that came into Spain for either side from foreign governments but rarely, if at all, on the internal manufacturing capabilities available to both sides. He was a stickler for discussing roads, railroads, and harbors. Those who knew him at the time pointed out how obsessed he was with reading maps and explaining exactly what the topography and locations were for even the most mundane events.[2]

Madrid   No. 6382

July 23, 1936

Subject: Spanish Situation—Military

(Report telephoned to Legation at Lisbon for forwarding to the Assistant
Chief of Staff, G-2, War Department.)

Best information available but not wholly reliable.

Rebelling militaries hold line Zaragoza-Soria, Aranda de Duero-Segovia-
Salamanca and all important cities north of this line. West, Caceres-Badajoz.
South, Albacete, Granada, Cordoba, Sevilla, Cadiz, Algeciras and all Morocco.
The Canary Islands and probably part of the Balearics are also held by the rebels.
Probably 2,500 Moroccan troops have been transferred to Algeciras and Cadiz.
Rebel hydroplanes control water immediately adjacent to last named ports.

Government troops dominate Madrid and Barcelona, the Catalan provinces
and in all probability the Eastern Mediterranean littoral from Barcelona to Malaga.
The Navy seems inactive except some few ships preventing transfer of Moroccan
troops to the mainland. Reports widely circulated that many rebel naval officers
have been killed and ships taken over by crews. The government forces dominate
the air in the environs of Madrid controlling the airfields of Cuatro Vientos, Getafe and Barajas. The government military forces control Madrid and environs
northward to Lozoyuela, eastward Guadalajara, westward Avila and southward the
battle is now in progress for the control of Toledo. Government forces are reported
moving from the direction of Lerida against Zaragoza and from Madrid in two
columns, one against Segovia and the other against the rebel position at Somosierra, on the Burgos road south of Aranda de Duero—at which points imminent
battle is expected.

Madrid

In the battle against the rebel troops in Madrid, the government forces practically
destroyed the 31st Infantry Regiment of Sappers and Miners, attacking these units
in their barracks. Some 100 officers and some 200 civilians are reported to have
been shot immediately upon surrender. The Signal Regiment at El Pardo escaped
in trucks from the government cordon and joined the rebel forces at Segovia.

Six thousand socialistic youths organized as militia have been armed by the
government and have been used principally in conjunction with the Asalto police

forces for the protection of Madrid. Few regular troops in Madrid which are reported loyal are being utilized for defense. The Madrid Guardia Civil is reported as loyal to the government but they are sparingly employed in the defense of the city.

The most serious situation confronting Madrid is the question of the food supply which is slowing growing less and less, fresh goods practically being cut off the market at the moment. I have participated in the organization of the Embassy with Mr. [Eric] Wendelin, the only member left in Madrid and the commercial attaché, to meet any likely situation which may arise. Beds and blankets from the Ritz Hotel and food supplies have been obtained and a thorough organization of the Embassy effected to house all American citizens if necessary.

The rebel movement is being directed in the south by General [Francisco] Franco who flew from his command in the Canary Islands to Morocco, establishing his headquarters at Tetuan and Ceuta and by General [Emilio] Mola in the north with headquarters at Burgos. The general plan seems to have been to gain the line Zaragoza westward to Salamanca and consolidate to the north and simultaneously to take over Cordoba, Sevilla, the ports of Cadiz and Algeciras and bring to the mainland an expeditionary force from Africa of 15,000 men. The plan for the north, up to the present moment, seems to have been perfected, while that for the south has been interrupted by lack of sufficient sea control to continue the transfer of African troops to the mainland.

From a military point of view it looks as if the government has confronting it a most difficult task to break the rebellion should the rebels continue to hold the positions they now occupy.

The military decision for the moment would seem to depend upon the result of the impending battles immediately to the north of Madrid and this is my estimate of the situation at this particular hour of this date.

In conclusion it might be stated that this movement, although dominated by the military forces, is believed to have the support of the great mass of Spaniards who are opposed to the political creed and doctrine of the extreme Left and who, regardless of all else, demands for Spain law and order and the protection of life and property.

No request for reports will be necessary as this office will report daily if practicable to obtain any outside line of communication.

Madrid   No. 6383
July 24, 1936
Subject: The Spanish Military Situation
(With reference to Report of July 23 on the Spanish Military Situation,
the following is reported by telephone to the Legation at Lisbon for
forwarding to the Assistant Chief of Staff, G-2.)

Information received this morning seems to verify and in general establish
reliability of the situation and estimate reported yesterday.

South
The government claims that loyal forces occupied Cordoba are disputed by radio
announcements picked up from Cordoba a few hours ago that troops from Africa
occupy the city. If this be true, it is more or less convincing that General Franco
has landed additional troops at Algeciras.

East
No further information.

West
No further information.

North
The rebel forces reported at Somosierra are in position on the range to the north.
The road column of the government forces, upon reaching the pass at Somosierra,
met a surprise attack by rebel planes, which completely demoralized this force and
caused a disorderly retreat southward which late yesterday afternoon was stopped
by large reinforcements hastily organized and sent northward on the Burgos road.
The government forces moving against Segovia have reached Guadarrama, which
was shelled yesterday by rebel artillery from the pass now in control of the Segovia
rebel forces.

From the information now available it is difficult to determine the plan of
the rebel forces to the north and northwest. However, it would seem that they are
not yet prepared for a determined advance on Madrid, but seem to be occupying
positions "in readiness" and organized to stop any further advance of the attacking
troops from Madrid.

Toledo

The rebel troops in Toledo are occupying the Alcazar and hill which dominates the city and are making a heroic defense of this position against tremendous odds; although they number no more than 1,000 mixed troops, they are holding the attention of nearly 3,000 government troop forces and socialistic militias.

Barcelona

Direct telephone conversation with the American Consulate this date states that practically all churches in Barcelona have been burned; that the city is more or less in the hands of the communistic groups and that the government is slowly losing the little control it now has. The Export line *Exeter* is expected to arrive in Barcelona this evening and in all probability some 80 Americans will be evacuated.

Madrid

Madrid has been comparatively quiet today as practically all available troops have been sent to the south, to the east and principally to the north in the defense of the city. Armed militia in private automobiles commandeered by the government are patrolling the streets and through lack of responsibility are making it dangerous for pedestrians. The red flag is more in evidence today than ever, many government buildings, including the A.B.C., opposite the Embassy, are flying the red flag and practically all vehicles in the streets.

The government seems in control of the situation and the principal utilities, water, gas and electricity which are functioning normally, although food supplies are getting shorter and shorter in the city. However, the real pinch has not yet confronted the population.

The organization of the Embassy is functioning splendidly. We have converted the building and grounds into an improvised hotel and are now housing and caring for some 120 people. Medical, nurse and sanitary organization [is] excellent and food supply ample. In addition to normal city water supply, the Embassy building has an individual reservoir of about 600 gallon capacity.

From a military point of view the government still faces a difficult task with the decision for the moment still depending upon the result of the impending battles immediately to the north of Madrid.

San Sebastian

Reports confirmed by London Radio announce heavy fighting now going on for the mastery of the city. Radio also announces British landing parties from cruisers in the harbor are moving to the British Embassy to afford protection to British subjects.

Latest information just received, the source of which is London, radioing news alleged from Lisbon, is to the effect that a rebel government has been established at Burgos called "Junta Provisional" including the names of Generals [Miguel] Cabanellas, [Mola], [Fidel] Davila, [Miguel] Ponte and Franco.

Madrid   No. 6387

August 10, 1936

Subject: Military Uprising against the Government

1. General development of the revolt

While rumors of an impending military uprising against the [Santiago] Casares government were freely circulated and unquestionably planned for some future psychological hour. The assassination of Sr. [Jose] Calvo Sotelo caused such violent reactions as to precipitate the revolt which has plunged Spain, Morocco and her insular possessions into a civil war, the magnitude of which seems to have transcended all similar happenings in her long and turbulent history of political revolution.

On July 18th the first news reached Madrid that the army of Spanish Morocco, the Balearic Archipelago and the Canary Islands had revolted against the government and that the rebels had complete control of these areas under the leadership of Major Generals [Manuel] Goded and Franco who at the time of the uprising commanded the Balearic and Canary Islands, respectively.

Further successive reports confirmed the initial success of the movement which rapidly gained ground on the peninsula, especially in those regions where the rightist elements are strong such as Navarra, Castile, Leon and Aragon. In the south, General [Gonzalo] Queipo de Llano, who commanded the Second Organic Division at Sevilla, through surprise and decisive action, gained immediate control of the provinces of Cadiz, Malaga (except the capital) and Sevilla. The possession of Cadiz province was most important for the rebels owing to the two important ports of Cadiz and Algeciras where troops from Morocco could be landed. General Franco arrived almost immediately by plane from the Canary Islands at Tetuan and took over the Moroccan command and commenced the transportation of native troops to the mainland.

In the two important regions of Catalonia and Madrid the rebel army movement, through lack of quick decision, control by officers of the rank and file or action of local support of the government, not only failed but resulted in a complete subjugation of the revolting army units.

As regards the navy, general confusion and irresolution seemed to have prevailed among its personnel during the first days of the revolt. It is believed that many naval officers were implicated in the uprising and supported the army but that the loyal attitude of the crews to the government paralyzed their efforts and, in general, prevented at the outbreak the expected cooperation of the war vessels with the rebel movement.

On July 28th it was known that the cruiser *Almirante Cervera* (9,300 tons) with a crew formed almost exclusively of officers, had revolted against the government. The government claims that the remainder of the fleet is loyal and is cooperating in the suppression of the revolt. It is also known that, in most cases, the crews gained control of the ships after killing or arresting many of their officers.

The policy in the revolt followed by the army rebels consisted of declaring martial law in the communities where they were strong, seizing lines of information and communication and controlling the labor organizations which had received instructions to declare general strikes in the regions affected by the rebellion.

The government used the radio constantly to publish edicts declaring void the martial law proclamations issued by the rebels, disbanding the army units participating in the uprising and authorizing the enlisted personnel of same to quit their units. The Madrid radio also broadcasted many items and instructions from the trade unions tending to raise the morale of the masses and urging them to arms to fight against fascism. The labor masses, at least in Madrid and Barcelona, have responded with enthusiasm to the call to arms. It is interesting to note that, at first, the government, instead of organizing the civilians volunteering for service into military units, armed thousands of these extremists who, accepting no military control, grouped themselves in small bodies under direction of their political organizations thus giving the impression that anarchy reigned in Madrid. The lack of control and discipline in these armed bands naturally brought about excesses committed against persons and property which soon caused the government to restrict their use in Madrid, and to force the labor organizations to organize the *milicianos* along military lines, an objective now being gradually attained.

That the military revolt was recognized by the government in the beginning as an attack on the cabinet and its left tendencies seems supported by the fact that on July 19th Señor [Santiago] Casares Quiroga resigned and Señor [Manuel] Azaña appointed the Presiding Officer of the Cortes, Señor [Diego] Martinez Barrio, to preside over a new cabinet. The appointment of this government gave rise to a rumor that the moderate republicans desired to enter into negotiations with the rebels in order to put an end to the civil war threatening the entire country. However, this government hardly came into being before the extremist elements succeeded in the removal of Martinez Barrio and the substitution as Prime Minister of Señor [Jose] Giral, Minister of Marine of the Casares cabinet who retained this portfolio in the new government. Most of the ministers of the last government were held over in the new cabinet, except General [Jose] Miaja and Señor [Augusto] Barcia, Ministers of War and Interior, who were replaced by General Joaquin Castello and General Sebastian Pozas, respectively. Señor Sanchez Roman, a moderate, who was a Minister without portfolio in the Martinez Barrio cabinet, was not included in the Giral government.

The new government displayed from the beginning great initiative and energy in checking the military revolt. It began at once the distribution of arms to the members of extremist parties, organized an attack against the rebels and a campaign to force the army units, still wavering in their loyalty, to surrender or to side with the government.

2. The character of the revolt

While it is difficult to understand all of the intentions of the army leaders and political elements participating in the revolt, there are sufficient indications to believe that, in case of success, the restoration of the Monarchy is not among the aims of the rebels. The leaders claim that the military coup d'état has for its primary object the preventing of Spain from being converted into a socialist or communist State [and] from being destroyed by anarchy and chaos should the syndicalists gain the upper hand. These leaders justify their action on the grounds that since the February elections the government has been unable to maintain law and to check the program of the Soviet revolutionary movement.

In all documents captured from the rebels no mention is made of [the] Monarchy or fascism in the proposed organization of a new government. The edict declaring martial law which General [Joaquin] Fanjul had prepared for publication in Madrid and was taken after the failure of the movement in the capital ended with "viva la Republica". General Queipo de Llano, who leads the uprising on the South, revolted against the Monarchy and is a firm republican supporter and the same is true of General Miguel Cabanellas, who is the head of the military rebel government at Burgos. From documents seized and information now available it is evident that, should the revolt succeed, the rebels plan to organize a military dictatorship with the primary mission to crush extremist organizations and to restore law and order throughout the country. Later, in all probability there would be organized a mixed military-civil government along some sort of a corporative line similar to that now existing in Portugal, which of course might eventually turn into a form of fascism.

The Provisional Junta or Government established at Burgos, according to the latest reports is formed as follows:

President— Major General Miguel Cabanellas
Members: Major General Andres Saliquet
           Brigadier General Miguel Ponte (Retired)
           Brigadier General Fidel Dávila (Retired)
           Colonel Federico Montaner, G.S.
           Colonel Fernando Moreno Calderon, G.S.

Major General Jose Sanjurjo, leader of the uprising of August, 1932, was to be the President of this government but the airplane in which he was traveling from Portugal to Spain met [with] an accident which resulted in the death of the general.

3. The military situation

With further reference to Reports of July 23 and 24, telephoned to our Legation at Lisbon for forwarding by cable to War Department, a recapitulation of the main developments in the various fronts from the beginning of the revolt to the present is as follows:

MADRID

In Madrid, while the majority of the army officers were implicated in the movement, the military garrison for some reason failed to mutiny simultaneously with those in the other provinces. This lack of coordinated action in the beginning of the revolt proved a setback to the rebel cause as the government gained sufficient time to arm several thousand extremists (*Milicianos*) and to take the offensive. The Asalto forces and the Guardia Civil in part, assisted by the armed militia, surrounded, attacked and captured the principal barracks in Madrid. Similar action was taken against the nearby garrisons of Getafe, Cuatro Vientos airfield, Carabanchel and Vicalvaro, all of which almost immediately passed into the hands of the government. Most of the Madrid aviation remained loyal to the government and actively cooperated in the defeat of the local garrison.

Infantry Regiment No. 31 and the Sapper Regiment, assisted by some 400 civilian insurgents who had concentrated in their barracks constituted the nucleus of the rebel resistance in Madrid. At this barracks, Major General Fanjul, former subsecretary of war established his headquarters. These troops, inoculated in part by socialistic revolutionary propaganda, would not leave the barracks to assume the offensive. However, in the early morning of July 20th, the barracks were surrounded by the government forces and after a few hours of fighting surrendered. It is generally accepted as a fact that the militia shot some 100 officers and 200 of the armed civilians assisting the garrison immediately upon surrender. General Fanjul and several other officers were captured by police forces and placed in a local prison.

The Madrid extremists celebrated this victory by burning most of the churches which remained untouched and by assassinating a number of friars and nuns. Furthermore, armed militia bands began to take possession of the mansions and residences, particularly along Madrid's aristocratic avenue *Paseo de la Castellana* expelling the occupants and in some cases arresting them. These militia groups also began the searching of houses, arresting and in some cases executing without trial those persons suspected of rightist leanings. This anarchical situation grew so alarming that the government restricted, with some difficulty, the circulation of automobiles carrying such armed parties and issued orders entrusting uniformed police forces exclusively with the mission of searching private houses. Although the CNT (syndicalists) continue to ignore governmental orders, the situation has greatly improved and Madrid appears quiet with an aspect of comparative normalcy at the time of writing this report—a condition, however, due in the main to the absence of the manpower at the front.

After the suppression of the army revolt in the capital, the government forces subdued with relative ease the garrisons in the towns of Alcala de Henares and Guadalajara. The Signal Regiment at el Pardo (12 kilometers north of Madrid) succeeded in escaping in trucks and joined the rebel forces at Segovia.

Following the policy initiated at Madrid, the armed militia shot a number of officers and rightists at Alcala and Guadalajara after they had surrendered. At the latter place, the bodies of Major General Barrera (retired) and Brigadier General [Gonzalo] Gonzalez Lara and Admiral Fontela were found among the dead.

Government troops were sent to suppress the uprising at Toledo, where the Infantry Academy is located. The students and school staff, assisted by the local police forces and a few civilians, have made a heroic defense of the city against tremendous odds and are still holding the Alcazar and hill which dominates the city.

On July 22nd, the government sent troops to stop the advance of several rebel columns marching against Madrid from the north. The rebel troops gained the mountain passes at Guadarrama and Somosierra (from 50 to 80 kilometers from the capital) which are the key gates for an advance from the north on Madrid. The government apparently has massed its available strength, including reinforcements from Valencia, against these positions without being able to dislodge the enemy (July 22nd to August 7th). The losses among the government troops in these areas have been estimated as "particularly heavy". During the first days of the attack, the labor armed militia, lacking military training, discipline, organization and proper leadership, suffered great losses. The lesson learned at the front by the militia has brought about some sort of organization along military lines, although they still are formed in units of their own, without the command of regular officers and non-commissioned personnel. For political and other reasons they object to being grouped with either the regular army or police forces. Therefore, with this lack of control and leadership, this irresponsible armed citizenry, which numbers in Madrid alone with 25,000, will in any eventuality become a menace to society when withdrawn from the front lines.

CATALONIA AND EASTERN MEDITERRANEAN LITTORAL
Soon after the outbreak of the movement, railroad, telegraph and telephone communications between Madrid and the provinces were either cut by the rebels or used exclusively by the government. Consequently, the news concerning the revolt available in Madrid was greatly restricted and much confused. The government controlled radio and press in Madrid, as well as the radio stations in the hands of the rebels, began at once the announcement of propaganda which made it impossible for the people of Madrid to understand what was happening throughout the country.

At Barcelona, several infantry and artillery units revolted, the military authorities declaring martial law, in their attempt to take over the city; however, the Generalidad, assisted by the Police and Guardia Civil forces and armed extremists, succeeded in quelling the revolt after heavy street fighting which lasted most of the early morning hours of July 19th. Most of the aviation remained loyal to the government and is reported to have cooperated actively in the defeat of the insurgents. The number of casualties in Barcelona in the initial fighting for the control of the city is reported to have been about 300 dead and 1,200 wounded.

Major General Goded, who commanded the Balearic Islands, assumed the leadership of the revolt in Catalonia and, after its failure, was taken prisoner. The fact that the Guardia Civil and Police forces remained loyal to the government, taken with the indifferently inclined army enlisted personnel and, above all, the decided hostile attitude of the Catalonians toward the military, are the principal causes for the failure of the military movement in this region. General Goded is quoted to have said to Sr. [Luis] Companys, the President of the Generalidad, "I have not surrendered, my troops abandoned me".

The revolt was quite successful in the Balearic Islands although a few days later, the enlisted personnel of the Mahon (Menorca) garrison, rose against their officers and reestablished the authority of the government in this port. Mallorca and Ibiza still continue in the possession of the rebels.

The revolt in the remaining Catalan provinces also failed although some guerrilla warfare is continued in the Lerida province.

Barcelona has suffered greatly from anarchy as the armed extremists soon controlled the local government. Most of the churches have been burned and it is authentically reported that a great number of priests, friars and rightists have been assassinated by the armed militia bands. On July 31st the Catalan government resigned and Sr. Companys appointed another cabinet, presided over by Sr. Juan Casanovas, who, although classed as a republican, leans more to the left. In assuming office, Sr. Casanovas declared that the government's primary objective would be to intensify the fight against fascism. On August 6th the Catalan government was reorganized by removing all the socialist ministers, the whole cabinet being now composed of republicans. Evidently, this step has been taken with a view to check the growth of anarchy in Barcelona, but it is doubted that this measure will prove effective as the government is daily losing ground to extremists.

In the Mediterranean littoral provinces of Castellon, Valencia, Alicante and Murcia, where the extremist elements are very strong, the army made no serious attempt to revolt and finally, after the arrest of most of the officers, remained with the government. Columns of armed extremists and police forces were sent into the provinces of Cuenca, Almeria and Albacete, which had fallen in possession of the rebels, but, after some little fighting, were restored to government authority.

The *Gaceta* of July 24th published a decree creating a *Junta Delegada del Gobierno* (Local Governing Board) with jurisdiction over the provinces of Valencia, Alicante, Castellon, Cuenca, Albacete and Murcia, passing to this governing body the authority of the Central State. This board is under the immediate control of the Prime Minister and is presided over by Sr. Martinez Barrio, other members being the Minister of Agriculture and the subsecretaries of Agriculture and of the Presidency.

This local government reestablished railroad communication between Madrid, Valencia and Alicante and through this corridor, the capital is now being supplied.

The importance of the Valencia corridor cannot be overstressed as it is the only railroad line open to the coast, all other routes being cut off. In addition to food and other supplies, this route has permitted the sending of armed forces from the eastern littoral to assist the government in its effort to repel the advance of the rebel columns marching on Madrid from the direction of Segovia and Burgos.

SOUTHERN, WESTERN PROVINCES AND MOROCCO
Major General Gonzalo Queipo de Llano declared martial law in the provinces of Sevilla, Cadiz, Malaga, Cordoba, Granada, Albacete and Almeria, and notwithstanding the fact that the labor masses in these Andalucian provinces are controlled by the extremist organizations, the army quickly attained control over all of them except Malaga. In this latter province, the forces loyal to the government, assisted by the navy, succeeded in holding the province for the government although it is reported that the city of Malaga suffered great damages, part of the town being destroyed by fire.

General Queipo de Llano has established his headquarters at Sevilla and apparently is fighting against great odds, as the labor organizations, through strikes and their active or passive resistance, have contributed in great measure to check his military activities. Although news from this region is sketchy, it has generally been confirmed that the rebels have lost the provinces of Albacete and Almeria, but gained the province of Caceres and the city of Huelva from which capital progress is now being made in that province. Badajoz has been held by the government but fell to the rebels when these columns from Caceres and Sevilla united at Merida. The union of these two columns is the most important gain the rebels have made during the last week as it establishes intercommunication along the Portuguese border between the main rebel headquarters at Sevilla and Burgos.

The key to success in the Andalucian Section seems to lie in General Franco's ability to transfer troops from Morocco to the mainland, an achievement which would give great impetus to the rebel cause. However, up to the present time, the navy, which in general seems to have remained loyal to the government, has prevented the landing of any large expeditionary force of Moroccan troops past the rebel controlled ports of Algeciras and Cadiz.

In Morocco, all indications are that the military rebellion was a complete success as the problem of controlling the extremist organizations in Melilla de Ceuta was comparatively simple. Meager news only is available from this sector; however, the reports from the government are to the effect that loyal ships have bombed Ceuta, Melilla and Algeciras, the latter, according to these reports, suffered great damage.

NORTH, NORTHEAST AND NORTHWEST PROVINCES

Up to the time of writing this report, it appears that the rebels control the provinces of Avila (part), Segovia, Salamanca, Zamora, Leon, Valladolid, Palencia, Santander, Burgos, Alava, Soria, Logrono and Navarra. These thirteen provinces, in which rightist elements predominate or are very strong, form a continuous territory which constitutes the nucleus and heart of the rebellion. The government controls the littoral provinces of Guipuzcoa, Vizcaya and Asturias, except the city of Oviedo, where the rebels are surrounded by armed miners and which may be expected to surrender if not soon relieved. As regards the four Galician provinces (Coruna, Lugo, Ourense and Pontevedra) the situation is more or less confused although it appears that the rebels control most of this territory, particularly the Coruna province and the Ferrol Naval Base.

The three Aragon provinces (Zaragoza, Huesca and Teruel) are unquestionably in the hands of the rebels. The government through its headquarters at Madrid, Barcelona and Valencia is directing one of its main efforts against Zaragoza, important railroad junction and the headquarters of the Fifth Organic Division. The importance of this center is further intensified by the fact that it is the gateway of both direct rail and highway communication between Barcelona and Madrid. Government columns from Catalonia, Valencia and Madrid are reported to be operating against the Aragon provinces with a view to encircling Zaragoza and thus bring about its surrender. In estimating the situation in this center, it must be taken into consideration that this place is one of the strongholds of the anarchists and syndicalists.

The rebel forces occupy very strong positions on the ridges and passes of the Guadarrama mountains, some 55 kilometers northwest of Madrid, from where they have repelled all attacks from the government forces for the last fifteen days. The fact that the government continues concentrating its reserves and all available war material in this district seems to indicate that the impending battle for the Guadarrama passes may be decisive, at least in so far as the government control of Madrid is concerned.

The rebel forces now hold the southern slopes of this Sierra almost to the town of Guadarrama, which has been practically destroyed by rebel artillery fire, thus controlling Puerto del Leon (55 kilometers distant from the capital) and [the] gateway to Segovia and the northwest. The northern slopes of both El Leon and

Navacerrada (about 10 kilometers east of the former) passes are covered with dense pine woods which the government aviation has burned to some extent by means of incendiary bombs. The Somosierra pass (about 80 kilometers north of Madrid) is on the highway to Burgos and is located at the eastern end of the Guadarrama ridge. The rebels not only hold this pass but occupy the southern slopes almost to Buitrago (some 65 kilometers north of Madrid) where the government troops are entrenched.

4. Madrid life during the uprising

The street life in the capital has varied from days when anarchy seem[ed] to reign throughout to those of an almost normal daily existence. For days during the first two weeks of the revolt, the streets were infested day and night with armed militia bands firing off their guns without any provocation, searching pedestrians without excuse and entering private premises and removing property without authorized warrants. This condition began to cease when these bands were ordered to the front to stop the advance of the rebel columns approaching Madrid from the north. Owing to the absence of air power at the front, the streets are quiet during the day; however, there are enough of these bands still left in the city to make the streets unsafe after 10:00 P.M. when all lights are required out and firing commences and continues throughout the night. The city is in constant fear of being bombed from the air and many pass the nights in subway stations, basements and cellars. The food supply will be in no danger of an appreciable shortage as long as the Valencia corridor remains open, although certain foods like fish and dairy products are off the markets and scarcity is being felt in all meats, fruits and olive oil.

The government and the labor organizations have requisitioned all private automobiles, all of the leading hotels and most of the unoccupied private homes and apartments. The red flag is more in evidence each day, the *ABC* (leading right paper) and practically all of the private homes that have been requisitioned and most of the requisitioned cars fly the red flag. The flag of the republic is not flown over the National Palace, the home of the President, but instead the "President's flag" is hoisted. As this flag is red, with a comparatively small gold emblem in the center, many, including the undersigned, were led to believe that it was the socialistic red flag; however, it is evident that the flying of this bright red flag, the gold center being difficult to observe, from the ground, and the absence of the tri-color of the republic, is intended as an appeal to the masses.

It will be of interest to note here that as soon as the importance of the revolt was understood by the government, all the rightist officers of the War Department and particularly all of the General Staff were ordered to repair to their homes and await instructions. Also it should be noted under this heading of conditions in Madrid that great numbers of monarchists and extreme rightists have faced the firing squad and that the execution of these classes continues daily.

5. Closing

In closing, it is evident that the rebels in the past week have gained a slight advantage both in position and in the principal engagements, as noted below:

(a) The government troops have failed to dislodge the rebels from the passes in the Guadarrama and Sierras—the gateways to Madrid from the northwest and north.

(b) The government has failed to reach even the distant environs of Zaragoza from either the direction of Madrid or Barcelona. The above objectives have been unattained notwithstanding the employment of all available forces.

(c) The rebels have held the key points noted above, have consolidated their positions in the north and south regions and above all have succeeded in landing troops from Morocco. This latter achievement, attained in spite of the government control of the sea, made possible the securing of the Caceres-Merida-Sevilla corridor, paralleling the Portuguese border, which connects the north and south rebel regions.

(d) The gold reserve in the Bank of Spain gives the government a great advantage in the ability to purchase war material and supplies should the civil war be dragged out in time; however, this may be checkmated by some foreign nations' agreement (now under discussion) not to sell war stores, including planes, to either part to the struggle.

6. Pictorial review of the revolt

Enclosed herewith are newspaper pictures of action scenes of the armed militia, police and Guardia Civil forces and other interesting aspects of the civil war from the government side. While all the Madrid press is now controlled by government agencies, the newspapers in total are extremists in character which may be a significant straw to watch should the storm wind now blowing wipe away the military revolt.

Madrid   No. 6395
August 22, 1936
Subject: The Military Situation

With further reference to Report No. 6387 of August 10, 1936, no material changes have occurred in the military situation.

Madrid

Here in Madrid, the recruitment and armament of men of all ages who volunteer for service have continued without abatement, it now being estimated that not less than 50,000 militia from the capital and nearby towns and villages are in the ranks at the front or engaged in some activity in the city. Most of the forces thus recruited are serving under the direct control of the extremist political organizations, the efforts of the government to organize new regular units having met with little success, notwithstanding the fact that two replacements have been called to the colors. The recruits prefer joining the socialist, communist or syndicalist special forces, where, in addition to receiving high pay, discipline is lax and the commitment of excesses is more or less condoned.

The military situation at the Guadarrama passes remains practically unchanged. All efforts of the government forces to dislodge the rebels having proved unsuccessful, although a maneuver to outflank them in the direction of Avila seems to have attained some progress. It might be said in this connection that the government evidently considers the Guadarrama area as the principal front for it has unquestionably assembled its largest army in this vicinity, the strength of which is estimated to be some 30,000 men. In connection with the composition of the government forces at the front, it is believed that there are but few regular army troops and Guardia Civil, the bulk of the forces being militia.

The Toledo Alcazar and hill are still held by the surrounded rebel forces which continue to maintain a desperate and heroic defense against tremendous odds.

Eastern Mediterranean Littoral

The government not only continues in possession of the large eastern zone, which ensures communication with and the supply of Madrid through the Valencia and Murcia regions, but has improved somewhat its military position by certain advances of small Valencia and Catalan columns in the direction of Teruel and Zaragoza. However, the fact that the Catalan government has not sent a large attacking force against Zaragoza is being interpreted as the lack of interest of this section in the war out of its regional limits.

The island of Ibiza of the Balearics has been taken by the government; however, Palma remains in the hands of the rebels notwithstanding the government claims to the contrary.

The government forces are gradually advancing against the cities of Cordoba and Granada, both of which seem to be almost surrounded and are expected to fall unless they are soon relieved. The rebel forces are reported advancing from Sevilla against Malaga and are now in possession of the town of Bobadilla, an important railroad junction. Unless their progress is shortly interrupted it looks as if this important port of Malaga will pass into rebel hands.

General Franco, commander of the South Army, has now completely perfected the communication lines through the Caceres and Badajoz provinces, thus consolidating the recent junction of the north and south columns at Merida.

Moroccan troops seem to have been landed in some force as they have been noted engaged in active operation in this region, and have appeared as far north as Burgos. It is possible that a push eastward from the Merida-Caceres line supported by a troop movement south from Avila may be the blow the rebels are counting on in their drive for Madrid, or the main attack may come from Avila.

North

Although the government still holds the coastline from Irun-San Sebastian-Bilbao-Santander to the Asturian region, the rebels are desperately fighting for the control of Irun, San Sebastian and the Oviedo region making some slight gains in these parts during the last week.

General Comment

The past week has seen little or no military action of a major character. The general estimate is that neither side is able to make a push for any magnitude. The rebels seem to have devoted the past week to the consolidation of their positions north and south and in the recently gained corridor paralleling the important friendly Portuguese frontier. The government has been busy buying war material, principally from France, among which may be counted perhaps some 75 planes both bombing and pursuit types. The government seems to have the psychology that it is victorious as long as it prevents the rebels from entering Madrid. As a matter of fact, as the situation now stands, in baseball parlance, one good "inning" on either side with a couple of bases covered and a "homer" and the "old ball game" would "all be over".

Madrid   No. 6396
August 22, 1936
Subject: The Civil War Approaching a "No-Quarter" Struggle

Judging from reports received from reliable sources, supported in some cases by positive indications and direct observation as regards Madrid, the Spanish civil war is being characterized by hates and cruelties engendered by passions typical of a barbaric race. Both the Left and the Right appear to be seeking not only the military defeat of their enemy but his complete subjugation and in great part the annihilation of those who showed any political preference for one of the other of the parties now struggling for the final supremacy.

The "popular bloc" militia fighting at the front on the side of the government is reported as giving no quarter. The regular army units and police forces assisting the government are in general observing the rules and conduct of war but they cannot always control the militia and consequently the prisoners taken by them seldom reach alive the town prisons. Just a few days ago a government train transporting some 225 prisoners was captured by armed militia (women included) at Vallecas (near Madrid) which resulted in a horrible massacre [with] none escaping according to reliable reports.

The rightist population of the towns and villages in the hands of the local armed militia have suffered greatly, many having been killed. Rightist property has practically all been confiscated, this extending to homes and apartments vacated by the occupants for the summer season. In the war zones where the militia forces from the cities are fighting, these troops are reported to have committed great atrocities against the priests and wealthy inhabitants, particularly in the places which have been taken by the insurgent forces.

The Madrid press daily presents alleged cases of the utmost ferocity committed by the army forces in the South, where the extremist organizations control the labor masses. The rebel forces, particularly the Moors from Morocco, are charged with killing by the hundreds not only extremist affiliates but peaceful inhabitants, women and children included, particularly in the provinces of Huelva and Badajoz recently taken by the army forces. The lack of direct, accurate and reliable information from the districts controlled by the rebel army on the south and southwest makes it very difficult to know the situation in these parts. However, there are sufficient indications to warrant the belief that the rebels, who have been and are still confronted with the active or passive resistance of the major part of the population in those districts, are employing methods of terror and making generous use of reprisals.

The rebel radio at the Burgos station claims that the prisoners taken by the army are respected and given humane treatment. However, there are indications that during the fighting in the mountain passes near Madrid, the rebels are giving, in general, no quarter to the militia. Furthermore, some extremist fugitives from the northern section, who succeeded in reaching Madrid, claim that many socialist and communist leaders have been executed and that terror is being used to control the labor masses. However, it is believed, owing to the fact that the rightists elements are strong in most of the northern provinces, that any cruel measures taken would have been restricted to the leading Left agitators since no strikes have been declared to check the progress of the so called "National Army".

The rebel radio constantly announces that complete anarchy reigns in the districts controlled by the republican government, particularly at Madrid and Barcelona, of which word pictures are painted of the wanton destruction of churches by the masses, of the frightful massacres and vandalic acts committed by the militia and ending with appeals urging all patriots to join the "National Army" so that the present civilization may be saved.

The existing hatred which now divides the Spaniards into two classes each seeking final supremacy through the extermination of the other, is in a great measure the result of the violent political campaigns which the press and party leaders have waged during the last years. Since the beginning of the military uprising, the Madrid press, which is controlled by the Left Bloc, has been fomenting their hatred for the rightists in the use of all conceivable propaganda methods. Besides, the Madrid radio is constantly used by extremists of all denominations who in bitter speeches insist on the necessity of crushing the rebellion which they classify as a "fascist movement".

Señor [Indalecio] Prieto, the socialist ex-Minister and perhaps the leading spirit behind the government, in a speech delivered recently over the radio, stated that while he favored the utmost courage in battle, he condemned the use of cruelty to prisoners, who after all, he added, "are compatriots and their lives should be respected". This expression has brought to him a strong rebuke from most of the newspapers which state that "fascists deserve no mercy and should be completely annihilated". This hatred of "rightists" is so overwhelming that the government cannot escape its influence, and in consequence, although against Spanish tradition, some of the leaders of the revolt who were taken prisoner have been sentenced to death and executed (Major Generals Goded and Fanjul, Brigadier General Fernandez Burriel and Colonel [Fernandez] Quintana), and it is believed that the same fate awaits a number of others still to be tried.

Both the press and radio of the capital seem to have in view two primary objectives: First, to classify the military, the Church, the wealthy and the conservative elements as fascists who are seeking to overthrow the republic and to oppress the Spanish people. Second, to urge the government to issue edicts in regard to private property, which are communistic in character, although maintaining the position that the people's fight is for the Spanish republic. This type of press and radio propaganda is apparently intended to mislead the republican classes and thus secure their cooperation. However, the turn that events are now taking; the fact that the control of the government is becoming more and more in the hands of the extremist parties; the confiscation of the property of the rich by communistic and anarchistic groups; the taking over by the demanding of free service at all restaurants and bars; the lack of personal security of non-belligerents and the constant increase in the flying of red flags are self-telling indications which enlighten thinking republicans as to the danger which faces the republic from within its own ranks.

One of the most alarming aspects of the situation in Madrid and Barcelona is the fact that both governments appear to have relinquished their authority to the Marxist militia with regard to the arrest and trial of civilians suspected of rightist activities or leanings. Since the revolt began in Madrid, militia parties have been searching houses and arresting individuals, many of whom later appeared as corpses in lonely fields in the suburbs of the city.[3] It is clear from evidence available that in general such persons were not given a trial although several CHEKA [a Russian-style security force] boards function in the capital, where some of the prisoners are comparatively safe; but it is conservatively estimated that about 2,000 persons have been executed without trial in Madrid alone, many of whom as the result of a cause arising from some personal enmity. The government has prohibited the entering of houses during the night and has ordered that Asalto police guards accompany the militia searching parties; but such restrictions are of no avail as houses are now searched throughout the day—parties being accompanied by a friendly Asalto guard or two.

It is known that a considerable number of fascists who simulated extremist leanings and thus became affiliated with the militia, are using this means to get ahold of socialists and communists and kill them during the night. At least, a number of the corpses found, judging from their appearance, are reported to be laborers. Such fascist tactics are not new in Madrid as, prior to the revolt, there were sufficient reasons to believe that the antagonism which existed between socialists and syndicalists was in considerable measure fomented by rightist laborers infiltrated in the extremist ranks.

Wholesale massacres such as 500 prisoners, mostly naval officers, in a prison ship off Cartagena and similar killings of large rightist groups by communistic sympathiziers are reported occurring throughout Spain, the verification of which at this time is out of the question.

Madrid   No. 6401
September 1, 1936
Subject: Conditions in Tarragona and Malaga

The following extracts from consular reports on conditions in Tarragona and Malaga are submitted herewith for information:

Tarragona

What principle of authority is to be sought in this province and especially so in the town of Tarragona gives the impression that the syndicalist, communist and anarchist organizations are steadily gaining ground in their apparent aim to substitute entirely the governments of the Republic and Generalidad of Catalonia by their own delegates. Such delegates are daily more numerous and are to be found in all sort of public services and activities and most especially in the handling of the confiscated industries, buildings and valuables which are at once taken control of by the aforesaid labor organizations.

Houses are searched with unabating frequency, some of them having been searched as often as 7 or 8 times. In such operations religious signs or images, even those of great artistic or historic value, are with but rare exceptions torn to pieces on the spot. What money or objects of value are then found in excess of what the searchers consider should be sufficient to have at home are immediately seized and no receipt given in exchange therefore. Although at the present time searches are prohibited unless by judicial writ, they continue being performed by patrols of the armed militia whose power seems to rest solely on the guns they carry.

Citizens continue being executed by the armed militias of the radical organizations. In this town the sentencing tribunal is constituted by five men each from a different radical party, the procedure being unknown but no appellation being given the sentenced man. Executions are usually carried out between sunset and sunrise in the outskirts of this town but quite near too as the reports of the guns are easily heard. The corpses are left on the ground until after sunrise when the motor truck fitted for the purpose picks them up and carries them to the morgue. In most cases the bodies are buried after an autopsy without having been officially identified either because they are disfigured or because the relatives and acquaintances of the reported dead fear going to identify them, while in a few cases identification has been prevented by the armed militia stationed in the morgue.

Malaga

On the night of August 30th Malaga sustained effective and destructive bombardment from rebel planes. One bomb fell in a street leading to the railroad station killing some ten persons. Another bomb destroyed a government plane at Malaga airdrome located at six kilometers from the city. Nominal sum of bombs, one of which fell within three hundred odd yards of [U.S.] Consulate, were dropped in and around the port doing no appreciable damage. This is the first night aerial bombardment we have had.

Possibly rebels have not decided upon concerted effort to break the morale of the people by frequent bombings preparatory to an attack on the city. The rebels on one front are reported to be within some 45 kilometers of Malaga. Battleship *Jaime I* returned to Malaga on August 31st following repairs undergone at Cartagena.

Madrid　　　　　　No. 6403
September 1, 1936
Subject: Air Raids on Madrid

Madrid has been attacked by rebel planes on several occasions during the past few days. These raids have been carried out by a few modern bombing planes—usually two—which dropped bombs in the nearby aviation fields and in the vicinity of important government buildings in the capital, causing slight damages. It is believed that the main purpose of these air raids is to remind the population that Madrid is under a serious menace of being completely surrounded and besieged and that the government is impotent to prevent an attack from the air. However, the Madrid people have as yet given little indication of being effectively alarmed.

Madrid   No. 6411
September 18, 1936
Subject: The Military Situation

1. Changes on the various fronts
MADRID

In the capital, the recruitment of men of all ages who volunteer for service, or are more or less forced therein by the trade unions, continues unabated while large contingents of prospective recruits arrive daily from nearby provinces.

In the Guadarrama passes neither army has made any appreciable progress of late. The rebels have maintained their strategical positions dominating the most important passes from which a general offensive against Madrid could be launched while the government troops continue to improve their entrenched positions and the leaders to indoctrinate the rank and file with the old Verdun slogan, "They shall not pass".

The insurgent army has attained considerable success recently in pushing its lines eastward from the Oropesa (Caceres province) front to beyond Talavera (Toledo province), defeating in both places entrenched government forces and inflicting upon them heavy losses in both personnel and materiel. In the former center the government troops suffered a severe defeat, particularly the militia, one battalion of which was destroyed and another captured. The success of this offensive made possible the consolidation by the rebels of important positions in the Sierra de Gredos, southwest of the Sierra de Guadarrama, with which the encircling of Madrid seems to proceed slowly but methodically. The battle line now lies some 8 miles east of Talavera, the immediate objective of General Franco evidently being Maqueda which will give the rebels control of the road to Avila and thus permit a union of the forces on the battle fronts north, west and southwest of Madrid. The Maqueda position, only 35 miles from Toledo, will also give opportunity to move against this city where the gallant defenders of the Alcazar, now converted by artillery fire into a debris heap, still hold out in the basement of the fortress in an heroic defense that must in the end thrill the reader of the story of the "Siege of the Alcazar" and evoke the admiration and plaudits of the military students.[4]

Some rebel pressure and progress have now been recorded northeast of the Guadarrama Sierra, in the Siguenza (Guadalajara province) front, where rebel troops from the north have threatened any Madrid forces from uniting with the Catalan columns in making a combined attack on Zaragoza.

CATALONIA AND EASTERN MEDITERRANEAN LITTORAL

The government forces, assisted by several columns from Catalonia, have made considerable progress in the provinces of Huesca and Teruel, occupying about half of these territories. This front now is an almost straight north and south line which starts at the French frontier and passes just east of the capitals of those provinces, which are reported to be in grave danger of being taken should this loyal troop advance from the east be not checked.

An expedition of Catalan and Valencian troops landed at Mallorca (Balearic Islands) but after several adverse engagements with the rebels had to withdraw, some of its elements being sent to Madrid to cooperate with the government forces in the defense of the capital. The island now is completely in the hands of the rebels.

SOUTHERN AND WESTERN PROVINCES

While the government has several times announced the imminence of the fall of Cordoba, the garrison of this city, assisted by reinforcements from Sevilla consisting mainly of Moorish troops, has up to the present writing succeeded in checking further progress of the government forces against its defenses. The same applies to the city of Granada against which the government attacking forces appear to have made little headway during the last two weeks, notwithstanding the fact that the city is rather closely surrounded by the attacking columns which have placed it almost in a pocket.

In this region, the rebels have made no appreciable progress against Malaga as the force of the drive against this city has been naturally lessened by the necessity of relieving the government pressure against the Cordoba and Granada capitals.

NORTH

After heavy and bitter fighting, the rebel army succeeded during the first days of September to take the town of Irun, thus controlling the important rail and highway routes to France on that frontier. The general headquarters of the rebel army at Tolosa then ordered a general drive against San Sebastian, the capital of Guipuzcoa, which fell on September 13th. The bulk of the government forces succeeded in withdrawing in the direction of Bilbao taking with them a large number of prisoners they had confined in the San Sebastian prisons. From various reports it is known that the rebels suffered great losses in the Guipuzcoa engagements which necessitated a delay in their last successful attack on San Sebastian, thus permitting the government garrison to make its escape without appreciable losses.

The Basque nationals, whose political tenets, aside from a desire for regional autonomy, are strongly conservative and common to those of the rebels, appear to be severing connection with the government militia with whom they have been associated in the fighting in the Guipuzcoa area. It is reported that the Basques have denounced the excesses committed by the militia and that their inaction permitted the comparatively easy advance of the rebels against San Sebastian and that this Basque attitude may permit the subjugation of the entire province in a few days as well as an early successful attack on Bilbao which apparently is about to be initiated. That the Basque nationalists are not now on good terms with the government is further evidenced by the fact that the vacancy in the Madrid cabinet allotted to them has now been filled by a republican.

In Oviedo, Colonel [Antonio] Aranda, with his some 4,000 regular soldiers and police, while still surrounded by attacking miners, continues to hold the city and immediate surroundings; however, there are three army columns, which are now in Asturias territory, marching to his rescue from Galicia, Santander and Leon. The strongest of these columns, that of Galicia, is reported to be some 25 kilometers west of Oviedo.

Strength

Although an accurate estimate of the military strength of the contending forces is out of the question, owing to the lack of organization in the government and the absence of any reliable information from the rebel territory, there are available certain data which permit one to draw an approximate picture of the relative strengths of the opposing forces.

As regards the military strength existing immediately prior to the revolt, the following data assembled from published tables gives a fair estimate of the army and police forces in the territory now controlled by each side.

GOVERNMENT	REBEL	PENINSULA
Infantry	21,500	25,350
Cavalry	1,500	3,000
Artillery	6,950	9,000
Other arms and services	16,100	15,000
Police forces	18,700	12,000
Totals	64,750	64,350
Army of Morocco and Jalifian troops		45,000

As seen from the above, the peninsular military strength of the two forces was about balanced although there were a number of factors, which, taken into account, gave a marked superiority to the rebel strength. Among these factors was the decree of the Madrid government declaring "discontinued" the units which participated in the rebellion and as a result of which many soldiers from the garrisons stationed in Catalonia and Madrid returned to their homes, or joined the militia forces. The military units which were not disbanded were of little or no military value to the government as most of their commissioned personnel were either killed or imprisoned. This situation naturally brought about a state of confusion and disorder which prevented the utilization of these forces as units during the first days of the military uprising. Thus, the fact has been recorded in prior reports that the militia, assisted by loyal Guardia Civil and Asalto police, were the main forces used by the government in the beginning of the revolt, and this situation continues to exist.

The initial superiority of the rebel army was affected to a certain extent by the low morale of the enlisted personnel which had been systematically contaminated by revolutionist propaganda. This circumstance forced the rebel commanders to delay active operations until they could intermingle Moroccan troops and fascist and other rightist militia with the army units. On the rebel side too, the Guardia Civil, assisted by armed rightists, were in great measure responsible for the initial successes of the revolt, particularly in those provinces in which the right elements predominated.

The manpower strength of the contending forces may be better understood by reference to the following table showing the population under control of each of the belligerents. This table must be taken as an approximate guide only as several of the provinces are partially occupied by one or other of the belligerents and consequently apportionment in such cases is pure estimation.

POPULATION UNDER CONTROL OF	GOVERNMENT	REBELS
Galicia	—	2,580,000
Extremadura	100,000	1,085,000
Andalucia	2,080,000	2,850,000
Castilla la Nueva	2,835,000	210,000
Castilla la Vieja	350,000	1,390,000
Leon	—	1,895,000
Basque provinces	600,000	365,000
Aragon	300,000	880,000

Catalonia	3,170,000	—
Valencia	2,130,000	—
Murcia	1,045,000	—
Navarra	—	400,000
Balearic Islands	100,000	275,000
Canary Islands	—	600,000
Totals	12,710,000	12,530,000

The rebels, in addition to the above, control the Spanish Protectorate in Morocco, which has a population of about 800,000.

Consideration must be given to the fact that the population in any given province or area may not be loyal to the governing regime.

Taking into consideration that the mass of the population is formed of laborers, most of whom having been gained for the revolutionary cause during many years of intense propaganda, the government has a definite superiority of soldier material over the insurgents. In this connection it is of interest to note that an excess of volunteers, for whom no armament is available, exists in all governmental recruiting centers and this situation is not believed to exist in rebel territory. In the Madrid front alone the militia army is estimated at about 50,000 not to count some 25,000 militiamen who are under training in the city awaiting armament or are engaged in political or organizational activities. It is estimated that at the present time the Madrid and Catalan governments, in addition to some military units, have armed about 250,000 militia.

The military efficiency of the governmental forces is believed to be very low, not only due to the lack of unity of purpose and leadership, as the several political organizations are directing their own militia, but also to lack of training and discipline and to the absence of any trained commissioned and non-commissioned personnel. Should the government have organized its army along military lines exclusively, a considerable number of the 10,000 middle aged officers retired by Sr. Azaña in 1931 might have volunteered for service, but owing to the revolutionary principles of the militia, which are adverse to military discipline and professional leadership, very few officers have joined. Furthermore, the many instances of officers executed on the battlefield by the militia units after unsuccessful engagements for alleged treason in misdirecting them, are contributing to discourage the seeking of field service by officers who feel themselves professionally disliked and always under suspicion. Thus the majority of militia units are commanded by newly made officers and non-commissioned personnel of little or no military experience. As regards training, the soldier militiaman practically receives his military education at the front and first fires his rifle, if at all, in combat.

The uniform of the militia is the *mono*, the blue one piece blouse and trousers used for work, known to us as *overalls*.

With regard to the rebel army, no positive evidence is available as to its present strength except that some 20,000 Legion and Moroccan troops have been transferred to the rebel peninsula force and that the regular army troops are being gradually expanded with the contingents derived from the "calling to arms" of five annual replacements. Furthermore, voluntary enlistment appears to be open in all the territory controlled by the insurgent army for the Legion and the various fascist and rightist military units, which, like the *requetes* (traditionalists), preserve their distinctive organizational character and bear, together with the Moroccan troops, the brunt of the campaign.

It is believed that while the insurgents have relatively more abundant war materiel than the government, owing to the fact that they control the headquarters of five of the eight military divisions, whose materiel depots exist, plus those in Morocco, they seem to be confronted with a lack of Spanish manpower from which may be recruited sufficient voluntary personnel. However, the transfer of Moors to Spain continues within the limitations imposed by the fact that the government controls the Mediterranean coastline and Gibraltar Straits. As the supply of manpower in the Protectorate appears abundant, it is expected that with the coming autumn fogs over the Straits, the rebels will be in a position to accelerate the crossing of Moroccan troops. At present, judging from statements published in the local press, of prisoners taken by the government forces, the rebels are in numerical inferiority on all battle fronts except those of the north.

Arms and Ammunition

The supply of arms and ammunition available to the two forces being of vital importance and increasingly so should the concert of European powers make effective a neutrality that would prevent war materiel shipments to Spain, the following information giving a brief summary of the location and materiel produced by the various state war factories is believed to be pertinent to the subject matter of this report:

Factory of Trubia. This factory, which is located some 19 kilometers southwest of Oviedo, is in the possession of the government, and apparently is one of the main objectives of the rebel army columns which are advancing to rescue the capital city where the military garrison is surrounded by the miners. One of these army columns is reported now to be 6 kilometers west of this factory. The Trubia arsenal produces special steel, light and medium guns, gun ammunition, armored cars, helmets and other war materiel.

Factory of Oviedo. This factory is located in Oviedo itself and is at present under control of the insurgent army. Rifles and machine-guns are manufactured here, the normal daily production being some 200 rifles and a few machine-guns. At Lugones, some 8 kilometers north of Oviedo, there exists a factory of military brass for ammunition which is in the possession of the government.

Factory of steel arms of Toledo. This factory, on the Tagus River very near Toledo, is devoted to the manufacture of steel arms and rifle ammunition and is in the possession of the government. The insurgents, before withdrawing to the Alcazar, took with them important parts of the machinery with a view to prevent the utilization of the factory by the government. It is further reported that bombing by the rebel aviation has caused serious damage to the factory installations.

Factories of Sevilla. There is here a gun factory which is equipped with modern machinery and tools for the manufacture of guns up to 15.5 cm. caliber and ammunition for same. This factory is also equipped to produce rifle ammunition, hand grenades, shells and military equipment such as gun carriages. At Sevilla, there is also located a military pyrotechnic factory which is equipped to produce large quantities of rifle and pistol ammunition, fuses, percussion caps, skyrockets and high explosives. Both factories are controlled by the rebels.

Powder factory of Murcia. This factory produces ordinary and nitrocellulose powders, nitro-cotton and nitric acid. It is under the control of the government.

Powder factory of Granada. This factory is located some 8 kilometers from the city. It manufacturers all kinds of explosives, such as trillite, etc., its daily production capacity being 2,000 lbs. of nitro-cotton and 5,000 lbs. of nitric acid. It is controlled by the rebels; however, the government forces surround rather closely on three sides the city of Granada and its aviation is reported to have bombed this factory causing considerable damage.

In addition to the State factories, the Constructora Naval Co. operates artillery workshops at La Carraca (Cadiz) and Reinosa (Santander) where guns for the navy and army, ammunition for same and other materiel are manufactured. The workshops of Cadiz are in territory occupied by the rebel army, while those in Santander are under the control of the government, although very near the battle line. At Plasencia (Guipuzcoa) there is a gun factory and in this province there are also many factories of firearms which could readily be turned to produce military armament. Most of the Guipuzcoa province is at present in the hands of the rebels. The province of Vizcaya, now in the possession of the government, is a highly industrial province, producing much iron and steel, where are located a number of small arms factories.

The Navy

The situation as regards the navy was at first decidedly favorable to the government owing to the fact that the majority of the vessels fell in the hands of crews which remained loyal to the socialistic regime. This government naval superiority, however, was considerably changed when El Ferrol, the largest and most important naval base of Spain, was taken by the insurgents during the last days of July. Upon capturing this base, the insurgents manned with their own personnel the cruiser *Almirante Cervera* [(9,385 tons) and the destroyer *Velasco* (1,337 tons). They also succeeded in placing into service the battleship *España* (16,400 tons) which was undergoing repairs at the El Ferrol docks. The *Canarias*, a 10,000 ton cruiser about to be delivered by her constructor to the navy, later joined the rebel fleet and, further, it is believed that her sister ship, the *Baleares*, which is near completion, may soon be added to the naval strength of the insurgents.

The first four warships named above, assisted by a number of auxiliary vessels stationed at the El Ferrol naval base, have taken an active part in the operations against Irun and San Sebastian which culminated in the recent capture of these cities by the rebels. They have also shelled strategical places along the littoral of Vizcaya, Santander and Asturias and have and do now control the northern and northwestern coastal front from France to Portugal.

The naval base at Cadiz is also in the possession of the rebels. Here the only warship controlled by them, the gunboat *Dato*, was recently disabled by gun fire from the battleship *Jaime I*.

Practically all the government naval forces, which include the 10 available modern destroyers (2,120 tons), and 12 submarines, the *Jaime I* and the cruisers *Libertad* (9,385 tons), *Miguel de Cervantes* (9,385 tons), *Republica* (6,450 tons) and the *Mendez Nuñez* (6,140 tons) are engaged in preventing the transfer of Moroccan troops to the peninsula and in controlling the Mediterranean coastline from Gibraltar to the French border. Some of these ships, among them the *Jaime I*, have been seriously damaged by the rebel hydroplanes and coast batteries.

The naval bases at Cartagena and Mahon (Balearic Islands) are under control of the government. It is of interest to note that neither of these naval bases has docking facilities for large ships. At Cartagena, there are under construction a few destroyers while Mahon is used solely as a submarine base.

The fact that the government vessels are under control of "committees" appointed by the crews, with no officer leadership, has materially reduced the combat efficiency of the fleet, which, up to the present, except for an unsuccessful raid in northern waters by submarines, has made no attempt to seek an engagement with the rebel squadron.

Plans and Estimates

Referring to the plans of the government and rebel forces, which were characterized in the main as defensive and offensive respectively, the unfolding and development of which are now revealed, is convincing of the correctness of the estimates of this office outlined in previous reports. The rebels continue the consolidation of their northern position and are apparently striking for the coastlines of the provinces of Vizcaya, Santander and Asturias—the centers of which are found in the capitals of Bilbao, Santander and Oviedo. Great impetus has been given to the consummation of this movement by the recent taking of Irun and San Sebastian. In the South, the rebels have maintained their positions with slight gains in the vicinity of Cordoba and Sevilla, which included the recent taking of Ronda and a determined push against Malaga which now promises success. The consolidation of the rebel holdings in the South and North, through the complete occupation by General Franco's troops of the Sevilla-Merida corridor, was the greatest blow delivered to the government's cause since the beginning of the revolt. This occupation permitted the capture of Badajoz and gave free access to the friendly borders of Portugal. Besides, it has given an opportunity for a united rebel command to move eastward and which is now advancing against Santa Olalla with its first objective the securing of Maqueda and the gaining of the road 90 kms. north of Avila. The success of this movement will make possible a united battlefront with the forces occupying the Guadarrama and Somosierra passes. When this has been attained, the rebels will then be in a position to make a combined offensive against Madrid, utilizing one or more of their positions for secondary or holding attacks and launching from another their main drive against the capital.

The plans of the government seemingly have been based upon the initiative of the rebels, as its forces have been created by the advance of the army troops. However, the government has taken the offensive, with Catalan and Valencia troops, against the capitals Zaragoza, Huesca and Teruel. The government has also locally in spots attacked rebel strongholds such as Granada and Cordoba.

The rebels seem to dominate the air based upon the reports of the number of successful bombing expeditions and gun attacks they have achieved.

In closing, the undersigned desires to refer to a trip he made yesterday to witness the siege of the Alcazar at Toledo and to visit the battlefront near Santa Olalla. The firing on the Alcazar has practically ceased, occasional shots were exchanged between the defenders and besiegers as favorable targets appeared to either side. The officer acting as my guide, informed me that a corner wall of the Alcazar was prepared for demolition and would be dynamited that night. News today confirms the report that the enterprise was successful and that government troops had entered the basement with machine-gun and hand grenades—which, if true, foreshadows the early fall of this historic defense.

From Toledo, we passed through Torrijos, which had just been bombed from the air about an hour preceding our arrival and was afire and smoking in several places. Just beyond the town—in order not to attract too much attention to our car on the road from the overhead planes—we stopped off the highway under a tree for lunch. Later we proceeded on to Maqueda and thence to Santa Olalla, the headquarters of the government forces engaged with the rebels west of the town. The place had been visited by rebel planes just prior to our arrival and many buildings were noted in flames, smoke and battered down. I called on General [Jose] Asensio[5] and talked with him a few minutes—our meeting was in the street, the General apologizing for not offering me the hospitality of his quarters explaining, as he pointed to a pile of debris, that they had just been bombed.

The town showed the result of very thorough and accurate bombing the effect of which was noted on the very disturbed morale of the troops. The rebel attack which was well timed was launched with the bombing of the town, the combined result of which was to force a withdrawal. From the personal observations made during this visit to the government's army on Madrid's most vital front, lack of officer and non-commissioned officer leadership, lack of any system of either organization or supply and the total absence of both discipline and training are convincing that the troops on this front must go down in defeat unless something in the way of a miracle comes to pass.

The general impression here in Madrid at this writing is that the "Popular Front" is weakening fast and that if the rebel army is able to continue the advance and the attack—then the government must pass or go down in defeat.

2

Battle of Madrid and Other Campaigns
(October 1936–February 1937)

"It is apparent that the results of the bombing from November 1st to December 11th are not what might be expected from modern bombardment activities."

Col. Stephen O. Fuqua,
January 8, 1937[1]

The central military event of the first year of the civil war was the Battle of Madrid, more aptly described as a combination of battles and a loosely managed siege, which over the decades took on a near-mystical reputation as a heroic defense by the Republicans and strategically crucial to the Nationalists. The combination of battles and siege continued until the end of the war, insuring that Fuqua and others would continue to comment about Madrid for several years. However, a critical period in the military history of the war was the Battle of Madrid, which took place in the first half of November, when the Nationalists attempted to enter the city by way of the University of Madrid campus. Although the initiative was blocked, the government of the Republic, nonetheless, moved to Valencia on the eastern coast of Spain to avoid the risk of being captured by Franco's forces. Conventional wisdom at the time held that the Nationalists would seize the city. Madrid was now run by a *junta de defensa* led by Gen. Jose Miaja Menant (1875–1958), a career army officer. After the immediate battle ended, the siege and other neighboring engagements continued until late March 1939, when the Nationalists finally occupied

35

the city. The city was able to hold off the Nationalists in November 1936 through a combination of willpower and resistance to invasion displayed by the local defenders, and through substantial infusions of weapons and military advisers and aviators from the Soviets arriving between October and December. Additionally, some 8,500 men of the First International Brigade arrived in Madrid on November 8, providing badly needed additional troops that could be thrown into the battle. These events are why, in many dispatches below, American observers commented on the role of the Soviets, militia, and the International Brigades in Spain. Reading reports in the previous chapter and later in this one about Republican military affairs must seem confusing at times, because there were militia, foreign military units of volunteers and professionals, soldiers of fortune (especially aviators), and, of course, a tiny professional cadre of Spanish Republic soldiers.

The fighting in Madrid in November displayed all manner of combat, which goes far to explain the intense interest in the fighting expressed by career military officers in many countries. It involved aerial bombardment with relatively new classes of aircraft, myriad uses of pistols, rifles, machine guns, antiaircraft cannon, artillery bombardments, house-to-house urban warfare, and use of mixed military units (e.g., militia and foreign brigades, and even civilians); in short, the list of possible warfare activities proved extensive. Nationalist bombs dropped at night frequently killed several thousand residents daily, while during the day both sides fought intensely.

The quote at the start of this chapter is a reminder that beginning with the earliest days of the civil war and extending to the present, historians of military events of the 1930s displayed considerable interest in the role of air warfare in Spain, largely because in that war aircraft and tactics were used that were more advanced than those of World War I. The files of the American military attaché are replete with extensive, highly detailed discussions about the technical features of aircraft, tactics, quality of pilots, training, and so forth. Stephen Fuqua was not an expert on aerial warfare and thus wisely turned to others to write the technical descriptions of aircraft and tactics. Because the topic has been of such interest, both to contemporary military observers and historians, this chapter includes reports written by other American military officers to round out the story told by Fuqua.

The military establishments of major nations expressed intense interest in Spanish affairs by the late fall of 1936, a curiosity that they sustained right to the end of the war. In the files are many reports by American officers of conversations with their peers in German, French, and British military units, sharing information about what they learned concerning Spain. A few examples of "he said" reports of such conversations appear in this and subsequent chapters. Typical of the various war ministries, the U.S. War Department was explicit in seeking out information. The General Staff instructed Fuqua in November 1936 to report in detail on current military activities:

> The present operations about Madrid, involving the action of forces armed with post-war weapons in a major engagement, are of extreme interest to the War Department. Your cabled military reports have kept the division informed of the day to day changes in the situation and have been transmitted, in substance, to the Chief of Staff.
>
> It is desired that when time and opportunity permit, a comprehensive and detailed report of the battle of Madrid be prepared and forwarded by mail. This report should include, subject to the availability of information, an account of the offensive and defensive plans of the opposing forces and the manner of their execution, their strength in the combatant arms, and the combined use of these arms in battle, and the extent and nature of weapons employed.[2]

Fuqua remained in Madrid during the fighting, not moving to Valencia upon the transfer of government (hence, the embassy) until at least the end of the year. Because communications proved difficult during the weeks of fighting and beyond, many reports of events in Spain, especially in Madrid, came into the War Department from American officers stationed in Paris and London who often transmitted summaries of conversations with reporters, pilots, and others familiar with the immediate circumstances prevailing in Madrid.

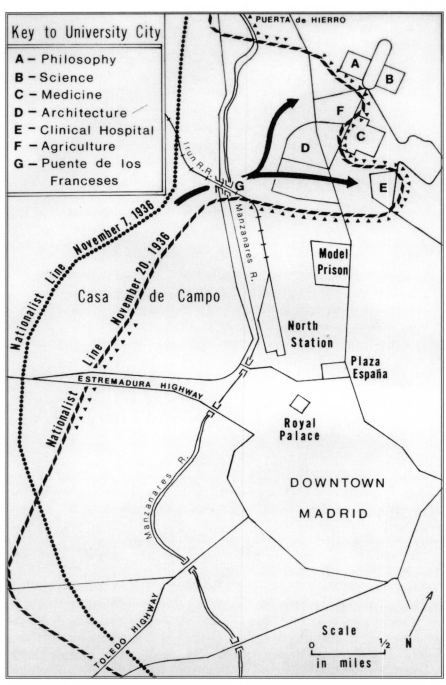

Key to University City

A – Philosophy
B – Science
C – Medicine
D – Architecture
E – Clinical Hospital
F – Agriculture
G – Puente de los Franceses

PUERTA de HIERRO

A
B
F
C
D
E
G

Irun R.R.

Nationalist Line November 7, 1936

Line November 20, 1936

Nationalist

Casa de Campo

Manzanares R.

Model Prison

North Station

Plaza España

ESTREMADURA HIGHWAY

Manzanares R.

Royal Palace

DOWNTOWN

MADRID

TOLEDO HIGHWAY

Scale
0   ½
in miles

N

Battle for Madrid, November 1936. Arrows indicate Nationalist advance, triangular symbols Republican lines held by anarchists. [Robert W. Kern, *Red Years/Black Years: A Political History of Spanish Anarchism, 1911–1937* (© 1978 by Institute for the Study of Human Issues, Inc.), 200.]

Madrid   No. 6427
October 22, 1936

Madrid-Guadalajara-Zaragoza Road

The farthest town held by government forces on this road is Algora, 140 kilometers from Madrid. About 1 kilometer southwest of the town is the limiting advanced position on a hill line with machine gun pill boxes and rifle pits directly commanded by a Madrid *bombero* (fireman).This position extends only three or four hundred yards [on] either side of the road and is occupied by some 200 men under the general command of a young lieutenant. The town is unoccupied, but there is a look-out in the church tower observing particularly towards Torremocha, which is controlled by the rebels. This front is reckoned as a quiet sector, the present relative positions of the contending forces having been held for some 6 weeks without either engagement or movement. At the occupied position the lieutenant and the *bombero* stepped on the running board of our car and accompanied us into the town. Here, we were greeted by the mayor, an escaped convict from the Cartagena prison, who was most courteous to us expressing his feelings of friendship in presenting us with a large jar of honey—significant of the leading products of this sector, this being the locality of large apiaries. The car, with a small American flag at the "helm", soon attracted the natives, who thronged about the vehicle. One fine looking old chap, putting his arm around me, said, "that the war would have been over a long time ago if it had not been for Germany and Italy helping the fascists, but that conditions would soon be better with the United States on our side." I immediately took the lead in shifting the conversation and left the old fellow to his thoughts.

It was interesting to note here that there had grown up between the two opposing forces a very fine esprit which permitted a town messenger from Algora to make daily visits to Torremocha, doing chores for the neighboring people of the two towns. In this connection, our guides told me that the messenger brought news of the enemy and, of course, they said, "we allow him to tell the fascists whatever he knows about us". The humorous side of the mission and duties of this common messenger, scout and spy brought forth some comment and occasioned the amusement the case merited.

The position, evidenced by the mentality of the troops was purely defensive in character, which was further fortified by the fact that the important points on the main road and all culverts for several kilometers back towards Madrid were being prepared for demolition.

North Madrid-Somosierra-Burgos Road

The farthest position north on this road occupied by government troops is a line running generally east and west across the road just north of Buitrago. Westward, it includes Villavieja and Navarredonda, thence the line runs southward along the road Gargantilla-Lozoya-Rascafria. The position extends eastward some 6 kms. to include the main water supply of Madrid—the Lozoya reservoir. The commanding officer of this sector is General Jose Galan, who three months ago was a lieutenant of Carabineros. The general seemed particularly pleased that a foreign military officer should call upon him and, on account of my nationality and office, he extended to me marked attention showing me his command and explaining the position of his troops. The artillery position on a ridge immediately south of Buitrago was well organized with 75s and some 6 inch pieces. However, the defensive character of the emplacements and dugouts gave no evidence whatever of any intention of passing to the offensive, and this deduction was verified by the general who informed me that he contemplated no offensive movement that his main mission was to defend the Lozoya water supply.

The organization of the position and general appearance of the troops were the best which have been observed. Unquestionably, the discipline and morale were superior to any of the troops I have visited. The only organized kitchen seen at the front was installed here, from which some 3,000 men were fed—the system being issues to "details" which carried the food to organizational P.C.s[3] for distribution directly to the men. This command has the distinction of being the only one that has never been driven from its positions. However, I am sure that the enemy facing this front has never seriously attempted to break it, for it appeared very weak, offering an easy advance against a most vulnerable right flank.

The Guadarrama Front

This position lies across the main highway some 55 kilometers from Madrid and about 2 kilometers northwest of the town of Guadarrama. The original position was at the divide, Puerto del Leon, about 10 kilometers from the town, which was occupied by the government troops shortly after the beginning of the revolt but was soon lost to the rebels. This front has been the scene of almost continuous fighting, the respective lines of the contending forces shifting back and forth between the pass and the town. The town was under artillery fire the day of my visit;

however, the bombardment was more or less routine and of a type that occurs daily. The crossroad just southeast of the town is subject at all times to artillery interdiction fire. The position is probably occupied by some five to six thousand men and is well supplied with artillery and machine guns. The artillery position is on the south side of a ridge paralleling the road to the Escorial, just south of the town. In general, the artillery type is the 75mm.; however, there are some 6 inch and 4 inch pieces—the individual guns are well placed and conventionally camouflaged.

The importance of the Guadarrama position lies in the fact that it is the key point dominating the main highway from Madrid to the northwest. A rebel advance of some 10 kilometers beyond the town of Guadarrama to Villalba would make the Navacerrada position untenable, throw back the government reserve position at the latter place and open the road north to La Granja and Segovia. It seems evident that the rebel advance from this position—which would be costly at the present time, is awaiting the cooperation of the successful drives west of El Escorial. The mission of this command is purely defensive, sufficient evidence being available that the troops were dug in to stay until driven out of their positions. The command of this front, since the relief of General Riquelme, has been changed so frequently that I was unable to learn on the day of my visit who then had this assignment.

The Alberche Front

This position originally covered the San Martin de Valdeiglesias area on the west side of the Alberche but was at Pelayos, the top of the river gorge, the day of my visit and since has been withdrawn to a line just east of Chapineria. The dam across the river near El Tiemblo, 10 kilometers northwest of San Martin, came into great press prominence as it was reported that the dam had been blown up by the government causing the impounded waters to rush to Talavera washing the rebels from the town and drowning hundreds. However, what happened was that the sluice gates were opened with a view of accomplishing what was reported but Talavera being some 110 kilometers distant, and the stream bed widening beyond the gorge, no appreciable rise in the stream was noted at the objective.

This front is particularly important and becomes more so now that the rebels are well on the east bank of the Alberche with almost level country lying between them and their main objective just 45 kilometers away. The scenes witnessed at Pelayos, where the church was in flames and militia mobs thronged the streets,

presented anything but what should be found in the advanced position of any
army facing an attacking foe. The commanding officer told me in person that
he did not have a machine gun or an artillery piece in his command but for the
benefit of his listeners said, "However, the absence of proper armament will not
change our determination to fight to the last man to stop the fascists from crossing
the Alberche". I knew at the time, from the untrained, undisciplined and lazy militia I saw about me, that there would be no tales of heroic defense for the Spanish
Civil War historian to record when the rebels come against Pelayos. In a few days
this mob was well east of Chapineria in a disorderly retreat.

The commanding officer of this front was at Navas del Rey at the time of
my visit and was particularly friendly to me, showing me his plan for recapture of
San Martin which was to be initiated that afternoon. I asked him why he did not
start now, remarking that time was precious and that he needed all daylight possible for the concentration of his columns on the objective. His reply was typical:
"After eating we will start". As it was 1.00 P.M. and the *comida* was to be at 2.00
o'clock, a ceremony that would last at least two hours, he was losing three hours of
valuable time. I heard later that his columns never reached the deployment point.
This front is generally recognized at this time to be in excellent shape—the training and discipline as well as organization and unity of command being far superior
to that observed in other theaters, save the troops of General Galan at Buitrago.
The command is not liberally supplied with machine guns and artillery and is being watched by interested observers to ascertain to what degree they will resist the
attack that sooner or later they must meet. The main defense line crosses the San
Martin-Brunete road at a point just west of the small stream about 5 kilometers
west of the latter town. When this line is broken, the Rebels will unquestionably
push to Brunete, establishing lateral communication with the Navalcarnero position. It is believed that the strength of this command is about 4,000 men, liberally
supplied with machine guns and artillery.

The Madrid-Portugal Road: The "Old" Talavera Front
This front came into outstanding prominence after the fall of the government's
strongly entrenched position just west of Talavera. The victorious march of the
Franco column along this great highway, driving back superior forces operating
in "friendly" territory, has been a great contributing factor to the advantageous
positions now held in the rebel encircling movement around Madrid. The column
since leaving Talavera has given crushing defeats to the government forces at Santa

Olalla, Maqueda, Santa Cruz and drove the militia troops from their Toledo positions rescuing the defenders of the Alcazar. The column, leaving a sufficient force to "dig in" for the defense of the south and east Toledo fronts, then proceeded northward on the main Madrid highway, again completely defeating the government troops in the important engagements at Olias del Rey, Illescas and Torrejon, their line now resting about halfway between this last named town and Parla.

During this northward movement on the Madrid road, the rebels cleared the north bank of the Tajo between Toledo and Aranjuez, working northward at the same time between the main roads from Madrid to Toledo and to Aranjuez, until their right flank lay across the Aranjuez road and the Valencia railroad just east of Sesena. After this achievement, the advance of the right flank column has kept pace with the forward movement of the center along the Madrid-Toledo road until now its right rests at Ciempozuelos, dominating the Valencia railroad, the Jarama Canal and the "four road juncture" at this point. The advance of the main and right columns has now obtained lateral communication along the entire front in this sector along the road Ciempozuelos-Torrejon-Grinon-El Alamo-Navalcarnero. To continue this front northward with lateral road communication will require the extension along the connecting road to Brunete, Valdemorillo to El Escorial, an advance to accomplish which may be initiated at any time.

My first visit to the "Talavera front" was during the attack on Santa Olalla referred to in [the] cablegram dated September 30, 1936 in which, from observations made at the time, it was definitely estimated "the complete government defeat, time dependent upon capitulating or defending Madrid," confirming similar estimate made in Report 6411—9/18/36.

My second visit was made when the government troops were at Valmojado, 12 kilometers southwest of Navalcarnero. Here, I had an excellent opportunity to see the troops in line and note their disposition in the occupation of a defensive position, notes on which are included in general comments following this report.

The command of this front has been until quite recently under General Asensio but who, a short time ago, in conventional parlance, was "kicked upstairs" to the non-active office of Sub-Secretary of War.

The strength of this command has undergone many changes, probably running from as high as 6,000 and as low as 2,000 men. The officer in command of the front line, at the time of my visit to Valmojado, gave me his strength as 600 men which with supporting troops and reserves probably would bring the total strength to 2,000 men.

Toledo Fronts Since Occupation by Rebels

EAST

After the capture of Toledo on September 28th, the militia retreated in great part southward toward Orgaz and Mora, while some few followed the south bank of the Tagus to Aranjuez. The rebels, upon taking over the city, took up a defensive position south and east of this town and, as noted above, began to clear the north bank of the Tagus in order to have this formidable obstacle covering their rear in their planned advance on Madrid.

The government troops, on noting they were not pursued, gradually returned to the railroad junction, some 10 kilometers east of Toledo, and took up a defensive position which the Valencia troops were establishing just west of the railroad station (Algodor—not named on map—location where the Algodor River crosses the railroad) at the time of my first visit to this sector. These troops, some 600 in number, were imbued solely with the spirit of the defensive; however, when they learned that the rebels were not marching eastward south of the river, but were moving up the river on the north bank, they advanced to within two or three kilometers of the east rebel defenses of Toledo and engaged in a feeble way the enemy on the north bank.

SOUTH

In order to see the conditions of the troops that had evacuated Toledo and to note their morale, we went south of Aranjuez via Ocana to Tembleque, turning west to Mora and Orgaz and thence toward Toledo. At Ajofrin, 20 kilometers south of Toledo, the commanding officer gave us a special pass to visit his front line which he described as being located 3 kilometers north of Burguillos. However, upon entering this town we saw no evidence of any troops beyond and were soon convinced that there were none between us and Toledo—a conviction which was established through talking to a native who informed us that the militia which had been north of the town had retired to Nambroca, the village 4 kilometers east of Burguillos. The native told us that one could go into Toledo by simply holding a white rag over his head and that the rebels had sent word to the town's people that no one, not resisting them, would be harmed.

On returning towards Ajofrin the captain was met and seemed much surprised and at a perfect mental loss when informed that he had no front line.

The troops observed were completely whipped and told of the horror of the rebel artillery fire preparatory to their evacuation of Toledo. They evidently were not of the same fighting stock as the band of heroes that fought in the Alcazar holding out for seventy-two days against the combined efforts of the government in the employment of rifle, machine gun and artillery fire, bombs from the air, dynamiting from tunnels bored beneath them, gasoline sprinkled and fired over them, as well as the promise of safety, should they walk out, by the Dean of the Diplomatic Corps. After seeing these troops, elements of the two thousand that had retreated under artillery fire from Toledo, my estimate submitted to the G-2 office was absolutely confirmed. I might add that every effort is being made to reorganize these militiamen in this section with a view of having them aid in a government offensive south on the Aranjuez road by striking north from Aranjuez and at the same time attack the east and south rebel positions in Toledo. However, the task is believed to be too great for these troops.

General Comments

Through the courtesy of the Spanish War Department, as the result of a personal call on Señor [Francisco] Largo Caballero,[4] I was given a document authorizing me to pass at will through the war zone and visit all Madrid fronts. It is desired to state that it is believed that this is the only paper of this character issued to a member of the foreign diplomatic corps in Madrid. The French military attaché has tried in vain to secure such an authorization. The mentioning of this document is believed to be important as this courtesy was extended on account of my nationality. This pass has enabled me to visit all Madrid fronts and to be the recipient of courtesies and attentions from all officials with whom I have had any contact. The authorization issued included freedom of circulation for my car and authorized the following parties to accompany me: Mr. Riley Williams, Worthington Pump and Machinery Corporation, former reserve officer, acting as my adjutant, Colonel Ramos, ex-Philippine constabulary officer (the gatekeeper at the Embassy) and one Embassy guard. My observations may be briefly stated as follows:

ORGANIZATION

The militia in general is organized in groups referred to as Battalions, Regiments, and Commands without any reference to strength. These organizations in general bear specific names which seemingly have a great appeal to militia psychology, such for example as:

> *Largo Caballero* (Prime Minister and Minister of War)
> *Thaelmann* (Noted German socialist)
> *Margarita Nelken* (Noted Spanish socialist)

Acero (Steel)

Hierro (Iron—Motorized machine gun unit)

Octubre (Commemorating the October 1934 revolt)

Martinez Barrio (President of the Cortes)

Leonese Rojos (Red Lions)

Alpino Juventud (Ski Battalion)

Pasionaria (Dolores Ibarruri—the Passion Flower—noted communist)

Cordoba (made up of Cordoba residents)

Fontana (made up of Valencia residents)

Mangada (named after the general commanding Escorial sector).

These units are politically controlled by the *comite* through whom the military leader functions. This leader is allowed a certain latitude in command, but all important questions must be acted upon by this body, which holds direct control over all matters pertaining to organization, discipline, training and supply. The relation of any separate unit to the military commander of a "front" or "position" is directed by the unit *comite* which at times, if not in accord with the policy of the central command, will move its particular group completely from this control. I saw this situation at Santa Olalla, while the action was in progress, when political organizations left the front without reference to the high commander and without opposition from him. This system of individual group action has probably been the greatest contributor to the crushing defeats administered to the militia by the rebel forces.

TRAINING AND DISCIPLINE

The militia organizations are hopelessly deficient in military training of any character and their discipline, in so far as the individual is concerned, is purely voluntary and in general is in proportion to the intelligence or to the obsession for the "cause" possessed by the militiaman. The attempt to train the militiaman in the "school of the soldier", as observed in the training groups in Madrid, could be characterized best by the use of the word *pitiful*. The disciplinary factor in connection with the "drill" of the "soldier", with and without arms, is not appreciated by the instructors, hence nothing in this line is accomplished. Have noted "drill masters" explaining in detail, for example, the movement "about face", stressing the importance and necessity for facing about as prescribed—but permitting the execution in a slouchy fashion—without assuming the "position of a soldier" in other respects. Not knowing that the drill book training, which exacts certain details of execution in such movements, was for the purpose of obtaining uniformity in execution, concert of action and the instilling of discipline—a "sergeant" I noted who was giving instructions was asked by a peasant type with whom he was having some difficulty, "Why learn this hard way to 'turn around' when it is so easy to turn like I have always turned?" I think the question was too deep for the drill instructors. However, this citation is general and most applicable to all close order instruction, which is wasted in that it is not utilized for disciplinary training. In fact, the subject with which this paragraph deals can be covered briefly by saying that the militia have no military training and discipline other than that which some have received through past army service.

SUPPLY

The supply systems follow that of organization, each political group taking care of its own personnel. Equipment, clothing, rations, ammunition and first aid are handled in this way so the confusion resulting can readily be understood. In moving up to the front, motor transportation of all types can be noted, marked with the particular organization for which the supplies are destined. I have heard that some of the "high toned" organizations, like the Largo Caballero Battalion, send up to the front the very best of food, including certain delicacies in this line that have long since been removed from the Madrid markets. However, the militia seems to understand this system and in one way or another are "making out" under it, for it is understood that they do not lack for supplies—at least those that are obtainable locally.

MORALE

The morale of the militiamen, singing the *Internationale* on the way to the front, reaches extreme heights fanned by the enthusiasm born in the belief that he is fighting not only the "fascist beast", as the rebel is painted, but for the establishment of a political regime that will give to him the old "forty acres and mule" of the "Reconstruction Period" in the South.[5] At the front, lacking the basic essentials of soldierly training, without proper equipment and armament and poor leadership, his first baptism of fire, from which he is compelled to retreat, destroys his morale and shakes his faith in the successful consummation of his cause.

UNIFORM, ARMAMENT AND EQUIPMENT

The uniform of the militia is the *mono* (overalls) of varying shades of blue and brown, however, lacking sufficient number of this garb, many wear civilian attire of non-descript character. The militia of course have no uniform armament or equipment. The artillery is of varying caliber 3 inches, 4 inches, and 6 inches. The infantryman is armed with the Mauser but until lately a number were issued shotguns of varying patterns as well as many types of American Winchester of a 44 caliber. Mortars and machine guns are scarce and few tanks are available.[6] The soldier has practically no individual standard equipment but carries a blanket roll, within which he places whatever he wishes. A belt, pouch or some form of ammunition carrier is issued to him. His headgear is what we term the "overseas cap", and is of many designs, piped with cords of various hues for organizational designation.

TRANSPORTATION

There is apparently no central system for delivery of supplies, this being done by organizational transportation or by trucks temporarily allotted for the purpose. On account of the comparative short distances of the fronts from the city, there exist no "field trains", as we know the term. The transportation utilized is, when practicable, the train service to the railhead and thence by motor truck to distributing points. Usually, however, it is by motor vehicle direct to the organizational receiving station. All motor vehicles, other than those of members of the Diplomatic Corps, were seized by the government at the beginning of the revolt, and while ample transportation was available for troops and supplies during the early stages of the revolution, there is now an actual shortage, due principally to inefficiency in both driving and upkeep, which has placed hundreds of vehicles in local repair shops, hopelessly inadequately equipped to meet the increased demands imposed.

COMMUNICATIONS

The militia organizations have no "signal units". All communications in the various fronts are handled by signal groups organized by the Spanish Telephone Co. and assigned to various sectors. Owing to the efficiency of the Telephone Company personnel, the communications, notwithstanding the many difficult local problems, may be said to be very satisfactory.

DEFENSIVE POSITIONS

The defensive positions, observed practically on all fronts, in general, violated most of the principles as to requirements. The cardinal precept of organization in depth and the location of machine gun positions coordinated to use cross fire and give flank protection were openly violated in all positions. The obsession to defend either side of a road—based upon the estimate that the enemy must approach by the highway—with both flanks uncovered and unprotected either by fire or a system of patrolling, seemed general. Keeping touch with the enemy by patrolling seemed an unknown art. In one case, two patrols were observed, sent out specifically to locate Moro cavalry, marching near and paralleling a road in the direction in which a short distance ahead was a friendly post. Hugging the road and the town edge was an expression of the militia psychology of safety first.

The defensive position which classifies all Madrid fronts, is nothing more than a line or double line of infantry troops occupying in most cases poorly dug trenches, badly located and unscreened, with both flanks "rest in the air". Whenever a town is available—the position is invariably in the outskirts, thus affording narrow streets for the important "get away" route. This organization of the defensive has permitted attacking rebels to flank the positions on all fronts with perfect ease. The main defense line for the protection of the city is shown [on] the accompanying map and is literally a line for there is no organization in depth. This line has now been broken and penetrated on three important fronts—Portugal Road, Toledo Road and Aranjuez Road. The rebel attack invariably follows the same plan—airplane bombing and artillery shelling by way of preparation, followed by an infantry advance against a flank or, if made against the front, the movement is preceded with a few tanks. In practically all cases the militia retire after the air and artillery bombardments, and in consequence, the rebel battle casualties are estimated very few.

Madrid   No. 6441
December 19, 1936
Subject: The Military Situation

The Madrid Fronts—General

After the methodic and successful advance of General Franco's columns, which, since the defeat of the militia at Navalcarnero (October 21), broke all defense lines of the government up to the very gates of Madrid, the military situation entered a new phase. The taking of the capital, which was anticipated and advertised by rebel press and radio as an easy task, suddenly developed, owing to several factors, into an undertaking of considerable magnitude confronted with many difficulties.

When on November 7th the Franco troops reached the Manzanares River, it seemed as a certainty from a military point of view that the fate of the capital was doomed. The sight of the demoralized retreating militia, the departure of the government from Madrid, the hurried escape of noted leftists, all combined to make the occasion opportune for the capture of the city by the advancing Nationalist columns, the morale and spirit of which were very high as a result of the uninterrupted series of crushing blows they had inflicted upon the enemy. However, the fact that General Franco did not order a general assault on Madrid, taking advantage of such favorable conditions, seemed to indicate lack of sufficient strength, as the changes of indecision made by some against this general are not seemingly justified, taking into consideration his demonstrated ability and past accomplishments.

While no accurate information is available as to the numerical strength of the Nationalist columns which reached the west and south suburbs of the capital, it appears from various sources and reports that these forces numbered some 40,000 men, a strength believed to be about one-third of the militia and other troops available for the defense of Madrid. Furthermore, it was clear that Franco's shock troops, consisting mainly of well trained and hard fighting Moors and Legionnaires, did not have behind them sufficient troops formed of the same high class material, but of army units, militia and police troops having a variable military efficiency. This may explain the failure of Franco in following up his advance to the Manzanares with a drive to take the capital at the most favorable opportunity. He gave a respite of a few days to his troops for the consolidation of their positions near the river, preparatory for further advance, at the same time he began to pound with artillery fire the Madrid line at several places in order to find out the vulnerable points of the city's defense. The government militia, far from abandoning their trenches as in the past after having been subjected to heavy artillery fire, made a rather resolute defense. This unexpected reaction caused the postponement of the final drive on Madrid.

A decision which must be reckoned from the information now at hand as a fatal military error. The weakness of the militia as a fighting force, its disorganization and demoralization, should have been known to the rebel high command in view of the almost uninterrupted march of the Nationalists from Maqueda and Toledo on Madrid, to say nothing of the estimates that should have been made by their reported system of espionage in the capital. Certainly, after the destruction of the Madrid defense lines at Navalcarnero, Getafe and Cerro de los Angeles which covered the three main highway routes from the south and southwest, Madrid could have been entered, in the opinion of the undersigned, without even a serious skirmish.

The *Junta de Defensa*, left in charge of the capital by the government, took immediate and excellent advantage of the halt by Franco's troops and began the reorganization of the Madrid defenses, utilizing the contingents which had arrived from Barcelona, Valencia and other places, among which there was one some 3,000 strong formed of foreigners, sent to reinforce the International Column. A Russian general, assisted by commissioned officers of various nationalities, assumed the direction of the defense of the city, while discipline was enforced on the militia, for the first time, through fear of punishment as those disobeying orders to hold fast faced death at the point of the pistols of their officers. The marked improvement in discipline, together with the numerical superiority of the government forces, now being equipped with abundant and modern material just received, bolstered the confidence of the people in the city's defense, which soon resulted in several attacks of the Nationalists, which although not attaining their objectives completely, nevertheless served to check further progress of the enemy.

On November 16th the Nationalists succeeded in crossing the river west of University City (the northwestern section of Madrid) and the following day took possession of most of the larger buildings of this educational plant now in the course of construction, but not without suffering great losses and facing a resistance from the militia formerly unknown. The efforts of the Nationalists in successive days to extend their foothold in this section encountered the same resolute resistance and in consequence it has been only with heavy losses that they have gained some additional ground in this section and in the adjoining Parque del Oeste.

At present, forty days have elapsed since the victorious Nationalist column reached the Manzanares River, and while a general drive on Madrid has not been attempted pending, it is believed, the arrival of reinforcements, both in men and materiel, they have made sporadic attacks which have accomplished little. As to the weakening effect of such pounding on the government forces, it does not appear to have amounted to much owing to the abundant reserves of manpower available to the militia forces.

Changes in Other Fronts

Since last report (No. 6427) the military situation on all other fronts other than Madrid remains practically the same. The unexpected resistance encountered by General Franco in his drive on the capital has evidently compelled him to withdraw forces from other regions in order to strengthen his Madrid columns, and, as a result, during the last three weeks the Nationalists have shown little activity in the various provincial sectors remaining, in general, on the defensive.

On most of these fronts, the government forces, responding to appeals made by the Madrid Junta de Defensa and the government in Valencia, urging them to attack the rebels without respite and thus cooperating in removing the pressure against Madrid, have shown a certain degree of offensive spirit during the last three weeks, without, however, any follow-on policy to local successes attained.

In the Asturias, the government troops launched during the last days of November an offensive, the main objective of which was to cut communications between Grado, a base of the Nationalist army in this region and the capital, Oviedo, which was also subjected to strong attack. This general offensive was repulsed, both sides suffering heavy losses, particularly the government militia, which for some ten days did not renew its attacks. The situation in Asturias, while no exact information is available as to the respective opposing positions, seems to be as follows: The Nationalists hold Oviedo, a small protecting zone north, east and south of the city and a corridor to the west ensuring communication with their base at Grado (some 40 kilometers from the capital). West of the line Grado-Pravia, all the littoral of the Asturias province and an extensive zone south of same until the Galicia region is controlled by the Nationalists. The government holds the important seaports of Aviles and Gijon and the remaining territory of the province.

On the Bilbao front, the Nationalists have lost some ground in the Alava province, the militia under the autonomous Basque government having advanced as far as the village of Villareal, some 20 kilometers north of Vitoria, the capital of the province. It is believed that the offensive against this city has little chance of progressing any further as the Nationalists have sent reinforcements which have reestablished the situation formerly existing. Furthermore, the mountainous character of this district and the frequent rains and fogs now occurring are naturally a handicap to offensive operations. However, it is evident that this government attack on Vitoria has cooperated in an indirect way in aiding the defense of Madrid.

The Santander militia have advanced into the territory of Burgos province and are now in the vicinity of Villarcayo, where all indicates that this government offensive has been stopped by the Nationalists.

In the Huesca and Teruel sectors, the situation has not appreciably changed. It appears that the Catalan government, bothered by its own problems and internal anarchy, has not made a real effort in organizing a strong offensive in these districts, where only minor engagements have taken place.

A new front has been established northeast of Toledo where a government column, mostly formed of troops from Valencia and Alicante, is menacing the rearguard of the Nationalist troops attacking Madrid. This column was assembled at Chinchon and faces the rebel lines at Pinto, Sesena and Anover de Tajo which they have attacked although without appreciable results. Still another front has been recently established southeast and dangerously near Talavera, the main base of the Nationalist army operating against Madrid. Government troops, probably taken from the Aranjuez sector, reinforced by contingents from Albacete and Alicante, launched some three weeks ago an attack against Talavera which, while not strong and was repulsed with heavy losses, appeared to have caused considerable concern to the Nationalist command. These government forces seem to be now on the line at San Bartlome and San Martin de Montalban. The situation in the Cordoba, Granada and Malaga fronts appears to be unchanged.

Paris   No. 23, 066-W
January 7, 1937
Subject: Air Combat Operations. Aviation in Spain

Recently several American aviators, among them Messrs Acosta, Schneider, Lord and Perry arrived in Paris after having flown for the governmental forces in Spain. From what could be gathered it appears that they quit the government forces because their pay was not forthcoming. It is believed that all, except Mr. Lord, have returned to the States.

Though there is no way of checking the accuracy of Mr. Lord's statements who, for some reason or other, is staying in Paris, the following is submitted for what it is worth:

It appears that the American flyers were stationed in Bilbao and vicinity where they flew mostly sports planes in their bombing operations. They were under Spanish command which was poorly organized and from what can be gathered it appears that they spent most of their time in easy living though they did on occasion fly certain missions. When they first arrived at Bilbao, 25 lb. bombs were carried and dropped over the side of the plane; later however what planes were available were equipped with a type of bomb rack. At times they flew even cabin ships and Mr. Lord is an authority for the statement that his observer on one occasion being equipped with a Lewis machine gun proposed, should enemy ships be met in the air, to fire through the window without bothering to open it.

In Mr. Lord's opinion, most of the Russian aviation is concentrated around Madrid where they have, according to him, over 200 planes. There were, however, some Russian planes in the Bilbao area on their own airdrome, where efficient organization obtained. They had a system whereby four planes were ready at all times to take to the air. The ships were on the field and the motor of a truck was connected up with the propeller and the ships warmed up every hour. The aviators fully equipped and ready to fly with their mechanics stayed in a dugout beside their respective ships and when the alarm was given the truck motor was started and the ships warmed up immediately. By the time the aviator had donned his parachute, climbed into his seat and was strapped in, the plane was ready to take off. In other words, by means of this system they were able to taxi down the field and take to the air in about a minute.

Russian influence is strong in all matters pertaining to aviation. It appears that when Lord required money, he applied to his *Commandante* (Spanish) who in turn called up the Russians in another part of town, and on occasions money was forthcoming.

As far as could be ascertained from Mr. Lord, aviation operated by the government forces themselves in Spain is poorly and haphazardly organized and equipped, while the Russians are very keen and on the job. In this connection he stated that he saw Russian planes bearing the Boeing-Curtis mark and that they appeared to be comparatively new. He further stated that on the docks at Alicante he saw crates piled high containing airplanes and airplane parts.

He added that on one occasion when the Italians bombed the town of Alicante, an Italian warship in the harbor directed its search lights on the town, thus outlining targets. Italian aviators from their base in the Balearic Islands bombed the town, dropping something like 400 bombs.

It is not known exactly why Mr. Lord is staying in France. Last night he visited the Spanish Embassy and he was told that at the present moment there were something like 100 bombers in France which it was desired to move into Spain. They stated in addition that 60 new bombers had been received very recently by the government forces. Efficient bombers have been lacking.

Mr. Lord stated that last night he met a French aviator in Paris who had gone to Spain as a sergeant at the outbreak of the civil war and who had knocked down something like 14 enemy planes. He had just received a very handsome bonus in gold and a *commandante*'s commission and uniforms. The Frenchman was in Paris on a short leave.

When Mr. Lord was flying in Spain his uniform was garnished with communistic symbols—a crossed scythe and hammer on each lapel of his tunic, and a red star on his hat with a huge red kerchief around his throat.

Lord may be dickering with the Spanish Embassy here in Paris with the idea of flying planes from France to Spain for the government.

Comment
All of the above must be taken with several grains of salt. When Lord's comrades return to the United States, they will undoubtedly be quizzed by the State Department and the War Department and his story can be checked.

It is believed that Lord is in the game for what he can get out of it, whether it be flying for this or that government, or in selling his story to some newspaper publisher.

The method of starting Russian planes with a truck motor is quite common and is used very often in Russia. Compressed air machines for starting are also employed.

Sumner Waite

Lt. Col., Inf., Asst. Military Attaché

Paris   No. 23, 106-W
January 18, 1937
Subject: Revolutionary Movements. Spain

The Assistant Chief of Staff, G-2 of the French Army has furnished the undersigned with a summary of events in Spain, army, organization and estimates concerning German and Italian assistance. [The first several pages of this report are not reproduced here. —Ed. Note]

Operations
When the military insurrection broke, the government disposed of very few regular troops and not over 200 officers. Of this number a goodly portion became disgusted with the government forces and joined the rebels. Rightly or wrongly the men and NCO's [noncommissioned officers] serving with the colors did not inspire confidence and were discharged and soon lost in the confusion.

The government called up three classes and created a volunteer army. The result was not happy. They finally assembled approximately 40,000 men with comparatively no military organization. Cadres were practically nonexistent. Members of the bourgeoisie and artisan classes in the towns had been caught and refused to answer the flaming appeals of the recruiting officers.

Only a comparatively few dazed and not very intelligent peasants, attracted by the pay of two duros a day, presented themselves for enlistment. From the materiel standpoint, the government appeared to possess a large number of factories and warehouses. But stocks were low and the trained factory hands had fled or had been killed. In many instances the rebel commanders had been careful to transfer to selected depots important supplies of arms and munitions. Accordingly at the outset, the government disposed of no leaders, few men and very little materiel.

The government forces consisted only of militia which had been armed hastily with knives, revolvers and various types of rifles.

Everywhere it was necessary to improvise. Each party, each syndical or political organization requisitioned indiscriminately transportation, equipment, etc. They fought savagely among themselves for the automatic weapons seized in barracks. Each party established its own column, composed of its own men, supplied by its own means and acting without regard to a general plan. It was the epoch of atrocities. One saw girls carrying pistols as they would a flower and pale adolescents playing at warfare and assassinating the bourgeoisie on the street corners.

On occasion these disorganized forces were thrown against rebel troops. The latter were not very strong but at least they were disciplined and obeyed orders. There, the subaltern leaders did not fail even though they were mediocre, but the men were not dependable. Previously soldiers had obeyed their officers passively but after the first surprise had been dissipated they exhibited a certain reluctance to carry out orders. Many were divided between their respect for the military hierarchy and a hidden class spirit which incited them to join their fellows across the barrier. When the insurgents were not entirely victorious, numerous desertions occurred.

There remained the "Phalangistas"—a formation hardly indoctrinate with fascism whose chiefs were prisoners and who themselves were but little better than white militia, anarchistic and inconsistent. Then there were the *carlistas* (*requestes*) of Navarre and the forces overseas—the original troops behind the movement, Moroccans and Legionnaires, professional soldiers, attached faithfully to their officers.

But these troops, well trained and capable, were in Morocco and the government navy patrolled the Straits of Gibraltar. It was, therefore, necessary to await the arrival of transport planes from Italy in order to ferry small groups to Cadiz and to Algeciras. Not much happened during the month of August except a few isolated combats in which the nationalists were generally victorious but lacked the will to exploit their successes.

On the other hand, raids were executed which required the maximum of nervous energy for short periods of time. The expedition completed, the adversary massacred, the men returned to their homes, to the factory, or to the rendezvous of the party and the force was dissipated.

However, out of the general anarchy which prevailed, there emerged two rebel personalities: a national, General Franco, a regional, the Carlist Chief, del Falconde. The first made himself the supreme commander from both the military and political standpoint, while the second with his mountaineers played the covering forces to the arrival of the Moroccan units. As soon as Franco disposed of some *banderas* (battalions) he immediately dispatched them into Estremadura in order to connect up the northern and southern sections of insurgent territory and at the same time separate Madrid from Portugal. He took Badajoz after 24 hours of street fighting, then he continued on toward Old Castile in order to effect liaison with General Mola. The latter with his forces, mostly Carlists, had been content to hold the Sierra front and to harass unmercifully the route from France. On the receipt of reinforcements in small lots, General Mola pushed them into the defiles of Navarre, broke the nationalistic aspirations of the Basques, already demoralized by two months of guerilla warfare, infiltrated toward Irun and San Sebastian, and conquered finally all of the Guipuzcoa.

By the end of September the government forces had lost the west and northwest of Spain. They had only Catalonia, New Castile, the Levant and certain areas around Bilbao, Santander, Oviedo on the Cantabrian coast, and Malaga in Andalusia.

What was General Franco to do? Continue his pressure to the north of Madrid or against the routes of the Levant in order to isolate the Valencia supply base? The latter of course was THE solution but a local episode caused him to abandon good strategy for a plan based on sentiment. In Toledo, sixty kilometers west of Madrid, some cadets and Guardia Civils mixed with *Phalangistas* had assembled in the Alcazar and resisted the violent Red assaults for several weeks. The relief of the Alcazar would be heralded world wide and would no doubt deliver a mortal blow to the governmental forces. A small column commanded by General [Jose Enrique] Varela was thrown quickly on Toledo and became involved in the pursuit of governmental militia which fled in disorder toward Madrid.

Willingly or unwillingly, General Franco was engaged in an attack on the capital. The combats which preceded the march on Madrid encouraged the white commander to attempt to take the city by assault. Never had the government forces shown themselves more incapable of resistance. Talavera, Ilsacas, Navalcarnero seemed to spread panic. Roads filled with fugitives, villages to the rear lodging idle troops, fronts held weakly by discouraged combatants, a disorganized government abandoning bit by bit a harassed town only waiting to welcome the victor, such were the favorable reports received at General Franco's Headquarters when the nationalist advance guards arrived before the Manzanares bordering the western confines of the city.

Why is it that two months later Madrid is still offering resistance? The answer is this: The "intimidation bluff" practiced by the nationalists failed while the "resistance bluff" of the government succeeded.

Before Franco's weak infantry had reached the first houses in Madrid, the nationalist general staff had ordered 18 planes (Junkers) to drop several thousand tons of explosives on the western part of the town. Immediate surrender was anticipated. Instead however, the infantry as it attempted to cross the Manzanares received heavy fire, inflicting losses and stopping their advance. For the first time since Talavera militiamen were encountered who apparently had the will to fight. The nationalists faltered, their "intimidation bluff" had failed.

A few days later the same "desire of resistance" was discovered to the north. Small groups of troops barricaded in buildings refused to surrender. Fearing sanguinary street fighting, the nationalist leaders did not exploit their success. They expected aviation to precipitate the fall of Madrid. But in Madrid everything had changed. The government had departed, a handful of extremists was in command. The "resistance bluff" had succeeded.

The outskirts of the town were defended by several thousand men. There were Communists who knew little about fighting but knew how to die. There were also foreigners who had some experience in soldiering and whose numbers were increased daily by international reinforcements. Supplies in materiel were received as well as Russian tanks, cannon, and airplanes which gradually equaled rebel aviation. The directors of the movement were Russian commissaries who worked behind the Council of Defense.

The history of the first resistance of Madrid is replete with lost opportunities on the part of the nationalist commanders. Timidity, lack of vision, and the limited experience of Moroccan troops prevailed together with internal difficulties and the lack of reserves. As the weeks go by, one is astonished that General Franco has neither reestablished direct communication with Old Castile by surrounding the small groups of militia entrenched in the Sierra, nor has he cut the important supply artery—the Valencia-Madrid road.

Having played poker to the limit, Franco now lacks reserves. Covering a front of sixty kilometers from Toledo to Madrid, sometimes within two kilometers of Red advanced posts, they have been reduced to the defensive. Government counter offensives, however, have failed.

Comment

Evidently Franco put too much dependence on his aviation during his first days before Madrid. The Reds refused to be scared. It becomes increasingly evident that while aviation may to a large extent help prepare the way, the effect is fugitive and as soon as the bombers have passed the defenders come out of their holes. To move forward, take and hold positions, the pressure must be constant.

The time element is playing into the hands of the government. The longer Franco dawdles at Madrid, the better organized will be the Reds when he meets them in the open. Only recently the Reds have made large purchases of gas masks of the conventional type in France. According to a French industrialist, M. Marcel Bogrand, whose acquaintance was made a few days ago and who is interested in the manufacture of such products, the war will soon be carried on *sans merci*, in other words one side or the other is preparing to use gas.

Conservative opinion seems to be that unless Franco takes Madrid in the near future and is able to secure replacements and reinforcements, his chance of success will be greatly diminished.

Waite

London   No. 38512
January 25, 1937

The following items were derived from an unbiased source in London enjoying unusual facilities for obtaining reliable information. It is requested that the subject matter, if widely circulated, be consolidated with other information on the same subject, so that its source will remain unidentified.

One of the most interesting features of the struggle is the effectiveness of the German anti-aircraft guns have been identified. They are completely equipped, officered and trained German organizations which arrived in Spain as units and have operated similarly. In action, the guns are arranged in a square with sides of 250 yards and are fired with parallel laying, so that they threw up four streams of shell, the bursts of which are arranged approximately as the guns. Their fire is known to have proven extremely effective up to 12,000 feet, although their range is greater. (The assumption with regard to the personnel is that they are volunteers in the sense that the men of the units were placed with their backs to a brick wall and told that any man who did not care to volunteer could take one step backwards).

The German bombing plane has proven extremely reliable and remarkably capable of self-defense with its own machine guns. These German planes, however, are protected by flights of Italian fighters, in which both the pilots and the planes have proven themselves extraordinarily effective. As a rule, this Italian effort proceeds at about 20,000 feet, from which height they successfully attack the Russian assailants of the German bombers.

It is interesting to note that the Italian pursuit planes and pilots form a complete complement to the German bombardment planes and pilots, and it is reported that this happy state of affairs has been a matter of mutual congratulations to the Italian and German authorities during the recent visit of [Hermann] Goering to Rome.

For some time it was a mystery as to how the Russian pursuit planes managed to attack Franco's bombers so quickly after the latter approached Madrid. The explanation hitherto offered was that the Russian pursuit planes were extraordinarily fast, but it has recently been developed that the real explanation is not the super speed of the Russian planes but the fact that their landing field is actually in the city of Madrid, and so they have no horizontal distance to cover before going into action.

One of the remarkable features of the war so far has been the amount of punishment the inhabitants of Madrid have taken from bombardment. Most military critics have hitherto assumed that continental bombardment of a civil population would completely disorganize the community life, but this has not proven true in Madrid.

The Russian tanks which have been identified are of two varieties, the light and the medium (11 ton). The light tank has been a failure. The 11-ton tank has been much more of a success, although it has suffered from the fact that its treads were made of synthetic rubber. This material has not only disintegrated under use but is particularly susceptible to gasoline and heat and explains the press reports that tanks have been put out of action by throwing petrol on the tracks.

It is believed by this observer that enough has transpired in Spain to prove that tanks can make no successful attacks by themselves but must be supported by infantry. It seems evident that the only use of tanks has been as infantry tanks and that no commander has yet resorted to the theory that tanks are best used in wide turning movements.

One of the lessons which the Germans took very much to heart after the war was the effectiveness of tanks in the attack. It is commonly believed that the disastrous day of August 8, 1918, was fundamentally the result of the use of British tanks.[7] With their customary thoroughness the Germans, therefore, have developed two of the finest anti-tank weapons in the world, one of which is a shoulder rifle and the other a proper anti-tank cannon. Against these weapons it is the belief of this authority that any advance against infantry in position by lightly armed tanks is sure to result in disaster unless the attack is made by such great numbers of machines that even considerable losses cannot halt the momentum of the attack.

Reliable information has been received to the effect that the French are already modifying their tank design as a result of the demonstrated success of German anti-tank weapons. Further information is available to the effect that the Germans have recently carried out large scale tank attacks, participated in by hundreds of machines, advancing in waves. These machines were opposed by German anti-tank weapons firing non-explosive projectiles with a reduced charge, with the result that only 12 percent of the tanks suffered direct hits. This experiment, it is said, was repeated five times, but nothing as yet is known as to the number of tanks engaged, their speed or the distance over which they were susceptible to anti-tank fire.

Nobody likes the raids, least of all the Militia. They show their displeasure by firing off their guns. A volunteer worker from the British Consulate was walking home when the Embassy raid took place. He had reached the broad Calle Velasquez when rifle shots and the whizz of bullets made him fling himself on the ground, while an irate gentleman posted behind a tree fired fifteen shots across the avenue, to which an apparently equally irate but less wasteful comrade replied with six.

Raymond E. Lee

Lt. Col., F.A., M.A.

Paris   No. 23, 126-W
January 26, 1937
Subject: Major Military Operations. Operations in Spain

In conversation with the German Military Attaché on events in Spain, he made three observations which are deemed of interest:

a) That aerial bombardment was not producing the results that most everyone had anticipated. That it was entirely too transitory in its effect and as yet lacked the necessary timing and coordination with the ground forces. That it could not, or at least had not, been sufficiently effective to drive the ground forces from positions held and once the aerial attack was completed the defenders were able to meet the opposing forces as heretofore.

b) That the German planes with General Franco were not entirely satisfactory and were not showing the speed and maneuverability desired.

c) That the Germans were highly pleased with the latest model of antiaircraft guns. That there was a battery of the latest type now with General Franco and that these guns were highly effective. This last statement was confirmed by Mr. Lord, the American pilot who served with the government forces.

H. H. Fuller
Lt. Col., F.A.
Military Attaché

Paris   No. 23, 140-W
January 28, 1937
Subject: Major Operations. Operations in Spain.

In conversation with the British Air Attaché, France, the following information concerning the air activities in Spain was given me.

Russian Planes

The Russian pursuit planes and bombers are by far the fastest ships in Spain. These planes have not, however, been very effective. It was stated that the reason for this was due to the lack of maneuverability of the planes and their instability as gun platforms. This lack of maneuverability and instability of the gun platform was due to the fact that in constructing the planes they have designed a comparatively short fuselage. Consequently, in any aerial combat the gunnery was extremely inaccurate; the same is also said of bombing operations.

In this connection, the Liaison Officer of the French Army with the Air Service, stated in a conversation January 27, 1937, that the Russian planes in Spain, although exceedingly fast, were not well built and the Hispano-Suiza engine barely lasted 100 hours in the air. He said that the French were very much concerned as to why these Hispano-Suiza engines, manufactured by the Russians, were so short-lived and that they, the French, intended to purchase 3 to 4 of the latest Russian airplanes with Hispano-Suiza engines.

He stated that the Russians were now building an experimental laboratory and manufacturing plant for airplanes in the Caucasus at an altitude of 12,500 feet in order to test planes at that altitude.

Italian Planes

The British Air Attaché stated that the Italian pursuit ships in Spain are extremely fast, easy to maneuver and the pilots unusually efficient; that practically all the Red planes brought down have been shot down by Italian airplanes.

German Planes

The British Air Attaché stated that the German pursuit planes are not coming up to expectations as to speed and maneuverability and that they were not considered in the same class with the Italian pursuit ships; nor were they considered as efficient as the present British plane of similar type. On the contrary, the German bombers which have a heavy duty oil engine (Juno) are extremely efficient, fast and very stable in the air. That the Germans are well pleased with the bombers they now have in Spain. That the Germans are now extremely accurate in their bombing activities and are constantly improving.

Speaking of the German aviation, the Liaison Officer of the French Army with the Air Service stated that the Germans are not satisfied with the efficiency of their Air Force at the present moment. They believe that the pilots are not ready for combat as they have not received sufficient training. That many of the commanders of squadrons, groups and wings were officers who have been transferred to the Air Service from other branches of the army and, therefore, have not the experience necessary to command air units. The expansion of the German Air Force has been entirely too rapid to permit it to be moulded into an efficient fighting force.

He stated that the Germans have not been satisfied with the performance of their pursuit ships in Spain. He stated, however, that it was difficult to determine whether the unsatisfactory performance has been due to the inexperience of the pilots or to some inherent fault in the planes but that they, the French, were inclined to believe that it was more a question of the inexperience of the pilots than inferiority of the materiel.

That Germany had recently sent a few of its latest model planes to Spain and was now sending some of her best pilots.

That they were confident that the Germans were turning out 300 planes a month; that this information was substantiated by the British.

French Airplanes

The British Air Attaché stated that a civilian friend of his who had recently returned from General Franco's sector brought back a piece of a French plane which had been shot down in combat and proved to be a Loire 46. This plane is reputed to be a very efficient type; it has not yet been incorporated in the French air force. Several of these planes were sent to Spain from France in October. Sixty have been ordered by the French Government.

German Anti-aircraft Artillery

The French Army Liaison Officer with the Air Service stated that the French have information that the German small caliber anti-aircraft artillery was extremely efficient and highly satisfactory to the Germans. This is substantiated by American pilots, who were flying for the Madrid Government. They stated that a number of planes had been brought down by German anti-aircraft guns.

Comments

British and French contacts state that accurate information on air activities in Spain is difficult to obtain and that reports are often misleading and contradictory.

Apparently, foreigners are not permitted to visit Russian aerodromes. American pilots who were with the Madrid Army state that they were not permitted to visit aerodromes occupied by the Russians nor were they allowed to fly Russian planes.

Fuller

Paris   No. 23, 151-W

February 2, 1937

Subject: Major Military Operations. Spain

The following information reference Spain was obtained from Mr. H.D. du Berrier, an American born in North Dakota in 1906 and a graduate of a military preparatory school in Wisconsin.

He has been flying for the Government forces since October and claims to have received $1,000 per month payable in London and a $1,500 bonus for each plane knocked down. He is supposed to have disposed of two.

He also flew for Haile Selassie during the Ethiopian campaign and was taken prisoner by the Italians.

At present he is publishing a series of articles in the *Petit Parisien* on his experiences and is looking for a selling job with an aviation concern in Holland. He is also understood to be in liaison with the opposition in Greece and claims to have an offer to take charge of the opposition air force in case anything should break. He does not intend to return to Spain and states that he is not in favor of the Red cause. To use his expression, the Russians "are plenty tough" and he is very happy to be in France. He joined up with the Government forces for the money.

His story sounded rather "pat" and only a summary of the conversation is given. He quit Spain on the pretext of recruiting foreign aviators.

According to him, the Russians are in control of all aviation activities and are putting into effect their own organization. Russian aviators are well trained, practically all of them started as parachute packers and advancing through the different echelons to the grade of pilot. He states that when Russian aviation is present in force the Government controls the air. Their pursuit is very fast and well armed while their bombers present no dead angles to the attack of hostile planes.

As a rule Russian airmen do not mix with foreign aviators, but on one occasion he had an opportunity over a drink or two to engage one in conversation. The latter had much to say about the excellence of Russian aviation and added that as soon as any new military plane reached production in the U.S., Russia had the plane and was engaged in turning out the identical ship.

Du Berrier did most of his flying from a field to the south of Alicante. He often flew over the town where the Russians were building a large aviation assembly plant.

In his opinion German aviators put up the best fight while the Italians are not so good. Italian pursuit is fast but their combat activities consist in a burst of machine gun fire and then they are on their way.

Air combat regulations have been published and pilots are given black board talks on the clarification of air tactics and regulations.

According to du Berrier, the hand of Russia is seen everywhere in Red Spain. The cinema is used daily to teach the approved methods of street fighting, such as the best way of shooting a man out of a window, etc. The movies are reinforced by flaming posters.

Waite

Paris   No. 23, 172-W
February 8, 1937
Subject: Major Military Operations. Operations in Spain

Bombing

German bombers, though not fully protected by pursuit, fly low and perform accurate and effective bombing. Most of the bombs are equipped with delayed fuses and make a crater from 30 to 40 feet in diameter and from 6 to 10 feet in depth. Where buildings have been hit, several floors have been penetrated before the explosion occurs which appears to be up rather than out.

For some time there were numerous flights over Madrid at high altitudes from which fragmentation bombs were dropped. The planes were said to be Italian. The marksmanship was poor and there were numerous duds.

During the early days of the siege of Madrid a number of fires were started by incendiary bombs from Italian planes; the populace, however, were able to handle such fires and comparatively little damage was done.

The Russians have been doing some bombing, but their operations have been carried out at high altitudes. From what can be learned, their marksmanship has been poor. Most of their bombs are said to weigh about one hundred pounds and are of the demolition type.

Russian pursuit planes, though superior to Franco's, do not seem to stop his bombers. Whether they are unable or do not want to take the chance is unknown.

According to M. Cornillon of the French Air Ministry, the poor showing and ultimate loss of the twelve (12) French Potez-54 bombers were due to M. Cot's stupidity in sending the planes to Spain without bomb sights or sighting devices of any kind. About the only bombing equipment the planes had was the necessary bomb release mechanism. The question of accuracy rested on good guessing by the pilot. Consequently, the ships were of little use to the Government forces. The pilots were forced to use foreign fuels, no doubt Russian, and the engines gave trouble from the start. It is known that the Russians are bringing in fuels from Baku.

The French planes were used when Madrid was about to be attacked and at that time the Government forces were flying at low altitudes. It appears that Franco's anti-aircraft guns were responsible mainly for the loss of the French planes.

Waite

3

Campaigns in Central Spain, Fall of Malaga, and Battle of Guadalajara
(January–April 1937)

"German anti-tank gun and anti-aircraft artillery have been satisfactory while their planes and tanks have been unsatisfactory. This is interesting, since the German doctrine is one of attack, yet it is their defensive weapons which have been good and their attack weapons poor."

Lt. Col. Hayes A. Kroner,
March 1937[1]

In the first few months of 1937, the civil war scaled up in intensity far beyond what was evident in the second half of 1936. It was in early 1937, for example, that major campaigns and battles began to occur one after the other. The fall of Malaga to the Nationalists in February followed by the Republican victory at the Battle of Guadalajara in March both involved thousands of troops, with military forces from Russia, Germany, and—most dramatically with respect to Guadalajara—Italy and International Brigades and various volunteers on both sides, such as airplane pilots. Yet these campaigns were linked to the larger objective of defending Madrid by the Republicans and its seizure by the Nationalists. Malaga gave the Nationalists a Mediterranean port and reduced the length of their southern battle lines as they continued to drive toward Madrid, while one could argue that the defeat of the Nationalists at Guadalajara led to a constellation of actions and circumstances that made it impossible for Franco to take the capital for another two years. The complexity, order of magnitude, and significance of Malaga and Guadalajara to the Spanish Civil War is comparable to such American Civil War campaigns as the battles around Fredericksburg and the Wilderness.

Fuqua and his military colleagues pieced together a remarkably accurate account of military affairs in the spring of 1937, which were borne out by historians over the next seven decades. Their explanations of the technologies involved, in particular of aircraft, and Fuqua's clearly written descriptions of military strategies, campaigns, and their importance are remarkable. They make it clear that to the trained eye, one could see clearly many of the features of the military side of the war. To be sure, much was not discussed, such as the massacre of some 2,500 individuals by the Republicans in Malaga and the Nationalist execution of some 4,000 in the same city after Franco's troops occupied the city. The only time in this war when General Franco de facto turned responsibility over to a foreign army to wage a campaign was at Guadalajara, where he essentially allowed Italian officers to have their head. He would never do that again. Fuqua was one of the first individuals not fighting on either side of the war to report in considerable detail the overt role of the Italians at Guadalajara, while other colleagues had provided the U.S. War Department a rich volume of details regarding air warfare.

The Battle of Guadalajara was quite important. The city, located north and east of Madrid, was part of the larger process of defending and attacking Madrid. The battle fought between March 8 and 23, 1937, was intended, in collaboration with action at Jarama, to serve as a pincer movement to surround Madrid. The Nationalists had 50,000 troops for the effort, the Republicans eventually 35,000. The Republicans claimed victory in this battle and, to be sure, Madrid was protected. Franco did not fight any further at Guadalajara, leaving the city to fall to his forces in March 1939. Both sides lost roughly 2,000 dead each and similarly sustained about 4,000 wounded on each side. So by any measure of the day, it was not a small operation.

Weaponry was of considerable interest to all military observers and they must have had puzzling moments as they reported on the use of everything from old shotguns and homemade bombs to the deployment of rifles and machine guns long favored by advanced armies of the world and to the use of state-of-the-art antiaircraft weapons and aircraft side by side with World War I–vintage technologies. Even cavalry operated in Spain in the early months of 1937, dutifully reported on by the Americans. Reading these dispatches demonstrates that American officers in various parts of Europe were now collecting information about the civil war, such as views of French and German officers, pilots from various countries, and inter- views with newspaper reporters and other visitors to Spain. The volume of material coming out of the American Embassies in London and Paris increased particularly. Fuqua deferred to younger military officers when it came to discussing aircraft, and they dutifully sent dispatches into Wash- ington, D.C., when Fuqua was out visiting battlefronts around Madrid and Valencia and Republican forces after the Battle of Guadalajara.

Madrid-Valencia   No. 6456

January 27, 1937

Subject: Military Situation

East. Madrid-Guadalajara-Zaragoza Road

In the third week of December the nationalists launched an offensive in this sector which pushed their lines dangerously close to Guadalajara, their vanguard advanc- ing up to a few kilometers from Taracona located but a short distance from that provincial capital.

This advance followed the direction of the highway and formed a wedge as progress on the remaining parts of the front did not keep pace with the attack carried in the direction of Guadalajara. Very recently strong reinforcements sent by the Government not only stopped this advance, but recovered part of the lost territory. The best information available indicates that the rebel line is located a few kilometers south of Jadraque and then runs northeast facing the Government positions at Matillas, Mirabueno and Algora.

Guadalajara-Soria Road

The Government troops have continued their advance in the zone comprised be- tween the Rivers Berneba and Sorbe and while the situation in this sector is con- fused owing to the fact that the territory is mountainous, sparsely populated and away from important roads, it is believed that the spearhead of the militia reaches the vicinity of Pradona de Atienza, some 10 kilometers southwest of the important village of Atienza.

Escorial Front

The nationalist advance on the northwest front of Madrid has created a difficult situation to the Government troops occupying this sector. As a result of this offensive the nationalists have pushed their lines up to some distance north of Villanueva del Pardillo, thus controlling part of the Escorial-Las Rezas road and have taken possession of the Coruna highway from the last named village to the capital. Although the Government forces on the Escorial sector have free access to the stretch of the Coruna road comprised between Las Matas and Guadarrama and from which at Villalba and Torroledonee[2] branch out second rate roads which connect on the east with the Madrid-Burgos highway, the communication of troops on this front with the capital is at present difficult and may cease completely should the nationalist offensive progress in the direction of Fuencarral. At present this village is under range of Franco's guns.

Changes on Other Fronts

The offensive launched by the Government troops on the Asturias, Santander, Bilbao and Aragon fronts with a view to force the nationalist army to abandon the siege of Madrid in general may be said to have attained very little, therefore, failing in this main objective. It will be recalled that the poor offensive spirit of the militia is a result of the lack of discipline and organization still existing among the Government forces. Another adverse factor is the obvious failure in achieving coordination of effort among the various semi-independent local governments and with the Largo Caballero cabinet.

Fighting on the Oviedo sector has been maintained on a larger scale but the miners have had to contend there with numerous and well trained nationalist troops, Moors and Legion units included, which, even though confronted with adverse conditions, have succeeded thus far in preventing the fall of this city. However, the militia positions seem to have somewhat improved, particularly on Mount Naranco, which dominates Oviedo.

On the Huesca and Teruel sectors the situation has not appreciably changed. Nothing except the political rivalries and internal anarchy existing in the Catalan and Valencia regions may explain the fact that these two cities, which since the beginning of the revolt have been closely surrounded by the radicals, continue as yet in nationalist hands. Since last report both cities have been subjected to considerable pressure; but, in the end, the advance of the militia forces has been checked and all that they have gained has been to press their lines a little closer around both provincial capitals. Recently it was reported that the Government forces had cut the Teruel-Zaragoza road a few kilometers north of Teruel, but the latest information indicates that the road is again open. The danger that the Teruel spearhead represents for the Government need not be emphasized. It is a potential threat to the land communication between Catalonia and Valencia.

The Nationalists have launched an offensive on the east of Cordoba, following the Guadalquiver River, as a result of which about 10 villages, including the important towns of Bujalance and Montoro, have been taken. This advance is of considerable importance since it has reached a depth of some 40 kilometers through one of the most fertile, rich and densely populated regions of Andalucia. Their lines are already in the Jaen province, some kilometers past the villages of Porcuna and Lopora. This movement has been apparently a tactical maneuver to attract Government troops from the Madrid front. When the Cordoba offensive was in progress the nationalist drive on Madrid was stopped, a fact that induced the Government to withdraw some of its best shock troops from the capital—elements from the Galan and International columns—and send them to the theater of operations. These reinforcements suffered heavy losses but seem to have checked the rebel offensive. The weakening effect on the Madrid Government lines was attained, a fact which no doubt made possible with less effort the rupture of the militia front in the Majadahonda-Pozuelo sector.

On the front northeast of Toledo nothing of importance has occurred since last report. On the Malaga front several villages in the mountainous district south of Ronda have been taken recently by the nationalists.

On January 14th nationalists occupied Estepona and the following days advanced toward Malaga and are now reported to be checked by Government [forces?] in the vicinity of Marbella. The last few days [the] rebel advance south of Granada has carried the line to a point seventeen kilometers north of Motril. Nationalist line now extends from a point north of Motril through Alhama and on unknown curve or arc to vicinity of Marbella.

Since January 12th increased activity [of] rebel ships along Mediterranean Coast. On the night of the 20th port was shelled with but little damage.

Griffiss

Valencia   No. 6457
January 28, 1937
Subject: Valencia Air Raid Shelters
To: The Assistant Chief of Staff, G-2

For the past several weeks air raid shelters have been under construction in Valencia. This office has been following the progress with interest but work has been slow and definite details lacking. The following information was obtained by Mr. [Edward H.] Knoblaugh of the Associated Press and given to this office.[3]

Aerial bombardments which have so much death in Spain seen will hold little terror for the inhabitants of this Levante capital.

The poorest city in Spain a few months ago, Valencia is being equipped with ultra-modern bomb-proof shelters which will make it one of the safest in Europe.

Forty-six refuges of reinforced concrete believed built so strongly that not even the most powerful of aerial bombs will penetrate them are nearing completion.

With capacity ranging from 1000 to 4000 persons each they will afford protection against death from the skies to nearly 1,000,000 [handwritten column comment shows someone checking the math: 4000 x 46 = 184,000—Ed. Note] human beings in the event Valencia should be subjected to bombardment. Eighteen hundred workmen are engaged in the gigantic project which involves the expenditure of some fifty million pesetas.

The city exposed to the sea as well as air attacks previously had virtually no defense against bombardment. Those who had seen the more substantial edifices of Madrid crumble under the shattering force of heavy aerial bombs realized just how little protection Valencia offered.

Water lies so near the surface in most parts of the city that few buildings have basements. The difficulty of securing solid resting for buildings in the treacherous undersoil has compelled extreme lightness of structure.

There might be some measure of safety in the lower floors of the taller business buildings whose foundations rest on great floating slabs of concrete, but the average apartment house of Valencia would crumble like paper under the impact of a 225 pound bomb or heavy projectile.

In both Madrid and Barcelona there are deep subways to which residents flock when air raid warnings are sounded, but Valencia has no subways.

The shelters decided upon were designed by technicians summoned by the Government from all parts of Europe. They are being placed at strategic points throughout the city with the larger number in the outlying workers' districts where houses are cheap and fragile affairs. Vacant lots and the centers of broad boulevards were the sites chosen.

Diggers working in relays excavated broad pits going down until they were halted by seepage through the underlying clay. Retaining walls of reinforced concrete from three to six feet thick were put in place, some with removable wooden moulds others with permanent inner facing. In these pits tabular shaped galleries were constructed with twisting ramp entrances at either end.

A protecting cover of six feet of reinforced concrete shields these galleries and on top of this an eight foot layer of earth. The original plans called for only a four foot concrete roof but technicians increased this to six feet after seeing how supposedly bomb-proof subways in Madrid had been crushed through by the more powerful bombs.

Drinking water, toilet facilities, and benches for women and the infirm are to be provided.

Tentative sites for additional shelters are being mapped in [the] event the population of Valencia, already more than double its 400,000 census rating, should be further increased by refugees.

It is of interest to know that the War Department has had nothing to do with the construction of these shelters. The entire project and work is being carried out by the Defense Committee of Valencia. Some time ago the War Department was questioned on this subject and knew nothing of the details.

This office is of the opinion that it will be many weeks before any of these shelters will be completed. The statement relative to capacity of shelters is believed exaggerated. Nothing has been seen of any such magnitude. At this time considerable propaganda is being put out by the Ministry of Propaganda.

Griffiss

Paris   No. 23, 186-W
February 11, 1937
Subject: Air Combat Operations. Major Military Operations.
Interview with German Military Attaché

The following information was secured from General Kuhlenthal, German Military Attaché, by the Military and Naval Attachés of the United States.

Situation in Spain

General Kuhlenthal stated that, several months ago, he had written a personal letter to General Franco, advising General Franco that a frontal and direct attack against Madrid would be useless and costly and that it would be better tactics to completely envelop Madrid and cut off all communications in the general directions of Valencia and Barcelona. General Franco's reply to this advice was that the Germans should furnish him with more soldiers as he did not have enough. General Kuhlenthal stated that General Franco was the outstanding soldier in Spain and had sufficient ability to meet the demands of the situation in Spain, but it was doubtful if he was a soldier of the caliber that would be successful in a European war.

The German planes in Spain were not satisfactory in that they lacked the necessary speed and maneuverability; that the pilots were inadequately trained and, as a consequence, their aerial gunnery and bombing was not effective. He thinks that it will take four years of intensive training to develop pilots to a point where their aerial gunnery, bombing and dive bombing will be reasonably effective.

He said that Germany had spent large sums in developing anti-aircraft artillery, almost as much money having been spent on this as upon aviation. He stated that the trend in Germany was towards the small caliber gun of 23mm and 37mm. That the Germans believed that guns of this caliber, with huge muzzle velocity, ranges up to 7000 or 8000 meters and having a rate of fire of 300 to 400 rounds per minute were superior to all other types. He said the 23mm. antiaircraft cannon which Germany had sent to Spain was an excellent weapon and had accounted for approximately 50 percent of all planes brought down. This cannon has a range of 6,500 meters, fires 300 rounds per minute, and a very high muzzle velocity. Fire is controlled by a telescopic director which is separate from the gun but the guns automatically follow the director. The plane is reflected on a graduated mirror which enables one to accurately estimate the speed and to calculate the angle of ascent and descent.

When questioned about supplies and munitions being sent to Spain from Russia, the General said that all of that was finished and intimated that it was due to the blockading of the ports and not to a desire on the part of Russia.

When asked if he knew where General Franco was obtaining money he said that the International Telephone & Telegraph Company had furnished some ten million dollars and was handling all arrangements for loans. As a compensation for the money given Franco had promised the company a complete monopoly of telephone and telegraph service in Spanish territory.

General Kuhlenthal stated that the most difficult operation at the present time was the proper control of planes in the air; that aerial operations in Spain had shown distinctly that control in the air was lacking and that aerial combats never produced any coordinated attacks and resulted in individual combats; that almost without exception they defeated their own ends. He also stated that aviation was now proving very costly to build and to maintain in comparison with the results obtained; that it took a tremendous amount of high explosive bombs to accomplish even meager results. As far as he knew all bombing in Spain was done with the horizontal and no dive bombing had taken place.

General Kuhlenthal said that Franco ought to be able to win the war by July. He expressed this so it sounded more as a hope than as a certainty.

Unity of Command

General Kuhlenthal was tremendously interested in unity of command and was quite familiar with the discussions and writings on the subject which have recently taken place in France. In his opinion one command for the Army, Navy and Air Forces was absolutely necessary in both peace and war; that to bring into the picture unity of command at the commencement of a war would not be sufficient; that the plan for the operations of the three services must be carried out in time of peace and that mutual cooperation would not produce the desired results. He admitted that no plans had been made for the use of the German fleet in the World War and that this lack of plan and the fact that in the early stages of the war a single command for both the Army and Navy had not been established contributed more than any other one factor to the loss of the war by the Germans.

He stated that he was absolutely opposed to a separate Air Force. With a separate Air Force, military and naval operations would inevitably suffer, that the results from operations would inevitably suffer, that the results from operations in the air alone were negligible and that until such a time as the Air Force was able to coordinate air activities and operations with those of the ground troops but little more than morale effect would be gained. He felt also that the morale effect to be secured by bombardments from the air would soon disappear after the commencement of hostilities, that people very quickly became used to shelling and to aerial bombing and took it as a matter of course.

Nationalization of War Industries

General Kuhlenthal displayed strong interest in the present nationalization of war-making industries now taking place in France. He stated that he lacked the necessary assistance in his office to adequately follow industrial mobilization and technical developments in materiel. He stated that, after 3 1/2 years in France, he himself could follow political events and the general trend of military organization and tactics, but that it was impossible to follow industrial mobilization and technical developments without the necessary personnel. He stated that Germany's industrial mobilization was largely patterned after that of the United States.

Fuller

Paris   No. 23, 210-W
February 19, 1937
Subject: Major Military Operations. Spain

The following information was obtained from Señor Trias de Bes and Señor Tobra, through Lt. Webber, CAC (DOL). The two Spanish gentlemen recently made a trip of two weeks through the central and northern parts of White Spain. They are ardent followers of Franco, consequently what they have to say must be taken with a certain amount of reserve.

They emphasize the fact that the morale of the Spanish people in White Spain is exceptionally high and that the rank and file have great confidence in General Franco. From their point of view it is only a matter of time before the Nationalists will be the masters of all Spain. The people are solidly behind the troops at the front and are perfectly willing to make every sacrifice in order to assist the progress of the rebellion.

It was noted that there were few policemen in the towns, every available man being with the Army. Notwithstanding this, there is more order, the streets are cleaner, and there is a great spirit of cooperation everywhere which is quite foreign to what is taking place in the cities and towns of "Red Spain". Women and older men do war work in the factories for which they receive no pay.

All the major cities visited: Burgos, Valladolid, Salamanca and even Pamplona are doubling and tripling their population due to the exodus of refugees from Barcelona, Valencia and other parts of "Red Spain". It is therefore very difficult to secure lodgings, even for a night.

Food is plentiful, the only commodity of which there appears to be any shortage being rice. An excellent four course dinner can be obtained for six pesetas. Meat comes from Galicia and fish from San Sebastian and other parts of the

Cantabrian coast. Vegetables, eggs and wheat are in abundance in Aragon, Leon and Castilla, while a plentiful supply of assorted fruit comes from the south and the Canary Islands.

Franco, through his Finance Minister, has checked carefully every ounce of gold in White Spain and has made negotiable by means of a stamp only the number of paper pesetas which can be backed by the available gold. The peseta of White Spain is worth about twice as much in foreign exchange as the pesetas from Red Spain.

Spaniards admit that they have seen German and Italian units passing through some of their cities. They comment freely on the neatness and excellent equipment of both.

They are particularly proud of the fighting qualities of the Moors and comment happily on the ruthlessness of a people who but a few years ago were deadly enemies of every true Spaniard. It is said that the Moors have first chance at looting and are allowed to keep or sell anything they may obtain.

Some far sighted German manufacturers have cashed in on the Spanish desire of display and have made many varieties of pins and badges for the patriotic Spaniard to wear. These pins include the emblems of the *Requetes* (Carlists), *Falangistas* (Fascists) and about a dozen other styles and variations. A rather significant emblem is a pin called *Los Cuatro Amigos* (The Four Friends) which carries the flags of Germany, Italy, Portugal and Spain.

Comments

At luncheon yesterday which Colonel Fuller attended, the German Military Attaché made the statement that there were approximately 40,000 Italians in Spain. He did not mention the number of Germans. He also stated that Franco was well fixed for men and supplies for some time to come.

The Guaranty Trust Company gives the exchange value of Spanish pesetas today as:

60 French francs = 100 pesetas (Government)
110 French francs = 100 pesetas (Nationalist)

Therefore, the peseta issued by Franco is nearly, not quite, twice the value of the Government variety.

Others who have traveled in White Spain including journalists report plentiful supplies, order and cleanliness, while in the rear areas of Red Spain just the opposite obtains.

Commander Chandler, the Assistant Naval Attaché, fresh from a trip to Madrid, Valencia and Barcelona reports shortage of supplies in the rear areas, much disorganization and suspicion everywhere, as well as lack of unity of effort and command. From outward indications, it would appear that the Government organization is on the verge of a break.

Waite

Paris   No. 23, 219-W
February 23, 1937
Subject: Major Operations. Spain

The decision to prevent the recruiting of volunteers for the Spanish Civil War is now in effect and on 6 March the patrol system for the purpose of enforcing nonintervention will become operative.

While no doubt both sides in Spain have supplies and men to last some time, it is reasonable to suppose that action taken by interested countries will shorten to some extent the period of hostilities. Strict enforcement of the regulations laid down by the Committee of London will in a sense guard against the growth of the Spanish Civil War into a general European conflict.

At the moment it would appear that General Franco has the initiative though at the present writing Governmental forces have reacted in the north.

Franco's tactics appear to have entered the phase of attacking the Government on all fronts which of course signifies that he disposes of considerable means and the ability to move rapidly across difficult terrain. It is evident therefore, that he has received considerable outside help.

The fate of Madrid seems to hang on the fight going on to the southeast of the city. The Valencia road has been cut at one point at least and traffic has been detoured.

Not only have Franco's troops made substantial gains, but it would appear that all is not well politically with the Government. The extremists can't seem to agree and the anarcho-syndicalists are giving Caballero plenty of trouble.

According to reports the Russian Ambassador has been recalled to Moscow. He has been considered all along by most observers as the spark plug of the Government organization. Perhaps Russia plans on a change of tactics with an eye to the future.

From now out it is reasonable to believe that the Spanish conflict enters a different phase with the Spaniards themselves fighting it out more or less along their own lines.

Waite

Valencia   No. 6473
February 27, 1937
Subject: Valencia Air Defense

During the period December 3, 1936 and February 27, 1937 Government planes stationed at Chiva Airport, Valencia, have made frequent bombing raids on Teruel. However, it was not until after the Government raid on Zaragoza that the Nationalists retaliated against Valencia. If the flying fields in the immediate vicinity of Valencia are used for other purposes than as bases for the air defenses of Valencia then it is but natural that reprisals will be made. The city cannot hide behind the cloak of foreign diplomatic presence while it makes war materials and uses its airports as bases for bombing missions without suffering the consequences.

As of February 26, 1937 the air defense of Valencia consists of:

a) French Squadron at Chiva composed of 2 Potez-54, 3 Nieuport-62 and 5 Breguet-19.

b) Russian Pursuit Squadron of 18 "Mosca" monoplane pursuit. This squadron arrived at Chiva on February 24th. The equipment is reported to be new and to have been assembled but recently.

c) Russian Pursuit Squadron of biplane pursuit stationed on emergency field—unknown—between Valencia and Teruel and about sixty kilometers from Valencia.

The ground defenses consist of:

a) Bomb-proof shelters. None of these shelters has been completed. A survey was made this morning and it is estimated that the ones started in the middle of December are about three-quarters completed. They should be completed in another two weeks. The work has been extremely slow. Many additional shelters are under construction ranging

    in progress from just breaking ground to the half-way mark. A future
report will describe the shelters in detail.

b)   Anti-aircraft guns have been placed on the roofs and pent-houses of
many of the larger buildings in the city and at the port. The Navy Yard
has but two anti-aircraft emplacements and there is only one small gunboat with anti-aircraft in the outer port. The air fields have inadequate
anti-aircraft defense.

c)   The types of anti-aircraft guns in use are the Hotchkiss 7.62 calibre and
the Oerlikon 20mm. I have not seen the latter.

The air defense plan is merely that of the alert system. Patrols are not flown,
but the Russian airplanes are said to be constantly on the alert. From the experience of the previous air raids and attacks from the sea on Valencia and due to the
fact that action has started before the warning signals have been sounded, it is my
opinion that the alert squadrons will not be effective until after the raid has been
made. There is no protection from an approach from the sea.

    In normal times the population of Valencia was 400,000 people. During the
past several months the number has risen to over 800,000. The tragedy that will
result from a well organized bombing raid on this city is all too apparent.

Griffiss

[The following is an undated, unsigned, unknown-authored transcript
that was in the files following the previous report.—Ed. Note.]

The estimates as to the size of armies that I recall, before the influx of foreign
volunteers, was about 38,000 for the insurgents and around 200,000 for the leftists. These figures have to be changed, of course, by the addition of German and
Italian volunteers.

    Weapons used have varied from the extremely primitive to ultra-modern.
Everything from crude dynamite bombs, old shotguns, to latest design rifles, latest type of anti-aircraft, etc. In the matter of artillery the insurgents used 15.5 and
.75's and towards the end some larger siege guns (obviously rather old German
types). Also a larger number of ordinary field guns—three inch or so.

    In the way of tanks, there have been small whippet tanks and large (medium
size affairs). The Reds used Russian tanks (alleged) with a one-pounder cannon
as well as machine guns. Both sides have had a fondness for armored cars; of the

homemade variety. The fighting also saw the use of armored trains, also something which seems to appeal to the Spicks, although their use was never efficient.[4]

Tanks, in my opinion, and I have seen the same opinion expressed repeatedly, have not justified themselves in the present war because of modern weapons of defense [and] because of their use for the most part as a separate weapon of attack rather than as the advance attacking unit for infantry.

One of the most effective methods of putting the tank out of commission, as practiced by the Moors, was the use of bottles of gasoline tied to hand grenades and thrown at the tank from close range. The gasoline, thus ignited, turns the tank into an oven and forces the occupants out.

I personally saw leftist tanks which had been mired and trapped by their own clumsiness, with the cockpits smeared with blasted bodies, the result of hand grenades being tossed into the interior.

The Germans also sent in their special anti-tank tanks, a very trim little weapon on its own carrier, and especially good at keeping tanks off roads. The Germans, so I was told, also sent in special anti-tank cartridges, a very highly charged cartridge with remarkable powers of penetrating steel. All in all the tank hasn't done so much.

Most of the airplanes seem to have been shot down in dog-fighting in the air rather than by anti-aircraft; this being due, to a certain extent, to poor gunnery and not having sufficient anti-aircraft to really lay down a barrage in the air.

Interesting and disconcerting to the rebels was the introduction by the leftists of the very fast bombing plan which, although it couldn't maneuver as fast as the pursuits, could outspeed them easily. Air forces have not on the whole affected the expected demoralization of the population behind the lines. Witness Madrid, the Alcazar, Oviedo. There has been extensive property damage, however, through the use of really large air bombs.

Up to the Madrid fighting the war was largely what must be called highway and semi-guerilla warfare. The tactics of the insurgents have been, and still are, to use the highway; while the main force moves up the highway or near the highway, small groups of fascists or Carlist volunteers branch out at either side, travelling by truck, to "clean-up" enough territory to provide a safeguard.

There has also been a good amount of mountain fighting in which small mountain artillery and cavalry has been used to good effect. The war has seen a rather extensive use of cavalry; in some cases a rather sensational use, the cavalrymen using their horses to arrive fresh at some difficult spot and then dismounting and fighting as infantrymen.

The military lesson for the future seems to be the increasing mechanization of transport (Spain's excellent roads made it easy for trucks to be used) and the invention of scientific defense against scientific attack.

There is also excellent proof, it seems to me, of the inability of air attack to achieve very much by itself aside from property destruction. Land forces, it would seem, must still bear the brunt of the attack, especially in the securement and holding of really important objectives.

To the extent to which the Spanish fight has not been stationary warfare (as was the World War) there has been emphasis on the advantage of striking hard and swiftly with strength enough to follow up an advantage. In spite of everything it would seem that it is still the little men with guns who do the dirty work, and who will do the dirty work in wars to come, despite machine guns, airplanes, tanks, etc.

Casualties in the Spanish war (direct war casualties) were admittedly very small up to the Madrid show. It used to be popularly estimated that 70 percent of the casualties were by execution; only 30 percent by actual fighting.

Paris   No. 23, 265-W
March 10, 1937
Subject: Major Military Operations. Air Combat Operations.
Air Equipment & Tactics

Tactics

There are certain tactics which have been tried out during the present conflict and the results of which should be of interest. Since they bear little relationship one towards the other it is thought best to set them down separately.

a) The fast Russian bombers shortly after their arrival here made repeated attacks on the trenches. Their method of attack was to fly very low and very fast along the trench, dropping bombs at intervals and sweeping the trenches with machine gun fire from a gun fitted forward. These attacks were very successful at first owing to the surprise with which they were delivered. Subsequently several bombers were destroyed during these attacks and they have been discontinued.

b) The fast monoplane Russian 1.16 fighters have proved a very great success and are claimed to have destroyed a great number of enemy aircraft.

Pilots attribute their success mainly to the great volume of fire which they can deliver by virtue of having four very fast firing guns.

c) The military authorities always endeavor to obtain air cooperation in attack. They claim that the value of the morale which the presence of their own aircraft instills in the troops is in excess of any material assistance which they can give.

d) Much damage to aircraft was caused during the early stages of the conflict by air attacks on airdromes. This is now minimized by parking aircraft all around the perimeter of the airdrome and away from buildings and well separated from one another. When possible aircraft are changed from one landing ground to another almost daily, and these tactics are used effectively around Madrid where there are many landing grounds. The Russia 1.16 and French Dewoitine fighters have been handicapped in these tactics by their fast landing speed.

Equipment
AIRCRAFT
All the service aircraft now in use by the Government are of Russian or French manufacture. There are many civil aircraft such as Douglas Airspeed Envoys, D.H. Rapids, and Fokkers, but although these were used for bombing in the early days of the conflict they are now kept for communications only. An American pilot informed me that eleven American aircraft thought to be Boeing P.12's arrived at Bilbao on January 24th but I have not yet been able to confirm this. The following brief particulars of aircraft in use are submitted.

Russian Fighter 1.15
Single seater biplane with Wright Cyclone engine. Four Vickers guns, two firing through the propeller and two wing guns. I am informed that this aircraft is a Russian development of the Boeing P.12. The engine is larger than originally fitted in the P.12. These aircraft are strong and maneuverable but without very high performance. I saw four of these fighters at Albacete, and I am told that there are considerable quantities in this country.

Russian Fighter 1.16
Single seater monoplane with M-25 engine of 900 HP. Two very fast firing machine guns of make and caliber unknown fixed in the wing and firing outside the propeller, and two Vickers type firing through the propeller.[5]

I am informed that these fighters are developed from the Boeing P.26. The under-carriage has been made retractable and folds along to lateral axis of the aircraft and under the fuselage. The wings have been made shorter and are of cantilever construction, this dispensing with wire bracing. The maxium speed of these machines is between 285 to 300 mph and they land at 85 mph. The engine fitted is a Russian development of the Wright Cyclone known as the M-25 and gives a maximum output of 900 HP. I saw between 20 and 30 of these aircraft at Alcala and I am told there are more at other airdromes.

Russian Bomber (8.B.)

Mid-wing twin engined bomber fitted with two Hispano-Suiza of 850 HP. Built under license. Retractable landing gear and very clean lines. Bombs apparently mounted internally. Two machine guns (make not known), one fore and one aft. I am informed by a qualified person that this bomber is a development of the Martin bomber and built under license. I saw one of these aircraft being assembled at Valencia and have been informed by British pilots that at least a dozen of them were operating from Cartagena in December. It is thought that there are many more of them and that it is these aircraft which carry out long distant raids such as those recently made on Cadiz and Ceuta.

French Aircraft

A considerable number of Breguet 19's are still used for reconnaissance but they are very old, unreliable, vulnerable, and inefficient. Together with these Breguets must be classed the Nieuports-62 which are still used for escort to the Breguets but could not be compared with the more modern fighters.

Potez 54

There are several of these aircraft in use and I have seen four at Chiva airdrome, near Valencia. Owing to their vulnerability they now are employed for night bombing raids or for bombing sectors which are not well defended by fighters. Other types of French aircraft have been used in small numbers and often without their correct armament.

Miscellaneous Aircraft

The Hawker Fury which gave excellent service here for many months proved, by virtue of its good maneuverability, high performance, reliability, slow landing speed and ease of control, especially suitable for conditions prevailing in this country. It was popular with all pilots.

The few Vickers Vildebeests which remain with the Government are said to have weak landing gears and so far as I can ascertain they are not used. (This information was received during a casual conversation with a Spanish lieutenant and may not be reliable).

The insurgents still employ Fiat, Heinkels, and Junkers. The Fiat and Heinkel appear to have very similar performance but the Heinkel, I am told, is better armed and manned and is more to be feared than the Fiat. The Fiat on the other hand is said to be maneuverable. The Junkers still carries out most of the bombing on Madrid and in spite of its slow speed it seems to be difficult to destroy. Although many Junkers are reported to have been brought down I have not yet met an English person who has seen one destroyed and to the best of my knowledge there are no wreckages in or around Madrid.

ARMAMENT
Bombs

It appears that most of the H.E. bombs[6] dropped on Madrid were approximately 100 Kg. although it is certain that far larger bombs were dropped on occasions. I will not attempt to give any further opinion on this as I was never able to see either an air raid or specimen bombs which had failed to explode. More accurate information could undoubtedly be extracted from reports submitted by other officers.

Incendiary Bombs

A very large number of incendiary bombs have been dropped, both on Madrid and elsewhere. Specimens of these have already been sent for examination. These bombs were dropped twenty-five at the same time and a comparatively large number don't ignite. The damage done by these bombs has been surprisingly small as they can be extinguished quickly with earth or sand (but not with water or fire extinguisher). It appears that they are more effective by day than at night as owing to the fact that the bright flame with which they burn at night always reveals their presence and immediate action is taken to extinguish them. During daylight, however, they may remain unnoticed during the excitement of a raid and so have time to ignite the roof of buildings on which they fall. It is thought that they are used at night more as a means of illuminating targets for the bombing aircraft than as a means of destruction.

Machine Guns

Apart from the guns fitted to the Russian 1.16 fighters, most of the machine guns appear to be Vickers, which still give good results in spite of their comparatively slow rate of fire. I can find no indication that either cannon or large caliber guns have been used by either side and Government pilots assure me that they have not been used by them.

Personnel

At the outbreak of the conflict most of the Spanish pilots departed to insurgent territory. Of those who remain a fair number are restricted in their flying owing to the several cases of aircraft having flown across to the insurgents. Consequently, the present pilots are mostly foreign adventurers. Attempts are being made to train new Spanish pilots but one cannot visualize the Government air forces dispensing with foreign pilots for many months yet.

The only organized assistance comes from Russia and the Russian aircraft are flown and maintained by Russians. From all accounts their knowledge and flying ability are good although somewhat elementary. Their discipline appears to be excellent and they have any amount of courage.

There are a great many French pilots who are from the Reserve of the French Air Force. It is not known at present how these are to be employed but it is said by the British pilots here that a French squadron is being formed. It appears also that several aircraft have come here from France to be tried out under war conditions. It does not appear that they ever arrive in large numbers but from time to time one hears of a new machine having arrived from across the border.

The British and American pilots here are diminishing in number, most of the Americans having already left, and the British beginning to follow suit. This is due to two reasons: firstly, that the Government are not fulfilling the extravagant promises made to them in London and, secondly, that they are given aircraft to fly which are so old that they are dangerous enough without even going into action and would stand no chance against any of the insurgent fighters. A British-American squadron was formed in Valencia but has not been a success and now only eight pilots are left, all of whom are contemplating returning. With one or two exceptions, the British pilots who have come out here have been totally inexperienced and have damaged a large number of aircraft. This may account for their difficulty in obtaining their correct salary and better equipment. The few who are left are at present responsible for the defense of Valencia, all the Russians recently gone to the Madrid front. They are equipped with Breguet 19's (which have no front gun) and with which they do both coastal and inland reconnaissance, and with Nieuport 61's for fighter defense, so that the defense of this large community is totally inadequate.

Fuller

Paris   No. 23, 307-W
March 25, 1937
Subject: War Operations in Spain

There are enclosed herewith three *Bulletin d'Information de Quinzaine* (Fortnightly Bulletin of Information) prepared by the French Air Ministry, and covering war operations in Spain during the periods: I-February 1-15, 1937, II-February 16-28, 1937, III-March 1-15, 1937. These bulletins contain details on military operations in Spain with which G-2 is already familiar. Other points of interest are given below.

I—Period February 1-15th

This bulletin gives an account of the political situation in Spanish Morocco, which is far from favorable to France.

German activity is manifesting itself in the military and economic spheres. Colonel Kunzlent was assigned to the Staff of the Spanish Zone at Tetuan; German citizens Wilhelm Schultz and Scholte are very active in the organization and command of the Tetuan air base; HISMA air lines tires: to ensure German influence over Spanish Morocco; to serve as liaison between Germany and Spain for the delivery of war materiel and food supplies in exchange for raw materials, oil and fruit; to supply the rebels in war materiel and chemical products. Italian influence is manifesting itself mostly in Tangier. More schools are being opened and the local Fascio openly supports the Rebels.

As regards aviation (Russian personnel and materiel—about 150 planes) the Government appears to be superior to the Rebels, both in quantity and quality and especially in so far as pursuit planes are considered. The I-16 is faster and more maneuverable than its opponents: Heinkel 51 and Fisat CR 32. The Italian pursuit plane CR 32 has good characteristics and is superior to the corresponding German type Heinkel 51.

Bombing planes, Italian as well as German, are inferior to expectations. Italian planes, in particular, are disappointing in their results. These planes are robust—more so than German planes—but bombing results are reported to be ineffective, both from accuracy of aim and efficacy of the projectile. This is attributed to the poor training of the bombing personnel and to the poor quality of the explosive used. Government pilots are more courageous, have more audacity, and are better trained. The Germans are reported as being better trained than the Italians, and very audacious in spite of inferior materiel. They are especially good for cooperation with ground troops. Italian aviators are much more careful—to say the least.

Attack aviation, as used by Government air forces, is also practiced by the Rebels, as shown by operations between Malaga and Motril.

ANTI-AIRCRAFT ARTILLERY

The following defense is adopted by Franco: Towns and their suburbs are divided into 5 zones (concentric circles with the center of town as center). The larger radius is from 60 to 65 Km. long. The smaller circle contains the town, the 2nd has a radius of 10 Km. around the town, and includes the guns and A.A.[7] machine guns. The area between the 10 Km. and 60 Km. circles is divided into three almost equal parts, with observation and listening stations, connected by telephone and radio, and also connected to the two center zones. This organization is said to be copied from the Germans. In Germany, however, the first two zones extend to 50 Km. around towns where war industries are located.

II—Period February 16th-28th

Bombing missions are usually protected by pursuit (6 to 10 bombers protected by approximately 30 pursuit). According to official communiqués, the Government pilots brought 20 Rebel planes down while the Rebels brought 21 Government planes down between February 15th and February 27th. It is, however, impossible to determine which are due to aerial combat and which are due to anti-aircraft artillery.

12,000 to 15,000 left Italy for Spain during the same period.

The following German air units are reported to be in Spain:

Richtofen Pursuit Squadron	Berlin	Heinkel 51
Immelmann Pursuit Squadron	Lubeck	"
Schlesissheim Aviation Group	Munich	"
Schwerin Aviation Group	Lubeck	"
(specialized in dive-bombing)		

Czechoslovakia is reported to have sold 16 bi- and tri-motored bombers to Government Spain. Holland is reported to have sold 10 Koolhoven bi-plane reconnaissance planes.

As far as efficiency goes, the various planes in service may be listed as follows:

Bombers-SB Maticuska (Russian)
Savoia, Caproni (Italian)
Junkers 52 (German)
Pursuit I-16 (Russian)
CR 32 ((Italian)
Heinkel 51 (German)
I-15 (Russian).

The German A.A. artillery is reported to be excellent and to be the only one to obtain very good results.

Italian tanks are not efficient, due to insufficient armor protection.

III—Period March 1-15th

Information received from various sources permits to state that the number of planes in service is approximately as follows:

General Franco: 110 bombers (Junkers 52, Savoia 81, Caproni 133), 100 pursuit (Fiat CR32, Heinkel 51, Arado).
Government: 70 bombers (SB), 80 pursuit (I-15 and I-16).

This includes only first line modern planes which have proven their worth in actual service. No mention is made of observation planes; however, the Rebels have Romeo 37's and Heinkel 45's while the Government has Russian two-seaters, type R-5.

The Government pilots brought 4 planes down during that period and the Rebels 6.

A total of some 50,000 to 60,000 men were sent by Italy to the support of the Burgos Government. It is reported that Italian volunteers will be permitted to settle in Andalucia, after the war is over, in exchange for this help. This may eventually be a menace to Gibraltar.

There are only a few old Breguet 19's at Nador and a few Heinkel seaplanes in the Lagune, Spanish Morocco. The Rebels have the following A.A. materiel:

—The heavy A.A. gun of 88 mm., vertical range: 10,000 m., cadence: 15 to
   20 shots a minute.

—The 37 mm. automatic gun.

—A machine gun at rapid rate of fire (probably the Dreyse, 20 mm.).

This A.A. artillery is very accurate at low and medium altitudes and forces
the bombers to fly at 4,000 meters, thus limiting their use. The Government
forces lack anti-aircraft weapons. Rebel bombers can operate at altitudes of 2,000
meters.

The morale effect of bombardment over civil populations is not very great,
as they gradually become accustomed to it. The precision of fire varies greatly. An
isolated spot is rarely hit. Bombing aviation operates usually in groups and no
plane must leave the formation without a good reason for so doing.

A homogeneous patrol of bombers is not vulnerable to enemy pursuit planes;
pursuit has a chance only when the formation is broken through artillery fire, etc.,
and in that case the isolated plane is an easy prey.

PERSONNEL

Practically all the Government aviation is Russian. A few Spanish pilots have recently completed training and are beginning to be seen. Practically all Rebel planes
were flown by Italian and German personnel. Some Spanish pilots are now flying
these planes. On the Madrid front, the Italians are preferred as pursuit pilots while
the Germans usually fly the bombers.

                                                                        Fuller

---

Valencia   No. 6486
March 4, 1937
Subject: The Fall of Malaga

The most important military development of late has been the Nationalist
offensive against the province of Malaga, which was initiated on January 15th and
culminated on February 8th with the taking of this important city after a series
of brilliant operations in which the government forces suffered a complete defeat.

Although during the latter part of December, 1936, the Nationalists conducted minor operations on the Ronda sector, during which they captured a number of villages located in this mountainous district, there existed few indications

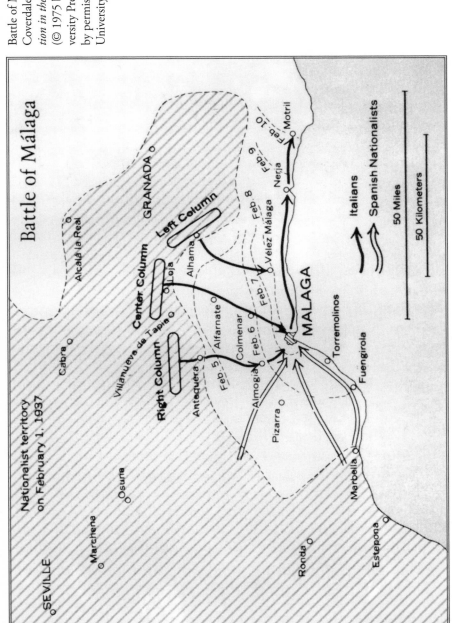

Battle of Málaga. [John F. Coverdale, *Italian Intervention in the Spanish Civil War* (© 1975 by Princeton University Press), 208. Reprinted by permission of Princeton University Press.]

Battle of Málaga

Nationalist territory on February 1, 1937

Italians

Spanish Nationalists

50 Miles

50 Kilometers

SEVILLE

Marchena

Osuna

Cabra

Alcalá la Real

GRANADA

Villanueva de Tapia

Loja

Alhama

Center Column

Left Column

Right Column

Antequera

Almogía

Feb. 5

Colmenar

Feb. 6

Alfarnate

Feb. 7

Feb. 8

Vélez Málaga

Feb. 9

Nerja

Feb. 10

Motril

Pizarra

MALAGA

Torremolinos

Fuengirola

Marbella

Ronda

Estepona

that a big drive was contemplated against Malaga. The magnitude of this offensive was further screened owing to the necessity for reinforcements demanded by the operations in progress on the Madrid front, and, further, at this time, a successful push was being carried out in the direction of Jaen, the final objective of which seemed to be the important lead mines in that region. However, this last movement proved to be merely a local tactical maneuver with which the Nationalist command succeeded in diverting the attention of the government troops while it made preparations for a drive on Malaga. The well thought out plan has been carried out in such a masterful way that the conquest of Malaga and the province is no doubt one of the most signal Nationalist successes since the outbreak of the civil war.

The offensive was initiated on January 15th by a surprise attack, with the cooperation of the navy, on Estepona[8] (about 80 kilometers west of Malaga) which penetrated the loyalist defenses and was followed by a determined push which drove the militia east of the important town of Marbella. In order to check this offensive, the Malaga command sent reinforcements to this vicinity, but the Nationalists, who had concentrated a force on the west of Granada, launched a sudden attack which in one single advance pushed forward 35 kilometers, capturing the strategic town of Alhama, near the western limit of the province of Malaga. Before militia reinforcements could arrive at the theater of operations in this sector, the Nationalist troops occupied dominant ground positions threatening the coast corridor—the only communication open between Malaga and the government territory to the east.

A rainy spell of some two weeks followed the above success, during which time active operations were paralyzed. However, it is now known that this period was advantageously employed by the Nationalists in the organization of five strong columns which from the Marbella, Ronda, Anteguera, Loja and Alhama sectors were to effect a simultaneous drive on Malaga.

That the government considered the Malaga situation very grave was evidenced by the fact that instead of rushing strong reinforcements through the open eastern coast corridor to defend the city, on the first days of February [it] ordered a general offensive against the Cordoba, Jaen and Granada enemy fronts with a view to force the Nationalists to withdraw troops from the Malaga sector. This offensive was particularly directed against the Nationalist positions of Pozoblanco, Montoro, Villa del Rio, Lopera, Porcuna and Alcala, but although General Queipo de Llano's troops lost some ground on those fronts, none of the above towns were taken, the attacks, in general, being repulsed with heavy losses for the government forces.

The general offensive against Malaga was launched on February 6th. The various Nationalist columns, assisted by the firing of their covering aviation and warships, broke the enemy resistance on all local fronts and from that time no serious attempt was made by the government forces to oppose the rebels. The militia, in a rout which developed into a panic, fled to the mountains and through the highway leading to Almeria. The city of Malaga was taken without resistance on the morning of February 8th and the victorious Nationalist troops then continued practically unopposed their advance through the remaining Malaga littoral and the coast corridor of Granada up to the border of Almeria province which they reached about February 15th. Further advance seems to have been checked or voluntarily stopped in the vicinity of Ugijar and Adra, where the line seems to be in the process of consolidation.

It should be taken into consideration that as the territory through which this victorious offensive has been conducted is roughly 200 kilometers long by 40 in depth, and mostly of mountainous character, some time will be required before the Nationalists will be able to take full possession of the rearguard zone and assume control of the numerous towns and villages therein comprised, the population of which is, in general, politically hostile to them. Nothing except the complete defeat administered to the government forces and the resultant panic which spread throughout the population can explain the sweeping Nationalist advance through such extensive territory, so well adapted to defensive warfare. It is reported that, in order to increase the terror of the militia and people fleeing from Malaga in complete disorder, the aviation, as well as the ships along the coast, constantly swept with gun fire the human stream retreating along the Almeria highway, and that those escaping in motor vehicles knocked down many fugitives who blocked their only road to safety.

Comments
The military and political importance of the disaster suffered by the government in the Malaga region need not be emphasized. The Nationalists captured important war materiel and supplies, since the government troops in their confusion and panic abandoned much of their armament, ammunition and equipment, being prevented by the element of surprise from making it useless to the enemy. The government forces sank two gunboats and endeavored to destroy other defense installations in the harbor, which had been converted into an auxiliary naval base, but, in general, the damage caused was small and will be easily repaired. The booty in the port included a number of commercial vessels and a few armed coastal craft.

Malaga province and the Granada littoral zone, which has fallen to the Nationalists, include very rich agricultural and prosperous industrial districts, most valuable from an economic viewpoint. This fact, united to the commercial and fishing possibilities of this extensive Mediterranean littoral, so close to the Spanish Moroccan Protectorate, enhance the military value of this important region. In reckoning the military value of Malaga, one must consider that it gives to the Nationalists an inside Mediterranean port along the Spanish coast to which foreign personnel and supplies may have access without passing Gibraltar; that it brings the North African ports of Ceuta and Melilla in direct communication with a friendly port without the necessity of passing through the Straits and that it gives the rebels a sea port of some magnitude from which sea attacks may be launched along the hostile coast line to the French frontier and besides offers a protected hydroplane base.

Furthermore, it will be recalled that prior to the conquest of Malaga, the Nationalist front in that region, now no longer necessary, extended for about 250 kilometers, thus requiring a considerable occupying force which, united to the reinforcements sent to carry out the offensive, probably exceeded 60,000 men, most of whom will be soon available for new drives against Almeria, Jaen, Madrid or toward the Catalan provinces.

As to the causes which may have produced the surprising defeat of the government forces in Malaga, they have not as yet been clearly determined. Popular voice charges the Malaga command with treason and cowardice. This accusation is supported, to some extent, by the fact that the authorities had made preparations to abandon the city to its fate before the final rebel drive materialized. The local command authorities escaped in a ship, ready for the purpose, taking with them all the money and valuables they could commandeer. However, it is clear that the existing disorganization arising from the lack of coordinated effort among the various local governing agencies, the absence of discipline in the militia and, above all, the failure of the government to send sufficient independent columns (mostly CNT [Confederación Nacional del Trabajo]) operating in the neighboring fronts are also among the causes responsible for the disaster. The weak resistance offered by Malaga, which was the strongest communist center in Spain and over which they have ruled for some seven months, does not speak well of the constructive capacity and ability for the organization of this party.

While for two days the Caballero cabinet prohibited the press to mention the fall of Malaga, considerable publicity is now being given to the loss of this region with a view to create a reaction which would assist the government to overcome the difficulties with which it is confronted. These, as is well known, may be traced mainly to the lack of unity of command, to party rivalry, to the absence of a regular and strongly disciplined army and, finally, to the revolutionary excesses committed by the syndicates which are a handicap to secure cooperation from certain classes.

On February 14, 1937 a large parade was organized in Valencia by all political parties forming the Popular Front, which was attended by some 200,000 persons, demanding full power for the government, the establishment of compulsory military service, the elimination of disloyal officers from the army, unity of command and other measures conducive to winning the war. A similar popular reaction has been manifested in other places led by the press which is conducting a campaign to arouse the feelings of the people against fascism and to bring about submission of all parties to the authority of the government. However, now remains to be seen whether the reaction caused by the Nationalist success in Malaga and by the imminence of further rebel blows, effects any improvement in the situation, as past experience shows that the extremist parties have been liberal in promising cooperation and discipline but very reluctant or otherwise unable to obtain these essential unity requisites among the masses.

In connection with the fall of Malaga the following paragraphs are quoted from a report made by the American Consul at Gibraltar who visited Malaga some 5 or 6 days after it was captured by the Nationalists:

"Careful inquiry revealed that 40,000 troops were available for the attack on Malaga, including nine columns of Italians to the number of 15,000. The latter were fully equipped and included units of field artillery for support. Not all the Italians passed through Malaga but some went round and continued eastward. Casualties in taking the town were slight, probably not over two or three hundred. There appeared to be no uneasiness about the possibility of a counter attack.

"One large Italian flotilla leader, the *Pessagno*, and a large hospital ship, the S.S. *Heluan* were in port, as well as two small Spanish insurgent gunboats, the *Canovas del Castillo* and *Canalejas*. Several cargo vessels of apparently Spanish registry were also in port. The U.S.S. *Kane* and a French aircraft carrier, *Commandant Teste*, were anchored outside the breakwater, and the German cruiser *Koln* came to anchor just as the U.S.S. *Kane* got underway to return to Gibraltar. In connection with the French destroyer *Alcyon*, which called soon after the fall of Malaga, was so unwelcome that insurgent officers turned their backs on French officers ashore rather than salute them. It was said that a protest had been lodged with the military authorities and it may be that the *Commandant Teste* is remaining until the representations are acted upon".

Valencia   No. 6488
March 4, 1937
Subject: The Military Situation

Madrid Fronts

Northwest. The Coruna highway and Pardo sector. Since the victorious drive launched by the Nationalists during the first days of January which resulted in the occupation of the zone comprised between Las Rozas and Aravaca, and gave them control of the Coruna highway from the former place to the Cuesta de las Perdices, near the Manzanares River, no serious attempt has been made by the Franco troops to push their lines farther in this sector. The natural barrier opposed by the Manzanares River, considerably swollen by heavy rains, and, above all, the formidable lines of defense organized by the government on this front, have apparently discouraged fresh rebel attempts at completing the investment of Madrid by advancing in the direction of Fuencarral. The government forces have launched several attacks against the Nationalist positions on this front but have failed to make any appreciable progress, since their objective was to dislodge the enemy from the Perdices heights which overlook the Puerta de Hierre—the northwest gateway to the city.

University City and Parque del Oeste. The salient formed by this front has been the scene of almost daily engagements since it was taken by the Nationalists on November 16th. At first, these attacks were almost always initiated by Franco's shock troops, particularly Moors and Legionnaires, to whom this most dangerous spear head was entrusted. The attacks, which were usually made during the night, seemed intended to keep them in constant alarm and fear. Only the low offensive spirit of the militia at the time could explain the maintenance by the Nationalists of this precarious foothold, which was surrounded by the enemy on three sides. After the successful Nationalist drive on Pozuelo and resulting expansion and consolidation of their lines in the Casa de Campo, the base of the wedge formed by the University City and Parque del Oeste was enlarged and became better protected. However, in spite of this improvement, the initiative of the attack from that time on has generally passed to the government forces, which, having attained a higher morale and better organization, have launched frequent attacks in this sector. The Nationalists, not daunted by the losses suffered, have made a very steadfast and heroic defense and have managed to hold most of the buildings they originally occupied in University City, although they have lost some of the ground they conquered in the Parque del Oeste. One of the buildings most furiously assaulted by the government forces, although without success, has been the Clinic Hospital, which has been partially blown up by mines, and for the possession of which both sides have sacrificed hundreds of lives.

The Madrid fronts are accurately stated as they were personally visited and checked by the undersigned [Fuqua] during his visit to Madrid on March 3-5.

Remaining fronts—Manzanares River. As is well known, the Nationalist front extends, at a short distance from the western bank of the Manzanares River, from the vicinity of the Puente de los Franceses (between the Parque del Oeste and the Casa de Campo) as far as the junction of this river with the Jarama, of which it is a tributary. The situation here, except at the confluence with the Jarama, which is dealt with under a separate paragraph, has not appreciably changed since the Nationalist drive reached the Manzanares on the first days of November. The government troops have launched frequent surprise attacks on the Carabanchel, Barrio de Usera and Villaverde enemy lines, which, while failing to make any important progress, nevertheless attained some slight advantages for the consolidation of their front. The most important attack was directed (January 14th) against the dominant position called Cerro de los Angeles, west of Getafe. The government troops, some 8,000 strong, obtained an initial success through a surprise attack which, however later, through a violent counter attack was completely turned, the Nationalists remaining in full possession of this important height.

Jarama front. This new front was established on the first days of February as a result of a determined Nationalist drive during which Ciempozuelos, San Martin de la Vega and La Maranosa were taken and the government forces driven to the eastern banks of the Jarama from about 10 kilometers north of Aranjuez up to its confluence with the Manzanares in the vicinity of Vaciamadrid. On February 10th the Nationalists succeeded in crossing the Jarama near San Martin de la Vega and in successive days their offensive, although confronted with strong resistance by the government forces, progressed as far as [the] firing range of Arganda and Morata de Tajuna, where it was stopped voluntarily or otherwise.

The importance of this advance is considered very great as it gives the rebels control, at close firing range from dominant positions, of the Madrid-Valencia highway, in the stretch comprised between Arganda and Vaciamadrid, thus mak-

ing more difficult the supply and communications of the capital with the eastern
littoral by forcing detours to the east through Alcala de Henares. Furthermore, it
will be recalled that at La Maranesa was located the army chemical warfare center and school. The loss of La Maranesa, together with the hills dominating the
Valencia road, represent a heavy blow for the government which has ordered its
troops to dislodge the enemy from these positions at all costs. The government
counter offensive was initiated on February 17th by the best militia shock forces
and several international brigades, resulting in a bitter struggle which raged almost without interruption for five days; throughout this offensive the government
troops fought well but were unable to push their lines forward but a few hundred
meters in the direction of La Maranesa owing to the vigorous defense offered by
the Nationalists. It is known from a well informed source that during this battle,
the government troops, which advanced in close formation, suffered about 10,000
casualties. During this battle, strong air squadrons from both sides cooperated and
carried on fierce engagements, as a result of which a considerable number of rival
airplanes were brought down. However, as on the ground, neither contending party appeared to attain a decisive victory. Señor del Vayo, the *Comisario de Guerra*,
announced that this was the greatest battle of the war and that in the fierceness of
the fighting with Germans arrayed against Frenchmen, it was a miniature Verdun.

Continued offensive against Oviedo. The Asturias government forces,
assisted by strong reinforcements sent by the Santander and Vizcaya provinces,
have responded with a desperate effort to the orders received from the Caballero
government "to take Oviedo at all costs". As is well known, the Nationalists have
succeeded, although with considerable effort, in keeping a precarious hold on
Oviedo, which has been more or less closely surrounded on three sides since the
war began. Their control of the city and of the narrow western corridor, ensuring
communication with Grado, has been maintained only at the cost of heavy losses
and by means of keeping there a large force, barely sufficient at times to hold its
ground against repeated attacks by the miners.

The present government offensive, which was initiated on February 20th and
has not yet completely ceased in spite of the resistance encountered, has produced
a series of most bitter and bloody engagements, during which both contending
armies, particularly the Marxists, have suffered very heavy losses. The attacks were
directed, not only against the Nationalist positions defending the city, but along
the whole corridor containing the communications from Oviedo to Grado. The
Marxists had abundant war materiel, including tanks and numerous aircraft, but
all indicates that their offensive was met everywhere with a most obstinate and

heroic resistance and that their efforts directed at completely isolating Oviedo and to take it by assault, have in the main failed, although they have succeeded in entering the outskirts of the city, particularly the San Lazaro district, where house-to-house fighting still continues.

The news released by the Nationalists and the government concerning this offensive is most contradictory, as the latter claims important progress, while the former in their official communiqués by radio state that all attacks have been repulsed with heavy enemy losses, which are claimed to be more than 12,000 casualties, about 3,000 of which were left within the Nationalist lines.

Nationalist offensive on the Teruel Front. In the Teruel sector, which was visited by the undersigned in January, the Nationalists have launched (February 20th) an offensive which progressed from Calamocha as far as 8 kilometers west of Montalban, on the Tarragona road, their lines being now past the villages of Vivel del Rio Martin, Fuenferrada and Portalrubio. This appears to be a strategic movement to attract the attention of the Catalan government which is evidently fearful of a Nationalist drive which threatens its land communications with Valencia. The fact that the Catalan government has not as yet responded to the appeal of the Caballero government for an organized and coordinated attack against the cities of Teruel and Huesca, further confirms the belief expressed in prior reports to the effect that the Catalans, being absorbed by the problems arising from the anarchistic elements existing in their territory, are rendering little assistance to win the war.

Valencia   No. 6505
April 2, 1937
Subject: The Guadalajara Drive—Italian Participation Therein

On March 8, 1937, the Nationalists initiated a strong offensive in the Guadalajara sector, which, judging from orders issued by the high command, had as objectives Guadalajara and the important town of Alcala de Henares, the capture of which would have completed the investment of Madrid and the cutting of its lines of supply with the east, still open through the Guadalajara-Cuenca highway and other secondary roads.

The Nationalist troops drove from their positions south of Algora, using as an axis of advance the Madrid-Guadalajara-Zaragoza road, breaking the enemy lines and occupying Mirabueno, Castejon de Henares and Almadrones. The gov-

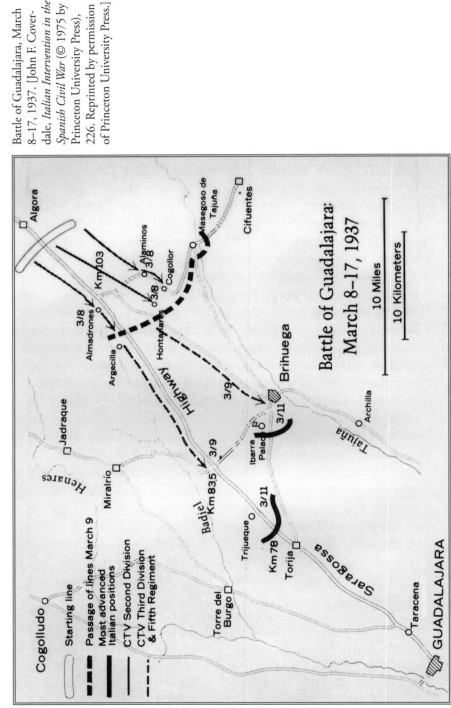

Battle of Guadalajara, March 8–17, 1937. [John F. Coverdale, *Italian Intervention in the Spanish Civil War* (© 1975 by Princeton University Press), 226. Reprinted by permission of Princeton University Press.]

Battle of Guadalajara:
March 8-17, 1937

10 Miles

10 Kilometers

Cogolludo

Starting line

Passage of lines March 9

Most advanced
Italian positions

CTV Second Division

CTV Third Division
& Fifth Regiment

Algora

Km 103

Alaminos
3/8

3/8
Cogollor

3/8
Almadrones

Argecilla

Hontoba

Masegoso de
Tajuña

Cifuentes

Brihuega

3/9

3/11

Tajuña

Archilla

Jadraque

Miralrio

Henares

Badiel

Km 835
3/9

Ibarra
Palace

3/11

Trijueque

Km 78
Torija

3/11

Saragossa

Highway

Torre del
Burgo

Taracena

GUADALAJARA

ernment troops, being taken by surprise and overwhelmed by the superiority of the attacking force, offered a weak resistance, retreating in disorder towards Guadalajara. On the next day (March 9th) the Nationalists, practically unopposed, quickly advanced on a front of about 30 kilometers occupying a number of villages, among which were Jadraque, of considerable strategic importance, located on the Guadalajara-Soria road, and Brihuega, some 35 kilometers northeast of Guadalajara. A spell of rainy and cold weather interfered greatly with this offensive, checking the advance of the mechanized units through the open fields which became practically impassable. In the meantime, strong reinforcements, consisting mainly of international troops hastily sent by the government, were concentrating between Torija and Trijueque to stop the invader.

On March 11th, the Nationalist columns [that] advanced on the Zaragoza-Guadalajara road began to encounter considerable resistance, in spite of which, however, they succeeded in pushing their lines as far as Trijueque (79 kms. from Madrid and 24 from Guadalajara). On this same date, a column from the Soria Rebel Division took the important town of Cogolludo and the village of Membrillera located to the west of the Guadalajara-Soria road, a movement which on March 12th progressed as far as Espinosa de Henares, on the railroad from Madrid to Zaragoza.

During the five days of this successful offensive, the Nationalist communiqués claimed that the government forces had suffered some 2,500 casualties and that about 300 prisoners and important war materiel had been captured. Furthermore, it was reported officially by the Nationalists that their aviation had brought down 19 government airplanes, either as a result of brilliant air engagements in which the hostile fleet had been clearly defeated, or by their anti-aircraft guns.

On March 13th, the government forces, which in large numbers had concentrated under cover of the forests south of Brihuega and Trijueque, apparently deceiving the enemy as to their real strengths, not only stopped the Nationalist drive, but, assuming the offensive, defeated the Italian troops advancing via the Zaragoza-Guadalajara road forcing them to retreat in the open country north of Trijueque. As to the exact strength of the troops which the government assembled in this sector, no accurate information is available, but it is estimated that there were not less than 10 brigades, formed of international volunteers and the best militia shock forces under Brigades Commanders [Enrique] Lister, Mora and El Campasino, all of them well equipped and supported by about 30 bimotor bombers and 60 pursuit planes. As a rule, the brigades in which the popular army is now organized, each consists of 7 battalions, of about 800 men.

This successful counter-offensive was much emphasized by the government and the Republican press, which represented it as a great victory, claiming that 14 guns, 60 machine-guns and a large number of prisoners, including a major, all of Italian nationality, had been captured. The fact that these Italian prisoners had been taken was used by the Minister of State as a basis for his statement concerning the participation of Italian regular units in the Spanish civil war. Señor del Vayo, in his note to the British government declared that in the Guadalajara front "there were engaged 4 mechanized Italian Divisions, plus 3 special brigades of German and Italian troops".

The persistent bad weather prevented major operations on this front until the early morning of March 18th, when four government columns, supported by 80 tanks and strong air fleet, launched an attack, the objective of which was the village of Brihuega. The battle lasted all the day and, after the Italians had been dislodged from the key positions they occupied in the vicinity, this village fell to the government forces by 10:00 P.M. Again, the government claimed a great victory, stating that the Italian troops had fled in disorder, abandoning 6 guns, 60 trucks and a large number of machine-guns, rifles and other war materiel.

The Nationalist command issued a statement by radio denying the military successes claimed by the government, saying that they were "completely fantastic," referring particularly to the capture of such quantities of war materiel and to the alleged participation of regular Italian army units. However, regarding this participation, it was admitted that Italian and other foreigners were fighting on the Nationalist side forming part of the Legion units. As to the reason for the paralyzation of the Rebel offensive, this was ascribed to the heavy rains, which had made the ground muddy and had swollen the rivers, all bridges over which had been blown up by the retreating government troops. In spite of this statement, it was clear that, although the character of the victory had been exaggerated by the government with a view to improve the morale of its forces and to arouse the feelings of the people by emphasizing the invasion of foreign troops, the Nationalist offensive had been checked and the Italian units repulsed, having lost in their retreat the villages of Trijueque and Brihuega.

On March 20th and 21st the government forces continued their advance occupying the villages of Muduex, Utande, Yela and Masegoso, their vanguards reaching kilometer No. 95 of the Guadalajara-Zaragoza road. By March 22nd, the Nationalists, firmly entrenched in the positions to which they had withdrawn, seemed to have checked the counter-offensive of the government forces, which had recaptured more than half of the territory lost. As regards the right of the Nationalist line, located across the Guadalajara-Soria road, all attacks of the government forces were repulsed, Franco's troops continuing in the vicinity of Padilla de Hita and Espinosa.

The government claims that during the counter-offensive of its troops in the Guadalajara sector, about 300 Italian prisoners were taken and that the materiel captured amounted to 24 guns, 200 machine-guns and 70 trucks. During this counter-offensive, the government aviation appeared to outnumber and dominate the Nationalist air force, bringing down some ten to twelve enemy planes, among them being two modern bimotor Junkers, which, according to a press report, used oil as fuel.

From March 22nd to date the government forces have made no attempt at a further advance, devoting their efforts to the consolidation of their positions. It appears that the government, having used almost all of its available forces to stop this grave menace to Madrid in the Guadalajara sector, now lacks trained reserves and must necessarily give a respite to its troops before they are in a position to undertake a major operation. It has been reported by the Madrid press that the Italian troops in the Guadalajara sector have been either withdrawn to the rearguard or entirely removed from that front, as the Nationalist front lines there are now occupied by Spanish forces. This cannot be confirmed, however, there is a current report, now unverified, that these troops have been transferred to the Teruel sector via the main Alcolea-Molina-Monreal road for use on the Montalban front.

Comments

The undersigned covered the Guadalajara front on April 1st visiting the government front lines on the Soria-Guadalajara road, the Guadalajara-Zaragoza road and the road from Brihuega to kilometer 81 on the Zaragoza road. The government front line as of this date was as follows: From West to East. Humanes-Hita-Muduex-Utande-Km. 95 (Guadalajara-Zaragoza road)-1km. north of Yela-Cogollor-Cifuentes.

The attitude of the troops observed was unquestionably defensive which observation was fortified by the elaborate trenches and wire entanglements being constructed.

While it appears that the operations in the Guadalajara front have not reached their final stage, it is probable that perhaps a decisive battle may still be fought in this region, the recent happenings in this sector are very interesting from a military viewpoint and besides they throw considerable light on the participa-

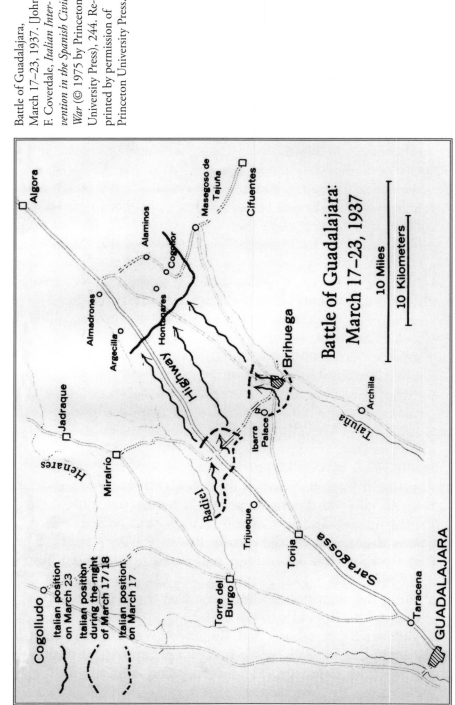

Battle of Guadalajara, March 17–23, 1937. [John F. Coverdale, *Italian Intervention in the Spanish Civil War* (© 1975 by Princeton University Press), 244. Reprinted by permission of Princeton University Press.]

Battle of Guadalajara: March 17–23, 1937

10 Miles

10 Kilometers

Cogolludo

Italian position on March 23

Italian position during the night of March 17/18

Italian position on March 17

Algora

Aleminos

Masegoso de Tajuña

Cifuentes

Almedrones

Cogollor

Argecilla

Hontanares

Brihuega

Archilla

Jadraque

Tajuña

Henares

Miralrio

Ibarra Palace

Badiel

Trijueque

Torija

Saragossa

Torre del Burgo

Taracena

GUADALAJARA

Highway

tion of Italian troops in the civil war, an intervention which until now could not be sufficiently substantiated with proofs unless such have been obtained in the Malaga region.

Judging from statements issued by the government and from articles which have appeared in the press, the Guadalajara drive was almost exclusively carried out by Italian troops. This claim is supported by the fact that all the prisoners taken by the Republican forces in this front (about 300, including five commissioned officers) were of Italian nationality. Furthermore, the considerable quantities of war materiel captured, such as tanks, guns, gun-carriages, machine-guns, etc. are unquestionably of Italian make, not to count important documents, issued by the Italian command, some of which have been reproduced in the press. However, it is not believed that these forces consisted of four Italian Divisions of regular troops, but that the Italian battalions participating in this drive were formed of officers and men, with some past service, who have been more or less voluntarily drafted for service in Spain, but which could not be classified as regular units. This point is considered of importance as the military efficiency of the Italian regular army is no doubt superior to that demonstrated by these battalions of volunteers in the Guadalajara front. The effort of the government to present these forces as the best regular units of the Italian army and emphasizing their defeat at the hands of the popular militia is calculated to bring about further international complications. In this connection, it might be stated that most of the credit for this victory belongs to the "Antifascist International Brigades", a fact which has been carefully omitted by the government.

Judging from available information, the Italian units which have participated in this offensive were motorized, equipped with modern and abundant materiel and were assigned this offensive mission in the sector including the Guadalajara-Zaragoza highway and region east of the road. The "right of the line" seems to have been entrusted to Spanish Nationalist troops, belonging to the Soria Division, which took Cogolludo and other villages west of the Guadalajara-Soria road, the general objective of which, aside from cooperating with the advance on Guadalajara, was apparently to threaten the Somosierra government front from the rear.

While the Nationalist command has repeatedly stated that the victories claimed by the government forces were "fantastic", the facts tell this story—that the Italian units were halted when they were victoriously advancing along the Guadalajara-Zaragoza road, that later a crushing defeat was inflicted upon them at Trijueque and Brihuega heights, and that along the Zaragoza road the retreat continued for about 20 kilometers, the first disaster of any consequence suffered by the Nationalist cause since the war began. The responsibility for this defeat does not appear to be imputable to Franco's command, as the right of the line, confined to Spanish troops, successfully stood all attacks. Furthermore, it will be recalled that since the beginning of the war the Nationalists have launched several offensives, all conspicuous for the method and prudence with which they were conducted, and to their credit it may be said that the positions conquered were never lost to enemy counter-attacks.

It appears that the Italian command, over confident in its materiel and organization, under-estimating the numerical strength and military efficiency of the enemy, reckoned that the taking of Guadalajara and Alcala, thus completing the investment of Madrid, was an easy task. Perhaps the facility with which Malaga was taken contributed greatly to mislead the Italian high command, although the obstinate and successful defense of Madrid against the best shock Franco troops during the last four months, and the slow but steady progress made by the government forces along organization and discipline, were known facts which should not have escaped the Italian leaders. It is believed at this time that the military mishap encountered by the Italians in the Guadalajara front may be traced in great measure to the poor combat efficiency of their units, the mass of which were formed of soldiers without sufficient training and war experiences, and to the bad weather they encountered which strained their physical resistance, and perhaps more than all to the severe bombing and strafing to which they were inflicted by the Government Russian air fleet of some 80 planes. Many Italian prisoners have declared that they were unemployed laborers in their country and that they had enlisted in the army as a means to provide sustenance for their families. It also appears that the small Italian tanks were not a match for the Russian [tanks], about half of which are of medium type, equipped with [a] high powered anti-tank gun in addition to machine-guns. The government made a desperate effort to repulse the "Italian" invader by withdrawing its best shock forces (mostly formed of international brigades) and most modern materiel from the Madrid and other nearby fronts. It is believed that these withdrawals were replaced by the recruits obtained from the recent calling to the service of five replacements.

It has been noted that the weakening of the lines in the Madrid government fronts was not taken advantage of by Franco's army in launching a decided offensive against some vulnerable sector of the capital. It is true that when the Guadalajara drive was stopped, some attacks were directed upon the government positions in the Jarama front, and also, that the rainy spell then prevalent interfered with major operations, but the relative inactivity of the Spanish Nationalists at a time when all indicated that a general drive on Madrid had been prepared, might indicate lack of sufficient forces after they were compelled to send reinforcements to reestablish the situation on the northeast.

Prior to and during the victorious stage of the Guadalajara offensive, the Nationalist radio stations boasted that the immediate capture of Madrid was a certainty. Therefore, the government success in checking this drive, while it may not have forced the Nationalists to abandon their plans, has evidently delayed the attainment of this important undertaking. The government's victory in the Guadalajara sector has lifted its morale to the highest point yet attained and the employment of Italian troops by the Nationalists has offered the Spanish State Department opportunity for excellent propaganda in its foreign presentation of this subject.[9]

Valencia   No. 6510
April 4, 1937
Subject: Visit to the Italian Prison Camp

Through the direct personal courtesy of Colonel Aureliano Alvarez Coques, the Chief of Staff of the Spanish Army, the undersigned visited the Italian prison camp at Valencia. He was received with military honors, the guard being turned out and presented to him. He was met upon arrival by the commanding officer of the prison and by him was presented to all of the officers of the prison garrison. He was escorted through the barracks, mess halls, kitchens, et cetera and was encouraged to talk to the Italian officer prisoners and to the soldier prisoners in his own way and to those of his own selection.

Notes of the Visit

The prisoners visited were those captured in the Guadalajara sector in the Nationalist drive of March 8th. The Spanish commanding officer of the prison stated that all of the Italian prisoners captured in the above sector were confined to this prison and that those who had been in Madrid, with the exception of three men, had been transferred to this garrison. The prison organization unit reviewed consisted of an improvised battalion of three companies, each about 100 men strong. The commissioned personnel consisted of five officers, one major and four lieutenants.

I was later presented by the Chief of Staff of the Valencia Command with a roster of the Italian prisoners captured in the Guadalajara sector, which, it will be noted contains the names of 299 men.[10] This data, in connection with the strength of these Italian prisoners, is presented in more or less detail, in view of the newspaper reports and exaggerated claims sent out of Spain to the effect that several thousand Italian prisoners had been captured.

Questions were asked [of] individuals as they were passed along the inspection of barracks, the answers to which gave the undersigned the following impressions:

a) That none had service in Abyssinia.

b) That most were peasants from the farm lands of Italy. Only two questioned lived in a city.

c) That an unusual number of them were married and had two or three children.

d) That their ages ran from 25 to 40 years.

e) That none of them were members of the regular Italian Army.

f) That all of them had some military training, mostly that given a conscript serving with the colors.

g) That they had left Italy wearing the uniforms and equipment furnished them by their government during their service with the colors.

h) That they were volunteers for some sort of "service overseas", not knowing that their destination was Spain.

i) That they were shipped direct to Cadiz and then trucked to Valladolid where they entrained for Zaragoza.

j) That they were generally—from appearances—lacking normal intelligence.

k) That they lacked any true soldier character and were willing to make the communistic salute and color their remarks to please their captors, particularly in denouncing "fascism" and embracing "communism".

l) That they were probably organized into "all Italian units" with numerical designations after leaving Italy.

m) That they were captured in a surprise attack by a Spanish column without resistance on their part and, from the records, with little loss of life. In this connection, the Spanish General Staff furnished the undersigned with the names of four dead identified as Italians.

Observations made during the visit produced the following impressions:

a) That they showed lack of proper soldier training by their inability to assume properly the "attention" position of a soldier, to render prescribed salutes or to march in step.

b)   That their barracks were dirty and disorderly arranged, no attention being paid to uniforms, in the arrangement of bunks, bedding or equipment.

c)   That they were dirty and unkempt personally, their uniforms poorly worn with coats and jackets invariably unbuttoned.

d)   That they were responding to communistic propaganda being implanted by leading communist men and women of Valencia planted in their midst.

Note: The Spanish Propaganda Section has furnished newspaper men and others with a copy of statements of selected prisoners.

London   No. 38695
April 20, 1937
Subject: Employment of Troops in Domestic Disturbances.
The Civil War in Spain

Opinions expressed in official and private circles in London now suggest that there is possibly no more than a 50-50 chance that the Insurgent Forces will win in the Spanish Civil War. It is, of course, significant that this opinion has been reached since the defeat of the Italians with Franco on the Guadalajara Front in the latter part of March. And in connection with the above, it is of interest to make a record here of one so-called "official view" of the circumstances surrounding the Italian defeat. This is given below in substantially the same form in which it was recently heard.

Apparently, the plan for the Italian advance in the direction of Guadalajara-Madrid was made with considerable secrecy. It was to be an attack with mechanized forces, but it is well to differentiate between "mechanized" and "motorized", and from what has been learned, it is believed that the cross-country, armored-fighting vehicles were few in number. The strength of the attack was designed to be its mobility and surprise and for this purpose the greater part of the Italian forces were motor-borne.

It appears that the advance got underway successfully, and under cover of some pretty bad weather it was thought that the move could be kept secret.

It so happened that a lone Russian observation plane (operating for the Madrid Government), while undertaking a casual flight over this area, discovered the long lines of motor columns advancing towards Guadalajara. The Russian observer returned at once to his aerodrome, and gave the alarm to the Madrid forces.

Because of the fact that the Russians had built for themselves numerous concrete runways on their aerodromes, it was possible to put into the air a large number of bombing planes from what would otherwise have been exceedingly heavy
and boggy fields. It is said that these planes attacked the Italian motor columns
in a bold and effective manner with machine guns and bombs. They machine
gunned the jammed-up Italian masses much along the same lines as is practiced in
"attack aviation" by the U.S. Army. So persistent and effective was the Russian air
attack that it is a wonder, really, that the Italians were able to make any defense at
all. As a matter of fact, the Italians were able to make considerable advance in one
or two areas in spite of that terrific confusion.

The Italian attack was finally stopped, however, by the International Brigade, especially dispatched from Madrid. It is said that the effectiveness of the International Brigade's defense was mainly due to the quantity and efficiency of the
French Artillery supporting the Brigade (French Artillery in this instance meaning French guns manned by Spanish artillerymen who were French trained, and
in some cases, French led). The execution of the French artillery is said to have
completed the rout of the Italians, and in spite of some considerable bravery and
some really able and tactical dispositions on their part, the Italians finally broke
and fled from the field.

The Italian flight is reported to have been a "complete flight". They abandoned every conceivable form of equipment. There were Italian guns, rifles, machine guns, pistols, knives, personal equipment of officers and soldiers, and an
almost inconceivable mess of damaged motor vehicles. The casualties suffered by
the Italians are not definitely known, but they are said to have been very high.

The defeat of the Italians on the Guadalajara front must have been a "pretty
bitter many for the Duce". Some persons have stated that they don't see how it was
possible for the Duce to "hold himself in" after this great defeat, but the British
point of view is, on the whole, complimentary to the Duce and the Italians, i.e.,
relatively so. In a British view, the victory of the Madrid forces was purely "fortuitous." It is believed that the Italian leader, with the Duce's consent, gambled on
the state of the weather to provide satisfactory cover for a mass movement entirely
by road, mostly during daylight. They gambled on the fact that there had been
little activity in the Guadalajara area for some time, and that there had been little
aerial observation, particularly during the very bad weather of that period. From
this point of view, it was purely bad luck that one Russian aviator who had been
instructed to cover the area generally, discovered through the mist of that day in
March the Italian motor columns advancing towards Guadalajara, and the bad

luck facing the Italians was still further reinforced by the fact that the Russians were able (with their foresight of some months before) to send off an effective number of airplanes from their concrete runways, although their air field was badly bogged.

The events of the latter part of March, according to several views expressed in London have, therefore, considered altered the estimates which have previously been more favorable to the Insurgent than to the Government Forces. From several quarters it is now suggested that a sort of stalemate is more likely than a victory by either side. Those holding to this opinion now suggest that the happiest solution would be for both sides fighting in Spain, in their "dilemma of exhaustion", to acknowledge a so-called independent military leader, and after destroying the dissenting elements who might persist in objecting to such a solution, to combine in liquidating the situation. Those who have made this suggestion are not able to name a suitable person at this juncture, around whom opposing elements in Spain would rally; but it is not improbable that they rather wish that this solution might now occur.

Hayes A. Kroner

Lt. Col., Inf., Acting M.A.

[No city cited; probably Valencia.—Ed. Note]

June 1, 1937

Subject: Further Report on the Guadalajara Offensive and Counter Offensive

The information contained in this report has been obtained directly and indirectly from the General Staff here in Valencia. The delay in the preparation of a report covering any further information on this campaign was made necessary by the lack of available details obtainable, the slowness with which the Spanish General Staff assembled pertinent data and the passage of time required to evaluate the items gathered by the press and other agencies. As this campaign was the first real major offensive involving an advance and the employment of open-order tactics, the lessons which may be drawn from it may be reckoned of some value.

The Guadalajara Front

Based upon the undersigned's visit to this sector in the early part of March, it was truly properly classified as a "quiet sector". From his personal observations and information gained from conversations with officers and men at the front, the lines were lightly held with poorly trained militia. It is reported that it was not until the 11th of March that reinforcements were brought up, which consisted of three battalions going into action near Trijueque. In this connection, it is of interest to note that the Spanish high command, even at this short distance from Madrid, was unable to get troops in any number to this front until five days after the nationalist advances had been initiated. It has been reported that the appearance of the Government ground troops in any appreciable number was after the retirement of the Italians had been initiated.

The strength of the rebel advance is of course unknown, and the only available estimate is that furnished by the Government, which in all probability is greatly exaggerated. Claims run to four and even six divisions; however, the evidence would place the Italian force at three divisions.[11] The Government mentions a third division in its communiqués which was partly motorized, a portion of the infantry and artillery being truck-borne. One or two companies of tanks of the Ansaldo type were reported with these troops. These tanks are mentioned by a military officer as "having shown their defects," that their "cross country performance was poor" and that "they cannot 'standup' to the Russian mediums". Judging from what the undersigned has heard from all sides, taken with his own observations previously reported, the Italian troops were of a decidedly poor order, low morale and lacked basic training. These troops possessed no outstanding arms or equipment worthy of any comment, except a 20 mm. combined anti-tank and anti-aircraft gun, the characteristics of which have been requested by the undersigned. The divisions were undoubtedly hastily formed and in all possibility lacked that basic element for the success we call "teamwork".

The invaders were caught by a surprise attack in a rain storm, three thousand feet above sea level, in a strange land. The cold rains huddled them in their motor trucks, dampened whatever little soldier ardor they may have had for fighting and made them an easy prey for the Iberian lads fighting in the shadows of their own homes, aided by men of adventure and courage, who had come great distances for a cause and braving danger for this great moment of combat. The road sides and cross country routes were soft and sticky—too much of an obstacle for the Ansaldo to negotiate. The column was denied ground facilities for dispersion—it hugged the road, in fact, its inflexibility was more that of a convoy than a mechanized force. This was the picture, to some extent, of the Italian advance when the low flying Russian planes swept over the long line of trucks anchored to the Guadalajara-Zaragoza road. Such a movement in daylight on a great public highway certainly evidences lack of reconnaissance efficiency and a complete misconception of the danger existing from the near presence of enemy planes (Russian)—the efficiency of which had been well established and should have been known by the Italian high command.

The most remarkable fact in connection with the concentration of the Italian divisions on this "quiet sector" was that [the] Government high command knew nothing of the movement until the storm broke on the 8th of March and even then it was some five days before a real appreciation of the conditions became apparent and when a reasonable estimate of the situation was made. The credit which might be given to the Italians for such outstanding success in the secrecy of their concentration is to a great extent discounted by the non-existence of a Government Intelligence Service and by the fact that the Russian plane observations never extended to any reasonable distance. It is of interest to note that this truck movement on the road was more or less obtained through accident by a loyal plane observer.

Plan of Advance

So, at the beginning of March, probably three divisions of Italians had been concentrated in the area Siguenza-Alcolea-Medinaceli, opposite the Government line La Toba-Mirabueno-Abanades. This front crossed the Madrid-Zaragoza road at Km. 110, and was consequently 56 Kms. from Guadalajara and 81 Kms. from Alcala de Henares. The Italian plan seemed to have Guadalajara as the first objective and Alcala de Henares as the second. The main column (including motorized units) was to follow the Zaragoza road and as soon as it had cleared Almadrones the first division (motorized) in support was to move on Brihuega and thence down the Tajuna valley. Both columns were to push forward rapidly and gain the Guadalajara-Cuenca road.

The Advance

After a three hour bombardment, the drive was launched on the 8th of March, the main attack directed between Mirabueno and Abanades. The weakly held Government front line was crushed at once and by the late afternoon, the main column had reached Almadrones, where Government supporting troops had formed, holding up the advance until the next day. On the 9th of March, although the Government resistance had been supported by some troops from Guadalajara, the advance pushed through to Gajanejos in which vicinity it remained halted on the 10th. This may have been due to a Government counter attack of some strength on the 10th, which resulted in the taking of some forty Italian prisoners and to allow the left division to catch up, having been delayed through some minor engagements. On the 11th, the advance was energetically resumed, the main column gaining Trijueque. It will be noted that this advance, considering particularly that it was composed of motorized troops operating against weakly held positions by a poorly organized militia, must be considered very slow. It had covered from Km. 110 to Km. 77, 33 Kms., about 20 miles, in a four day forward movement in enemy territory. However, this slowness of movement of this advance may have been occasioned by the fact that this motor column, some 20 Kms. in length, was tied to the road and that it was delayed to allow the left division to gain its relative position on the flank. Notwithstanding the causes cited above, the delay of this advance must be credited to the Government (Russian) air force which went into action on March 11th, and from that time on dominated the air.

The Counter Attack

On the morning of March 12th, the Government air fleet (Russian) in low flying attacks, struck this motor column, strung out along the Zaragoza road, and gave it a terrific beating, definitely halting the movement with complete demoralization of the troops. This surprise attack from the air is reported to have caused a panic, the effect from which the Italians never recovered. This pandemonium which now raged in the Italian column was noted by the Government troops, which are said to have attacked at this time, although they had been retiring defensively during the previous days. With practically no resistance, the loyalists captured a large number of trucks filled with ammunition and war materiel, 12 field guns, and 2 combined anti-aircraft and anti-tank guns. As a result of this action the Italians must have commenced their withdrawal on that night, the 12th-13th, as the Government troops took Trijueque on the 13th unopposed.

It has been reported by an officer of the Government air forces that the Russian squadrons in this attack made 8 sorties, dropped 492 bombs and fired 200,000 rounds of small ammunition.

The casualties which resulted from this air attack, the panic and defeat which followed cannot be estimated. They are reported in the thousands, perhaps five thousand would be the average claim.

It must be emphasized here that the Government counter offensive with ground troops—although claiming a victory over "great opposition"—was nothing more than exploiting a success gained by a surprise air attack of Russian planes—in fact, it was more in the nature of a mopping up action than a combat.

The demoralizing effect of this attack from the air can best be summed up in the realization that a division, possessing immeasurable superiority in men, equipment and fire power over a weak enemy that had been defeated, what might be termed a rear guard action on the previous day, withdrew in disorder, taking with it the left flank division.

The Retreat

That the Government ground forces contributed little toward this victory is evidenced by the fact that their combat pressure was so weak as to cause them to lose contact with the Italians on the 14th and 15th of March, and that they lacked all power and cohesion sufficient for an organized pursuit. The Defense Junta at Madrid did not seem to realize what had happened, as evidenced by the fact that under its direction Valdearenas, 4 Kms. from Trijueque, was not occupied until the 15th of March and then unopposed by the enemy. It was not until the 16th that the Government air forces attacked Brihuega, finding only a rear guard left by the Italians which had to remain until the main column had cleared the cross road near Almadrones. This attack was delivered by some 30 bombing planes protected by pursuits, which are reported to have discharged 120 bombs and fired several thousands of rounds of ammunition. The attempt on the part of the rebel's air force to counter attack was feeble and uncoordinated and accomplished no positive results.

On the 17th, a Government force of three brigades attempted to surround Brihuega. These brigades made some progress between the Tagus and Tajuna and threatened one of the lines of retirement from Brihuega, capturing some few prisoners. It appears that the main Italian resistance was centered around Brihuega. The garrison of the village was probably two battalions of infantry, several machine gun platoons and two batteries of 75's. The village was attacked on the 18th. In the afternoon some small units managed to make their escape by the Almadrones road. At about 8 p.m., under cover of darkness, the Italians with difficulty evacuated the village, leaving to the Government forces some hundred prisoners, 60 trucks, 6 guns and a considerable number of machine guns. The air attacks on this garrison during the day of the evacuation had much to do with the Italian retirement. The first attack is reported to have been delivered by fifteen machines dropping 360 bombs and firing some 12,000 rounds of small ammunition, while the second attack, under more intense conditions was carried out by a bombing squadron protected by 45 pursuits, which on completion of their protective role, emptied their belts into the village.

On the 19th and 20th of March, the Government troops advanced without encountering any appreciable resistance and on the 20th, they reached the line running eastwards from Km. 95 on the Zaragoza road to Cifuentes and westward to the Soria road at Hita, a front line position which was visited by the undersigned in the early part of this month and remains unchanged at this date. The Government air forces not only played the important role in this drama of defeat and withdrawal of the Italian divisions, but on the 20th initiated the most violent attack which had taken place during this campaign. To the north of Almadrones, Algora and Navalpotro, 80 Government planes attacked the enemy's concentrations, dropping 610 bombs and firing 100,000 rounds of ammunition.

Closing Comments

Lack of combat ability and military leadership on the part of the Government ground forces, in not taking advantage of the opportunity afforded them by the brilliant successes of the air force must be attributed to them by the student of this campaign. The part that these foot troops played was minor and secondary, yet, there was before them a chance for great military renown and position of achievement—a goal attainment, however, which required those basic military qualities unpossessed by the Government infantry.

Notwithstanding the Government claims, its ground forces were not only incapable of taking the offensive, but did not do so. It is evident, with the exception of the three international Brigades participating, that the Government forces were militia, improved somewhat since the days of Talavera and Getafe but still lacking the training for open warfare maneuvers and offensive combat. Unquestionably this militia has lost its inferiority complex, evidenced completely in its recent attempts at the offensive, but instead it has acquired that valor of ignorance so conclusively demonstrated in the thousands of dead piled up on the banks of the Manzanares in the recent, hopeless and futile frontal attack against probably the strongest section of the fortified rebel line in the Casa de Campo.

The undersigned, being an infantry officer and having had some part in the development of the present efficiency of his arm in anti-aircraft training and being familiar, to some extent, with the maneuver tests in the field of activity at Fort Benning, desires to warn the student of the Spanish civil war not to learn a wrong lesson from the successful achievements of the air service in this and other offensive operations.

The undersigned recalls the success attained by the rebel planes in bombing and strafing in the nationalists' triumphant march along the Extremadura road to the outskirts of Madrid—many of these air attacks against ground troops he witnessed and in several instances he was uncomfortably close to the action scenes. In these cases, as in the Guadalajara sector, the ground troops were either poorly trained or not trained at all, and consequently were paralyzed with fear and ran in all directions freeing themselves in many instances from their rifles if such became a hindrance to their seeking some kind of cover. Not the slightest attempt was ever noted of the infantry soldier employing his rifle against an enemy plane. Through lack of training, he has no confidence either in himself or his weapon against the war machine.

It is interesting to pause and endeavor to construct a picture of what might have happened, for example, on the Guadalajara road when these Russian planes swooped down on this motorized column had this command been properly trained in anti-aircraft combat—say training equal to that of our 29th infantry. Let us assume that these trucks carried machine guns—fixed mounts—with an occasional truck-mounted 50 cal. And prepared—as they would be for air combat—traveling on a great highway in day time, in a hostile country with the knowledge that the enemy was not only air active and superior in the skies, but that his landing fields were not far distant. Let us say that these trucks were filled with soldiers equally trained to those of our regiment mentioned, that upon the siren or other signals adopted by the columns announcing the presence of the hostile air fleet the men detrucked orderly and in accordance with their training instructions took to firing.

[The rest of the dispatch is missing from the file.—Ed. Note]

4

Daily Routine of War and the Fall of Bilbao
(April–July 1937)

"The power of the Government appears to have been weakened by the fall of Malaga. Although no signs whatever of demoralization exist in Madrid, there are for the first time indications of pessimism and political disintegration on the part of the Central Government."

Fuller,
April 1937[1]

As the opening epigraph suggests, the rebel forces of General Franco were increasing their pressure on Republican forces. In the period covered by the dispatches in this chapter, while the number of military engagements was few, they were bigger, involving larger concentration of troops on both sides, more use of artillery and airpower in a coordinated manner, and with greater consequences. The chapter ends with a discussion of the fall of Bilbao, the heart of Spain's industrial sector, to the Nationalists. In the spring and early summer of 1937, a variety of cadencies become evident in the historical record that demonstrate the war's now pervasive features.

Both sides by now had put together armies populated with tens of thousands of troops, variously equipped but obviously armed and provisioned at levels not evident in the early months of the war. As the following dispatches demonstrate, there was an influx of airpower from German and Russian sources, along with a ragtag group of pilots and miscellaneous aircraft from various countries. The same could be said regarding artillery but to a lesser extent. Many battlefronts were established, complete with networks of trenches and artillery positions, but also with minimal war-fighting activities. Indeed, many dispatches reported no activity evident at various fronts, and thus those documents are not presented. It appeared that both sides were settling down to a long, drawn-out affair, even though both sides did choose to launch larger campaigns that were specific in scope, such as continued attacks on Madrid's environs and the initiative to the north in the Basque country.

The volume of discussion among attachés and other military observers from various countries remained high in this period. Besides reporting on events, there was considerable discussion about the strategic use of airpower and tanks. In the 1930s, both sets of technologies were the subject of considerable conversation in military circles in Europe and North America. It was in this period, for example, that the German army officer who became so famous in World War II for his use of tanks, Erwin Rommel (best known as "the Desert Fox"), worked out his thinking about the strategic use of tanks, publishing what rapidly became a classic work on the subject read by generals in many armies, including Gen. George S. Patton. The German general (later field marshal) benefited from the growing experiences of both sides in the Spanish Civil War.[2] The war was clearly an open book for all those, both civilian and in uniform, interested in military affairs. These dispatches offer specific and useful differentiations between what the propaganda put out by both sides said about military issues and what troops on the ground reported to the American observers. In this group of dispatches we also find rare, contemporary eyewitness comments about how naval warfare in the war was waged and about the construction and use of trenches.

Valencia   No. 6531
April 26, 1937
Subject: The Military Situation
Madrid Fronts

The relative calm which existed on all Madrid fronts during the latter part of March and first days of April was broken early on the morning of April 9th by the initiation of a general government offensive. This movement soon developed into a battle of considerable magnitude, practically restricted to a small north-western sector, raging almost without interruption for four days and ending apparently with the exhaustion of the attacking army. This belief is supported by the fact that the government forces, which had suffered terrific losses during the battle, stopped their attacks on April 13th without having attained any important objective. That Franco's troops were also considerably weakened after the effort made to repulse this offensive was evident since they did not counter-attack in force to gain the ground lost in the Casa de Campo, which, although amounting to a few hundred meters only, nevertheless made their communications with the University City sector more difficult.

This offensive of the government forces is believed to have been launched in a desperate effort to relieve the situation in Vizcaya, where the Nationalist Army of the North, evidently reinforced with troops taken from the Madrid and other fronts, had broken the enemy lines north of Villarreal and gained several strategical mountain passes from which a final assault against Bilbao was being prepared and seemed imminent. The fact that the loyalist attacks on the Madrid fronts were repulsed from the beginning clearly indicates that the above purpose was not attained.

Without detracting from the splendid defensive combat of the Nationalists in repulsing this offensive (the participation of Italian or German troops was not claimed by the government), the results from this new Madrid offensive show the great advantages which Franco's troops derived from modern fortifications to be able to stand the attacks of a great superior force equipped with abundant war materiel.

The available information is to the effect that the government employed in this drive about 50,000 of its best shock forces to break the enemy lines in the small zone of the Casa de Campo and Cuesta de la Perdices, [and] that these forces were supported by about 150 guns, by some 120 Russian tanks and by a large air force in absolute control of the air; however, the offensive failed.

Northwest. Coruna Highway, Pardo and Escorial Sectors

On April 9th the government offensive was launched on all Madrid fronts, apparently with a view to confuse the enemy, but the main drive was made on the following day against the corridor, perpendicular to the river, in the hands of the Nationalists, which ensured communication between their positions in the Casa de Campo and University City. The attacks were launched simultaneously from the south, through the government positions in the Casa de Campo and Coruna highway paralleling the river and from the north, through the Pardo, against the Cuesta de la Perdices, as is called the stretch of the Coruna road after it bends at the San Fernando bridge—about a km. of rather steep grade in the direction of Aravaca.

The immediate objectives of the government troops appeared to have been the isolation of University City and the taking of the Garabitas and El Aguilda heights, dominating the river and from which the Nationalists, besides protecting the University City salient, frequently shelled Madrid. From April 10th to April 12th several international and shock militia brigades attacked in this sector, but notwithstanding the determination shown by these troops, they failed to attain any of the above objectives. However, the Nationalists lost a few hundred meters on the Cuesta de la Perdices, the top of which now appears to be occupied by the government forces and in the vicinity of the Puente de los Franceses, a loss which, although small in itself, affects adversely the communications of the Nationalists with University City, which now appear to be dominated by enemy fire.

On April 10th the attack was made by some 20,000 men, mostly forming part of International Brigades, about 3,000 dead. On April 11th the offensive was renewed with six brigades of fresh troops (about 30,000 men) in the hope that the enemy could not resist this new onslaught, but the attacking forces suffered such great losses that it appears that the Thaelmann, Dimitroff and El Campesino Brigades were almost annihilated.

The Nationalist lines proved to be so well fortified and they defended them with such energy that the government columns suffered terrific losses. While the Salamanca official communiqués fixed the losses in this particular drive at 9,000 dead, which appears excessive, it is conservatively estimated that, in all Madrid fronts, the loyalists had some 14,000 casualties.

A strong government air force commanded the air during this offensive. The communiqués issued by the Valencia Ministry of Air claimed that it bombed effectively enemy positions and that special squadrons for low flying subjected them to heavy machine gun fire. It was noted that notwithstanding the intense firing from the numerous and efficiently handled Nationalist anti-aircraft artillery, no government plane was brought down. The government suffered great losses in the tank units participating in the battle, Salamanca official communiqués stating that 36 tanks were disabled either as a result of anti-tank artillery or from other causes.

All attacks against the Nationalist lines at Aravaca and Las Rozas were repulsed. In El Escorial, Las Navas and Robledo de Chavela sectors, there was considerable fighting and the government claimed that its forces attained an improvement in their lines, which is probably true; however, it does not appreciably alter the relative situation in these fronts.

University City and Parque del Oeste

Particularly on April 10th, the buildings and positions in the hands of the Nationalists in this sector were subjected to heavy bombing by the government aviation and to furious attacks tending to prevent the garrison from cooperating in the defense of their lines in the Casa de Campo which protect access to this salient. As usual, the defense of this front was confided to units of Franco's best shock troops, which once more did honor to their fame by not only repelling all attacks but by effecting a sortie at a critical moment of the battle, thus greatly cooperating in saving the situation for their cause. The bravery displayed by the Legion *bandera* which conducted this attack has been rewarded by the collective promotion of all its members. The government forces apparently succeeded in destroying the temporary bridge which had been constructed by the Nationalists over the Manzanares river for communication with the Casa de Campo.

Manzanares River

All attacks launched by the government forces during their general offensive (April 9th) and on the following days on these fronts were repulsed, the only losses of the Nationalists being a few houses on the Extremadura road near the Military hospital, at Carabanchel.

It may be noted here that during the days preceding the claiming of this report Madrid has been more heavily and more consistently shelled than ever before. Morning and afternoon during the past week there has been literally a rain of shells falling generally in the business areas centered around the Gran Via. Some twelve shells struck the Telephone Building during this period doing great damage; however, no casualties occurred in the building. It is believed, as the rebel aviation is reported in the Bilbao area, that the Nationalists have used their artillery instead of their air services in the continued effort to weaken the Madrid defense particularly to remind the garrison that their artillery positions in Carabanchel and the Casa de Campo were still intact after the recent government offensive in that section.

General Comment

Attention is invited to the importance given by the Nationalists to their offensive against Bilbao and by the Loyalists to their drive on Teruel. It is generally believed that both sides have massed their available strength in these localities to attain their objectives in the two campaigns now well underway. It would seem that the taking of Bilbao from a military standpoint would carry tremendous weight and react most favorably to the rebel cause and this fact had much to do with the government staging a counter show in the organization of the Teruel offensive. However, the Teruel salient continues to be reckoned as a threatening dagger pointing at the Mediterranean coast line and much defensive effort has been expended to prevent an advance from this city to the sea. Besides, Valencia feels the nearness of the Fascists as long as they hold this important road junction connecting up Cuenca and Valencia with the Saragossa region to the north, registered by a great sign in the Plaza Castelar, the main square of the city, reminding all that "the front is only 150 kilometers Teruel—Valencia". Should either side succeed in attaining its objective such success will be broadcasted far and wide not only for the military advantage thus gained but in establishing the fact that it possesses the ability to organize a major offensive and drive it through to successful attainment. However, the converse of this deduction must be drawn by the observer on the side lines, for, should neither the Nationalists nor the Loyalists gain their objectives in their drives on Bilbao and Teruel, he may rightfully conclude that neither side, at least at this time, has the "punch" remaining for anything like a "knockout" blow. From this, one may go still further and vision that the present front lines may be the basis for a division of Spain into two parts—a thought which might be considered premature yet must be given consideration as a solution to a stalemate war in view of the intense hatred existing between the Loyalists and the Rightists and the fact that the political creeds for which they are killing each other lie at the opposite ends of the poles of government.

Paris   No. 23, 443-W

May 25, 1937

Subject: Armament and Equipment . . . Tanks in the Spanish Civil War

It is now possible to evaluate to a certain extent the type of tank used and method of employment.

The Nationalists employ a light German tank (new type) and the Fiat-Ansaldo used by the Italians in Ethiopia. The Government uses two types of Russian tanks, T 26 and T 28.

Nationalists
Light German tank.

CHARACTERISTICS:

Maximum speed per hour	50 kms
Crew	2 men
Armament	Twin machine guns turret mounted
Armor	Insufficient. 15mm/m maximum
Weight	About 6 tons

This tank is similar to the light Landwerk tanks which are better known and which have approximately the same maximum speed per hour, 55 kms; armor, 9 to 13mm/m in thickness; radius of action, 200 to 220 kms; weight, 4.8 to 6.8 tons.

Light Italian tank Fiat Ansaldo. This tank was successful in Ethiopia due to the terrain and the mediocre resistance encountered. It is modeled after the light English tank Mark VI.

CHARACTERISTICS:

Maximum speed per hour	45 kms
Crew	2 men
Armament	1 machine gun placed forward or twin machine guns
Armor	10mm/m (approximately). The two known types of Fiat Ansaldo tanks have armor 9 to 13mm/m in thickness.
Weight	2 to 3 tons
Radius of action	100 to 110 kms

Government

Powerful light tank T 26. This tank resembles the light Vickers Armstrong tank of the A and B type now used in Siam,[3] Turkey, Bolivia and Poland. The Russians employ it to exploit the infantry success.

CHARACTERISTICS:

Maximum speed per hour	30 kms
Crew	3 men
Armament	One 37mm/m or a 47mm/m gun and machine gun turret mounted, or 2 MG's turrent mounted.
Armor	13mm/m (insufficient)
Weight	8 1/2 tons
Radius of action	Approximately 150 kms

Medium tank T 28. This tank is designed to operate deep within hostile lines. It is similar to the Vickers Armstrong medium tank of 18 tons.

CHARACTERISTICS:

Maximum speed per hour	40 kms
Crew	5 or 6 men
Armament	1 45mm/m and 1 machine gun in the main turret and two 7.62mm/m machine guns in two lateral turrets
Armor	25mm/m (estimated)
Radius of action	Approximately 180 kms

The above two types have serious defects and are liable to destruction by fire. The T 26 is a hybrid.

The Nationalists have light tanks, armed only with machine guns incapable of penetrating armor 25mm/m or even 13mm/m thick, beyond a range of several hundred meters. The Government forces, on the other hand, have powerful light tanks and medium tanks armed with guns though the former are insufficiently protected. From a tactical point of view the Nationalist tanks are of the type suited for distant or near reconnaissance or for gaining contact. The Government tanks, on the contrary, are less speedy, heavier, more powerfully armed, have thicker armor (especially the T 28) and are of the combat type.

Because of the differences noted above, Nationalist tanks must endeavor to avoid combat with the heavier vehicles. "Combat between tanks," writes Lt. Colonel Perre in the *Revue Mensuelle des Officiers de Reserve* (February 1937), "has the rigidity of combats between armored ships. Whatever be the quality of the crews and the skill of command, the fight can only be successful against a ship of the same class. The light cruiser which meets a battle cruiser must turn away or face destruction. The tank meeting hostile tanks, better protected and with more powerful armament must do the same". The foregoing, however, was learned at Villers-Bretonneux, 24 April 1918, and Niergnies-Seranvillers, 8 October 1918.

Government anti-tank weapons are of French manufacture (probably 25mm/m caliber) and able to penetrate the thin armor of the German and Italian tanks. On the Nationalist side there are some excellent German guns, 37 mm/m (long) which have been very successful against both the T 26 and T 28 tanks. The superiority of the anti-tank guns on both sides is all the more evident due to insufficient artillery. Moreover, precise information on the emplacement of anti-tank guns is difficult due to atmospheric conditions and the difficulties of liaison between the various arms.

Anti-tank defense by means of mines has been efficient. Further, it has been observed that on occasions two determined men have immobilized tanks by means of flaming gasoline or hand grenades, as prescribed in the regulations for German anti-tank detachments. Tactical errors have also contributed to the loss of tanks.

Since December 1936, no attack has been launched without the support of tanks. The number has increased steadily which indicates the value attributed to tanks of both belligerents. At first, both sides parceled out all available tanks. Mass action, therefore, was out of the question. The ten, twenty, or thirty tanks engaged in local actions rarely left the road and were soon destroyed by enemy anti-tank weapons and artillery.

Last March, however, when the Nationalists launched their attack against Madrid from the direction of Guadalajara, 200 tanks were engaged and in one bound advanced 50 kms. on a front where, previously, costly efforts had resulted in insignificant gains. The attack unfortunately was not supported by either porte infantry or artillery which should have occupied the positions conquered and consolidated the results obtained. Failing to receive close support, the tanks advancing 15 kms. per hour were soon isolated. Under such conditions it was only natural that a Government counter attack recaptured 30 kms. of ground. It can be stated now that in the gun against armor fight, it is the former which has won the day south of the Pyrenees.

For the combat tank speed and radius of action are less important than armament which should include a gun and sufficient protection. Against an enemy capable of laying down accurate fire, medium and heavy tanks must be employed.

By medium type is meant a tank similar to the Russian T 28 resembling the 18-ton Vickers Armstrong tank.

In another article published in *La France Militaire* of 8 May 1937, and emanating from a Russian correspondent of *La Renaissance*, the author states that except for a few isolated types, the materiel employed in the civil war is not that which the nations involved would use in a future war. The test of the above types, however, has a certain importance since this material was constructed after the World War and, therefore, lacked combat test. While this constitutes a sort of mass test and the conclusions derived, therefore, are common knowledge, the same cannot be said of the test of more recent types which are kept secret. Hasty conclusions, therefore, should not be drawn regarding the superiority of the material of this or that nation.

This goes on to say: "The German press which, in general, is rather sparing with its compliments concerning Soviet materiel remarks on the Soviet superiority in tank armament; the employment not only of the machine gun but also guns of small caliber gives them superiority over the Italians. On the other hand, the French and Polish military press emphasize the insufficient armor of the Soviet tank, not only as regards thickness but also lack of protection for vital parts. The important conclusion, therefore, is that the armament and armor of the tank are no less important than speed, which confirms the accuracy of the French thesis and leaves in question the Italian and Soviet idea of speed to the detriment of armor."

Comment
The Spanish Civil War appears to have demonstrated the need for a heavy tank for close-in combat.

Waite

Paris   No. 23, 461-W

June 2, 1937

Subject: Major Military Operations. Air Combat Operations

[The first section summarizes the Battle of Guadalajara with nothing new from earlier dispatches, so they were not included here. —Ed. Note]

Conclusions
There is no doubt during the period under review, the Government held complete air superiority. According to the figures published in press communiqués it appears that their losses amounted to one R.5 and one S.B. brought both down by

A.A. fire, but from other reports it is learned that several more aircraft were lost in the low attacks on the motorized column. The Insurgents are said to have lost six Fiats and two Junkers. The tremendous success of their air force must have been a surprise to the Government themselves as well as a nasty jolt for the Insurgents and for Mussolini. (It is fairly definitely established that the columns were almost exclusively composed of Italian materiel and personnel). On the other hand, one must not overlook the part played by the weather and the way it favored this side; if the Insurgent columns had been able to leave the road, or if the Insurgent aircraft had been present on March 12th, or if the Insurgents had had their A.A. defenses properly organized, perhaps by now Guadalajara would have fallen and also Madrid.

Nevertheless, the fact is that 150 aircraft, manned by personnel of various nations and with no academic training and equipped only with simple and elementary accessories, were able, by using tactics which are in no way new or complicated, to defeat a mechanized army of 20,000 men and 2,000 vehicles.

TRAINING OF PERSONNEL IN PEACE AND WAR

Accounts of the tactics and formations adopted by both sides during the present conflict are very varied and the few examples given below are ones with which everyone is in agreement. It had moreover become very strongly impressed on all the pilots here that peacetime tactical training is merely a stepping stone to the tactics which will follow in war time. When confronted with an enemy, it is essential to study carefully not only his tactics but also his ground and air equipment and to base war time training accordingly. Consequently, peacetime tactical training should allow a degree of flexibility which will make any changes of tactics a simple undertaking.

Most of the pilots complain that their peacetime training did not include enough air gunnery. They state that results obtained with camera guns do not give a true indication of the accuracy of their fire. It is thought, however, that this does not apply at home (England) and that many countries which train with camera guns do not have an accurate system of marking. They also accepted the value of tracer bullets and of teaching pilots to observe the tracer at the target and of its trajectory and not at the gun end.

FIGHTER TACTICS

Russian fighters have developed the head-on attack which is used successfully against the Junker 52's. The principles incorporated in these attacks are applied to all operations carried out by fighters. The I.15's with their armament of four guns and light bombs carry out the actual attacks whether they be on ground or air targets whereas the I.16's are used for protection. A squadron of I.15s in flight is composed of 11 aircraft, a center flight of three and two wing flights of four aircraft each. The role of the two extra wing aircraft is protection in the event of enemy fighters escaping the I.16's higher up, and their methods of executing this role is to turn and face head-on any approaching enemy fighters. Thus the biplane fighters concentrate their energies on attacking major objectives rather than in becoming involved in dog fights. The I.16s on the other hand engage immediately all enemy fighters and thus prevent them attacking the I.15s. They are capable of diving as fast as the Fiats or Heinkels and so can keep on their tails, should they attempt to go to the rescue of the bombers which they are escorting. The I.16s are not particularly maneuverable, but can always depend on their speed to get out of the tight corner and their attacks are very much of the "hit and run" kind than those of the more easily handled I.15s.

GROUND ATTACK BY FIGHTERS
The I.16 fighters were originally equipped to carry four 10-lb bombs but the racks were not a success and the only form of ground attack in which they very occasionally indulge is by diving and using their two very fast firing guns. The I.15s on the other hand carry out a great number of ground attacks. Each aircraft has four Vickers and can carry eight 10-kg. bombs. The bomb release is said to be very badly situated in the cockpit and pilots prefer to drop their bombs fairly high at about 1000 feet and continue the dive using their guns to about 300 feet.

BOMBING TACTICS
Very little is known about the tactics used by Russian bombers, or regarding the success they obtain in high altitude bombing. It is known that although they can usually depend on their own speed for defense, they are often escorted by fighters who fly at the same level as the bombers. The bombers have recently carried out night attacks and have on more than one occasion used the following rather clever ruse to great advantage. One bomber flying at a considerable height proceeds some distance ahead of the main formation of bombers. Some five miles behind this machine and flying very low comes an R.5 ground attack biplane. When the bomber crosses the target all the searchlights, which also probably control A.A. units, come into action. It is then the duty of the R.5 to attack these lights from very low with bombs and gunfire. It appears that the R.5 usually takes the searchlight operators

completely by surprise and manages to extinguish the lights in readiness for the approach of the main bombing formations.

It has been noted that the R.5s normally carry out their gunnery against troops, convoys, etc., very low, at probably not more than 100 feet. But to release their bombs they usually "zoom" to four or five hundred feet. This may be in order to obtain penetration or it may be that their bombs are not correctly fused for them to be dropped lower. These aircraft have armor plating protecting their more vital parts and their armament was described in previous reports.

AIRDROMES AND COMMUNICATIONS

As I have previously reported, there are a great deal of temporary landing grounds which have no accommodation or facilities of any kind. The Russian aircraft, by continually changing their base and by nature of their dark green camouflage which makes them difficult to see when on the ground have become practically immune from air attacks while on the airdrome. All stores, personnel and supplies for these aircraft travel by lorries, presumably at night. These grounds are directly connected by telephone with an observation post which is on the roof of the *Telefonica*, the highest skyscraper in Madrid. Thus whenever any enemy aircraft are observed either over Madrid itself or over the Madrid front, their presence is immediately communicated to the fighters. Wireless is not used to any great extent and the fighters are not equipped with R.T.[4] but use well standardized signs to communicate their intentions to one another. The units seem well disciplined and pilots and formations successfully cooperate with each other in this manner.

PARACHUTES

All pilots and observers on both sides are equipped with parachutes and should an individual be so unfortunate as to have to jump it is now understood that he is a fair target for the enemy aircraft. This was expressed very well by another Air Attaché (believed to be Captain Griffiss, U.S. Army Air Corps) in one of his reports which was seen by the writer. "This is the first aerial war of any importance in which both sides are equipped with parachutes. Since coming to Spain I have heard time and again the old argument as to what should be done by a pilot who suddenly sees an opponent floating to earth in a parachute. It is interesting to note that most of the old timers stick to the spirit of chivalry whereas most of the younger chaps look at the proposition in a modern light. My opinion is that the romance of the parachute disappeared as the romantic spirit of aviation changed to a clear-cut science. The Air Force is but one of the many components of any army and as such bears equally the responsibility of the destruction of the enemy. The sparing of a pilot's life in combat is on the same footing as an unauthorized and local armistice. Both may be the direct cause of future operations. The pilot whose life is spared may not on the morrow fly against his chivalrous opponent, but he may bring death to others not only in the air but also on the ground and may be the direct cause of the failure of the High Commander. No pilot has the right to assume such a responsibility. The aerial war of the future as far as combatants are concerned will be devoid of all feeling and sentiment." Peace time training should include every method for the destruction of the enemy and it is not going too far to recommend gunnery practice against dummies, floating down in parachutes. In Spain, both sides are shooting airmen dropping from parachutes. I do not know for certain which side started the policy but at this time it is in full swing. I have been told that the Russians are mighty efficient at the art and never lose an opportunity.

TRAINING

Although the vast majority of skilled personnel on the Government side are foreigners to Spain, the training of both pilots and mechanics had not been neglected. Although there are no figures available it is known that a great number of pilots are under training both at Los Alcazares, near Cartagena, and also in Russia. It is said that some have also been trained in France. The policy is to allow these pilots to filter into the existing Russian units and so eventually be capable themselves of forming units. At present there are many Spanish pilots flying I.15s who have proved themselves very efficient. In order to obtain skilled mechanics conscripts of the years 1932, 1933, and 1934, have been called up and are under training in Murota and Barcelona. They form four battalions.

AIRCRAFT PERFORMANCES

The high performance of the Russian aircraft has surprised most nations who were of the opinion that Russian factories produced only aircraft somewhat out of date and built under license. Although they have certainly improved on the performance of the aircraft they copied, they have at the same time cut down accessories to a minimum and increased their landing speed. Their machines are admirably suited for this conflict because the landing grounds are large and they are not required to operate at very great heights where heating, oxygen, etc., would be required. It appears that at great height the Insurgent machines, which are built more on the lines of the aircraft in England, would have a distinct advantage both in equipment and performance, but at the same time it is significant that in "sunny Spain" it is seldom that aircraft operate at above 15,000 feet and the order of the day is usually low attacks. The aircraft themselves are said to be crudely built and not well finished but they certainly serve their purpose and their armament is exceptionally good.

JUNKERS 86

During March Junkers 86 aircraft with heavy oil engines were found to be operating for the Insurgents. On March 16th one of these machines was brought down at Alcala de Henares and since then two more are said to have been destroyed. These bombers not only have a good performance but are well armed with three turrets, each carrying two guns. The Russians claim that although they are difficult to attack they have a blind area on either side, behind the twin rudders.

Fuller

Valencia   No. 6562

June 1, 1937

Subject: Relative Efficiency of the Contending Armies—General Considerations

The slow but nevertheless constant improvement attained by the Government forces along the lines of organization, discipline and morale has been evidenced during the offensive operations which they have recently conducted on some of the fronts. These offensive movements, although failing to reach the desired objectives, clearly show that the Government has now an army, still in need of much improvement it is true, but nevertheless an army strong in numbers, well supplied with modern materiel and equipment and having excellent soldier material capable of being developed into a good fighting force under proper leadership. The Republican army has demonstrated that it possesses considerable courage and stamina for defense, and lately, through organization, training and war experience, to have attained a certain offensive capacity. It is true that the international brigades continue to be used as shock forces in conjunction with the best Spanish units, but owing to the man power requirements of large scale operations, practically all troops have participated in combat and they have shown considerable fighting spirit, which, however, is beginning to be dimmed by the failure of recent offensives.

However, what the army principally lacks and what is absolutely requisite for ultimate victory is unity of command and trained leadership and until this has been attained no major offensive on an extended front can hope for successful attainment.

At present, as regards the army—the Catalan and Basque separatist forces are still more or less a mosaic of army units and party militia forces—the Republican troops are in general organized along conventional lines forming a regular army, and considerable improvement has been observed in the training, discipline and uniformity of equipment. The use of political flags in the army has been forbidden and now the Republican colors are exclusively displayed. The syndicalists, for well known reasons, while accepting the principle of superior command, continue controlling their own units and the appointment of their own officers, although they now form part of the regular army and as such are organized. This control by the political parties is what prevents unity of command and forbids the essential military factor of responsibility of leadership.

It is well known that during the first months of the war, the Nationalist command used exclusively as shock troops native Moroccan forces, Legion units, Requete (Traditionalist) and Falange (Fascist) voluntary militia. The regular army troops sparingly participated in combat, as the soldiers, owing to compulsory recruitment, were not considered dependable as many of them had been contaminated with revolutionary propaganda. Taking into consideration this handicap, the efficiency demonstrated by the Nationalist regular army units, since they gradually became reorganized and employed in the front lines, indicate the success which has been attained by the Franco government in the formation of a loyal regular army.

While many voluntary units continue to be used as shock troops, the bulk of the Nationalist army is now formed of regulars obtained from drafting all youths fit for military service between the ages of 21 and 27 years. The relative small number of Nationalist soldiers who have passed over to the Government side shows that the propaganda conducted in rebel territory has considerably counteracted the Marxist spirit which formerly permeated a large part of the labor masses. However, the Nationalists continue keeping a close watch over regular army conscripts through non-commissioned and commissioned personnel, in the selection of which great care is exercised. Furthermore, it appears that in the front lines regular organizations are intermingled with voluntary, Moorish and other units of unquestionable loyalty.

In order to determine the relative loyalty of conscript troops, the Nationalists are using great care and discrimination when effecting the mobilization of replacements. In general, they seem to be employing the method of carrying out the recruitment of personnel by regions and provinces instead of mixing recruits from various division areas as was more or less customary in the past. In this manner, besides establishing a sort of competition among units from the various regions, they are in a position to know the degree of Marxist contamination to which enlisted personnel had been previously exposed.

The four Galician provinces and Navarra, Alava, Guipuzcoa, together with the Castile region, have supplied military units which have distinguished themselves in the war. Thus we see that the conquest of San Sebastian was almost exclusively accomplished by Navarra and Alava requetes and regular units which at present are actively participating in the operations against Vizcaya. The bulk of the troops which have defended Oviedo against the combined efforts of Asturias, Santander and Vizcaya militia, were formed of Galicia regular battalions, the presence of which has also been noted in Madrid and Vizcaya fronts. These Galician battalions have everywhere demonstrated absolute loyalty to the Nationalist cause and admirable courage and stamina. During the recent Government offensive on the Madrid front the Canary Island battalions were reported to show great courage in resisting the attack of superior forces. In general, it may be said that all Nationalist regular units have given a good account of themselves and there has not been recorded a single case of collective desertion, or a tendency to mutiny, a fact which shows both the ability and success of the Nationalist high command in the organization of its army.

As regards foreign assistance, it is clear that General Franco could not maintain the war without the support he is receiving from Germany and Italy, which supply most of the materiel used by the Nationalists. It is common knowledge that the rebel aviation is almost entirely German and Italian, both with regard to personnel and materiel, and that the assistance rendered by these countries in furnishing numerous artillery and other military experts has been in great measure responsible for whatever successes may have been attained. However, it must be remembered that the participation of foreign units in the Spanish war is common to both sides. The Republican aviation and tank service are practically entirely Russian, as previously reported. The "Antifascist International Brigades" have saved the situation for the Republican Government in many cases, particularly on the Madrid front, however, up to the present, the participation of foreign units as such on the Nationalist side has not produced any outstanding result. It should not be forgotten that the first important defeat suffered by the rebel cause was due precisely to the poor combat efficiency of the Italian troops on the Guadalajara front.

In conclusion, the estimate is submitted that the efficiency of the Nationalist forces based upon the factors of training, discipline, leadership and unity of command is superior to that of the Republican army.

Valencia   No. 6558
June 1, 1937
Subject: The Military Situation

As a result of conversations with all manner of persons during the past few weeks, including some who have just returned from the rebel lines and the government positions at Bilbao, supplemented by personal visits to the Madrid and Jarama fronts, the following estimate may be of interest at this time.

The failure of the loudly heralded major offensives of the government on the Madrid front, facing the Casa de Campo and the University City, the checking of the drive from the Pozoblanco region by the rebels, where the Valencia foreign press were transported to write of the expected victory, the disaster in the attempt to cut the Zaragoza highway to Teruel, the fiasco of the drive on Toledo and that on the Jarama front to free the Valencia road from rebel interdiction fire, the failure of the Catalan troops to stage an offensive against Huesca or Zaragoza to relieve the Nationalist pressure on Bilbao, and the continued retreat of the loyal forces in the Basque region, in addition to other causes mentioned below have shaken the government's faith in itself and given ample proof to the military student that the loyal force lacks the training, discipline and leadership sufficient for major offensive operations.

There is a rumbling in Catalonia, where the proverbial ear [is] not held to the ground to hear sufficient well founded charges against the Central Government, to warrant the fixed opinion not only that the Catalans may not be counted upon out of their own region but that no offensive operations may be expected by them as long as the Nationalists continue their defensive attitude on the Aragon front.

A visit to the Madrid fronts yesterday on the north side of University City, into the Casa de Campo and to the Franceses Bridge sector, where I have stood in most of the front line trenches, is convincing that the war spirit of the loyal troops is on the wane, that they have no unity of command and that their failures in successful offensive attainment has destroyed their initiative. Further, my impression is deep that the long stay in the trenches has given the militia a "trench psychology" which has anchored them to their rabbit holes of safety and destroyed all vestige of the spirit of the offensive. My observations, upon which are founded the expressed views above, are further fortified by the conversations I have had with both officers and men in which the "fed up" spirit for fighting, lack of enthusiasm in their mission and weakness of faith in their cause are definitely apparent.

Paris   No. 23, 508-W
June 22, 1937
Subject: Major Operations. Basque Front

The following copy of a report prepared by the Naval Attaché's office is forwarded as of interest:

I visited St. Jean-de-Luz on 16 and 17 June, for the purpose of obtaining first-hand information of the fighting on the Basque front. My best source of information was the British Consul from Santander, Mr. Bates, who left Santander the evening of June Tuesday, 15 June.

Santander

The food situation at Santander is acute. Now that Bilbao harbor is closed, the Spanish Nationalist Navy has four warships and innumerable trawlers blockading the port. Between 14 June and 15 June, 10,000 refugees from Bilbao arrived in Santander, making the food situation desperate. At the request of the Civil Governor of Santander, the British Consul has asked his Government to evacuate refugees from Santander under British Navy escort.

General Situation

The port of Bilbao is closed, the Nationalist artillery having the roadstead under fire. Two Spanish Government cargo vessels attempted to enter Bilbao on 16 June; both were sunk. Bilbao is cut off on three sides, only the west side being still open. The main Bilbao-Santander road has been heavily bombed and is closed to motor traffic. The French Consul evacuated Bilbao on Tuesday, 15 June. He was forced to use side roads, and required 3 hours to reach Castro Urdiales (36 kilometers), where a French destroyer picked him up.

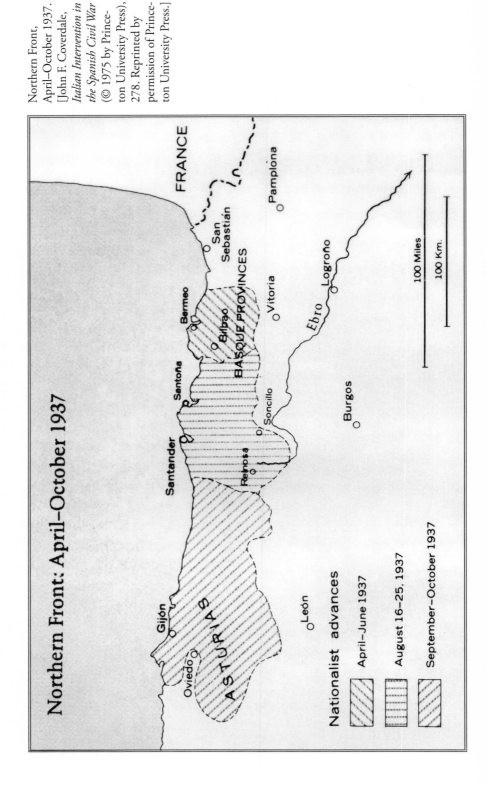

Northern Front, April–October 1937. [John F. Coverdale, *Italian Intervention in the Spanish Civil War* (© 1975 by Princeton University Press), 278. Reprinted by permission of Princeton University Press.]

Northern Front: April–October 1937

FRANCE

Pamplona

San Sebastián

Bermeo
Bilbao
BASQUE PROVINCES
Vitoria
Logroño
Ebro

Santoña
Santander
Soncillo
Burgos
Renosa

Gijón
Oviedo
ASTURIAS

León

100 Miles
100 Km.

Nationalist advances

April–June 1937

August 16–25, 1937

September–October 1937

Mr. Bates estimated that, after the fall of Bilbao, Santander would hold out for not over 2 weeks, and after Santander falls the rest of [the] Government [of] North Spain will give up. According to Mr. Bates, the brunt of the fighting on the Government side has been borne by the Asturias and Santander soldiers, the Basques themselves being half-hearted and surrendering whenever possible. Two thousand Basques at Galdacano surrendered to the Nationalists and asked for permission to fight for them. General Franco has promised to pardon all Basques except the political leaders.

Aviation

The Nationalists have complete control of the air. The Government planes on the Northern Front at the beginning of May have all been destroyed. The airport west of Bilbao has been ruined by bombs. The Valencia Government has managed to get 20 pursuit planes to the Northern Front. The present status of these planes is as follows:

At Santander (Bates counted them)	6
At Biarritz airport (I saw them)	4
Shot down over Santander (Bates)	4
Destroyed on the field at Santander (Bates)	5
Shot down near Bilbao	1

The planes in the French Air Ministry hanger at Bayonne-Biarritz-Parme airport are Russian Mosca (I-15) biplane fighters. They were chased into France by Nationalist aviation, and landed at Biarritz, one of them cracking up. The planes are interned; the Spanish pilots have been sent back to Spain.

Mr. Bates saw the last air battle over Santander, a week ago. Three Nationalist tri-motor bombers, with a small fighter escort came over. They were attacked by eight Government fighters, four planes landed on Santander airport, two of them cracking up. The airport was the target for Nationalist bombs, and five Government fighters were demolished.

Sinking of *España*

Mr. Bates investigated the *España* sinking thoroughly. The findings of his investigation were as follows:

a)   Two Breguet-19 planes from Santander attempted to bomb *España*: as she was sinking after having struck a mine. No bombs fell on or near *España*.

b)   Bates was talking to the Civil Governor of Santander when Madrid
     called him by radio and asked for details of *España*'s sinking. The Civil
     Governor replied, without hesitation, that *España* had been sunk by bombs
     dropped by Government airplanes!

                                                                     Fuller

---

Valencia   No. 6569
June 14, 1937
Subject: Distribution of Troops. Air Situation at Bilbao

The Assistant Military Attaché for Air of the British Embassy has just returned to Valencia from a visit to Bilbao and Santander. Captain Pearson most
cooperatively gave me the following interesting points of his trip.

Due to the influence of Russian supervision during the past several months
in the Air Ministry at Valencia, both Captain Pearson and I have been forced
to adopt the policy of waiting for the right moment before officially requesting
certain types of information. Captain Pearson was led to believe that by personally visiting the North he would have ready access to installations and airdromes.
However, upon his arrival at Bilbao he found that the Air Headquarters was extremely reticent about giving out any information and side-tracked him on every
move to visit the airdromes. It was only by going directly to the President of the
Basques that Captain Pearson was finally able, through the War Department, to
visit one of the fields and in having some of his questions answered. The President
was most helpful.

Prior to May 25th the air defenses of Bilbao and Santander were totally
inadequate. The destruction of planes both in the air and on the ground has been
heavy and as of May 27th Captain Pearson was told that the fighting strength in
the North was aircraft: 17 bombers, Russian bimotors; 25 pursuit, mostly biplanes
but a few monoplanes [for a] total 42. Ground troops: 50,000 men at the Bilbao
front; 35,000 men in reserve [for a] total 85,000. On May 24th this office cabled
a Military Report stating that, "Reliable information indicates important Government aircraft transfer movement from Guadalajara Sector to Santander. Reported
fifteen Koolhoven F.K.-55 pursuit en route Bilbao."

Since then it has been reported that about 80 planes have been sent in all
to the North Front. The exact proportion of types is not known, but contacts
have stated that the larger percentage is of the Russian biplane pursuit type, the

I-15. The 15 Koolhoven F.K.-55 pursuit planes reported to have been sent from Holland, route unknown, have caused considerable interest in air circles at Valencia. The performance of these planes will be closely followed. I have also been informed that five American Vultee attack bombers, of a total of sixteen that were landed in France, have already been flown to Santander. So it is apparent that every effort is being made to bring into play the striking power of the Air Force.

Captain Pearson stated that the Basque Government was extremely put out due to the fact that not so long ago the Valencia Government sent a man to Bilbao to become Minister of War. The story goes that the Basques promptly shipped this man back to Valencia and continued with their own personnel, but with the result that little or no future help was received from this Government. This took place during the regime of Señor Largo Caballero. As early as May 1st the Valencia Government had planned to send aircraft from the Madrid and Guadalajara Sectors directly to Bilbao but the squadrons remained at their stations. Then with the advent of Señor Prieto as Minister of National Defense the squadrons were immediately dispatched, but by a different route. A glance at the map will show that the triangle formed by the points Guadalajara Sector, Lerida and Bilbao is practically a triangle with the base running from Guadalajara to Lerida. For some overcautious reason, which was much against the desires of the pilots, the squadrons were ordered to fly first to Lerida, take on gas and then procceed to Bilbao. The first attempt was most humiliating for the Government Air Force. Twelve biplane pursuit and five single motor attack were forced off the Lerida-Bilbao course by bad weather and landed at Pau, France. I have been told that a few others landed at Bayonne, France. After considerable discussion the planes were permitted to return to Spain after several had been deprived of their machine guns. I was told by a contact at the Air Ministry that the French certainly profited by the above flight for some of the guns that remained in France were of the new Russian types. The Air Ministry then ordered that the squadrons should fly directly from Guadalajara to Bilbao. This was done over a period of four or five days.

Airdromes

One of the main difficulties with which the Government has had to contend is the lack of landing fields in the area between Bilbao and Santander. The Nationalists, on the other hand, have several well situated fields for air operations. During the past several weeks the Government has been constructing temporary fields, but the rugged nature of the terrain has made it necessary to locate those fields at extremely vulnerable points. At the present time there are airdromes at the following places at Bilbao: Lujua, Lejona, Abanto, Llodio; between Bilbao and Santander: Playa de la Arena, Laredo; Santander: Astillero, Santa Cruz, Torrelavega. Most of these landing areas are of the emergency class, but all are large enough to be used by all types of Government planes.

The Basque Government is manufacturing all types of bombs that are being used. The factory that formerly operated at Guernica has been moved to Bilbao and at present there is another one at Galdacano. Near Santander is another factory making both bombs and ammunition.

Nationalist Equipment

The types of planes that have been employed in the North Front are the Junker-52, Junker-86, Heinkel-111 and Heinkel-51. Captain Pearson was told that no Italian Fiat pursuit planes have made an appearance. It is further reported that all of the Nationalist planes brought down have been manned by German personnel. The bombs used have been of both German and Italian manufacture. The German bombs range in weight from 50 to 150 kilos and have electrical fuses with slight delay action. All these bombs are of the same general construction, only differing in size, weight and charge. The Italian bombs are reported to be of the instantaneous type.

Nationalist and Government Air Activity

From the very beginning of the Bilbao offensive it has been evident that the Nationalists have had air supremacy. This advantage has enabled the ground troops to operate with little or no air opposition and with considerable air support. On the other hand, the morale of the Government troops has been seriously affected by the lack of Government air cooperation. However, with the reception of aircraft equipment from the Guadalajara Sector, the Government situation immediately showed improvement but of extremely short duration. The reason for the failure of the Government Air Force to make a better showing in the North has been a puzzle to this office and the only logical explanation is one that was given [to] me by a member of the Air Force. As has been reported previously, the Spanish pilots who have received training in France and Russia are being returned to Spain and have gradually taken over the work of many foreign pilots. Most of the Russians, with the exception of the pursuit monoplane pilots, have returned to Russia and there are very few pilots of other nationalities left. It is said that the training the Spanish boys received in Russia was excellent, but that the instruction received at the French schools was totally inadequate. When these Spanish pilots first returned to Spain they were placed in squadrons led and commanded by foreign pilots, but as time went on the leaderships were gradually turned over to the Spanish personnel. True to nature, "two Spaniards, one civil war", the Spanish personnel with many petty jealousies quickly and adversely affected the efficiency of these tactical units. The original idea of the Spanish Government to have an Air Force made up of Spanish personnel was based upon the probability that all foreigners would be removed from Spain. If that should develop the Government has made a fine step forward, but in my opinion the Air Ministry has made a big mistake during the past two or three months in encouraging foreign pilots to leave the country. Of course, such a statement is easy to make now but I have been told that the Government is quite anxious to have certain foreign personnel who have already left Spain return to their flying jobs.

The above may not be the only reason for the poor showing made by the Government Forces in the North, but personnel differences certainly would be a tremendous factor. Once again it is possible to learn a lesson or two from past operations:

No matter how fine aircraft equipment may be, it is necessary to have personnel adequately trained and possessing a high state of morale and loyalty.

An Air Force is an invaluable striking weapon on both the defense and offense and when cooperating with troops that have the heart, courage and leadership to advance its value is tenfold.

Every operation since the Guadalajara affair of March has shown the value of low bombing and ground attack work by both specially equipped attack planes and pursuit types.

The most formidable Air Force in the world is dependent upon its ground installations, whether of a permanent, temporary or emergency nature, for its efficient employment.

At this writing the situation at Bilbao is becoming extremely serious for the Government. It is impossible to send ground troops to reinforce the defenses and the only means by which aid can be sent is through the air. The question is whether or not the Government will rush additional aircraft to the North in hopes of saving the day, knowing all the while that such a move might seriously deplete its Air Force through destruction on the ground. The lack of past support is difficult to understand.

Griffiss and Fuqua

Valencia   No. 6583
June 25, 1937
Subject: Drastic Measures to Enforce Discipline in the Army

As is well known, one of the causes responsible for the military defeats suffered by the Government is the lack of a high standard of discipline in the Republican Army. Notwithstanding the fact that the situation of almost total lack of discipline noted in the first militia units, has been gradually improved, and that the army is now organized along military lines, it is evident that the results attained are far from satisfactory.

The Government is now resorting to drastic edicts and measures which reveal the admission of a low state of morale and lack of confidence in the ultimate victory of the extremist masses unless organized and controlled. Furthermore, the publication of these edicts indicates in great measure the panic which has seized the Government after the recent Nationalist victory in the Bilbao region and the failure of the Aragon and other offensives launched to relieve the rebel pressure in the North and to divert attention from the defeats being administered to the loyal army by the Franco "rebels". *Diario Oficial* No. 148 of June 21, 1937 published several decrees in the preambles of which the necessity for enforcing discipline at all costs is strongly emphasized.

One of these decrees provides the following penalties for desertion and other military crimes:

Desertion in the face of the enemy is defined to include those recruits who fail to report for service within three days of the designated date for their incorporation to the ranks. Those found guilty of this crime will render their service in disciplinary units, and after the termination of the war will be required to work from 6 to 20 years in concentration labor camps.

Absence without leave from the ranks will be considered as desertion and will be punished with penalties which include death or service in disciplinary units and concentration camps up to a period of 12 years.

Anyone abandoning without order his military post in a war zone will incur the death penalty or will be sentenced to serve up to a period of 20 years in concentration camps after completion of his service in disciplinary units. The same penalties will be imposed on those who mutilate themselves to evade military service, by those who disobey orders in the face of the enemy or refuse to join designated posts or fail to perform the missions entrusted to them.

Any doctor who issues a false sick or disability certificate with a view to exempt anyone from military service will be sentenced to from 2 to 6 years of imprisonment and a fine ranging from 2,000 to 10,000 pesetas.

Any member of the army who in the face of the enemy or being ready to engage in an action, is the first to turn his back to run, will incur the death penalty and may be killed on the spot as an "exemplary punishment".

Anyone who, while in the performance of duty, insults or attacks a superior may be sentenced to death or to serve 12 years in concentration camps.

Another decree provides that those charged with the commission of military crimes, punishable with the death penalty or imprisonment for 30 years, or other offenses affecting discipline and morale which require immediate action, will be tried by a summary court martial.

Furthermore, another decree provides that all officers must serve in the front line for at least three months. Those officers who have not as yet fulfilled this minimum period of service at the front, are required to apply for such assignment within 15 days from the date of this decree. Officers failing to comply with this order, in addition to whatever military responsibility they may incur, will lose their grade and will be compelled to refund all pay received since their appointment as officers.

The undersigned has just returned from a visit to some of the rest area camps in the Alicante and Denia sections and was surprised to find these places frequented in large numbers by members of the International Brigades, and who seemingly had lost interest in the front. Several Americans and Britishers were questioned and all showed satisfaction in being away from military control and evidenced no enthusiasm about returning to their organizations. Many had been away as long as three weeks with no dates fixed for their returning to their commands. From what I saw and learned, I feel sure that these happy communities will soon be cleared of these large groups of "deadbeaters" from the International columns. It was evident that the Spanish soldier resents these foreigners living here in ease and luxury instead of at the front for which duty they had volunteered for service in Spain.

Valencia   No. 6608
July 14, 1937
Subject: Naval Engagement near Valencia—July 12, 1937

The undersigned was fortunate in having spent the night of July 11-12 at his beach house near Perello, which enabled him to have a bird's eye view of the Naval Engagement that took place on the morning of the twelfth.

At 6:30 AM firing was heard and upon going to the roof of the house I saw one cruiser matched against three destroyers. Information received later stated that the cruiser was either the *Canarias* or the *Baleares*—they are identical and I personally checked their pictures—but no names were given to the loyal destroyers. The tactics of the cruiser were interesting in that the ship steamed back and forth parallel to the coast at a distance of about eight or ten thousand yards. The destroyers were in the vicinity of Cullera Point and used hit and run tactics.

Before continuing with the engagement it is necessary to describe the present local situation that exists between Perello and Las Palmeras, both small beach pueblos twenty-five kilometers south of Valencia. During the time of the Madrid evacuations several hundred children were taken to Perello and Las Palmeras and at this time both places are crowded. Then with the Valencia bombardments of May the majority of the Diplomatic Corps made arrangements for living quarters outside of Valencia proper. The British Embassy and some Legations have moved with all personnel to the vicinity of Las Palmeras. The United States Embassy Chargé d'Affaires has taken a large villa at Torrente, inland and about ten kilometers from Valencia. I have a personal beach house near the British Embassy and between Perello and Las Palmeras. The members of the International Telephone and Telegraph Company are occupying a villa a few hundred yards from the beach and directly behind the British Embassy. It is therefore evident that besides the several hundred refugees living in this vicinity there are also quite a number of foreigners.

Continuing now with the morning's action it was apparent that the rebel cruiser was dominating the situation firing many more shells than the destroyers. I could not understand why the destroyers insisted in remaining in the vicinity of Cullera Point, but presently the reason was evident for a merchant ship slowly rounded the Point and headed toward Valencia. The destroyers gave forth a tremendous amount of smoke either in an effort to shield the merchant ship or in the process of acquiring more speed. No matter what the reason the efforts were fairly good. The merchant ship was neglected for a few minutes while the *Canarias* concentrated on the destroyers and the latter maneuvered for favorable positions. However, the *Canarias* never left her beaten path knowing full well that the destroyers would not follow the merchant ship along the coast for such an action would have placed the destroyers at a terrific disadvantage. Nevertheless, the destroyers several times made sorties against the *Canarias* but their four or five inch guns were no match for the eight inch ones of the rebel cruiser. The destroyers did not advance far north of Cullera Point while the merchant ship was slowly but surely drawing away from them in her advance up the coast. From the time that the merchant ship had first been sighted it had been gradually getting closer to shore so that when three-quarters of the distance from the Point to Las Palmeras it was about 800 yards offshore.

Then the inevitable happened. The *Canarias* suddenly transferred its fire against the merchant ship, four shots falling short and two on shore extremely close to the Swedish Legation. The destroyers at once made every effort to draw the rebel fire on them and for the next few minutes the *Canarias* let the merchant ship alone. Naturally this apparently doomed ship must have thought that with the previous overs and shorts the next salvo would finish her career and consequently headed a bit more toward shore. When approximately opposite the British Embassy she was not more than six hundred yards offshore. The general situation at this moment was such that the *Canarias*, the merchant ship, the British Embassy and the ITT House were in one straight line. I suddenly saw the flash from the forward two top turret guns of the *Canarias* and immediately focused my glasses on the merchant ship. The first shell struck the water about one hundred yards off the starboard beam. The second struck immediately in front of the ship and so close to it that before the spray had completely disappeared the ship had passed through it. The ship had not been hit, but my thoughts were transferred from the fate of the vessel to that of my neighbors. More shots might mean some more overs and firing of that type would undoubtedly have caused some uneasy moments.

However, either through good luck, thoughtfulness on the part of the *Canarias* or because the merchant ship had turned a little more toward shore, which might have given the impression that she had been struck and was being beached, no more shells were fired in its direction. When the vessel passed in front of my house I noticed that it was a tanker riding extremely high and apparently empty and was not more than four hundred yards offshore. I was greatly surprised when I saw flying from the mast at the stern the flag of France. The *Canarias* and the destroyers disappeared to the southeast and only a few more shots were heard.

Comments

It was later learned that the merchant vessel was a Spanish tanker called the *Campilo*. It evidently had been to Denia or Cullera and had deposited its load. For the past several days there have been Government destroyers in these waters but I do not think that these warships were specifically escorting the *Campilo*. It is more probable that the destroyers came to the aid of the *Campilo* after the *Canarias* had been reported offshore. As for the presence of the *Canarias* this is an excellent example of Nationalist espionage. The Madrid offensive is in full swing and all the Valencia air defense has been withdrawn. The *Canarias* knew it and took full advantage of the opportunity. Many merchant ships arrive off Valencia about sunrise. The *Campilo* was no exception.

Naval Activity

I was greatly impressed by the fire superiority of the *Canarias* and the rapidity in which it fired in salvos of twos. So much has been said about and against the Government Navy that I fully expected the destroyers to immediately turn and run. To the contrary these vessels stayed right in the fight and on several occasions made valiant efforts to place some effective shots. Roughly estimating I judge that some one hundred and fifty shells were fired, the *Canarias* alone firing about eighty. Many of the rebel shots fell close to the destroyers, but the effects of the Government fire was not so easily determined. I saw no hits and none have been reported. The accuracy of fire was not impressive. The engagement lasted two hours and fifteen minutes. It has further been reported that three additional destroyers were along the coast between Cullera and Denia.

Aircraft

If the *Canarias* was actually in waiting for the *Campilo* it was for some other reason than for the cargo. If there was something aboard this ship of extreme importance then it is possible that the Government destroyers were escorting her. This action took place between 6:30 AM and 8:45 AM on the twelfth. The *Campilo* made the Valencia port and docked alongside of a British merchant ship. At 5:20 AM the following morning the Nationalist aircraft attempted to finish the uncompleted mission of the previous morning. Again they were unsuccessful.

Griffiss

Valencia   No. 6613
July 17, 1937
Subject: The Military Situation

Jarama Sector

I visited this sector on July 11th solely to determine the accuracy of the recent government reports of "repelling renewed rebel attacks" to cut the Valencia-Madrid highway. These propaganda announcements were broadcasted through foreign press agencies here and appeared in headline news—at least in France—to the extent that the American Ambassador in Saint-Jean-de-Luz wrote me a personal letter, under date of June 30th, as follows: "I see that the recent rebel attempt to cut the Valencia road has been a complete failure and that they have suffered heavy losses".[5]

In my visit to this front, I reached the south end of the bridge over the Jarama River (km. 20 from Madrid), a position which I had visited many times before. I had [an] opportunity to talk with the bridge guard on the spot and learned definitely what I had already been told by General Staff officers—that there had been no Rebel offensive in this sector. The routine Rebel artillery firing, which, for some reason, is heavier on some days than on others had been taken advantage of for government "counter battery firing", the combination of which was proclaimed and broadcasted in the foreign news as "a heavy rebel attack repelled by loyal forces". The hour of my visit was quiet although I was informed that Rebel artillery had been active in the early part of the day in what might be termed "interdiction fire". It will be noted that the Chinchon Road joins the main Valencia Road at this bridge head. This point is also near the narrow gauge railroad which has been out of commission for some time but now is being feverishly restored to service as a supply route between Torrejon de Ardoz (km. 15 Madrid-Alcala de Henares Road) and the Arganda sector of the Jarama front. Further, it may be stated that where this narrow gauge railroad crosses the unimproved road 5 kilometers west of Arganda is located the C.P. for this front. The whole atmosphere of this front registered not only tranquility but there existed neither evidence of recent nor immediate activity in this sector.

Guadalajara Sector

On July 8th, I explored the Guadalajara front bordering the two main road systems traversing this sector. On the Guadalajara-Zaragoza Road, I found complete quiet. Conversations with men on this front proved conclusively that the constant government reports of attacks and counterattacks in this region were purely products of the imagination of the propagandists.

The Usera Drive

Usera is a south suburb of Madrid lying just across the Manzanares between the Aranjuez Road and the Toledo Road. The front here, locally designated with the name of this suburb, covers about 2 kilometers and includes the small group of houses and trash dump known as El Basurero. This offensive was initiated on July 5th, with much publicity, with a view of breaking the Rebel lines east of

Carabanchel Alto, having as its ultimate objective the Campamento, km. 7 Extremadura Road. There were some 10,000 men and 35 tanks assembled for this offensive which continued for three days with a net result of carrying the line to km. 6 on the Toledo Road; however, the immediate front south of Usera was practically unchanged. I visited this front in the afternoon of July 9th and these comments are based upon personal observations and conversations with a major and a captain in whose front line P.S. [perimeter station] I was entertained with a glass of ice cold beer, some salty fish and much conversation. In the course of our talks they spoke of this "great drive" pointing out the ground that had been gained. Incidentally, they informed me that their present P.C. [platoon commander] had been in this exact place since last November. The only battle scar signs I observed was a "wounded" government tank hanging over the enemy's trench line just to our front perhaps a hundred yards distant. Without obtaining too much information directly concerned with the "battle", I did receive a definite impression that it was a determined and prepared effort to break through the enemy's line, that it was coordinated with the big drive to the northwest of Madrid, that it was a complete failure and that the government troops suffered great losses.

The Casa de Campo Front

I covered this sector in the afternoon of July 10th. Upon my arrival within the "campo", I went at once to the P.C. of the Lago's front and found the same officer (Major Sorinborf—phonetic spelling—a Georgian Russian) there in command [who] I had visited on two previous occasions.

The major seemed very pleased to see me and with some "boasting" remarked "that we would get into the car as the front was some distance". In fact for the past six months the line had passed on the east bank of the lake, with the slight gains shown in my last situation report. Some time about June 16th, in a night attack, the flanks of the Rebel front west of the lake were turned and the entire position fell into the hands of the government troops. The gain in depth was probably about 600 meters and in width about 800. The geographical center of this captured position is a hill on which there was an edifice, now in ruins, known as the Casa Iglesia. The "Major", who was inclined to boast a bit, spoke in detail [about] how his plan had completely taken the "fascist idiots" by surprise, that they had neglected to cover their flanks entirely, that he had taken a few prisoners and killed many of the enemy and had captured some materiel including several weapons. He showed us a captured machine gun—an Italian Breda of normal type—and a quantity of small arms ammunition definitely of Italian origin.

There were noted several pieces of equipment, viz: Hotchkiss machine gun, gas mask, hand grenades with 12" wooden handles through the center of which passed the fuse carrying a five second powder train. Also, there was observed a projector and grenade with vanes adapted for long range—the type of which was one of the many forms used in trench warfare. There was also a mortar similar to if not the Valero design which has been previously reported upon in detail.

This captured position was of particular interest to the undersigned as it was the first opportunity that he had had to inspect field fortifications constructed by the Rebels. As he walked through some 600 yards of trenches, he noted the generally poor class of work in this engineering field performed by the Rebels. The fire and communicating trenches, gun positions, loopholes, insets in the trench walls for storing material, comfort stations and rest niches had either been reconstructed or newly built. This position, which had been occupied by the Rebels for some six or seven months was poorly organized from a military point of view as to safety and comfort. Communication in depth and laterally was poor and the sanitation was horrible. If this entrenched position represents the Rebel type of fortifications on the outer circle of Madrid, they are not comparable to the trench constructional standards seen on the inner circle.

Vizcaya and Santander Fronts

Contrary to the opinions expressed in the government press that the death of General Mola, like that of General [Tomas de] Zumalacarregui while besieging Bilbao during the Carlist war, would make the turning point towards the failure of the siege, the Nationalist army, in a formidable onslaught which began on June 12th, pierced at several places the so-called "iron belt", and in one week of brilliant operations took possession of Bilbao and all towns on the west bank of the Nervion estuary.

For several days after the Nationalist offensive began, government official communiqués gave little details of the course of the operations in Bilbao, stating only that its forces were checking the advance of the enemy in "a most heroic way". However, on June 22nd the government admitted the evacuation of the city and announced that the line had been withdrawn west of the Cadagua River, retaining control of the Bilbao industrial and mining center. However, no serious attempt at Resistance was made on this line and the victorious Nationalist advance soon dominated these important centers.

According to available information, on June 12th, after subjecting the Basque defenses to a severe artillery fire and aviation bombing by some 80 planes, the Nationalists broke the "iron belt" at several places northeast of Bilbao and, in spite of the desperate resistance offered by the enemy, within two days had advanced to within a short distance of the suburbs located on the western bank of the Nervion estuary. It has been reported that the air raids made by the Nationalists in this zone, to pave the way for their advancing ground forces, were "terrific" and that the many tons of bombs dropped practically destroyed several villages and set afire large stretches of pine forests, thus adding to the terror of the population and retreating government forces. The Nationalist aviation was in complete command of the air.

The drive then was extended to the Orduna sector where a large force, said to consist of 9 brigades, after breaking the front, swept up the Nervion valley threatening to cut off the retreat of the Basque Nationalist forces which, entrenched on the heights close to Bilbao, were endeavoring to interpose a last barrier to the invader.

By June 16th all the government defenses protecting Bilbao, including Galdacano, the strongest point of the "iron belt" had been taken. The column advancing from the south crossed the Nervion making rapid progress towards Bilbao from the southwest while the coastal column crossed the estuary at Las Arenas taking Portugalete. The situation of the troops defending Bilbao became so critical that, had the order of withdrawal been delayed, in all probability a large part of the government forces would have been completely surrounded.

The Nationalists have reported that, at first, the retreat of the government forces was orderly but that such soon converted into a rout in which they abandoned considerable war materiel and lost about 6,000 prisoners. However, it appears that the main part of the government forces were able to withdraw taking with them most of their artillery. After the fall of Bilbao, the Nationalist advance encountered little resistance, the most important engagements occurring in the vicinity of Valmaseda, where an attempt by the government forces to stop the enemy proved unsuccessful. Up to the present writing the line of Rebel advance follows roughly the Santander border. The Nationalists have occupied Sierra Castro Aler which dominates a large zone in the Santander province and appear to have crossed the border on the littoral towards Castro Urdiales, an important town in the Santander province. However, the operations against Santander seem to have been stopped for the present owing to the military demands of the situation on the Madrid front.

Contrary to what was expected, the Basque separatists succeeded in preventing the destruction of Bilbao by the extremist elements, and the city may be said to have fallen practically intact into Nationalist hands. The industrial zones on the banks of the Nervion estuary appear to have suffered only comparatively minor damage and the Nationalists have announced that in a few weeks work will be resumed in most factories and workshops, particularly those connected with the manufacture of war products.

The statement contained in the manifesto issued by the government immediately upon the fall of Bilbao to the effect that "the whole population of Bilbao had preferred to abandon their properties rather than live under fascist rule", has not been confirmed by reports from other sources which indicate that a large part of the inhabitants of Bilbao remained in the city. It also appears from Nationalist broadcasts and foreign press dispatches that the light, water and other public utilities were reestablished in a few days, that new bridges soon replaced those blown up by the retreating government forces in the Bilbao zone and that normal activities are being gradually resumed in the city.

According to a Salamanca report, during the 90 day offensive on the Basque front, Franco's troops had "569 dead and 1,897 wounded". It was further reported that these comparatively light losses were due to the fact that the infantry attacks were always prepared by heavy and effective artillery firing and air bombing. In the attack against the "iron belt" not less than 440 guns and 169 airplanes were engaged in preparatory bombardment of the government positions. The Nationalists, according to the Salamanca report, lost only 3 planes during this offensive, 6 airmen being killed and 7 injured. The Nationalists further claim that during the Vizcaya offensive some 15,000 militia were taken prisoners or passed over to their side.

Comments

The loss of Bilbao with its industrial and mining centers is without doubt the heaviest blow suffered by the government since the war began and one which may lead to its defeat should the Nationalists be able to follow their victory by crushing the resistance of the loyalist forces in the Asturias and Santander zones. Judging from recent statements of General Queipo de Llano during his radio talks, the Nationalists contemplated "conquering the enemy zone in the North" before launching the final offensive against the Eastern regions. However, the Madrid government offensive has forced the Rebel generals to change their plans and to fight perhaps the "Gettysburg" of this war on the fields west of Madrid.

As this report closes, the government offensive, halted for the past few days, is pushing with all its strength towards Villafranca del Castillo with the Coruna Road beyond as the main objective and towards Boadilla del Monte for the Casa de Campo and University City goals.

In closing this narrative report it can be stated positively that the major offensive plan now in execution west of Madrid represents the best the government can produce at this time, it is the result of a long General Staff study backed by Cabinet discussions and final approval, and has been passed to the "Hero of Madrid", General Miaja, for execution. The importance of this offensive must be deeply appreciated by the Rebels for news reached me today—through Mr. [Walter] Thurston of the Embassy—that Mr. [Jose] Giral, Minister of Foreign Affairs, had just informed him that General Franco is in Navalcarnero. From my impression gained in official, military and diplomatic circles here, it is convincing that the government feels that this offensive is a play in the military game in which the stake is the Republic itself—as expressed by a friend in high government office: "The eyes of the world are on us, it means for us victory or defeat".

Paris   No. 23, 625-W
August 3, 1937
Subject: Military Operations—General. Report on an Interview with a
Deserter from the International column July 13, 1937

Introduction
On June the 11th, No. 3125454 Private G . . S . . who has served 13 years in the British Army with the Royal Scots Fusiliers and the Lincolnshire Regiment, reported at the British Embassy Valencia together with three other deserters from the English Battalion of the International Column. They had just come down from Madrid and had taken part in the first days of the big attack which is being launched by the Government forces in the sector between El Escorial and Las Rosas. Owing to his experience and his good record in the British Army he proved to be a useful informant on the progress of this attack and on the situation in general. Private G.S. came to Spain in December and had risen to the rank of Lieutenant; thanks to unofficial assistance he has now been able to return to England.

The International Column
The International Column is now incorporated in the Spanish Army although the various battalions of which it is composed retain many privileges not enjoyed by Spanish battalions. Thus, although these battalions figure in the official publications and documents in the same manner as the Spanish battalions and the Government is able to claim that the International Column no longer exists in practice

it forms the nucleus of the ground forces. The privileges given to its members are better food, extra luxuries, the amalgamation into units of men of the same nationality and the somewhat doubtful privilege of always being thrown in where the fray is thickest.

Personnel

Each battalion is kept up to a strength of 700 men and one company is usually manned by Spaniards. Most of the officers are Russians and in the battalions which have commanding officers of other nationality the second in command is invariably a Russian. The battalions are always kept up to full strength in spite of the tremendous casualties suffered, and it appears that there is never a shortage of volunteers. When the Government attack was launched on the 6th of July there were thirty-five international battalions which included one British battalion with a total of 650 Englishmen, two American battalions with a total of 1400 Americans, one Canadian battalion with a total of 350 Canadians. Also five Russian battalions. The remaining battalions were built up of men from every nation in Europe.

After the village of Quijorna had been taken on July 9th only thirty Englishmen were left and of the Americans only fifty.

The senior officer of the battalions which form the column is General Copic, a Czech who was once a politician in Czechoslovakia but whose views proved to be too extreme. The English battalion is commanded by a man called [Fred] Copeman who, it is said, was involved in the Invergordon incident.[6]

Equipment

The armament and munitions used by these battalions are all of Russian manufacture and considered to be very good. The rifle issued is the Russian 1924 type of .303 calibre. The artillery most generally used is 9.2 and 6 inch field batteries. The Russian tanks are thought to be superior to those of the Insurgents. The Russian automatic rifle is not issued to international battalions and is only used, with much reserve, by Spaniards, but Private G. . S. . had an opportunity of operating one and spoke very highly of it. He stated that the mechanism is similar though not identical to the Lewis gun, and that the only stoppage which occurs is a "double feed" which can be easily cleared.

Morale

Private G. . S. . was questioned on the morale of the Spanish troops, and in particular the conscripts. He asserted that he had no knowledge that large numbers and even complete units of Spanish conscripts had deserted to the other side, and stated that in his sector during the offensive only 26 persons had gone over whereas a far larger number of Insurgents had come across to the Government line. It must be remembered, however, that the news given to the soldiers is carefully censored. He mentioned that when the Spanish battalions appeared to be discontented they were put with the international battalions and given the same privileges for a period in order to improve their morale. Desertion is not easy. There are frequent pickets on all roads and when the opposing trenches are close to one another sentries are posted out at night in pairs and at short intervals where they remain facing in opposite directions, one towards his own lines and the other towards the enemy.

Aviation
Private G. . S. . was of the opinion that on the Madrid fronts the Government air force was very superior to that of the Insurgents, so much so that it was able to supplement the artillery and tanks in their respective duties.

The Government Offensive
In the Government offensive which began on July 6th the Insurgents have been driven back to the SW and a Government salient has been formed which runs from Escorial and includes Villanueva de la Canada, Quijorna and Brunete, but not Villanueva del Pardillo nor Majadahonda. The objective seems to be Navalcarnero, thus pushing round behind the very strong Insurgent positions on the SW of Madrid, which proved to be impregnable to attacks by the Government forces in May. Although the offensive has met with initial success it has cost so many men and the positions held by the Insurgents are so strong that it is doubtful whether it can be maintained.

Conclusion
On being asked why he had originally come out here and also why he had deserted, he stated that before enlisting in the British Army he had been a moulder, but after 13 years service he had found himself to be out of touch with his trade and could not find employment. He was attracted out here by the money offered and by the spirit of adventure. As a married man with no children his wife was entitled to 30/-per week to be paid by the Spanish Government through the Communist party in England (The wife of a married man with one child should get 35/- and with more than one child £2-0-0). While out here he had no means of knowing whether this money was being paid and several of his friends had managed to

receive uncensored letters which stated that payments were somewhat irregular. Also no compensation is given to wives and families in the event of a man being killed. These facts combined with the enormous casualty list during the last few months and in particular during the present offensive made him decide to desert and risk being shot.

He attributed the tremendous number of casualties and the successive failures of the Government forces to their senior staff officers, who are chosen for their political views rather than for their military knowledge and ability and consequently put their men at a decided disadvantage.

Fuller

5

Intensification of the War in the North
(July–November 1937)

"Most of the towns which have been taken by one side or the other have been in the main due to the artillery preparation."

Col. Stephen O. Fuqua,
Infantry, 1937[1]

During the second half of 1937, significant portions of Spain came under the control of the Nationalists, most notably large swaths of northern Spain. One of the most discussed events of this period was the Battle of Brunete, which took place in July 1937. Then, as now, it remains an important event for a number of reasons. In the first place, it was the largest military campaign to date in the civil war, lasting for almost three weeks and costing the lives of thousands of people. Brunete was a tiny village about fifteen miles west of Madrid and part of the broader campaign for the conquest of Madrid. It was fought in 100-degree weather and proved to be a violent affair. Military historian Raymond Proctor, like the military observers commenting in this chapter, considered the planning for the battle "brilliant, but its conduct stupid."[2] The Republicans wanted to break the Nationalist assault on Madrid and this was the campaign they hoped would accomplish that objective. The military observers in this chapter explained what happened with clarity and in detail. To put the size of the engagement in perspective, keep in mind that about 23,000 Republican troops died while the Nationalists lost 17,000. The Republicans failed to achieve their fundamental objectives, gaining only minor pieces of new territory, while the Nationalist Army of the Center remained intact. The pressure on Madrid remained, and the Nationalists could return their attention to campaigning in the north, particularly in the Santander region.

The reports from the American military are remarkably similar to those written by historians decades later, demonstrating a clarity of reporting in the 1930s. As demonstrated in dispatches in earlier chapters, the American military took great pains to explain the events and their military significance. The only variance was that the American military presented events in a rather cold, dispassionate manner, minimizing the enormous suffering, losses, and horror of the campaign. For instance, some losing soldiers committed suicide, and Republican officers machine gunned their own men to prevent them from fleeing the battlefields.

This chapter ends with a detailed description of the American volunteers who served in the Republican army at Brunete, where they suffered so many casualties that two American battalions were merged into one after the fighting. Fuqua visited the Americans, and his description adds considerable new information about how they functioned that is not always presented in other histories of their role.

On a broader plane, however, this chapter documents many of the military campaigns of the second half of 1937, a period when the war evolved from ad hoc events into serious, large, sustained military campaigns by both sides. Any illusions anyone had that the war might end soon were shattered by the depth and substance of the war-fighting activities of both sides and of their respective allies.

June 28, 1937
Memorandum for the Chief of Staff

The following quotation from the *United Services Review*, published in England, dated Thursday June 10, 1937, on the subject of "Air Lessons from Spain", is quoted for your information:

"The air lessons of the Spanish Civil War are beginning to stand out more clearly, and among them is the fact that the bomber aircraft is a very difficult proposition to tackle either in the air or from the ground. It is a very important

Stephen O. Fuqua serving as General of the U.S. Army with the rank of major general, circa late 1920s–early 1930s. (*Courtesy of the Fuqua family*)

Stephen O. Fuqua, on his way back to the United States after serving as the U.S. military attaché during the Spanish Civil War. (*Courtesy of the Fuqua family*)

A building in University City, Madrid, in the winter of 1937–38. It was the site of intense fighting during the early months of the war. (*U.S. National Archives, RG 165, Box 1739*)

This was the only crossing on the Manzanares River in Madrid between University City and the rest of Madrid. Note its temporary nature, as all other paths into the area had been destroyed. Winter 1938. (*U.S. National Archives, RG 165, Box 1739*)

Nationalist artillerymen fire a Schneider Creusot 6-inch gun on Bilbao, June 1937. (*U.S. National Archives, RG 165, Box 1739*)

What is remarkable about this photo is that the machine gunner was chained to his gun by Republican military so that he would not retreat while serving at the Teruel front in February 1938. (*U.S. National Archives, RG 165, Box 1739*)

These are Republican prisoners of war captured by Nationalist forces during 1938. Many of them would be given the opportunity to switch sides and join the Nationalists, otherwise they were sent to a prisoner-of-war camp. (*U.S. National Archives, RG 165, Box 1739*)

These are the same Republican prisoners captured in the fighting north of Madrid during the winter of 1938. This photograph must have been taken soon after their capture, as there are no facilities for housing or incarcerating them, let alone transportation to move them out. (*U.S. National Archives, RG 165, Box 1739*)

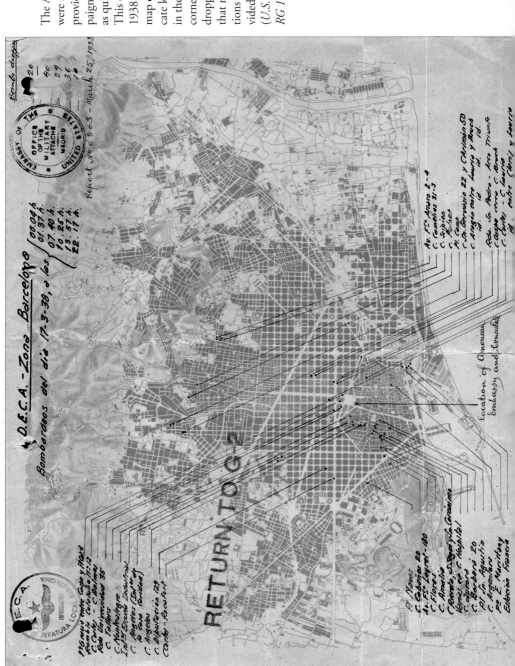

The American observers were asked constantly to provide maps of campaigns, cities, and towns as quickly as possible. This one, dated March 1938, uses a preprinted map of Barcelona to indicate key buildings. Note in the upper right-hand corner the tally of bombs dropped in the city and that most of the annotations are in Spanish, provided by local officials. (*U.S. National Archives, RG 165, Box 1739*)

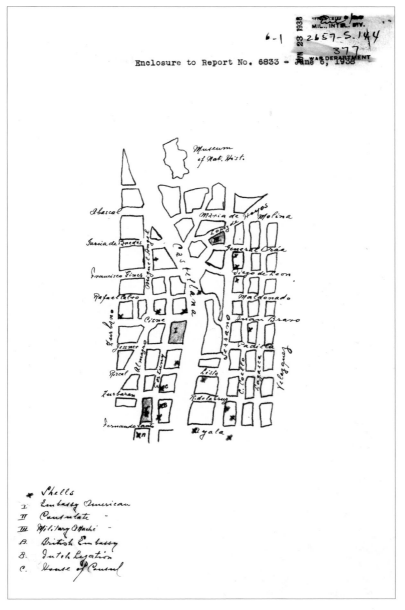

This is a hand-drawn map by the American military observers showing where key buildings were located in Madrid and where bombs had fallen in June 1938. Fuqua complained constantly about the lack of good maps in Spain; he was a stickler for using maps. (*U.S. National Archives, RG 165, Box 1739*)

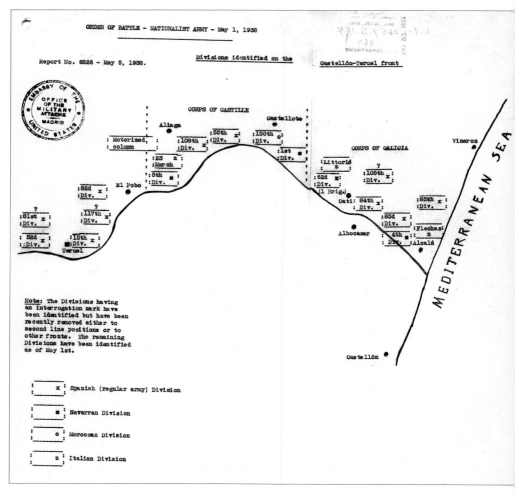

This perhaps is one of the most interesting maps to come out of the Spanish Civil War, because it was typed. One can imagine how long it took for a clerk at the U.S. Embassy to prepare this document. It shows the order of battle for the National Army at the Castellón-Teruel front, May 1, 1938. (*U.S. National Archives, RG 165, Box 1739*)

lesson, indeed, from our own defensive point of view. The basic fact to realize is that the superior speed of the fighter which once gave it dominance in combat with all other types of aircraft is becoming more and more a negligible factor. The modern bomber is not now so very much the slower of the two, and superiority of fire on the fighter's part is its main means to victory.

"But the bomber is also developing its defensive armament, with all-round fire to boot, and the gap between the two is closing in on this count as well. As regards anti-aircraft gunnery the results have been disappointing, even in the case of the German modern guns with trained crews. The fact seems to be that bombing planes in formation, bent on their mission, will be hard to deter from its accomplishment."

O. Westover
Major General, Air Corps, Chief of the Air Corps

July 6, 1937
Memorandum for the Chief of Staff
Subject: Evaluation of Attached Extract Submitted by the Chief
of the Air Corps

The extract quoted is included in the editorial comment of the *United Service Review*. This periodical is a British military weekly devoted to the interests of the Army, Navy and Air Force and considered to be impartial. The author of the extract and his source of information are not known.

The consensus of recent reports on this subject is to the effect that pursuit protection of bombardment formations on daytime missions is still considered imperative by both the Rebel and Government Air Forces, the proportion of pursuit to bombardment planes being as much as two or three to one. Exceptionally, some of the fast Russian light bombers (maximum speed of 248 mph) have operated without pursuit protection.

The Germans have come to the conclusion that their slow bombers (Junkers-52) first sent to Spain were deficient in both speed and armament as it has recently been reported that two new types of bomber, the Junkers-86 (211 mph maximum speed, with armament of 3 machine guns instead of 2) and the Dornier (250 mph maximum speed) have appeared in action. The German bombers have had to contend with Russian pursuit planes of great speed and much superior armament, viz: the I-15 with 4 machine guns each firing 1800 rounds per minute

[rpm], having a maximum speed of 240 mph and the I-16 with 2 similar machine guns and having a maximum speed of 290 mph.

The most efficient bomber in Spain has been the Russian SB-7 having 2 machine guns each firing at 1800 rpm and a maximum speed of 248 mph. This plane is on a par in speed with the German and Italian pursuit planes opposed to it. Nevertheless, when undertaking a mission in formation, it is normally protected by the Russian I-16 pursuit plane.

The present trend in Spain may be said to be toward more speed and more armament in the bombardment type planes. Some experienced pilots there have, in addition, recommended as essential provision of a light armored shield to protect the bombardment pilot and co-pilot.

It is the opinion of our Air Attaché in Spain (experienced most widely as a pursuit pilot) and of other qualified observers there that in spite of a reduced differential in the relative speeds of bombardment and pursuit planes, the latter will still have a decided superiority, when aerial combat is actually joined, because of their ability to concentrate a tremendous fire power from a selected angle upon the bomber being attacked.

The Division has no information to the effect that bombardment planes in Spain as powered and armed, have so far been able to match their pursuit adversaries in the concentration of fire power. Nevertheless, the pursuit planes are having more and more difficulty getting in position to hit the new bombers as the latter become faster and install more machine guns.

The statement appearing in the extract that, "as regards anti-aircraft gunnery the results have been disappointing, even in the case of the German modern guns with trained crews," is not borne out by the information at hand from reliable British, French and German sources and from Spain itself. German A.A. guns of 20-mm., 37-mm. and 88-mm. caliber have been consistently reported as very accurate and effective, particularly at low and medium altitudes, and have also forced opposing bombers to fly about 13,000 feet.

Nevertheless, it is believed to be true as stated in the basic extract that regardless of pursuit and antiaircraft defenses, a bombardment attack (of adequate strength and proper formation) determined to accomplish its mission in spite of losses, will succeed in getting some planes through to the target.

E.R.W. McCabe
Colonel, General Staff,
Assist. Chief of Staff, G-2

Valencia   No. 6643
August 13, 1937
Subject: The Military Situation
[The first half of this dispatch was omitted, as it reported on visits
to various fronts at Madrid, all described as quiet. —Ed. Note]

Brunete Offensive

THE TERRAIN

The almost quadrangular sector in which these operations were conducted is
bounded on the north by the road running generally east and west through Villanueva del Pardillo—on the east by the Guadarrama River—on the west by the
Quijorna arroyo and on the south by the road running generally east and west
through Brunete—an area of some 250 square kilometers. The longitudinal central sector of this area is easy rolling country and affords no terrain obstacles of
any consequence, while the eastern and western edges are cut up by the arroyos
that carry the surface waters to the Guadarrama River and Quijorna arroyo respectively. The water shed of this area, which was followed by column 3, parallels both
sides of the Villanueva de la Canada-Brunete Road.

THE EXECUTION

Three columns of about 4,000 men each left the vicinity of Valdemorillo—headed
towards Quijorna, Villanueva de la Canada, Brunete and Villanueva del Pardillo—
in the evening of July 5th in time to arrive at their respective objectives at daylight
of the morning [of] the 6th, the attack to be initiated and pushed home under the
commanding officer of each separate column. These columns will be designated
for easy reference in the order named above as Nos. 1, 2, 3 and 4. It might be
stated here that the tanks—approximately around 25 to 30 for each command did
not join the heads of the columns until just before going into action. This precau-
tion was taken in order to prevent the noise of the tanks indicating the presence of
troops, as the element of surprise was counted upon in estimating the successful
attainments of the missions. From reports these tank units arrived as planned and
were detrucked at the stations selected. However, the part in general played by this
weapon was not commensurate with the cost in effort, time, road requirements,
supply, etc. essential for its employment. The factors which lessened the maximum
attainable efficiency of this weapon are believed to be those mentioned in Report
No. 6587 of June 27, 1937.

Columns Nos. 1, 2 and 3 moved to their objectives across [the] country in the region between the Quijorna arroyo and the Valdemorillo-Villanueva de la Canada Road, No. 1 turning westward near Quijorna, No. 2 eastward opposite its objective and No. 3 continuing south toward Brunete. The Brunete column, considered the most important, was placed under the command of Lister whose brigade was the spearhead of this advance. The elements composing these columns were practically all units of the International Brigades.

Column No. 1 did not attain its objective until July 9th and only after severe fighting. Column No. 2, which profited greatly by the surprise factor, particularly true with the troops that took Brunete, gained its objective on July 6th. Column No. 2 found considerable resistance in the Rebel positions at Villanueva de la Canada, which fell after Brunete has been taken.

Column No. 4, which followed generally the road eastward to Villanueva del Pardillo, met great resistance and until heavily reinforced was unable to fulfill its mission, which it achieved July 11th.

The details of troop employment in these engagements are not available.

Large reserves were held concentrated in the general neighborhood of the road juncture north of Villanueva de la Canada, prepared to reinforce the columns in the attainment of their missions. As noted above, the resistance met by columns No. 1 and 4 made reinforcements from the reserve necessary. By some observers, and the undersigned is inclined to agree, it is believed that notwithstanding the presence of many elements, the combination of which caused the failure of this offensive, the one big contributing factor was the lack of pushing reserves into the Brunete position for continuing the drive southward to Navalcarnero as planned, i.e., the spearhead of the attack was too weak. It seems now that the resistance met at Quijorna and Villanueva del Pardillo and the failure to take the road juncture at Navalagamella decided the high command to stop the penetration and throw every effort into widening the salient in the direction of Majadahonda and to the east of the Guadarrama. As this effort failed and the Government line stabilized just east of Villanueva del Pardillo (where it is now) the southward push became anchored at Brunete until its fall to the Rebels on July 24th.

STRENGTH

The strength of the Government forces and equipment concentrated for this offensive are estimated—from one of our best informational sources—as being:

Personnel

Madrid front before concentration	90,000
Increase for July offensive	60,000
Total	150,000
Government losses—all causes—dead, incapacitated, etc.	20,000
Now in the Ejercito del Centro	130,000
Being withdrawn from lines for organization of Mobile Reserve Force within the command	30,000
Present strength of Madrid fronts	100,000

Losses

Rebel estimate of Government losses	30,000
Killed	10,000
Other causes	8,000
Government estimate of Rebel losses	
Killed	12,000
Wounded	8,000
Rebel estimate of own losses	5,000 (killed)
Government estimate of own losses	8,000 (killed)

Note: It is generally believed that the Government's losses were double those of the Rebels.

Equipment

Estimate for concentration . . . 250 tanks (included a large number of French Renaults), 200 guns, 150 planes. Note: Attention is invited to the attacks in the Sesena and Usera areas, which were merely of a diverting character, reference to which may be found in Report No. 6613.

The Corps units taking part in this offensive were the V, VI and XVIII in the Escorial region, the II Corps in the Usera front and the III Corps in the Aranjuez Sector.

The daily chronological history covering this front for this period, based on Government and Rebel reports follows:

July 17. Nationalists claim that Government offensive west of Madrid has failed.

Government reports a surprise attack at dawn by Moorish forces against positions occupied by XVIII Corps was repulsed with great losses to the Rebels.

Also a violent attack on Villanueva del Pardillo during the last hour of daylight was repulsed.

July 18. Nationalists report that in the Brunete-Villanueva del Pardillo sector the Government, during the present offensive, in addition to heavy personnel losses, has lost an antiaircraft battery, 4 anti-tank guns and 4 tanks.

Government reports a daylight attack south of Brunete after a terrific artillery bombardment. By noon the attack had extended to positions northeast of Quijorna, the Rebels being repulsed all along the line. Later the attack was localized around Hill 670 around which a violent battle raged the whole day. All lines of the Madrid fronts remained the same except for a slight withdrawal from a small hill on the front of the XVIII Corps due to a most terrific artillery bombardment.

July 19. Nationalists attacked energetically in various parts of the sector, the attack being accompanied by intense artillery fire. Government states that all attacks were repulsed.

July 20. Nationalist communiqué says that counter-offensive on Brunete front continues successfully, several more enemy positions being taken at the confluence of the Guadaramma and Aulencia Rivers, the Government wedge toward Brunete being gradually closed. Among war materiel captured were 7 tanks.

Government admits loss of Hill 660 east of Villanueva de la Canada after heavy fighting during which heavy losses were suffered by the rebels. Strong attack against Aulencia castle position repulsed. Attacks along the line Navalagamella-Perales also repulsed after heavy fighting.

July 21. Nationalists claim that desperate Government attacks in Brunete salient were all repulsed, 3 tanks being destroyed and one more captured.

Government reports heavy fighting on the front of the XVIII Corps. Also reports recapture of Hill 660 in a brilliant counterattack, and the capture of several trenches opposite the 150th Brigade in a surprise attack.

July 22. Government says all Rebel attacks on lines recently captured have broken down with heavy losses to the enemy. Also report capture of a ridge dominating the Perales River, obliging Rebels to withdraw to opposite bank. During the morning the Rebels unleashed a violent attack on the positions east of the Guadarrama River and north of the Brunete-Boadilla del Monte Road, being repulsed. A second attack in the afternoon was also repulsed with heavy losses to the Rebels.

July 23. After intense artillery preparation the Rebels attacked the Government positions on the Guadarrama, being in turn heavily counterattacked and not achieving any decisive results. According to Nationalist communiqué all territory which Government had taken west of Guadarrama River has been recaptured.

July 24. Nationalists claim capture of Brunete and great victory over enemy with capture of many prisoners and much war materiel. Government admits the abandonment of Brunete by the 11th Division after furious air and artillery bombardments. During the afternoon the 11th and 14th Divisions counterattacked, and late in the afternoon succeeded in entering one end of the town. As night fell furious fighting was taking place, the final result of the battle not yet determined.

The 39th Division also counterattacked in another sector of this front, combining with the 46th Division in dislodging the Rebels from several positions. The XVIII Corps was forced to abandon its position on the west bank of the Guadarrama taking up new positions on the opposite bank.

July 25. Nationalists claim all Government counterattacks on Brunete repulsed with heavy losses and destruction of 24 tanks, the victory being overwhelming for the Rebels. Government admits Brunete remains in Rebel hands after the Government attack at dawn which failed against the strong resistance of the Rebels supported by air and artillery bombardment.

The Fall of Brunete

The Rebels heavily reinforced with troops from Avila—reported transferred from the Santander front—broke the outer defenses of Brunete and entered the town on July 24th. The village was occupied by both forces during the 24th and until the retirement of the Government forces on the 25th. During these two days, it is reported that the contending forces were bitterly engaged in fierce hand to hand combat. From a participant, verified by other reports, information comes that the Rebel artillery fire was the most destructive of any occasion known during the war, equaling the inferno it produced in Toledo, when, through its fire only, the town was evacuated and fell to Franco's troops. The Government's retreat, having been planned well ahead of time, was orderly accomplished—the troops retiring behind occupied positions south of Villanueva de la Canada.

Was Brunete a Government Success or Failure?

In connection with the July offensive it is of interest to note the six-point brief prepared by the Government for propaganda purposes to show that the drive had not been a failure. This brief follows with comments by the undersigned:

1. By launching the offensive on the night of July 5th-6th resulted in releasing Santander from the pressure of the Insurgents.

   Comments: The offensive had been planned to relieve the pressure on Bilbao, but its consummation was so delayed that Santander had to be substituted.

This offensive did relieve the Rebel pressure on Santander but it is evident that such relief is only temporary in character as the Rebels are the masters in this region and can resume their offensive at will, which, according to best contacts, may be expected at any time.

2.   By taking the offensive the Government forced the Insurgents to concentrate their Troops and fight in a locality chosen by the Government and well prepared in advance. Further, it prevented the Insurgents from utilizing their strength against a front more favorable to them.

Comments: The statement contained in the first sentence of this second point is true but such reacts to the discredit of the Government for notwithstanding this situation, the preparation and advance was so delayed and disorganized that the Rebels who moved troops from great distances did so in time and with numbers sufficient not only to stop the drive but hurl the government troops well north of the San Martin de Valdeiglesias-Brunete-Boadilla Road. The claim in the second sentence of the paragraph is true to a limited degree. The Rebels, by stopping the first and only great offensive staged by the Government in a vital area, could not have used their troops in a more important theatre—although from a position point of view the Government had the advantage.

3.   In order to check the offensive the Insurgents were forced to expend their best shock Troops. The Government claims that it is in a better position to suffer losses than the Rebels.

Comments: This claim could be easily made by the Rebels as the best shock troops of the Government—the International Brigades—took the brunt of the fight suffering tremendous losses, some units being almost annihilated and all are now in rest areas being recruited and reorganized. Whatever claims the Government may make as to its better position to suffer losses, it is certain that it cannot afford to lose large numbers—as was the case in this offensive—of the personnel of its international brigades who have in all important offensives and defensives been the first line against the enemy.

4.   The Government estimates that the cost to the Insurgents approached the three hundred million peseta mark.

Comments: The value of this claim cannot be gainsayed. However, if it did not break Franco's bank, it might turn out to be a good investment in that it achieved the result of saving the Rebels' nearest and vital lines of communications to the west Madrid area and, above all, of proving in battle the superiority of the Insurgent troops over the Loyal forces even when the latter had the advantage mentioned in 2 above plus that of numbers.

5. Even though the geographical objective was not reached by Government troops, and even though the offensive was stopped and the troops forced to withdraw, the Government maintains that it is still in possession of two-thirds [of the enemy territory occupied during the offensive].

    Comments: This claim of possession is practically true and perhaps is effective propaganda among those unfamiliar with the military and terrain features of this theater of operations. If ground gaining was the objective of the offensive, the July drive would be considered a real military success but this was not the case. The object of the drive briefly was to release the investment of Madrid by cutting off the subsidiary line of communication—the road running east and west through Brunete and the main road artery near Navalcarnero. The main objective never was attained and the first though gained was lost. In fact, after the Rebels had driven the Government troops to the outskirts of Villanueva de la Canada (where they still remain) their attack ceased through evident lack of effort on their part as the Brunete road had been freed and further ground gaining northward would accomplish no good and certainly no military purpose. The road north from Villanueva de la Canada (the only line of communication) is under constant Rebel artillery fire from positions south of the town.

6. The experience and training gained by the Government troops during the open Warfare character of the fighting are claimed to be of tremendous importance to the future operations of the ground forces. The Government admits it paid handsomely in lives for the experience gained and states that its losses were eight thousand killed against twelve thousand for the Insurgents.

    Comments: The experience gained was shared by both sides, perhaps the Government troops learned much but it is generally accepted that the great lesson which was forced home to them was the same shown on other fields—lack of unity of command and officer and non-commissioned officer leadership. In regard to the comment of losses, it is more than probable that the numbers should be reversed.

Having commented upon the "6-point" claim of the Government why the July offensive was successful, the undersigned has undertaken to enumerate below a "6-point" claim why this drive was a failure, viz:

1. The postponement of the organization of the large units until such had to be undertaken in the period of concentration in the face of and under the

observation of the enemy. The principle of concentration towards the enemy is not only Napoleonic but basic, but to inject the factor of organization into the execution of this military axiom must court disaster. This necessarily caused long delays in the period of preparation, so much so that practically everyone in the "Street" knew of the projected offensive. In fact, days before, the Rebel radios announced it and on the north-west Madrid front the Rebel soldiers are reported to have yelled over to the Government trenches such jeers as: "When are you going to start your offensive?" "Hurry up and commence your offensive, we are getting tired waiting for it".

2.   Basically, the lack of unity of command and efficient leadership in the lower grades. This reason has been advanced by several who participated in the campaign.

3.   The disintegrating, undermining and demoralizing effect of the control by the political parties of their respective units. This was manifested by the extremists in their constant complaint that their men were not being equipped and supplied as were their political rivals—the Communists. Furthermore, the extremists claim that the Communists ran away, with the consequences that the brunt of the fighting fell upon them as evidenced by their losses.

4.   It was in the field of tactics that the Government forces failed, in all probability through the lack of trained junior officers and non-commissioned officer personnel. The well known military principle that the commander on deployment commits his troops to his subordinates was strikingly demonstrated in this offensive.

The strategy of this campaign and the plan adopted seemed excellent, and the offensive deserved to be successful. The attack struck the enemy at probably his most vulnerable point on the entire front. The plan included the element of surprise, although this factor was practically lost owing to the reason given in 1 above. The plan, if successfully executed, would have achieved far reaching results including the lifting of the siege of Madrid and possibly the cutting off of the Rebel investment forces to the west of the city.

5.   The economy displayed in the distribution of troops to the attacking columns turned out to be costly reminding one of the old saying of "sending a boy to do a man's job". The reserves for these columns should have been determined upon and followed in supporting distances—even if held in hand by the central command—until their need or not had been determined. The intervening objectives should have been taken immediately, by the em-

ployment of overwhelming forces, after Brunete had fallen in order that the southward push to the Extremadura Road could be prosecuted vigorously. The lack of the ability and experience of the high command and staff in the employment of large units might account for this failure, accompanied by the novice's fear of troop commitment in the attainment of an objective.

6.   The troops lacked individual and organizational field training, particularly in open order combat, weapon confidence and that team work so essential to success in battle. From information at hand, the International Brigades marched more or less independently of each other—the spirit of cooperation and that teamwork so stressed in our army was apparently absent.

Although the material for this report was written on August 12th the mailing has been delayed until this date, August 17th. Advantage of this is being taken to bring attention to the fact that the resumption of the Santander offensive is well underway and that the important town of Reinosa—km. 48 Santander-Palencia Road—has been taken by the Rebels in a five column drive as noted below from West to East. (1) Vicente de la Barquera-Cervera Road; (2) Torrelavega-Reinosa Road; (3) Santander-Burgos Road; (4) Valmaseda-Santona Harbor Road; (5) Castro Urdiales-Santander Road. As this report is being mailed, the information seems definite the advance of the columns No. 1, 2, and 3 is timed to precede that of columns 4 and 5.

The Reported Government Mobile Reserve

In this report may be included a mention of the visit of the undersigned to 36 Mobile International Brigade familiarly known as the Campesino Brigade. The importance of the visit lay in the fact that search was being made for reported concentrations in the Madrid area. After personal visits through the north, west and south Madrid fronts, it seemed evident that no large bodies of men were in the reserves or immediate back areas of these sectors. Information was obtained that the Government had sent all reserves, assembled for the recent Brunete offensive and the International Brigades that had participated, to rest areas in the Alcala de Henares region. The purpose of this concentration was in order that these units may be reorganized, re-equipped and rehabilitated with a view to their forming part of a strong mobile striking force being organized and held in the Madrid area for emergency use for stopping an enemy penetration or for filling a gap in the line, but more particularly for forming the spearhead of a drive planned for September when conditions would again permit the Government to turn from defensive to offensive tactics.

Fortunately, the undersigned had been given a letter and package from the family of the recent Governor of Valencia to be delivered to "one of the boys"— with whom a friendship had been developed some time back in Madrid. This errand, the delivery of a package of food, in some strange fashion, was better than a pass as it was an "open sesame" to all places and to all units. The search for the party addressed permitted visits in various parts of the Escorial and finally to the Campesino Brigade, camped about 3 kilometers east of Alcala de Henares in the valley of the Henares river. From the observations made during this visit, information collected and reports of others visiting in this Section, the conclusion was drawn that whatever mobile force is being organized and whatever its strength may be (reported 30,000) it is being assembled in this general area.

Dissensions

The Government communiqués covering the Andalucia and eastern fronts consistently and insistently announce discord in the enemy camp. Grave disorders necessitating the employment of firearms for quelling are reported frequently by the General Staff Information Section. These "uprisings against the foreigners", as they are defined by the Valencia Government, are stated to be of large proportions, particularly in Andalucia centered in the Granada region. There is no verification of these reports.

Closing Comments

In resume, it can be definitely stated that the Brunete offensive must be recorded as a military failure and that it is so recognized in the inner circles of the Government and the Central General Staff. The opinion expressed in the closing paragraph of Report No. 6613, on the importance of this offensive and its effect upon the Government, has been reinforced by occurring events and by the general sinking of that buoyancy of hope which pervaded the Government at the time of the launching of the July offensive. The peak of the military power of the Government, in the opinion of the undersigned, was attained in the concentration of the great striking force of some 60,000 men to "free Madrid from fascist fangs". The army of the Republic has lowered greatly, in both fighting power and morale, since the fall of Brunete and must, in order to lift its efficiency curve, undergo a complete reorganization, the effort toward which has now commenced. To say that it cannot "come back" or move forward to a higher state of efficiency than ever attained, is too much to prophesy but it is clear to the observer here that efforts beyond those employed in the past, with many fundamental changes in the organization of the army, must be applied before the Government may expect the attainment of battle success.

Valencia

August 16, 1937

Subject: Military Report

Military Attaché returning from Madrid reports that personal reconnaissance of all Madrid fronts furnished no evidence of reported troop concentrations for second Government major offensive in that area which was confirmed in interview with [Antonio] Ortega, commanding Army of the Center, who opposes major offensive at this time. Government organizing a mobile reserve reported of some 30,000 men in Central Area as striking army of all arms equipped and trained for future offensive or defensive action. Regular Army circles bitter against the Ortega assignment and fighting his commission as a general which promotion is still held up. No evidence of rebel offensive on Madrid front to the contrary indications point to next drive in some other sector plan not yet unfolded. Past estimates of recent Madrid offensive failure strengthened by occurring events reflecting that high tide of Government Military Machine probably attained in July shows receding signs. Reported activities on all fronts, although may attain importance, of local interest, only at present.

Valencia   No. 6645

August 19, 1937

Subject: Equipment and Other Data Obtained from French Sources

[The following information was obtained through French sources from French nationals serving with the Republican Army. —Ed. Note]

Russian Infantry Automatic Weapons

Briefly speaking, source considered that the Russian L.A. was an efficient weapon, though in no way superior to the French F.M. 24, whereas the machine gun was a failure. The wheeled mounting is clumsy and sticks in mud and dust owing to the smallness of the wheels. The canvas belt feed causes perpetual stoppages and destroys the gunners' confidence in the weapon. Water-cooled, the steam is visible up to a thousand yards.

Tactics

Source considers tactical training is non-existent on both sides. The Insurgents' superiority is artillery; however, it is very marked.

In the last defensive works constructed by the Government troops near Cordoba, under the supervision of Russian advisers, the following precautions have been observed. Trenches are constructed (with head cover and traverses) having only one exit, which is guarded by a reliable man. The trace of the work is circular in shape. The exit being guarded, the occupants are bottled up like rats in a trap when an attack takes place. They can, of course, use their weapons but, like cornered rats, they must fight and cannot leave expeditiously by the back door. Squads of well-armed *Komsomols* ensure the impossibility of a hasty departure of the garrison.[3] Source stated that only once had he observed the effect of a bomb upon a wire obstacle. He saw a 100-lb bomb drop in the middle of a wire fence of the usual type, some 15 ft. across. The blast tore up the pickets and flattened the wire to the ground making a gap about 20 ft. wide. During the attack on the Cerro Gordo near Puertollano, source was present at a successful attack by the insurgents, well supported by aircraft and artillery. The work attacked was isolated, occupied about 600 yards on frontage, and had a garrison of approximately 250 men. The hastily-dug trenches were too shallow, not being more than 2-3 feet deep.

A ninety-minute artillery preparation was carried out by three medium batteries (12 guns) and a thirty-minute air bombardment by thirty heavy bombers took place, 129 men being killed and 80 wounded. The survivors appeared stupefied and incapable of resistance. The attacking infantry, about 400 or 500 in number, surged forward in a mass and occupied the position without firing a shot.

General Information Regarding the Army of Andalucia

The Army of Andalucia is in [the] process of passing completely under Communist control. The political commissars are all Spaniards, 80 to 85 percent of them belong to the Communist or to affiliated parties. They receive their instructions direct from [Julio] Alvarez del Vayo, the Commisar General of Valencia. With every formation above the brigade there is a Russian military representative of the rank of colonel or lieutenant colonel. A Russian colonel with a numerous staff has his headquarters at Almeria and controls the army of the south. All the Russian military organization is unified under the control of one, Colonel Petroff, at Valencia.

These military advisers have no hand in politics but they often intervene in imperious fashion as regards the conduct of military operations. They are generally arrogant and imbued with a sense of the superiority of their race and caste. Relations with the Spanish commanders through the medium of interpreters (generally German Jews or Poles) are very difficult. Spanish commanders and staffs generally poor in quality and not up to their work and are helpless against Russian domination for they know that the powers of the Russian military advisers are practically unlimited. After each operation the Russian military adviser prepares a report, which is transmitted direct to Colonel Petroff, chief Russian military adviser in Valencia, who has direct access to Prieto, the Minister for National Defense. In spite of this attempt at complete domination of the Republican Army by relatively competent foreigners the results achieved are very mediocre. The Spaniards meet all attempts to impose a discipline and organization foreign to their nature with bitter hostility and invincible inertia. For instance, French source, who never moves without a trustworthy guard, has been frequently shot at. Mention has already been made of the measures adopted to ensure a determined defense. Any attempt at an offensive seems impossible. The population of the Jaen-Andujar district is frankly hostile. As an illustration, it was found necessary to cut down the olive trees to clear fields of fire. Those responsible were threatened with death by the peasants.

In short, source, an ardent supporter of the Republic does not leave one with a very favorable impression. Although not himself a Communist, he supported this "Musovite reign of terror" because he considered it the only remedy against general disintegration. But he doubts of its success in the face of an insurgent offensive. The Andalusian has no longer any desire to fight. It is only the fear of his commanders and his ten pesetas a day that helps him to maintain his family which keeps him in the ranks—and that only till battle is joined.

Undated
Subject: Military Report

The Nationalists' offensive in Santander region definitely resumed in five column advance against coastline east and west of Santander from Castro Urdiales to San Vicente. Columns moving north in west section of zone of operations gained key mountain positions Peña Labra and important town of Reinosa. Government reorganization of forces in Central area continues with probable completing date not earlier than September 1st. Government has concentrated some forces on East front for apparent minor offensive.

Quiet on all other fronts.

Paris   No. 23, 694-W
August 28, 1937
Subject: Operations North-West of Madrid 6-14 July

The battle of Brunete, if it may be so termed, is interesting, not so much from the tactical and technical point of view, as with regard to its repercussions on the future war effort of the Republic. As at Guadalajara in March, the main offensive role fell to the air force, due to a lack, among the ground forces, of trained commanders, staffs and artillery, and to the low standard of training, equipment and discipline of all arms. Mention has been made elsewhere of the stifling of Revolutionary enthusiasm by Communist Party discipline. Added to this, the infantry is yet incapable of maneuver and lacks sufficient mortars and automatic weapons. Elsewhere, too, has been mentioned the mechanical defects of the AFVs[4] almost all Russian, the indifference of their tactical handling and the indiscipline and lack of courage of their untrained Spanish crews.

The air force, on the other hand, although lately diluted with Spanish pilots, represents worthily the most efficient of Russian defense forces. It has already given proof of the strictness of the discipline which controls [it] and of the enthusiasm and offensive spirit which animates it. However, with material at least as efficient as that of the Insurgent air force, it is not surprising that the only coherent tactical conception that has emerged from the operations of the Republican forces has been a vigorous offensive in the air followed, if possible, by the occupation of ground gained on the part of a somewhat spineless and ill-equipped infantry assisted to a limited extent in their forward movement by the inadequate support of artillery and AFVs.

It was difficult, as in the case of the Guadalajara operations in March, to disentangle from the partial, frequently ill-informed and generally exaggerated Government communiqués the little truth which they contain and to deduce from the few facts and conclusions which are given here. For the same reason it is impossible to enter much detail. In fact, were it possible to do so, it is unlikely that any useful purpose would be served.

The Object

It is probable that the attack was initiated with the double object, firstly, of drawing off enemy reserves that threatened Bilbao and, at the same time, of disengaging Madrid and compelling the withdrawal of enemy forces before that city by cutting or threatening of their communications with Talavera and Toledo. It is incontestable, firstly, that the offensive came too late to save Bilbao and, secondly, that it has not so far compelled the withdrawal of Insurgent forces attacking Madrid. There is still the possibility of its being the means of saving Santander and the Asturias. Evidently great things were expected as, not only the Asturian Government leaders, but also most of the prominent members of the Valencia Government, emigrated to Madrid to watch the progress of the offensive.

Judging by the location and direction of the three attacks which took place, the destruction of enemy forces in Madrid and Jarama salients was apparently to be effected as follows:

(a) The first and principal attack, to be delivered in the area South of the Escorial, had Navalcarnero as its objective.

(b) The second, launched from Villaverde and Carabanchel, must have had as its objective the high ground west of Carabanchel.

(c) The third, in the Aranjuez area, was intended, it is believed, as a holding attack, to prevent the movement of reserves from the area South of Madrid. This attack might, if successful, have brought about the withdrawal of Insurgent troops in the Jarama salient, in combination with operations at Carabanchel.

Had these attacks succeeded, all the main communications by road of Insurgent troops in the Madrid and Jarama salients would have been either cut or threatened. These are: Road Madrid-San Martin-Avila; Road Madrid-Talavera; Road Madrid-Toledo.

For lack of adequate support the second and third attacks were a complete failure. The first and main attack, however, achieved considerable success from the outset; a breakthrough was affected, but unfortunately, on too narrow a front for successful exploitation to the depth required to achieve its object. Thenceforward it was the usual story of reserves used up in widening the breach, of surprise hence sacrificed and a consequent loss of momentum that brought the offensive to a standstill, having almost achieved its object.

The only result of a week's fighting was the formation of two fresh salients, one held by the Republican troops with its apex at Brunete, the second held by the Insurgents and formed by the failure of the Republican forces to neutralize Las Rozas and Majadahonda, immediately northwest of Madrid.

Government Ground Forces Engaged

In the main attack, apparently, three army corps took part: the V and the XVIII, supported to the East by the VI. In the two subsidiary attacks, two other corps took part, the III at Aranjuez and an unknown corps at Villaverde. The corps generally consists of two divisions, of three brigades each, the latter of three or four battalions. The infantry strength of a corps thus approximates to 15,000. The artillery support probably did not exceed 12 batteries, i.e., some fifty field guns per corps.

Nevertheless, for the Republican Army, this was a considerable effort. About 80,000 infantry were engaged, of which 50,000 took part in the main attack. Thus, 5/6 of the army of the Centre were employed, this being about a third of the Republican field Army. Four battalions of AFVs supported the attack, three in the North and one at Villaverde. Although these battalions are believed not to number more than 40 machines apiece, most of the Republican resources in AFVs must have been engaged, the total of their tank brigade not being more than 200 AFVs.

Ground

The ground over which the main attack took place was the broken and undulating country South of the foothills of the Guadarrama mountains. Although intersected by water courses, the general direction of the attack was parallel to that of their flow. Hence, serious obstacles to the employment of AFVs were, in all probability, few and far between. Sparsely wooded, the main obstacles to the progress of the attack were, as usual, the villages, easily convertible into strong points, against which AFVs were of little value, and air bombardment comparatively ineffective.

Narrative

5th July. Bombing of enemy positions facing sectors where attacks subsequently took place, except opposite Villaverde where, Insurgent positions being known to be strong, the Republicans tried to achieve surprise.

6th July. The air offensive began at dawn in the Northern sector. This consisted of an air bombardment of the enemy positions lasting from 6 to 9 hours, including reserve positions and a headquarters at Navalcarnero, where some petrol dumps were set alight. The number of machines engaged over the sector of the main attack is thought to have been in the neighborhood of 150. The infantry attack was delivered on a front of from 5 to 6 miles between Valdamorillo and the Guadarrama river. Apparently no resistance was encountered in the enemy forward positions and few prisoners were taken. It is therefore probable that survivors of the air bombardment took refuge in the villages.

The Republican troops effected a break through on a front of from 2 to 3 miles. Through this gap, infantry, supported by AFVs, exploited success to a depth of eleven to 12 miles. Brunete was taken at 1600 hours. On the flanks of this gap, Villafranca del Castillo to the East, and Villanueva de la Canada and Villanueva del Pardillo to the West, continued to hold out. The Republican troops were thus pent up in a narrow salient. The Insurgents state that they took 4000 prisoners. This figure is almost certainly an optimistic one. At 2200 hours the Republican infantry entered Villanueva de la Canada, after a heavy air bombardment of two hours, taking about 100 prisoners.

In the two southern sectors the infantry attacked at Villaverde at 1500 hours after an aerial bombardment and reached the 7 km. stone on the Madrid-Toledo road. There, this attack was held up, once and for all, at a considerable cost in casualties to the Republican troops. A half-hearted attack on Sesena was held up in front of the Insurgent forward positions.

In the North, the day's gains consisted of a salient 11 to 12 miles in depth, rather less than 5 miles in width at the base. This was contained by Villafranca del Castillo to the East and Valdemorillo to the East and Valdemorillo and Quijorna to the West, all of which were still held by the Insurgents. Brunete was in Government hands, although too weakly held. In any case, no further advance could be undertaken towards Navalcarnero until reorganization, consolidation and a widening of the gap had taken place.

7th July. In the course of the day the Republican troops attacked Quijorna unsuccessfully and the first Insurgent counter-attack took place in the air and on the ground. The Republican air force bombed Quijorna several times during the day as well as enemy reserves, being brought up to prevent the widening of the salient. On this day the Government lost air superiority and was attacked in the air on equal terms, according to their own statements. At the end of the day Government troops had closely invested Quijorna; the Guadarrama river had been crossed at Villanueva de la Canada. It is not clear whether Brunete was still in Government hands. But it is certain that elsewhere the Government offensive had been held up. No action of any importance took place at Villaverde or Sesena on the two sectors to the South.

8th July. Republican troops completely surrounded Quijorna, crossed the Guadarrama river and took Romanillo. The Insurgent air force was very active. The principal effort of the Government air force was directed towards the protection of the Western flank of the attack, more exposed to the threat of enemy counter-attacks. Chapineria and Navalagamella were heavily bombed, 35 heavy bombers taking part in the attack which took place at 1800 hours. Elsewhere, the Government air force covered an encircling movement east of the Guadarrama river with an exceptionally heavy bombing of Boadilla and the area surrounding it, where enemy concentrations had been reported between noon and 1600 hours. Insurgent batteries were also heavily machine-gunned and apparently neutralized. In addition, the Government machines carried out a thorough reconnaissance, not only of the front to the North and North-East of Madrid, but also along the railways by means of which reserves might be moved from the Basque provinces. In fact, the Government air force seems to have been more than fully employed. In addition to its normal role of medium and distinct reconnaissance, allied to the bombing of back areas, it carried out both protective duties and counter-battery work. As no enemy counter-attacks took place it seems to have accomplished its task successfully.

9th July. Quijorna fell into Government hands at 11 a.m., together with 200 prisoners, the first notable number taken by Republican troops since the beginning of the offensive.

The Government air force continued its task of protecting the Western edge of the Brunete salient against counter-attacks, engaging M.T.[5], columns to bring up reserves to Fresnedilla and Cobreros. Throughout the day, villages in the area Brunete-Navalcarnero-Madrid were bombed. Air reconnaissance was continued along the railways to the North of Segovia, Avila and Aranda de Duero.

10th July. For three days the Republican troops had made no progress. Neither Villafranca del Castillo nor Villanueva del Pardillo had been taken. The 75 to 80,000 men engaged on 6 July had everywhere been held up and heavily counter-attacked. Moreover they were hardly able to hold the ground gained. The Government air force appears to have been indefatigable, concentrating most of its attention on the salient between Las Rozas and Majadahonda and on the Madrid front, paying particular attention to communications and enemy centres of resistance. The Insurgent air force was becoming daily more active, dog fights more frequent and losses in machines heavier on both sides.

11th July. Early in the morning Villafranca del Pardillo fell at last, the Government claiming several hundred prisoners. The Insurgent defense of this village and of Villafranca del Castillo, over a period of five days, may be termed one of the chief causes contributing to the failure of the Government offensive, limiting, as it did, the width of the gap made in the Insurgent line. The Government air force assisted with continual bombing around the base of the Las Rozas salient, Boadilla, Sevilla la Nueva and Majadahonda. Anti-aircraft batteries which had been pushed up to the forward positions, were bombed at Brunete, Sevilla la Nueva and Romanillos.

12th July. Enemy counter-attacks were delivered against Villanueva del Pardillo, where fighting continued all day. These counter-attacks were apparently unsuccessful. The Government air force continued its action against the same objectives viz: Boadilla, Villaviciosa de Odon, Mostoles and Alarcon. The more supine the Republican infantry, amongst whom the action of some 10,000 men merely consisted of the very passive defense of a village, the more intensified was the offensive action of the Government aircraft in their effort to compensate for the shortcomings of their grand troops.

13th July. Insurgent troops North of Las Rozas salient appear to have withdrawn a short distance past certain points before the Republican VI Corps which had been under arms since the beginning of the offensive. Elsewhere there was apparently little change in the general situation. The Government communiqués were discreetly silent, probably underrating Insurgent gains to the West. From this moment all hope of a further advance Southward seems to have been lost. Nor, apparently, were the Government even able to hold Brunete and Quijorna. Judging by the small number of prisoners taken by the Republican forces, the Insurgents seem to have been able to hold up the Government advance with a considerably smaller number of troops than those at the disposal of their adversaries. In spite of this, the offensive spirit of the Republican ground forces, a frail plant of very recent growth, seems to have withered and died under the cold blast of determined opposition. To all appearances, the attempt to disengage Madrid seems to have failed.

14th July. The President, Ministers and other members of the Government returned to Valencia.

Conclusions

For reasons which have been previously enumerated, it would appear that the only chance of success held by the Republican forces lay in the successful action of their air force, as at Guadalajara. This success they came near to achieving, and in spite of the poor quality of the ground forces, they would have done so if the momentum of the offensive could have been maintained.

What seems more important is the effect on the conduct of the war of such a costly failure. Unfortunately the figures of casualties sustained are not available.

But they are known to be high. And the gravity of such a failure to the Government cause can only be measured in terms of war weariness and lowering of morale at a very critical period. Judging by the interest displayed by the leaders of the State, high hopes must have been set upon success.

It is perhaps early to judge of a temporary disappointment, nor should the determination and courage of Republican troops and their leaders be given too low a valuation. Perhaps the recent operations are only indicative of a phase. But there is no blinding the fact that the operations of 6-14 July constituted a noteworthy effort to pass from the defensive to the offensive and that at the first trial the Republican ground forces failed—and failed with heavy loss. Such a failure coming at such a time cannot augur well for the future.

Fuller

Valencia   No. 6711
November 1, 1937
Subject: Three-Day Visit to the Eastern Front

Through the courtesy of the Spanish War Department in providing the necessary special *salvoconducto* and the personal invitation of the former commander of the Washington Battalion to visit the "American units", the undersigned was a guest of the XV Brigade at Quinto October 25-27, 1937.

The visit was of unusual interest presenting not only an opportunity to see this particular front but affording a close up picture of the American volunteers in the Spanish army. The undersigned was literally taken into the "bosom of the family", housed and messed at Brigade Headquarters, shown the activities of the command, escorted through the battle areas of Belchite, Quinto and the present front facing Fuentes de Ebro and honored by having the brigade paraded for his review. Major [Robert] Merriman, the Chief of Staff of the brigade, was the host of the undersigned during his visit.

The Brigade-XV International Brigade, XV Division
ORGANIZATION, STRENGTH AND COMMAND PERSONNEL
The brigade is organized as other Spanish regular army units. Its present strength is 2,750 men, 500 of which have recently joined and are still classed as recruits. The brigade consists of the 57th, 58th, 59th and 60th Battalions which are racially organized as follows:

57th Battalion – 3 companies English and 1 company Spanish.

58th Battalion – 3 companies American and 1 company Spanish.

59th Battalion – 3 companies Canadians and Americans mixed and
          1 company Spanish.

60th Battalion – 4 companies all Spanish.

PERSONNEL

The commanding officer [C.O.] of the XV Division, to which the XV Brigade belongs, is General Alter—a Pole, who the undersigned has not met. The C.O. of the XV Brigade is Lt. Colonel Vladimir Copic, a Croat who was expelled from Jugoslavia for political activities. His wife and child are now living in Prague. Colonel Copic is a typical communistic internationalist, well educated, speaks several languages including English, handsome physically, fine appearing soldier type, neatly dressed, gives appearance of leadership and initiative, was in the Austrian Army during the World War. From reports of his subordinates, he is popular with his officers and men and holds the confidence of his entire command. He seemed proud to be in command of the American unit, paid glowing tributes to the fighting efficiency of the Lincoln-Washington Battalion both as regards to its combat value as a team and to the individual bravery and soldierly qualities of its members.

The Chief of Staff of the brigade is Major Robert Hale Merriman, who was at one time the commanding officer of the Lincoln Battalion. Major Merriman is a graduate of the University of Nevada, class of 1930, and is about 30 years of age. He claims California as his State. Upon graduation he passed from the ROTC unit of the University to the Officers Reserve Corps and attended the ROTC camps at Monterey, California 1931 and 1932. Major Merriman is the backbone and moving spirit of the XV Brigade; he is addressed as *Camarada* by all except those near to him and to these is he is known as "Bob". He is a fine manly type, over six feet in height, physically sound with the endurance of an ox, pleasing personality, filled with initiative, overflowing with energy, he moves about everywhere in the command honored and respected by all, he is unquestionably the dominant figure of the brigade, and the "Star" American in the "Volunteer" group. Major Merriman is married and has his wife with him in Spain. She does secretarial and hospital work and is now on duty in a "mixed capacity" at Albacete. Major Merriman was presented by the brigade commander with a handsome gold watch during my visit and in my presence "for his services to the Brigade and for his leadership and personal bravery in the recent campaigns of Quinto, Belchite and Funetes de Ebro". Major Merriman was badly wounded in his shoulder in the Jarama campaign and during the period of his convalescence was utilized in training troops in the Albacete region.

The Second in Command is Major Crespo, a Spaniard. I was told that this officer was purely a "figure head", common to all International Brigades, and that the office was created to keep the War Department posted on the brigade activities but more than all to give the impression that the International Brigades were officered in part by Spanish officers.

The staff of the brigade is mostly American with a mixture of British. The outstanding figures seemed to be:

Captain Dave Doran, a Californian without previous military service. Commisar Politico. A very wide awake, intelligent worker, who seems to concentrate most of his energy on planning talks for the Altavoz—how to win adherents from the rebels and make them pass over to the government side.

Captain Frank Ryan. American, Brigade Adjutant, is reported to have some military background.

Captain Malcolm Dumbar (English) is chief of operations. This officer explained to me the action of the brigade in the recent fighting around Fuentes de Ebro and the eastern front lines as they then existed. Captain Dumbar is a college graduate, possesses a keen mind, lots of initiative and energy. Highly thought of on account of both his efficiency and pleasing personality.

Captain D. Dart (American), assistant operations officer, is from Chicago, very active and energetic, bright mind, much relied upon in planning brigade movements and actions. Reported to have had some military background.

Captain Paul White—G-2 (American). Is from Oregon. Commands the scouts and publishes the local newspaper. He was formerly a newspaper reporter and has had some military service.

EQUIPMENT—INDIVIDUAL

There is no uniform equipment. Ammunition belts, packs, pouches, canteens and mess gear are of many varieties—none of which show any new development in this field. Practically everything in this line was dirty and showed no evidence of any attention towards cleanliness, care or preservation.

UNIFORM AND CLOTHING

Uniforms are of O.D. khaki[6] and corduroy types—worn mostly with varicolored lumbermen packets. Shirts of O.D. khaki and grey hues abound.

Headgear—overseas caps, helmets and civilian hats, Russian turbans and civilian caps (with ear muffs) of several varieties.

Underwear—heavy blue cotton with wool mixture, well suited for winter wear.

Footwear—boots laced and otherwise, heavy shoes of all types worn with and without leather leggings.

Blanket issues—one to each man, hardly enough for winter.

The uniformed appearance of the command in parade formation can best be expressed by the words "unclean and unsightly".

BARRACKS AND QUARTERS

The command occupied some monastery buildings. No attempt was made to obtain uniformity of arrangement of bedding, clothing and equipment. Articles were mostly dumped in individual piles on [the] floor near the walls. Total lack of camping expedients and the sanitary conditions can best be expressed by the word "horrible". The quarters of the officers were in former residences in the heart of the town. They were dirty, unsanitary and evidenced no attempt at tidiness.

The men were at rest and idle and would have welcomed I am sure, a real old time "post general fatigue day". If such an event had occurred, afterwards, in looking over their place policed, orderly and sanitary, I am sure that they would have had pride in their achievement, received a boost in morale and lifted their heads a bit higher in self respect and self esteem. Their leaders seemed to lack an appreciation of the far reaching effect of and sound benefits which accrue from close attention to policing personnel. The men in these units by their nature, temperament and experience readily adopt the idea that dirty bodies, hairy faces and tough looking exteriors give them a real "field soldier" appearance. However, when this type of personnel is led to the appreciation that "cleanliness is godliness" and that system and orderly arrangement are the essence of true soldierly qualities, they will follow the leader like the Spanish sheep follow the bell horned goat. These men of the International Brigades belong in the category often referred to in our army when we speak of a man as being "a good field soldier but rotten in garrison".

SOLDIERLY BEARING AND APPEARANCE

Seemed at a low ebb in and out of ranks. There was no evidence of results attained from closer order drills—men in ranks moved about at will and effort at exactness of execution and simultaneous movement seemed pitiful. There were few signs of either individual training or combined mass movements. The troops were paraded for the undersigned in a hollow square formation. No attempt was made to march by in review—a maneuver which in all probability could not have been executed without embarrassment to the leaders, a situation which they evidently foresaw and avoided.

MORALE

Judged from the stories of individual and group action in combat and observing the men in training squads, at mess and at play, their fighting spirit is evidently high. This can well be understood knowing the soldier types in these International Brigade units—in which they come from the four corners of the earth actuated by those impulses of adventure, wanderlust, hate, political faith which make for the "to do or die" spirit in men.

TRAINING

What little individual and group training this command has had has been inspired by our training regulations which are in the hands of the American instructors, who control the instruction. However, these teachers are handicapped in not having the power to impose a discipline requisite and essential in the school of training the student types that come and go with such disrupting frequency in these International Brigade Centers. At best, these soldiers receive only a few basic training principles, a bit of field service instruction, a touch of first aid and personal hygiene and not more than an introduction to their weapons with little or no target practice. Their group training is just as amended with the consequence that their movements lack cohesion and cooperation—uniformity and exactness of execution being unknown to them. What battle successes these men have attained seemingly have come to them through their strong conviction of the rightness of their cause, of their physical courage, of their personal bravery and through their indomitable spirit to win. Their failures, in most cases, were plainly caused by lack of efficient leadership in the lower grades and almost the total absence of proper field training.

ARMAMENT

The Infantry Cannon. The brigade has a group composed of three sections—each of which is armed with a 45 mm. infantry cannon. The cannon and ammunition— examined personally—are Russian manufactured judging from the Russian language markings. The officer who showed me the gun had been the section commander for several months, but knew nothing of the ballistic properties or characteristics of the piece. However, the following mental notes were made by the undersigned at the time of the observation: The carriage, split trail, barrel and mountings seem almost identical in design with our 37m. gun, increased, however, in size and weight to meet the greater caliber (34). No unusual or novel devices, in the construction of the piece, were noted. The marked comparative differences between the two pieces lay in the increased weight of the gun and carriage, but it had an oil compression recoil system, that it was not constructed with a view to dismounting in the field for man handling, that it was sighted in ranges up to 10,000 meters, that the wheel tires were heavy solid rubber tires and that it had unusually large gripping spades on the split trails. The tires showed little wearing as the piece is entrucked for all movements except for short distances, in the presence of the enemy, when it is rope hauled. The piece observed had fired in one day at Belchite some 1100 rounds over a period of about ten hours. There was no log kept for the gun, so the total number of rounds it had fired since it came into serve last February was unknown; however, it has been operated in all the campaigns since last February in which the brigade has participated. There are three guns assigned to the brigade—each being operated by a crew of 8 men.

The breach block is practically the same as on our 37mm. gun, opens vertically downward and ejects [the] shell after firing. Although the piece is sighted up to 10,000 meters, it is generally employed at its best ranges, 1500-2000 meters, in which distances protective cover is generally found. The barrel is susceptible to an elevation of 45°. The officer commanding has high praise for its accuracy of fire as he expressed it, "at 2000 meters I can pump shells through an ordinary window of a building". The gun is reported "tough". The piece observed—all parts painted olive drab—showed little or no signs of the hard usage to which the gun had been put. No part had been replaced except one small screw in the breech block handle mechanism and the firing pin examined showed practically no wear.

The shells used in this gun are of two conventional types both of which are about 18 inches long. One type is employed against tanks and although it does not contain a delayed fuse—it breaks only after great resistance. The other is used for firing against fortified buildings, ground machine-gun nests and "strong points" and is detonated on impact.

While this gun has played an important role in the fighting in which this brigade has been engaged, to the undersigned it has functioned more as an "accompanying gun" and perhaps this type of cannon may be of the type to fill the infantry's long cry for an "accompanying gun" approaching artillery caliber. The fact that this cannon cannot be readily dismounted and man handled makes it, in the opinion of the undersigned, unsuited as an organic arm for the infantry. Judging from the part it has played in battle, it has been more in the role of artillery. Certainly, on most of the occasions of its employment, an artillery piece of 75 mm. could have been used and to greater advantage, while the infantry has been deprived of a weapon that could really follow its lines into action.

The Rifle. The brigade is armed with a conventional type of rifle of Russian design manufactured in the United States about 1924. Caliber 30.

The Infantry Mortar. No mortars have been issued to the brigade—probably as this weapon is not desired. The brigade being most employed in offensive action and the type of mortars available in Spain being designed for trench warfare, will account for the absence of this weapon.

Hand Grenade. Every form of hand grenade on the military market is probably in use in Spain. The so-called "potato masher", the model issued to our infantry and a very small grenade, about the dimensions of an ordinary apple, seem to be the prevailing types.

Smoke and Gas. None are employed.

Pistols. No uniformity. Probably all standard makes on the market can be found in the brigade.

American Volunteers

AMERICANS IN SPANISH ARMY

The following well thought out estimate of the strength of the American volunteers in Spain was prepared for the undersigned by the Chief of Staff of the brigade:

Original strength	2,500
Losses—All causes, deaths, discharges and desertions and missing in action	500
Present strength 10/21/37	2,000

This figure can be broken down as follows:

With combat troops	900
In hospitals and rest areas	300
With non-combatant services, mostly Motor and Hospital units	500
	1,700

The figure above with combat troops 900 may be broken down as follows:

Lincoln-Washington Battalion	225
Mackenzie-Papinau Battalion	200
With other combat units: Artillery, Cavalry, Communications (mostly with Artillery)	475
	900

The Lincoln-Washington Battalion

The Lincoln Battalion was organized in the Madrid area in January 1937 and the organization of the Washington Battalion followed in April. The two were merged in May into what is now known as the Lincoln-Washington Battalion due to the reduction in the strength of both organizations occasioned by their great battle losses. The battalion is truly a "rainbow unit" for within its ranks may be found representatives from the 48 states of the Union and Hawaii and Puerto Rico. The representation from New York predominates with those of California and Ohio a distant second. In the unit may be found some ten negroes and a similar number of men of the Jewish faith.

The present battalion commander is Captain Philip Detro, a journalist from Houston, Texas, and a former member of the National Guard of Texas. Captain Detro is about 30 years of age, medium height, slim and of the "raw bone" type. He is reported to be "a good fighter of the true Texan brand". He could not be classified as a dominant leader and does not belong to the "fire brand" class. He is very modest in his manner and soft speaking in his voice. His ability to lead probably comes through these characteristics reinforced by strong convictions, initiative, courage and some military experience.

Mention will be made here of Captain Hans Amlie who organized the Washington Battalion and who commanded it during its short life. Captain Amlie is from Elkhorn, Wisconsin. Captain Amlie served in the U.S. Marine Corps 1916-1920 and in the 20th Infantry in 1921-1923. He was with the 2nd Division throughout its campaigns in France and was wounded twice in the Belleau Woods engagements. He was wounded in the July fighting in the Brunete campaign at Mosquito Ridge and again at Belchete where as he expressed it, "a bullet just parted my hair". I noted the hair "parted" in the middle to which he referred. During his service with the Marines he was at one time on the Marine Rifle Team which attended the National Competition at Camp Perry, Ohio. Captain Amlie's service in the American battalion in Spain has been marked with great distinction. He is the tall ungainly type, modest, phlegmatic, conscientious, courageous, possesses good judgment and lots of sound leadership qualities. With these characteristics, fortified by his six years' service with regular troops, two of which were in the World War, Captain Amlie has been an outstanding figure among the American Volunteers and probably can be included among the three leading Americans in the Spanish Volunteer forces. In this selected group the undersigned would include Major Merriman, Captain Amlie and Captain Johnson. The last named officer is here placed from heresay remarks and praises given to him. He formerly commanded the Lincoln Battalion and is now the head of an officers' training school. He is reported to be a graduate of West Point and an ex-regular army officer and seeks the background atmosphere avoiding publicity of any type. The undersigned expects to meet Captain Johnson shortly.

Captain Amlie was my escort during the trip of the Eastern front.

ENGAGEMENTS

The American battalions and the American-Canadian units have participated in the following major engagements:

> The defense of Madrid
> The Jarama actions—defensive and offensive
> The Brunete campaign—Villanueva de la Canada column
> The Quinto-Belchite campaign
> The Fuentes de Ebro campaign (the October Offensive).

Under the heading of engagements may be mentioned some notes on the Quinto-Belchite campaign and the recent battle for the Fuentes de Ebro, particularly as these were actions carried out almost solely by the XV Brigade and that these engagements have been mentioned by the high command as "an outstanding tribute to the fighting efficiency of the American Volunteers".

Quinto

The movement against Belchite was subordinated to the attack on Quinto, the success of which made possible the Belchite envelopment movement. The Quinto advance was made from the south with an artillery barrage laid on the strong isolated fortified ridge to the south of the town. While this artillery battle was in progress, a two brigade column circled well west of the town with Hill 161 as its objective; however, when nearly west of the town, the XV Brigade was told off to take the town from that flank, which it did after a two day fight, the second day being devoted to street fighting and the taking of the town citadel—the customary church on the hill. Hill 161 fell thus cutting off Quinto from Fuentes de Ebro and reinforcements from the north. The detached ridge south of the town fell by negotiations—the garrison of some 200 men surrendering. The success of this combined movement made it possible to push a force at once towards Medina, some 14 kms west of Quinto, which took the town almost in one onslaught. This victory cut the road between Fuentes and Belchite and permitted the latter town to be attacked from the north. The Chief of Staff of the XV Brigade informed me that the Quinto campaign was well organized and coordinated and that it was by far the best conducted offensive in which the brigade had participated. In fact, he added, it is the only one where there prevailed combined movement controlled by a central authority in the field with a definite purpose and fixed objectives.

Belchite

The advance on Belchite was made from the west and south fronts, the south column finally swinging westward through Ermita, thus cutting the road to Fuendetodos. The XV Brigade later was moved from the Quinto position to Codo just northeast of Blechite. Thus Belchite was completely surrounded and, in which situation, it so remained for 14 days. During this time, the isolated garrison was supplied from the air; almost daily rebel planes would drop sacks of food, ammunition and medical supplies. The reception field for the landing of the sacks was a sunken spot near the Cathedral and was well protected from hostile ground fire. (The spot was visited by the undersigned.) Throughout this fortnight, the town was hammered by some 50 pieces of artillery, from the nearby heights, of all calibers, during which time the village was literally battered to pieces. During a thorough inspection of the town not one single house was observed unhit and probably no place of this size has been so completely wiped out as was Belchite. However, during this period of bombardment the garrison hugged their dugouts, manned their posts and peppered the enemy's lines whenever exposed with a grilling machine-gun fire refusing to a man to quit their positions. This situation being so prolonged, and none of the troops advancing, the high command decided on the 14th day of the siege "to drive the rats out of their holes" and for this task the XV Brigade was selected. The troops left the vicinity of Codo for the cross road just north of Belchite and on September 1st launched the assault from that position with the road to Mediana as the axis of the advance. In the assault the houses were not entered until the 4th and during that day and the 5th the fight was "street to street, house to house and at times room to room". The town finally fell on the morning of the 6th after the garrison had been "shot out of their dugouts and hand grenaded from their house fortresses".

Belchite was a religious center and possessed four churches and several monasteries, all of which afforded the defenders strong "centers of resistance" which from the attackers' statements were held unto the last. Many stories are told by those participating of how "hard the fascists fought at Belchite", and of the many incidents occurring in the "house to house" hand to hand fights where the enemy died fighting and the cases of suicide "rather than be taken alive". The XV Brigade in this attack had 175 wounded and 50 killed.

Fuentes de Ebro

After Belchite the brigade was more or less out of the lines or remained in the quiet sectors until October 12th when it was ordered to the trenches facing Fuentes de Ebro, under orders to initiate an attack against that town. The Brigade entered the line the night of October 12-13 and launched the attack at noon of the 13th. The Brigade was disposed in the line on a two kilometer front—the left of the Mackenzie-Papinau Battalion resting on the Quinto-Fuentes road, the American Battalion in the center and the English Battalion on the right. The line extended northeast and at right angles to the road, the direction of attack being northwest against the enemy's front line trenches just south of the town and northeast of the main road. The axis of the advance was about 1500 yards in depth. The "jump off" was made from an interior sector, the left sector of the trench line being occupied by the 143d Catalan Brigade and the right by the 120th Catalan Brigade. The Spanish battalion of the XV Brigade was assigned to accompany the 45 tanks which preceded the attack on three separate lines of advance—one group of 15 moving south of the road on the left flank, a second group of 15 on the right flank and the third group of 15 along the axis of the advance. The center group was to pick up enemy machine-gun positions and destroy them, the flank groups were to cover with machine-gun fire the flanks of the advancing infantry line, penetrate the enemy's position and strike it from the rear and finally aid the infantry in entering the town. Each tank transported five infantry soldiers—in a prone position back of the turret—with the plan that these small groups would drop off on reaching the enemy's line and with their hand grenades storm and take the enemy's first positions. The machine-gun companies were assigned as reserves to occupy a position for firing, holding same until the infantry objectives had been taken or to cover the withdrawal or resist a counter attack.

The artillery was to lay a thirty minute barrage on the enemy's front line in preparation for the advance. The brigades on the right and left of the XV were to advance to a rolling ridge some 500 yards to the front, and there pound the enemy's line, particularly in front of the attacking brigade, with a devastating fire. What happened to this plan, as told [to] the undersigned by the Chief of Staff of the Brigade, follows:

The passage of the tanks across the trench line occupied by the brigade was the zero hour signal for the initiation of the infantry attack. However, the tanks were an hour late on their schedule. The right and left tank groups drove forward without relation to their infantry flank protection mission and entered the edge of the town where they were stopped by "ditches and barricades". The force of their forward movement having been spent, they became an easy prey, in fact, so easy that the enemy captured 22 without the necessity of rendering them unserviceable. The second phase of this fiasco battle was that the artillery barrage was laid upon the second instead of the first line of enemy trenches. The third and telling mishap occurred when neither of the Catalan brigades, on the right and left of the XV, advanced. In fact, these troops did not leave their trench positions.

Notwithstanding these deterring factors, the XV Brigade advanced to within about 500 yards of the enemy's line where it secured sufficient ground cover and partial screen to enable it to hold on, without being annihilated, until darkness set in under cover of which the elements withdrew to their original trench line. The losses in this engagement were exceedingly small—considering the grave danger to which the troops were exposed, 20 killed and 102 wounded out of an attacking line of about 1,000 men.

Thus ended the "battle" of Fuentes de Ebro which in the government communiqués at the time heralded not so much as a victory but "a success which will make possible the encircling of the town". The lines are now stabilized—the rebels just south of the town 500 yards and the government troops some 2,000 yards away—the line crossing the main road at kilometer 28 which means that distance from Zaragoza. Although the officers who described this action to me did not mention outright of "treason in the ranks", it was evident that they strongly suspected such. The Catalan explanation given for not advancing was that their brigades were not equipped nor prepared for offensive action as they had been assured in this trench assignment that their mission was "purely defensive". One of the officers remarked on commenting on this incident: "The Catalans are dug in for the winter".

As Quinto—as expressed above by the brigade Chief of Staff—was the best coordinated attack in which the XV Brigade had participated, so Fuentes was by far the worst.

Spirit of the Enemy

The "fighting efficiency" of the rebels based upon their performances at Belchite and Quinto was not only high but well in the category of heroic. Under the most adverse circumstances, they fought, cut off on all sides, to the very last, engaging in hand to hand mêlées and frequently committing suicide as a last resort to prevent capture.

Closing Comments

Herein, the undersigned desires to make of record the usual courtesies of the Spanish War Department in authorizing his trip to this front, particularly as it was closed at the time to all visitors. The visit to the American units was the consummation of a long felt desire as well as the result of an effort initiated some months ago.

The undersigned feels that he would be remiss in not emphasizing the fact that the Americans are held in high esteem in the Spanish army and at the War Department for their "courage and fighting efficiency" evidenced not only in extolling words but in the historical fact that in this war, where the shells have burst loudest and the bullets fallen thickest there the American volunteers could be found. These comments are embodied in this report with a sense of national pride regardless of the fact and with the knowledge of the status of the American volunteer in Spain in the home country as a law violator.

6

Lessons from the Spanish Civil War
(November–December 1937)

"The day is past when a people's militia can stand against trained troops by trained officers."

U.S. military instructor,
Fort Leavenworth, Kansas, 1937

This chapter begins with some brief accounts of events in the fall of 1937, but for military observers all over the world, they increasingly began commenting on the lessons of this war. After all, the fighting had been going on for nearly a year and a half by the end of 1937. Observations from the field, from such observers as Fuqua and others, were making their way into training programs and discussions about strategy and possible implications for new weapons systems. The centerpiece of this chapter is a lecture presented to mid-career U.S. Army officers at their training facility at Fort Leavenworth, Kansas, at the end of 1937. Historians are fortunate that the lecture was both written and preserved, as it represents one of the clearest and most useful summaries of events and lessons learned from a military perspective that we have. Through this document, for instance, we see the subtle professionalization and enlargement of the war. The epigraph at the start of this chapter was part of that analysis and a key point about the changed circumstances that emerged during the course of 1937.

Notes attached to the lecture acknowledged the sources for its content being a large variety of intelligence reports from U.S. military personnel attached to various embassies in Europe and to the press. However, the central source cited was Colonel Fuqua, about which the lecturer noted, "His information has been gathered in the front lines and often at the risk of his life."

Valencia   No. 6715
November 4, 1937
[The majority of this report is not reproduced here, as it was essentially comments on the inactivity of various fronts.—Ed. Note]

Closing Comments

The collapse of the last frontier in the north has destroyed all vestige of hope on the part of the people and has shaken their faith in the government to win the war. To the masses, the Nationalists have won the war and the man in the street is hoping that the final blow may be soon forthcoming. This cross section man of the people is tired of the inhibitions imposed by the conflict, he is weak and weary, war worn and hungry. He longs for peace and would joyously hail an armistice, but he dares not speak his thoughts for the eavesdropper is near and the executioner working strong. There is a desire in military circles that the committees concerned with the "foreign volunteers" will soon come here and a hope that in some way their coming may cause a cessation of hostilities, at least for the time being. This hope is reinforced by the belief that if the "firing is once stopped it will never be resumed".

The information coming from all sides is convincing that a rebel attack may come from any front or a combination movement on all fronts with the main attack organized to give a telling blow that will pave the road for the "Appomattox" of the war.[1] The government reports rebel concentrations on the Madrid, East and South fronts and evidently the Nationalists are doing just that and in this way are concealing on which particular front or fronts the main concentrations are being made. The undersigned plans leaving for Madrid on November 9th in order to study this front with a view of forming some estimate of the situation.

Copies of Military Reports—cable enclosure to Report No. 6715—November 4, 1937.

Valencia
October 22, 1937

Asturias defense has collapsed completely. Gijon, Oviedo and north region now dominated by Rightists. Government leaders escaped fleeing by sea and air to France, resulting revolt of civil community and surrender of troops without heralded last stand fight. Rightist prisoners unharmed released. Fall of north released estimated 70,000 troops for offensive on other front not yet exposed. Government has concentrated best troops and most reserves on East front largely at expense of Madrid area. Government East front offensives seem definitely stopped although attacking rebel Fuentes de Ebro-Sillero line continues. Action in Pozoblanco and Madrid areas continue at present of local importance only. Heavy shelling of Capital continues almost daily. Government planned movement to Barcelona estimated increased unfavorable reaction. It followed immediately military collapse in north.

October 28, 1937

Military Attaché returning from three day visit to East front reports: Teruel sector remains inactive, that recent government offensive Fuentes de Ebro-Belchite Sector has definitely ceased, heavy artillery and International Brigades being removed to rear areas for estimated transfer to another front. That most of ground gained in government offensive north of Ebro to Huesca has been lost to enemy. That Huesca to Jaca front again stabilized with rebel controlling road and railroad center at Cartiraza. Direction rebel offensive estimated in preparation not yet revealed although reports' varied sources seem to indicate major action Madrid area.

Berlin   No. 15, 595
November 24, 1937
Subject: German Estimate of the Military Situation in Spain

A responsible officer of the German War Ministry on duty in that branch of the G-2 dealing with Western Europe stated that it was now the opinion of the German War Ministry that Franco's ultimate success in Spain was certain. He estimated that in the course of the last five months Franco had gained about 100,000 men numerical superiority over the Valencia government. He estimates Franco's military strength now at about 500,000 men as against 400,000 for Valencia.

In particular he stressed the excellent results of the training carried out by Franco's men in the last six months and felt certain that with each month that passed, Franco's superiority would become more and more evident. He furthermore stated that the German army was pleasantly surprised with regard to the results achieved by their training cadres in Spain. In particular the high fighting qualities of the 6 Navarre Brigades, totaling in all 20,000 men, received wholehearted German acclaim. The officer went on to say that any army in the world would be pleased to number those fighting forces among its own units. In skill and bravery, no other unit of the Franco army approached this force, although in his opinion, if the war continued until spring, other units of the Franco army would be brought to nearly the same degree of fighting efficiency.

Truman Smith

Major, G.S., Military Attaché

Lecture

The Command and General Staff School, Fort Leavenworth, Kansas, 1937-1938

Lessons from the Spanish Civil War

December 1, 1937

General Franco raised the standard of revolt in Morocco on July 17, 1936, and started ferrying his Moors and Legionnaires across the Straits of Gibraltar in loaned or purchased German and Italian planes. He little realized that his coup d'état, almost at once, would take on the aspect of a World War in miniature. But even as German and Italian planes were being flown to Morocco, in Moscow Russians were nailing up the crates of other airplanes for shipment to the Spanish Government and the radical French Government was permitting the delivery of 22 pursuit planes, intended for the French Army, to their Spanish brothers of the left. The commercial planes of France in Spain were seized by the Government without eliciting a protest.

What kind of a man is Franco? Primarily a soldier. At 32 years of age he was the youngest major general in the Spanish Army. To him and General Sanjurjo go the credit for putting down the Moorish revolt after the efforts of many others over a period of 8 years had failed. Franco had never mingled in Spanish politics, and for this reason he was able to take over command of the revolt without alienating any of the many factions. He has proved himself an able leader, a conciliator and organizer: Insurgent Spain is now a well governed country. In spite of starting without any gold backing for his currency he has kept his peseta stable, while the Government, with seven hundred millions of gold, has seen its currency fall to half [its] value on the international exchange. Franco has united the disparate elements behind him to a remarkable extent, while the parties of the Government have devoted quite as much energy to fighting among themselves as to fighting Franco.

Internal Politics

Supporting Franco are the Alfonso monarchists, the Carlist monarchists, the Catholic Action Party, the Falangists of young Primo de Rivera and the Right Republicans. Franco's following is variously called monarchist, fascist, nationalist, insurgent, rebel, and white. They will be referred to as Insurgents throughout this lecture. On the government side are Socialists, Anarchists, Stalin communists, Trotsky communists, and left Republicans. These varieties of faith are further split by the autonomy movements in Catalonia, Viscaya and Asturias. The Government forces are variously referred to as Red, communist, republican, and loyalist. They will be referred to as Government forces in this lecture. The Spanish government is popular front, that is, in theory, a combination of the left parties. In actuality it is an involuntary coalition forced upon them by the war. The Trotsky communists have been driven underground and their leaders assassinated and imprisoned. But their secret press floods the cities with anti-government propaganda. The anarchists have been unwilling participants in the government. In May 1937 they revolted, but were suppressed with 1400 killed and 600 wounded. In Spain they make the bitter joke that the only country to respect the non-intervention agreement is Catalonia. The Stalin communists support the government during the prosecution of the war. But they remember the injunction of Lenin: "Accept all the obligations that are demanded of us, but when the hour of decision sounds, do not forget that the honor of a communist consists in not fulfilling them except in the measure in which they answer to the interests of the proletariat". The communists now control half the Government army, and 90 percent of the political commissars.

Foreign Assistance

Russia has been the chief purveyor of materiel and advice to the Government. It has probably sent five thousand technicians, aviators and military and political advisers to Spain. As a sidelight on the Soviet utopia the early Russian volunteers

seem to have volunteered primarily to escape Russia. They deserted at the first opportunity in Spain. Later arrivals have been selected from those who had hostages
behind in Russia. The kindly government has also furnished them with female
interpreters, who sadly know no Spanish; but that is simply another Russian para-
dox. Government aircraft have been principally Russian with some French and
American planes. Tanks and artillery are French and Russian. Russians run the
Tank and Chemical Warfare Schools. Aviators are sent to France and Russia for
flying training. Germany has sent Franco between three and five thousand technicians, aviators and military advisers. Italy has contributed 40,000 men—blackshirt volunteers; aircraft, tanks, artillery and small arms.

The International Brigades

Louis Fischer, a left wing correspondent in Spain, states that the International Brigades have never exceeded 15,000 men and that the total numbers received have
not exceeded 23,000. George Seldes, another pro-government correspondent, estimates them at from 40,000 to 50,000. From 1500 to 2000 Americans seem to
have joined. The International Brigades have been about half French. They are
composed of communists, adolescent idealists, military adventurers and criminals.
They had a leavening of World War veterans and initially the courage of men
fighting for a cause. They have usually gone into battle with two to four weeks'
training. How slight is their military experience is indicated by a description by
Louis Fischer who writes of Robert Merriman once a lecturer at the University of
California: "He left Moscow in December and by virtue of his ROTC training
soon became the chief officer of the first Lincoln Battalion". Now on his arms are
the three red stripes of a Spanish Captain. He is in command of a battalion which
the correspondent saw on the rifle range where "many of the men had handled
weapons before and they hit the target frequently".

Foreigners are unpopular with the Spaniards. The Russian military and
political advisers dare not move without an armed guard. They have never hidden their contempt for the Spaniards and are well hated in return. History has
furnished few more amusing pictures than the sight of Russian officers, only a
generation out of serfdom, most of them with little education and no military
experience, arrogant and imbued with a new-found pride of race, lording it over
the proud and sensitive Spaniards. And, little love is wasted on the International
Brigades. They advertised that it was they who had won the battles, and accompanied their narratives with aspersions on the Spaniards.

General [Emilio] Kleber, a Canadian-born communist and soldier of fortune was the first commander of the International Brigades. He was relieved of his command and practically disgraced. His crime seems to have been an undue fondness for publicity together with a critical attitude toward his superior, General Miaja.

General Miaja is commander of the Army of the Center, and defender of Madrid for the past year. He is an able soldier of the old Spanish Army and probably the only competent officer in the higher Government ranks.

In Morocco Franco was supported by about 20,000 Moors and 14,000 Foreign Legionnaires. The naval revolt had failed; warned by enlisted radio operators, most of the crews, which had been organized by the anarchists, had killed their officers and seized the ships. The uprisings in Seville, Salamanca, Burgos and the cities along the northern coast succeeded. After severe battles in Madrid and the cities along the Mediterranean, the Government retained control there. They also recaptured the north coast. Franco was faced with the problem of getting his troops to Spain across water controlled by the Government. He adopted the original solution of ferrying them by air. Some three to six thousand were crossed in this fashion. Two thousand more came in boats protected by bombers. Franco flew to Sevilla August 7th and assumed command of a force of 10,000 men. Three days later Merida was taken. Badajoz fell on the 15th, Talaverra the 25th and Toledo fell September 27th. Franco had marched and fought for forty days, making a two hundred mile advance. With eight tanks and a small air force, he attacked and scattered the militia in every battle. The militia never stood up to serial bombardment and when this was followed by the rumbling tanks, spitting fire and flames, they threw down their arms and ran for their lives.

At the Alcazar in Toledo, six hundred men had resisted the attack of five thousand militia for seventy days. Toledo is not on the direct route to Madrid and time was important. Franco, nonetheless, turned aside to relieve the defenders of the Alcazar. Five hundred of the six hundred defenders had been wounded when the militia were driven from Toledo. As it turned out this diversion was a major error on Franco's part. Two lessons can be drawn from the siege of the Alcazar. The first is the defensive power of a courageously held fortress. The second is the enormous value of such a defense. The five thousand men held attacking the Alcazar might have been sufficient to have stopped Franco's advance north.

Meanwhile in Madrid, according to war correspondents, soldiering was a great pleasure. The proletariat had seized the houses of the wealthy and made merry. The militia roamed the streets singing the International, and strutted their bravery, so far untested, in the cafes. Female militia was armed with rifles at a time when there were not enough to arm the men.

Censorship had kept news of the fall of Toledo and the succession of defeats from the populace. All the citizens had heard of were proletarian victories. Not until Franco had defeated the militia at Illescas, halfway between Toledo and Madrid, were the Madrilenos informed of the imminence of real warfare.

While General Franco's well trained and completely disciplined Moors and Foreign Legionnaires were carrying out trained officers' orders to the letter, Government volunteer companies were choosing their fronts by ballot, voting themselves leaves to go back for street rollicking at Madrid or leaving their positions undefended while they foraged (with excellent reasons, since the Government supply service was almost non-existent) for food. Officers, chosen by election, were wrecking the last remnants of discipline by quarreling loudly and bitterly about tactics, while their followers stood by laughing at them.

Franco and Mola had 40,000 men to capture a city with a million inhabitants defended by 120,000 militia. The attempt to take it by a frontal attack failed. Untrained militia, willing to fight, proved they could hold when protected by trenches. Franco managed to get a foothold across the Manzanares River in University City which he has maintained ever since. The defense was helped tremendously by the arrival of Russian planes and other equipment and the intervention of the International Brigades.

In connection with the frontal attack, Franco tried for the first time in history to the much discussed Douhet theory of massive bombing.[2] During November, December and January, the Insurgent air force shuttled back and forth bombing Madrid. What was the result? Nothing. People shook futile fists at the murderers in the sky and muttered, "Swine". Madrid has now had a front line in it for over a year and during that year it had been bombed and shelled heavily. The results are 3,000 killed and 14,000 to 15,000 injured. A quarter of the city is in ruins. But streets are cleared, tramways and subways still run. In spite of broken windows, burning houses, gutted buildings and blocked streets, life in Madrid continues. 800,000 people live there now. Fires attract no spectators—they are quickly put out.

Children soon accepted the explosions as in the natural course of events. The grown accommodated themselves more slowly. But bombing is quickly over. After each hurried rush for shelter one knows it is safe to go about business as usual. "Artillery fire is much worse—it continues". The telephone building has been hit 130 times and its elevators still run. Housewives shop for groceries or stand in queues when the supply is scarce. Cafes still welcome citizens in the afternoon for their orangeade and vermouth. In the evening, youths continue to stroll in the shaded streets.

Bombing, far from softening the civil will, hardens it. Terrorism has finally been tried and found wanting. Murder of non-combatants increases resistance and lengthens war. Spain has given the world one great lesson—that the bombardment of so called political objectives is futile; a waste of a powerful weapon. [Benito] Mussolini has read the signs—he has announced to the world that Italy, the birthplace of Douhet, the prophet of aerial terrorism, will not wage war on the civil population.

Following the failure of the effort to take Madrid by aerial bombardment and frontal attack Franco tried to envelop it. The Jarama offensive in February had for its object the envelopment of Madrid from the south. It succeeded in cutting all the rail lines leading to the coast. Franco had too few infantry to exploit his initial success. Reserves, moved from Madrid, counterattacked and held. The only highway leading south to Valencia came under artillery fire. From this time on all the supply to Madrid has come over 110 miles of highway. This highway starts at the railway end at Utiel and runs to Cuenca and Guadalajara. A limited amount of traffic goes over the southern railroad from Valencia, but this requires a long truck haul over secondary roads to Alcala de Henares and thence to Madrid.

The next effort to capture Madrid was made from the north and led to the much discussed Guadalajara battle.

The Guadalajara Battle

The situation: The failure of the attack on Madrid in November, December and January, and the limited success of the Jarama offensive in February had resulted in strengthening of the defenses of Madrid in these localities to such an extent as to make the success of further attacks improbable. The Guadarrama sector had been a quiet one throughout the war. An attack down the Zaragoza road, if made by surprise, would therefore offer an opportunity to outflank Madrid from the north. It would also cut the Valencia-Madrid highway going through to Cuenca at Guadalajara. Alcala de Henares was the center of the network of secondary roads through which all supplies moved into Madrid. There was an excellent prospect that the capture of these two places would force the fall of Madrid.

Terrain: The Zaragoza-Madrid highway followed the center of the narrow valley between the Tajuna and Henares River. It is a modern hard-surfaced road and, following the ridge line, does not cross many streams. At Almadrones a secondary branches off to Brihuega and follows the course of the Tejuna River to where it joins the Jarama River south of Madrid. North of the valley were the Guadarrama mountains.

Plan: Troops, principally Italian, were secretly concentrating in the vicinity of Siguenza. Two motorized divisions were to move down the two roads with a Spanish unmotorized division on the right flank and some unmotorized Italian troops on the left flank. It was thought that Guadalajara, 45 minutes distant, should be reached in about two days. The concentration of the troops was successfully carried out in complete secrecy.

Combat power: The composition of the Italian motorized divisions was as follows: Two infantry divisions, each of 3 battalions of about 650 men and 70 trucks. Each regiment had a battery of 65-mm mortars and a platoon of 45-mm mortars. Two battalions of field artillery, each of three batteries of 75-mm and 100-mm guns. One battery in each battalion was portee[3] and the others tractor-drawn. One battery of 20-mm combined AA and antitank guns. Thirty 3-ton tanks. One machine-gun battalion. One chemical company of flame throwers. Engineer, signal and medical detachments. The total strength of the division did not exceed 5,000 men. A hundred airplanes were to support the attack.

The Italian troops were blackshirt militia volunteers. None of them had any combat experience except a few who had engaged in the capture of Malaga. Most of them had reached Spain since the first of the year. The officers were mostly blackshirt volunteers without combat experience. The division commanders and staffs and some of the artillery officers were experienced and capable regulars.

The attack commenced on the 8th of March. It was completely successful and an advance of five miles was made to Almadrones where it was stopped by support troops. Rain and low-hanging clouds over the mountains prevented support by Insurgent aviation. Many of the Insurgent's temporary airdromes had become bogged with the incessant rains and planes were unable to take off. On the 9th the advance was resumed and the main column reached the vicinity of Gajanejos. It remained here during the 10th to permit the division on its left to come up on the road to Brihuega. This division had been delayed by the washout of a bridge which the Government forces had neglected to destroy in their retreat, rain accomplishing what inexperienced troops failed to do.

On the 10th a lone Russian pursuit ship on a casual flight discovered the columns of motors. It appears that the ground forces had made no report to Madrid, or had not realized the strength of the force against them. On the 11th the attack was resumed, the right column reaching Trijueque. The advance guard had reached Toria but was forced to withdraw since it had not been supported. The left column occupied and fortified Brihuega. On this day the first reinforcements of three battalions arrived in front of Trijueque from Guadalajara.

This was the situation, when on the 12th the Government aviation made its first attack on the right column, dropping 492 bombs and firing 200,000 rounds of ammunition into the column. The attack came as a complete surprise; pandemonium reigned. Weather had prevented the operation of the Insurgent air force and apparently the Italians had neglected antiaircraft precautions. This represented the limit of the Italian advance: twenty miles in four days. They had no air support, their trucks could not leave the road into the [unintelligible], their artillery was unable to get off the road to support them. The light 3-ton tanks were found to have little cross-country mobility in the [unintelligible] and swollen streams. Apparently at this time, the Italian command decided that surprise had been lost and gave up on the idea of further advance. Their withdrawal commenced the night of the 12-13th. With practically no resistance the Government troops captured a large number of trucks filled with ammunition, 12 field guns and 2 antiaircraft guns.

On the 13th Trijueque was retaken unopposed. The Government air force resumed its attacks, dropping 120 bombs on the left column and firing 50,000 rounds of ammunition into it. On this day the first Insurgent planes appeared. Bombers bombed the airdromes at Alcala and Guadalajara and fighters attempted to give direct support to the columns.

On the 14th and 15th several more aerial attacks were made on the column retreating from Trijueque, but these were not as effective since Insurgent air support kept the Government aviation busy. Brihuega was still held. On the morning of the 16th, 770 bombs were dropped on the Insurgent positions there.

In the meantime three Government brigades, the 11th and 12th International and a Spanish militia brigade, had been moved up the valley in trucks and taxicabs from Madrid. These attempted to surround Brihuega on the 17th, moving up the valley between the Tajuna and the Tagus. The column on the Brihuega road had to wait till the other cleared Almadrones before it could withdraw. The garrison of Brihuega, probably a rear guard, did not exceed two battalions, two batteries, and a machine-gun company. Their routes of withdrawal were threatened and they withdrew with difficulty during the night of the 18-19, losing about 100 prisoners, 6 field guns, 60 trucks and a number of machine guns. By the 20th the lines had been reformed.

Ernest Hemingway spent four days going over this battlefield and proclaimed it as a great defeat for the Italians as the Battle of Caporetto.[4] He insists that it was a victory of small arms. Actually, the foot troops played a minor part in this reverse. It must be considered an air victory. The Government staff orders to its reinforcements directed them to establish a defensive line along the line of Brihuega-Trijueque and to organize a line of solid resistance in rear of this. The flanks were to be protected by massive demolitions. Trijueque was occupied without resistance after the Italians evacuated it. The slight pressure maintained is indicated by the fact that for two days the Government forces lost contact with the column retreating from Trijueque.

Such lessons as can be learned are only confirmatory of what we already know. Troops in motors cannot fight. They are an ideal target for aviation. Air advantage is an essential part of the superiority of force required for offensive operations. New proof was given of the effectiveness of air attack on motors massed on a road.

Some rear-guard tank actions took place during the retreat. These showed that the light Italian tank was no match for the heavier Russian. The battle of tank versus tank goes to the tank with the heavier armor and armament just as is the case in naval battles.

The action also showed the tremendous morale effect of ground attack by aviation. Apparently the Italians huddled in the rain were incapable of reacting. The initial attack caused total disorganization. Throughout the Spanish conflict it is noted that air advantage is just as important for the morale of troops as is good artillery support.

The failure to depart Madrid by frontal attack or envelopment left Franco in a strategic dilemma. He was maintaining a front of about 780 miles in eastern Spain and another of 200 miles in northern Spain. It was impossible for him to hold his lines and at the same time to gather a sufficiently large offensive force for capture of Madrid.

The situation of Madrid was extremely unfavorable to the Government. All the rail lines to it had been cut. It had a vast morale importance to the Government. About one-third of the government troops were in its vicinity. To move these to other fronts required an initial movement by motor to a rail line leading to the coast and then a long haul by rail. By continuing to threaten Madrid, Franco could immobilize with a small force a third of the opposing army. He had about 100,000 men on the 200 mile northern front. Apparently the only way in which he could gain a large enough maneuvering force to end the war was to reduce the northern front. Franco's decision to hold on the main front and to reduce the secondary front, for which his available force was sufficient, was undoubtedly wise.

The situation of Franco and the Government with respect to railway transport should be noted. One-third of the Government army is held in the Madrid area, unable to reinforce other fronts except by long motor movements. The Government has railway lines leading vertically to the front at only seven points in its 780 mile extent, less than one line for each one hundred miles of front. Franco, on the other hand, has parallel lines over almost his entire front. Although theoretically he is on exterior lines he is able to reinforce any part of his front by rail with great rapidity. It should also be noted that the contour of his front is dependent upon the railroad net. The long front from Toledo to Merida represents little more than a guard for the rail lines. The last actual Insurgent attack was made in the vicinity of Don Benito with no other object than that of freeing the balance of the rail line parallel to the front leading to Cordoba. Franco's decision at this juncture was to hold on the main front and to reduce the salient in the north. This was started by a campaign against Bilbao.

Campaign against Bilbao

Because of the rough terrain, with deep, steep-walled valleys, it was deemed unwise to consider any type of campaign based on a quick drive on Bilbao itself. Reconnaissance had disclosed that the defenders had adopted the plan of digging trenches along every ridge, barricading the roads, and establishing machine-gun posts, which would cost many men to take by assault. It was therefore elected that the advance should be by indirect attack and flank movement around fortified positions to pick off enemy terrain piece by piece. It is interesting to note that during the weeks of advance, the defenders failed to solve these flank attacks and time after time allowed themselves to be dislodged from easily defended positions.

The advance by short steps fits well with Spanish psychology and climate. It enabled commanders to start engagements early in the day, reach objectives before noon, dig in, rest awhile, finish the day with registration by the artillery on the next objective, and rest up for the next day.

Aerial photographs were taken of the whole area. During the nine months of hostilities the Bilbao forces of some 90,000 men plus 4,000 to 8,000 political prisoners had built the "iron ring" and additional trench systems. According to estimates it would have taken 250,000 men to man the systems completely. Plans of the defenders were based on their ability to shift their forces from point to point. This was discovered early in the campaign and the attackers saw to it by use of local assaults, now here, now there, that there never were enough defenders at the point attacking to prevent the desired advance.

The attack would begin at daybreak with an artillery preparation laid on the front lines extending well to the right and left of the section to be assaulted. Then the position would be bombed from the air. Following this preparation the infantry and tanks, where terrain permitted, would advance on a narrow front. Tanks advanced with the first wave of infantry, not ahead of them.

At some points where machine-gun nests were hidden in the forest, attacks broke down. Usually immediate call for airplane assistance and dropping bombs enabled the attack to be resumed and the objective reached the same day. Enemy soldiers driven into the open were attacked by machine-gun fire from planes. The attacking Spanish troops always dug in the moment an objective was reached. Each unit carried a big flag to mark newly-taken positions to keep friendly aviators from attacking them. When the attack on the next objective was delayed by the weather or other causes, barbed-wire entanglements were laid, steel angle irons being used for uprights. Communications during the campaign centered in the headquarters of the German general of artillery at Vitoria, 20 miles southeast.

By the 2nd of June, 1937, the Insurgents had advanced to positions close to the "iron ring". For nine days thereafter fog prevented any sort of an attack. On the 11th a strong attack was made at Orduna, twenty miles southwest of Bilbao, to draw reserves in that direction. On the twelfth a concentration of sixty batteries opened fire on a three-mile front between Larrabezuia and Galdacono. At a point near the latter, a deep valley bisected the line of defense. Both sides of this valley were lined with reinforced concrete rifle pits, machine-gun nests and lines of trenches with barbed wire in front. All trees were cut from the slopes. For some reason the mouth of this valley was not fortified on the flat, save for a few trenches along stone fences. At the upper end, however, a cluster of strong points existed, which if properly manned, would have enabled the defenders to keep anyone from coming up the draw.

After a short artillery preparation the entire fleet of bombers dropped 42 tons of bombs. Immediately after the bombing a force of a thousand Carlist volunteers led the way up the valley and advanced deep into the countryside of the ring. They lost a number of men from fire of machine guns at secondary positions, but were not prevented from debouching right and left inside the ring. More troops followed and within a few hours the defenders had been driven from over a mile of the ring's line of strong points.

The further advance was continued without great difficulty. The Italian brigade followed along the seacoast. Bilbao surrendered June 19th. The Asturian leaders of the defenders wished to destroy the city but were prevented by the Basques, who had enough of them, and welcomed the conquerors as deliverers.

An example of the effect of the combined artillery and aerial bombardment is given by one instance where the Government position occupied 600 yards of frontage with hastily-dug trenches two to three feet deep. The garrison was 250. The Insurgents executed a 90-minute artillery preparation by 12 guns and a 30-minute bombardment by 30 heavy bombers. One hundred and twenty-nine were killed and eighty wounded. The survivors were stupefied, incapable of resistance. The attacking infantry occupied the position without firing a shot. When the iron ring was broken, Captain Murga, the engineer officer who had built the fortifications, was tried for treason and shot.

The balance of Government territory on the north coast was reduced in the same fashion. It should be noted that the defenders were at all times greatly inferior in the air. They had but few airdromes and these were bombed incessantly. They finally became unable to get into the air. The decisive air advantage of the attackers enabled them to operate both in the air and on the ground at will, with little danger of discovery and still less of air attack. Foggy weather and movement at night made it possible to effect concentrations for attack by surprise during the entire series of operations.

The Government had been able to give but little assistance to the defenders on the north coast. They had sent a commander to take charge, but the Basques would not accept him. They had also sent some aircraft, but when the military commander was returned to them they stopped any further direct assistance. They expected, without doubt, that Bilbao would be able to defend itself for a much longer period than it did.

Instead they planned a great offensive at Madrid with the army of maneuver they had been training all winter.

Battle of Brunete, July 6-30, 1937

The object of this attack was probably two-fold: One was to disengage Madrid from the Insurgent investment and compel the withdrawal of the forces before the city by cutting or threatening their communications between Talavera and Toledo. The second was to draw reserves from the forces threatening Bilbao. It came too late to save Bilbao, although it delayed the attack on Santander, and failed to force an Insurgent withdrawal.

Three attacks were planned. The first was to be delivered south of the Escorial with the objective: Navalcarnero. The second launched from Villaverde and

Carabanchel and the high ground west of Carabanchel as [the] objective. The third in the Aranjuez area, if successful, would have forced the withdrawal of the Insurgents in the Jarama salient and would have relieved the Madrid-Valencia road from artillery fire. Had these attacks succeeded, all the main insurgent communications in the Madrid or Jarama salients would have been cut. These are: road, Madrid-San Martin-Avila, Madrid-Talavera, Madrid-Toledo.

In the main attack three army corps took part, the V and XVIII with the VI in support to the east. The III Corps attacked at Aranjuez and the II Corps at Villaverde. The corps consisted generally of the two divisions each of three brigades of three or four battalions. The infantry strength was thus about 15,000 men to a corps. Artillery support was probably about 12 batteries per corps. About 150 tanks supported the attack. The air force of about 180 planes worked in close support of the ground operations. The government had made great preparations for this attack. The troops had been training during the winter and spring. So much was hoped of it that the entire government came up from Valencia as spectators.

The main offensive fell to the air force, due to a lack among the ground forces of trained commanders, staffs and artillery, and to the low standard of training and discipline of all arms. The infantry showed itself incapable of maneuver. The tanks, being Russian, gave the usual trouble with mechanical defects. The untrained Spanish crews, fearful and undisciplined, failed to make best use of them; and the tactical handling was indifferent. The air force was much better trained and disciplined. This lack of balance resulted, in the battle, in an apparent tactical conception that the air force would pave the way with a vigorous offensive and the infantry would occupy the ground they had cleared.

The attack was preceded by an aerial bombardment lasting from 4:00 AM to 9:00 AM, July 6. On the Villaverde and Aranjuez fronts the attacks started at 3:00 PM. They were quickly stopped and never succeeded in accomplishing anything. On the northern sector between Valdemorillo and Villanueva del Pardillo, a break-through was made on a three and one-half mile front reaching to a depth of eleven miles. Brunete was captured. Villanueva de la Cañada fell at 10:00 PM after a two-hour aerial bombardment. The following day the Government forces attempted to widen the flanks of the salient. Their efforts were met by an aerial counter-offensive and counter-attack by local reserves.

Quijorna was captured on the 8th and Guadarrama River crossed to the east of Villanueva de la Cañada. Not until the 11th was Villanueva del Pardillo taken.

In the meantime the Insurgent aerial activity was increasing. A large number of Insurgent antiaircraft batteries were brought in close to the front, and under cover of air support and antiaircraft artillery, Insurgent reserves brought from the north by motor moved in to counterattack. Quijorna was retaken and the eastern flank of the salient reduced. In the salient itself, constant aerial actions had destroyed all ability and will of the Government forces to attack further. They were few roads and these were bombed constantly. It became difficult for the Government forces even to get water.

On the 14th the Government offensive seemed to have bogged down and the members of the Government who had come from Valencia to Madrid returned again to Valencia. Their greatest effort of the war had failed. It had gained a little ground at great cost. A relatively small number of Insurgent troops had stopped the maximum effort of the Government.

The attack was renewed by the Government a week later. During this attack they succeeded in enlarging the salient to a depth and width of ten miles. It was met again by Franco, first, by the transfer of masses of aircraft and antiaircraft artillery. Three hundred and twenty planes were counted in the air at one time. The subsequent movement and concentration of troops for a counteroffensive was thus protected. These attacked, supported by large aerial concentrations, and moved the lines half way back to where they had been when the offensive started.

Government losses were extremely heavy in this offensive. The Guadalajara victory had steamed them up into the semblance of an offensive spirit. The losses of Brunete killed this little flame for good. The International Brigades were wrecked as spearheads of the attacks and never recovered. The Government has shown that it lacked the leadership, especially in junior officers and noncommissioned officers, to lead and carry through an offensive operation. This winter they claim to be training an army of maneuver of four or five hundred thousand men. They claimed the same last winter. But, since Brunete, all their offensives have been ghost offensives, designed for propaganda purposes and nothing else. What would have been called a trench raid in the Great War is hailed as a great victory in Government Spain.

The Brunete battle and the threat to Zaragoza in August delayed the reduction of the north coast to such an extent that Franco was unable to concentrate for a major offensive before winter. Apparently he had planned two offensives toward Lerida and Zaragoza and Huesca. Floods in the river valleys stopped the operations and were followed by weather which made them impracticable. He now has blockaded the Mediterranean coast of the Government territory and probably hopes to force a surrender without major fighting before spring. His bombers have been active, bombing lines of communication to Madrid and between Barcelona and Valencia, and the wharves and warehouses at the latter place are bombed frequently. Russian help to the Government is being greatly lessened by activity of submarines and bombers and by their own needs in the far east. Prophecy is dangerous but one can conclude that the war, if it does not end by blockade this winter, will close shortly after Franco starts his next offensive.

Conclusions

THE DISCONTINUOUS FRONT

Four hundred thousand men on either side are spread along a battle line 780 miles in length; more than twice the extent of the Western front in France. This is required by the threat of mechanized and motorized forces. An army can have no flanks; it must extend to impassable barriers. Aircraft and motors make the defense of such a front possible. The first reaction to attack at some thinly-held point is supplied by the transfer of large air forces which counterattack the troops in the open and furnish protection to the counteroffensive force which moves up in motors close to the line. We can anticipate in the future, if not a continuous front, at least a discontinuous front. Every envelopment will have to break through somewhere initially and then must be prepared to meet an aerial counteroffensive.

THE COMPLEXITY OF WAR

War has become increasingly complex. Only professionals are competent to direct it. The day is past when a people's militia can stand against trained troops by trained officers. The Government of Spain, even with considerable help from foreign advisers, has shown itself incapable of training and directing an army capable of offensive action.

THE NEED FOR A TRAINED INFANTRY

Slightly trained troops, if sufficiently courageous, will hold in trenches. But such troops are incapable of offensive action and maneuver. The Insurgents in the early stages of the war were relatively heavily equipped with planes and motorized equipment. The lack of infantry was glaring at this time. The slowness of Franco's operations can be ascribed primarily to [the] lack of a sufficient number of infantry.

ROADS AND RAILROADS

First class all-weather roads have assumed equal importance with railroads. The direction of operations follows the communications nets. Franco's front follows the rail net, but Madrid has been supplied for over a year, principally by a single road 110 miles in length. It is possible, in operations where larger scale bombing of railroads is undertaken, that roads, being more difficult to block, will be of greater importance than rails.

COMPOSITION OF THE AIR FORCES

The Government air force of about 485 planes has a ratio of about two to one in favor of pursuit. Relatively few observation and ground-attack planes are used. Pursuit and bombardment carry out observation and ground-attack missions with equal ease as well as their special tasks. The biplane pursuit is supplied with bomb racks and is an offensive ground-attack plane. The Insurgent air force of over 700 planes has a proportion of about two bombardment to one pursuit. It also has very few observation and ground-attack ships. However, it should be noted that both sides are convinced of the importance of ground attack and would like special equipment for the purpose. It appears that the American concentration of this form of air action is well justified.

BOMBARDMENT OF COMMUNICATIONS

Communications have proved more difficult to interrupt permanently by bombing than had been believed. Franco's rail net, close to the lines, functions. Trains move at night. Destruction is quickly repaired. Roads are even more difficult to interrupt. The Madrid supply road has been bombed constantly for a year and, though thousands of crippled trucks line the highway, supplies in sufficient quantity still reach Madrid. Trucks are chased into the ditches by pursuit ships and bridges are bombed and knocked out; but temporary ones keep the traffic moving.

POLITICAL BOMBARDMENT

The commander who orders the bombardment of the opposing capital is in reality issuing two orders: he orders his own capital to be bombed also. Retaliation is always the answer to such bombing. Government aviation bombed Salamanca: the expected bombardment of Valencia took place within three days. This was quickly appreciated in Spain, and practically all bombing operations are now conducted against legitimate military objectives.

AERIAL ATTACK OF TROOP MOVEMENTS

Mass movements by either foot or motor have proved impossible in daylight. An Insurgent regiment, in the early days of the war, marching south from Huesca to Zaragoza, was decimated by aerial bombardment. At Guadalajara motor columns were paralyzed. Movements are made most safely in small groups by motor in the daytime, and by motor at night. Since the early days of the war there have been practically no foot-marches made in Spain. Everyone goes by motor.

GROUND COOPERATION

If we have to conclude that bombardment of political and economic objectives have been a failure in Spain, and that communications still function in spite of aerial attack, on the other side of the picture, aerial cooperation with ground operations has proven vital and far more effective than anticipated. The capture of the whole north coast of Spain was made possible by the coordination of air action, artillery, tanks, and infantry. The usual procedure for an attack, as developed after a year of war, is an artillery preparation of an hour or hour and a half, followed by a thirty minute aerial bombardment of infantry and artillery positions and reserves. After that the tanks and infantry go forward together. Any strong points that hold out are reduced by a further call for aviation. The results of these methods at Bilbao, Santander and Gijon, were an advance day-by-day, except as interrupted by weather, strictly according to a schedule worked out at the beginning of operations.

In the defense, aircraft are quickly shifted and the first counterattack is by airplane. The attacking troops in the open have proved themselves extremely vulnerable. In the Brunete offensive they took cover in the villages and stopped fighting. Where men are well entrenched, the action of aviation has not proved effective. It takes the combined action of all arms to drive them out. The morale effect of efficient air support has proved as important as that of artillery support.

BOMBARDMENT OF AIRDROMES

Our military attaché estimated from trustworthy sources that the Government losses of 120 planes from April to August, 1937, were divided: 65 lost on the ground by bombardment of airdromes, and 55 lost in the air by aerial combat and antiaircraft artillery. During a period of fifteen days of the Brunete battle, when the Government air force was used principally for ground cooperation, it performed 23 missions on airdromes. Pursuit airdromes are habitually shoved close up, from fifteen to forty miles, from the front. One squadron was forced to change its airdrome three times in one day. Bombardment of airdromes has led to extreme measures of camouflage and deception: dummy airdromes with dummy planes on them; light houses on wheels which are rolled out onto the field when it is not in use, etc. Planes are painted green and scattered among the trees. The necessary dispersion of airplanes on the fields has required more time to take off than we count on at present.

PURSUIT VS. BOMBARDMENT
Pursuit has shown that it is still capable of besting bombardment when it meets it. At the present time a large number of modern planes are in use in Spain. The German Messerschmitt pursuit has a speed of 310 mph; the Russian I-16, a speed of 290. Modern bombers with speeds of from 230 to 270 mph are in use. The best defense of the bombers is their speed. In spite of considerable armament they all have been found to have blind angles which they can be attacked.

PURSUIT PROTECTION OF BOMBARDMENT
In the bombing missions over the front lines, bombardment is usually given pursuit protection. The reasons are that they are apt to meet defending pursuit in direct support, and also that these missions last for some time and the nearby pursuit airdromes permit occasional interception. For bombardment of distant rear areas, no pursuit protection is furnished. Interception has proved impossible, even when the warning net has functioned efficiently. Bombers are able to drop their bombs and be gone before defensive pursuit can take off and get altitude. Valencia gave up all use of defensive pursuit last April and now depends solely on antiaircraft artillery.

ACCURACY OF BOMBING
Bombing accuracy from high altitudes has been very disappointing. In the early phases of the war, Loyalist planes aiming at the Insurgents on the Spanish bank of the Bidassoa (boundary river) blew up a restaurant on the French bank in the village of Biriatou. None of the bombs fell on the Spanish side. The joke at that time was that the Government could not even hit Spain with their bombs. In rear areas large amounts of antiaircraft artillery have forced bombing operations up to ten thousand feet and higher and have decreased their effectiveness.

IMPORTANCE OF AIR ADVANTAGE
Aerial cooperation has become so important that offensive operations are apt to fail unless the attacker has air advantage and can maintain it. The Insurgent successes on the north coast and their successful counteroffensives at Brunete were made possible by air advantage. The Insurgents drove 8,000 Catalonians out of Majorca after they had made a successful landing, almost solely by aerial action. The landing

force had no air support at the time. The Italian defeat at Guadalajara was made possible by their lack of air advantage. Air advantage will fluctuate. Both quality and quantity of planes is required. In the latter part of the Brunete battles the Government air force had worn itself out by constant operation. They had made as many as 8 sorties a day at times. Although their equipment was superior in quality at that time, they did not have the opportunity necessary to maintain air advantage.

WEATHER AND AIR OPERATIONS

On the north coast, ground operations stopped to wait for weather in which the air force could operate, so valuable was their assistance. This reverses the procedure usually imagined wherein ground operations are theoretically conducted in bad weather to prevent interference and observation by aviation.

DEFENSE AGAINST AIR ATTACK BY TROOPS

The Spanish leaders seem to have been unable to induce their troops to deliver small arms fire on airplanes. It is easy from where we sit to scorn them as incompetent and to point to our 29th Infantry at Fort Benning and its accomplishments in defending itself from air attack. However, it is not wise to have too much assurance on the matter. It may well be that firing back at a 230-mile-an-hour ship which is firing at you from four machine guns and dropping high explosives all around you is a far different matter than firing at a towed sleeve in safety.

ANTIAIRCRAFT ARTILLERY

Antiaircraft has proved effective far beyond the expectations of everyone concerned. The 3" and 88-mm cannon have forced bombing operations to high altitudes. The 20-mm automatic cannon has been very effective at medium and low altitudes. To what extent the failure of bombardment of the docks at Valencia and of communications bottlenecks is due to antiaircraft artillery is not known exactly, but it is known that these objectives have been bombed constantly for a year. Air Commodore Charleton, of the British Royal Air Force, said, after a visit to Insurgent Spain, that the 88-mm German gun would pip off a bomber at 12,000 feet almost every time in the first three or four salvos. Reports in military circles in France early in the war credited the antiaircraft artillery with the destruction of 70 out of 100 Government planes destroyed during the early period. Even the less effective materiel at the disposal of the Government has forced the Insurgent bombers to fly high and has also made them undertake much of the bombing of objectives in the rear at night. Valencia, the seat of the Government, gave up pursuit protection six or eight months ago and since that time has depended on antiaircraft artillery exclusively for protection.

FIELD ARTILLERY

Field artillery has been inefficiently used. On the Government side this has been the result of their lack of competent technicians as well as their tactical ignorance. They seem to have asked their air force to do much that a capable artillery would accomplish. The Insurgent artillery was used very effectively in the reduction of the north coast. The capture of Toledo resulted from a seven-day artillery bombardment which by itself caused the Government forces to withdraw. The most important artillery lesson to be learned is the need for capable, well trained artillerymen. In the year and a half of war the Government has failed to make up for this initial lack.

TANKS

Tanks have been used in too small numbers to furnish conclusive lessons as to their effectiveness. In general, whenever attacking tanks have been met with antitank guns (120-mm and upward), they were either destroyed or immobilized before they had accomplished their aims. Without these means of defense they have been usually successful. Tank obstacles are effective. Apparently tank mines have not been used.

In April, 1937, when the Government first received a large number of Russian tanks, an attack was planned to the west of Madrid. Tanks were to be used independently and break through the position with the infantry coming after to occupy it. The Government was so confident that they invited all the correspondents up to see the great victory. Unfortunately, their planned operation had not been kept secret. Fifty tanks started up Garabitas Hill. Twenty-two fell into a tank trap, a long, wide, deep trench which had been dug and covered with trees and brush, and were captured. At other points on the line they broke through the outposts but were met with antitank fire. This together with mechanical troubles accounted for another 14 of them. Fourteen of the fifty which started out to win the war returned. This can be considered as an example of independent tank action against a well prepared defense. After this time tanks were never used independently. They accompany the infantry and are preceded by aerial and artillery preparation. In the Insurgent offensives in the north they have been used very effectively in spite of the rugged terrain. They reduce machine-gun nests that artillery missed. The infantry needs all the help it can get in offensive operations and tanks in close cooperation with the infantry have both a tremendous morale and physical value.

The Government tank actions have been greatly hindered by the poor training of the Spaniards. Many tanks were lost through mechanical troubles before they reached the battle. How much of this was deliberate is unknown, but it is suspected that cowardice played a large part. Tank crews need to be men of high courage and mechanical ability. The Insurgent tanks, manned by Germans and Italians, may have given much better results due to this fact.

Russian tanks are modeled on the English Vickers-Armstrong of 1930, with a larger engine. They have two types of turrets, one carrying two machine guns and the other carrying a 45-mm cannon and a machine gun. The general opinion of observers is that even light tanks will have to carry a cannon large enough for antitank action and armor sufficient to prevent penetration from small arms and machine guns. This would require about 7/8" armor and a tank weighing about 10 tons.

TRAINING, MORALE AND DISCIPLINE

Experienced leadership in the lower grades has been one of the most serious deficiencies of the Government army. With ample time to form a disciplined and competent force, they lacked a sufficient cadre, and have failed to do so. One reason is that most of the educated class are on Franco's side. Those caught in government territory were killed. In the navy, most of the officers were shot or else their hands, and feet, were tied and they were thrown into the sea, and many were washed up on the French beaches. The Government started with decided naval superiority. Very quickly the incompetent crews had the navy out of order; they could not fire the guns, and superiority at sea passed to Franco. Now there is no Government navy at sea.

Russian advisers of the Government introduced the system of political commissars. The commissar has his own chain of command; he spies and reports on the commander, lectures the men on the communist faith, and also theoretically maintains their morale and procures their food. On the other side of the unfortunate government commanders sit their Russian military advisers. These have their own chain of command, the channels going directly up to the Russian adviser of the Minister of War. So, officers without authority, constantly spied upon and hindered in every decision, interrupted in the exercise of disciplinary authority, have little chance of developing a cohesive army. The Spaniard, proud, individualistic and indolent, can be a splendid soldier. In the past he has marched over most of Europe. Franco is making him one again by use of ancient military standards of discipline and training. On the government side the Russian system is effectively preventing the development of an army.

The Government army for a long time was a collection of the various party armies. An Anarchist force held the Aragon front, a communist army the Madrid front, etc. The political commanders refused to cooperate with each other. Each claimed the other was favored in the distribution of supplies. All brands of political faith attempt to proselyte among the soldiers, each hoping to have control of the army, and thereby the government, when the war is over. At the present time the communists control about fifty percent of the army, and about ninety percent of the political commissars are communists.

Franco has been almost constantly on the offensive and has been generally successful except for the Italian setback at Guadalajara. The Government force has shown itself incapable of offensive action. Troops with amateur commanders and amateur staffs cannot maneuver, they can only stumble. The Government soldier contents himself with the *no pasaran* attitude. He is satisfied to stay in his trenches. Out of them, he seeks cover at the first sign of resistance. It has been many years since there has been a chance to realize the helplessness of untrained soldiers, officers, and staffs. The World War started with trained forces opposed to each other. In Spain a small trained force was able to chase the untrained militia at will. In a year and a half, the Government, lacking a trained nucleus, has been unable to build an army capable of offensive action.

PROPAGANDA AND CENSORSHIP

No discussion of the Spanish war is complete without taking note of propaganda. The Government, Russian advised, have shown themselves superior in this respect. Russians sit at the elbows of French, British and American correspondents, and censor their dispatches. Russian-directed propaganda floods all Spain. Stories of atrocities fill the people with fear of surrender. Fake victories keep up the civil and military morale. Defeats, when they have to be admitted, are labeled strategic retreats. Every Insurgent victory is followed by a Government victory in the press.

Loud speakers are taken into the trenches and there they blare to the opposing soldiers: "Kill your officers. You are cannon fodder to protect their fine estates. Why do you fight your comrades who are defending their homes? Desert and join your brothers. Here you will have plenty of food. We have liberty and democracy". Back comes the answer from Insurgent speakers: "Communists have deceived you.

You are not Spaniards. Tools of Russian thieves, lay down your arms. Stop fighting for Russian liars". And so it goes, night after night. Cities are bombarded with pamphlets. It is believed that Insurgent propaganda had a great deal of influence in arousing the Anarchist outbreak in Barcelona. It was suppressed with the death of 1400 and 600 injured.

Propaganda is also directed toward the outside world. Each endeavors to convince the world that its side is the just one and that the other commits unbelievable atrocities, although atrocities have been bad enough to require no exaggeration. Take the bombing of Guernica: actually it was not bombed; it was burned by the Asturians when they withdrew. G.L. Steer of the *New York Times* sent out the horrible news:

"First, small parties of airplanes threw heavy bombs and hand grenades all over the town, choosing area after area in orderly fashion. Next came the fighting machines which swooped to machine-gun those who had run in panic from the dug-outs, some of which had already been penetrated by the 1000-pound bombs which made a hole twenty feet deep. Many of these people were killed as they ran. The object of this move apparently was to drive the population underground again, for next, as many as twelve bombers appeared at a time dropping heavy and incendiary bombs upon the ruins.

"The rhythm of this bombing of an open town was therefore logical—first hand grenades and heavy bombs to stampede the population, then machine-gunning to drive them below, next heavy and incendiary bombs to wreck houses and burn them over the victims".

Such nonsense needs no comment before this audience. But it was believed all over the world. Preachers made their sermons on it. Though the entire story has been proved an invention, it has had an enormous influence in prejudicing the democratic countries against Franco.[5]

Propaganda is a weapon of war. The radio and the airplane have given the means to distribute it to the enemy as well as to your own soldiers and civil population. In Government Spain it has maintained the civil will. In spite of real hardships, the civil population has had its will to continue maintained by propaganda. It also has accomplished the miracle of gaining American sympathy for a Government which has assassinated 300,000 people behind the lines. Although the propaganda in Spain is fantastic and would have no effect on an educated public, material suitable to the population for which it is intended would undoubtedly be just as effective in other countries.

THE POWER OF THE DEFENSIVE

The defensive is still increasing in power. The increase in automatic arms requires almost complete destruction of the opposing trench system. The air forces of the defender can be moved in a few hours and start an aerial counteroffensive. Motors, used both tactically and strategically, rush reserves to the threatened points. Before the World War a school of thought in France held that the increase of fire power would rebound to the benefit of the offensive. Throughout the world, now, military men have included to believe that mechanization and motorization would be of the greatest assistance to the offensive. As it has turned out, mechanization, motorization and air power have benefited the defensive more than the offensive.

[This lecture was not signed.—Ed. Note]

7

The Teruel Campaign
(December 1937–February 1938)

"The Teruel series of engagements constitute the most important battle in which both sides have engaged since the Brunete campaign . . ."

Col. Stephen O. Fuqua,
1938

Over what should have been a respite from war and a joyous Christmas season of December–early January, and even extending through the cold and particularly snowy February of 1938, one of the most important military campaigns of the civil war took place, and when it was over, the nation wondered if now Spain might be closer than ever to the end of what had become a long, weary, and protracted war. It had all the elements of high drama: a well-thought-out Republican military plan, initial success for the Republicans, many large and dramatic events, counterattacks by the Nationalists who were initially knocked off their game, and much second-guessing of Franco's decision to divert his attention to Teruel, where ultimately he won the battle. Military lines proved important, serving as a buffer between central Spain and the eastern zones of the Republic, the Levante, and Catalonia. The community and province of Teruel is located in southern Aragon, and before the civil war it was a poor agricultural area. The Nationalists controlled the northern end of the province, the Republicans the eastern and southern ends. Its division between the two sides and its physical location between central and coastal Spain ensured that at some point it would be a major point of contention.

The dispatches below describe in considerable detail the events of December through February. However, keep in mind that this was a large initiative, not always made clear by Fuqua and others as they focused on the details of the events. The Republicans launched their offensive against the city of Teruel on December 15, 1937, with some 100,000 troops. All accounts of the campaign speak about how cold the period was and the extensive snowfalls that played havoc with both armies. Losses on both sides were staggering. Franco's appeared to be about 14,000 dead, another 16,000 wounded, and another 17,000 ill (from frostbite, among other ailments). The Republicans suffered casualties of each type and probably exceeded those of the Nationalists by 50 percent.

The last dispatch in this chapter opines if the war will soon end as a result of this victory. The Nationalists followed up Teruel with campaigns in Aragon and the Levante in March 1938, cutting off Catalonia from central Spain. The Italians sent more assistance to the Nationalists, while people inside and outside Spain began to wonder if the Republic could hold out much longer.

The Americans' reporting on this campaign was their best to date as measured by the speed of the analysis and volume of details. What is not published here and remains in the files as part of the specific dispatches partially reproduced in this chapter are the translated daily summaries of Republican and Nationalist bulletins, which, more than for previous campaigns, were the most accurate to date on the daily details. A full reading of those would have made this chapter much longer but reflect the back-and-forth motions of the campaign over the ten-some-week period. The American reporting is enriched by the fact that Fuqua visited the Teruel sector while the campaign was under way, providing personal insight that alone would have been of sufficient quality and importance to justify the publication of this book. It is not to be missed.

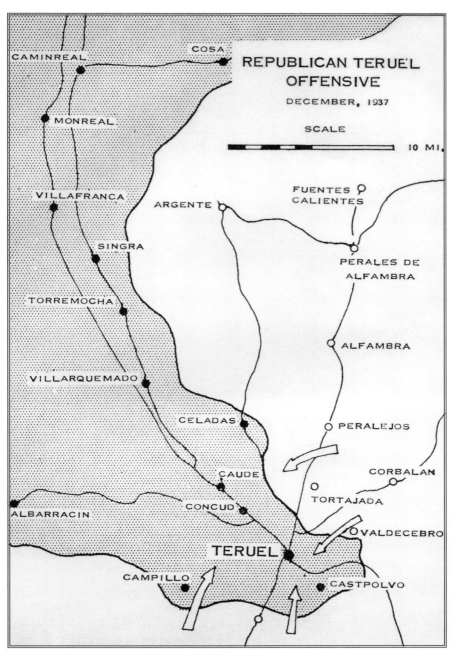

Republican Teruel Offensive, December 1937. [Verle B. Johnson, *Legions of Babel*
(© 1967, The Pennsylvania State University Press, University Park, Pennsylvania 16802),
128. Reprinted by permission of Pennsylvania State University Press.]

(Madrid) Barcelona
December 18, 1937
Secretary of State
Military Attaché's Report:

Government troops concentrated in first instance for defensive missions on east front taking advantage of long delay of expected Rebel drive—augmented by International Brigade units including American and English battalions shifted from central front—launched a major offensive December 15 to sever Teruel Zaragoza communications and capture Teruel. Government communiqué today announces first phase of movement successful claiming capture of Villastar, Campillo, San Blas and Concud, thus completely encircling Teruel cutting off its communications with Zaragoza.

Thurston

(Madrid) Barcelona
December 22, 1937
Secretary of State
Military Attaché's Report:

Government announces Teruel entered last evening by Loyal troops after seven day offensive of eighteenth and twentieth corps augmented by units of International Brigades of Carabineros and Asaltos numbering about 50,000. Cold and bad weather conditions extremely hard on both ground and air troops. Government aviation seemed superior in both independent and cooperative missions including reconnaissance bombardments and attacks against rebel troops and supply concentrations and especially against troops advancing to the front. The success of this offensive should have a beneficial morale effect though it is too early to judge its military importance. However, but slight Barcelona enthusiasm is noticeable.

Thurston

Barcelona
January 3, 1938
Secretary of State
Military Attaché's Report:

The battle for Teruel entering third phase. During the first phase December 15 to 29 Government successfully advanced entering city December 21 but was unable to completely dislodge rebels. From December 29 to January 2 Nationalists heavily counter attacked and on December 31 claimed to have relieved besieged garrison and to have inflicted severe losses on Government troops.

Third and present phase characterized by terrific fighting under adverse weather conditions, by increased use of artillery and aviation, by rebel determination to retake lost territory and by use of the less enthusiastic tone of Government communiqués.

On December 27 it was reported and later confirmed that Government troop concentrations were taking place vicinity Alcaniz. The Fifteenth International Brigade was then located near Alcorisa where it had been since December 16. Reliable contact reported in event of continued success at Teruel that Zaragoza was to have been next Government objective. However, on December 31 the Eleventh and Fifteenth International Brigades moved to Teruel sector.

Thurston

Barcelona   No. 6755
January 12, 1938

[The text below appears to be several dispatches written at different times but all submitted together. It is not clear if Fuqua wrote all of these, although they were submitted under his name. Most of the text, if not all, was, however. Large portions not substantive to the story or redundant from earlier reports (e.g., aircraft used in the war) have not been reproduced below.—Ed. Note]

The Spanish Situation, January 4, 1938

I entered Spain on December 9 and remained there until December 22, during which time I visited the following places by automobile: Salamanca, Toledo, Madrid front, University City, Merida, Sevilla, Jeres, Valladolid and Burgos, all of which are in the possession of the Nationalist government. Salamanca, where I spent about four days, is the seat of the civil Government, and the Army General Headquarters is at Burgos.

MILITARY TACTICS

Generally speaking the only troops actually available for attack among the Nationalists are the Tercio (the Foreign Legion), the Moors and the regular army. The requetes and Falangistas, due to insufficient training, have been very little used as shock troops but it is likely that they will be used more in the future as their training improves.

As far as it was possible for me to observe, the spirit of the officers and men is excellent. They are well equipped and armed and their ration is if anything more abundant than that of the British troops on the western front during the World War. I talked to officers and men both on the Madrid front and on the rear and was much impressed with the offensive spirit they displayed. Everyone to whom I spoke was optimistic and all expressed the desire to take part in the attack then being prepared and seemed confident, perhaps overconfident, that the end of the war was in sight. They seemed to have no doubt whatsoever of their superiority in every way to the Government troops. This was previous to the attack on Teruel but I doubt very much if this has greatly affected their morale.

The Nationalists claim that they now have an army of some 700,000 men and I observed large numbers of recruits drilling in various parts of the country. I am inclined, however, to think that this estimate of 700,000 is perhaps somewhat exaggerated.

It is reported that the projected Nationalist attacks were to have been made at Huesca to the north, at Guadalajara near Madrid and possibly towards Almeria in the south. The purpose of the Huesca attack was to cut off Government territory from the French frontier, through which it was receiving the greater part of its supplies. Due to the nature of the terrain, which is very mountainous and easily defended, I am convinced that this attack could not be successfully carried out in the winter. The attack at Guadalajara was to have been made by the Italian troops at the special request of Mussolini in order to retrieve the Italians' previous defeat.

METHOD OF ATTACK

The Nationalists in attacking use artillery barrage though with fewer guns than on the western front during the World War, and infantry attack by infiltration, similar to the method used in France towards the end of the World War. On the other hand, the Nationalists report that the Government troops attack in mass—in the Russian system—and that anything gained is paid for by disproportionately heavy losses. If this is true it would indicate that the morale of the Government troops is low and that they lack sufficient leadership among subordinate officers.

Nationalist officers with whom I talked, stated that the Red plans were always excellently drawn but that they generally failed because of poor execution on the part of subordinates. One Nationalist officer who had been at the French École de Guerre stated that the plans showed strong evidence of having been drawn up by French superior officers and that they followed closely the theories prevalent there while he was a student. This may be taken for what it is worth.

The Nationalists claim that the only efficient troops that the Reds now have are in the International Brigade, but that the Red militia is so badly organized and led that it is of very little value, though not lacking in courage.

Teruel is a pocket extending into the Red lines and was the nearest point to Valencia held by the Nationalists. It seems obvious that the attack by the Reds was made at this point because they feared further advance by the Nationalists in the direction of Valencia. While completely surrounded, the Nationalists claim that the town itself has not surrendered and they are counter attacking in force. The Nationalist plan of attack was disrupted by the Governmental attack on Teruel, but will doubtless be resumed as soon as Teruel has been relieved.

The Nationalist front, unlike that of the World War, is not a continuous line of trenches but a succession of strong points which cover the intervening ground. Apparently there is only one line of defense. Remembering the series of defense lines in the western part of France I found this somewhat surprising in view of the fact that the part of the front which I visited had been held for some time. Then I asked the captain in command what would happen if the Government troops broke through their first line, his only reply was: "They won't".

PERSONAL OBSERVATION

The most impressive thing to anyone acquainted with conditions in France during the World War in Nationalist Spain is the small number of troops in the rear areas. At Salamanca, the seat of Government, there was practically no evidence of military occupation at all and there were very few troops in the streets. The same applies to Sevilla, where practically all the troops I saw were obviously new recruits with new equipment.

During an 800 kilometer drive in an automobile only very occasional small groups of troops were met with and the railroads, roads and bridges were apparently not guarded at all during the day. At night near the front lines, automobiles were not allowed to pass, but during the day they circulated quite freely and were only stopped by civil guards who were usually satisfied with a word from the driver that he was on official business.

Work in the fields was apparently going on as usual and the olive oil factories near Sevilla and the wineries and distilleries at Jeres, which I visited, were carrying on their work as if the country were at peace. Food was abundant and cheap everywhere and beyond the presence of an occasional man in uniform there was no evidence that the country was at war. Prisoners of war working in the rear areas, of which I saw large numbers at Toledo and Sevilla, were dressed in ordinary civilian clothes and were not heavily guarded.

This I found surprising as apparently it would have been very easy for them to escape because it would have been impossible to distinguish them from other civilians. The Spaniards told me it was not necessary to guard them heavily or clothe them differently from the others because they were satisfied as they were.

In the early part of the war, due to the fact that all the ammunition factories were at Barcelona in Governmental territory, the Nationalists were obliged to import practically all the ammunition they used. It is now said however, that they have set up factories in Spain for the manufacture of their own ammunition and that in a very short time they will be self-sufficient in this respect.

At the Madrid front at Carabanchel, which I visited, the Nationalist positions completely dominate not only the positions of their opponents, but the city of Madrid itself. All the high ground is occupied by them and with field glasses it is easy to see people walking in the streets of the city.

An attack started from this point should enable the Nationalists to take a considerable part of the city with no great difficulty, but this would naturally involve the destruction of a great part of Madrid with house to house fighting, and they believe the terrain gained would be disproportionate to the destruction and losses entailed. Furthermore, the Nationalists claim that, while the taking of Madrid would have a great morale effect, the fact that the Government is no longer there would prevent this from having the effect of ending the war, which was the main purpose of the original attack on the city when made. In addition they say that Madrid is more of a liability than an asset to the Government, as its possession necessitates the feeding of a million and a half people, which, if the city were taken, would fall on the Nationalists.

The main purpose of the Nationalists now is to cut off Governmental territory from the French frontier, through which it is claimed they receive large quantities of war materiel and supplies, and to decisively defeat the opposing army. The cutting off of supplies from France and the defeat of the enemy forces in the field will, the Nationalists believe, automatically bring about the surrender of Barcelona and Madrid, and this result they hope to obtain by their next offensive.

Refugees from Barcelona, of whom I met a number in Sevilla, said that they had heard from relatives and friends in Barcelona that the city was completely demoralized and would surrender at once if Franco's offensive in the north were successful. Some of them were so optimistic as to believe that they would be home by February or March at the latest. A report was current among them that Barcelona authorities, because of their dissatisfaction with the Valencia Government, with which there has been considerable friction, had offered to surrender to France if he would grant them autonomy and that he had replied that he would accept only unconditional surrender. One gentleman from Barcelona, who spends a great deal of his time in the United States, said he hoped to sail on the *Saturnia* with me on February 2nd after he had an opportunity to visit his home.

Military Situation
THE GOVERNMENT OFFENSIVE
From information now available the Government's plan for the encircling and capture of Teruel was as follows:

> Three division columns were launched simultaneously:
>> Column 1. From the line south of Rubiales with Campillo as the objective.
>> Column 2. From the line north of Villel with Villaster as the objective.
>> Column 3. From the line near Tortajada westward to the road fork just south of Caude or Caudete.

The object of this movement was to gain the line—which had previously been selected for defense. Simultaneously with the advance—three division attacks were launched in an encircling movement against the city. Considering these divisions at a strength [of] 9,000 men plus the forces of the reserves, it is estimated that the plan called for the employment of some 70,000 men. The propaganda issued by the Government that the concentrations for this action were for the purpose of resisting an expected rebel drive had its effect—producing even here in Barcelona a complete surprise.

It is thought that the plan was brilliantly conceived and masterfully executed. It stands as a tribute to the genius of General [Vicente] Rojo, the Chief of Staff of the Republican Army, who finally gained Mr. Prieto's approval after the latter had opposed the project. Mr. Prieto argued against the plan on the grounds that the probable losses incurred in storming the Teruel defenses would outweigh the importance of the victory if attained. However, General Rojo convinced him that the plan could be initiated as a surprise attack and that the gaining of the defensive position would permit the encircling of the city and then from this cordon a gradual reduction of the interior defenses and that as a result of this procedure the losses would be small.

The success of the attack can be well attributed to the surprise factor. This statement is further fortified by an opinion expressed by a correspondent with the Franco forces who, in conversation with the undersigned, said of the attack, "The reaction on the Nationalists was STUPEFYING SURPRISE" [Fuqua's emphasis.—Ed. Note].

The plan contemplated the use of Spanish troops only, the International Brigades having been concentrated in the Montalban-Alcaniz region. It is understood that this concentration had in mind the launching of an attack in the direction of Calamocha, however, this did not materialize as in all probability it was called off after the Nationalists initiated their major counterattack against Teruel.

The Government offensive against Teruel began on December 15th. The following is a summary of the daily communiqués issued by the Ministry of National Defense during the first days of the drive showing the progress of the operations with additional comments and data obtained by this office from other sources.

Dec. 15. "At 3:45 PM the Galiana position was taken. At 5:00 PM the Concud village, and dominating heights north and northwest of the same, together with San Blas and other important positions were occupied. At 7:00 PM the Campillo village fell".

A glance at the map shows that during the first day of the operations the columns which through surprise attacks broke the Nationalist lines north and southwest of Teruel practically attained the isolation of the city. The Government communiqué does not mention that the infiltrations which made possible this important advance were attained, according to Nationalist reports, during the previous night and early morning hours of the day. Once the front was broken, the large force prepared by the Government, supported by abundant artillery and masses of aviation, succeeded in overwhelming the resistance of the Nationalists who fought desperately to protect the encirclement of Teruel.

Dec. 16. "In addition to taking Height 1076 (west of Teruel) and other points, the positions reached the day before were consolidated by our troops".

Throughout this day the government forces were on the defensive and successfully repulsed all counterattacks of the Nationalists who received reinforcements brought from nearby back areas. The Government aviation controlled the air and bombed and strafed effectively enemy concentrations and the reinforcements being rushed to his aid.

Dec. 17. "The important positions known as the Muela de Villastar and Las Hoyuelas fell (8:40 AM). During the remainder of the morning and early afternoon, important positions in the western vicinity of Teruel were taken".

In view of the failure of the Nationalist counterattacks and notwithstanding the fact that the cold weather and snow continued even greater than in proceeding days, the Government forces continued their advance, now against the city, taking important positions southwest of same. At the same time, another column of Government troops advanced in the direction of the Albarracin Sierra in order to protect and consolidate the encirclement of Teruel. The Government aviation continued controlling the air and, when weather permitted, bombed and ground strafed enemy concentrations.

Dec. 18. "During the morning, La Granja and other positions in the south sector were taken. In the afternoon, the enemy resistance at Galiana and Muela de Teruel, the latter a height of great strategic value, was finally reduced".

Throughout the day the main efforts of the Government troops were directed toward taking the strong enemy positions, which were surrounded in the rearguard, between the exterior line Campillo-Concud-Celada heights and the city.

Dec. 19. "Escandon Pass-Valencia-Teruel Road and Pancho Villa and other positions fell to our forces while the Villastar column reached the outskirts of Teruel. In the afternoon, the village of Castoalbo, Castellar and several important positions in the outskirts of Teruel, including the cemetery, were taken".

The fall of Escandon Pass and the progress of the south column advancing from Villastar placed the Government troops in a position to initiate the assault on Teruel which was launched in the evening and gave them the possession of some buildings on the outskirts of the city.

Dec. 20. "After consolidating the position taken from the enemy at Escondon Pass and south of Teruel, a general attack on the city was launched. Our troops continued their progress in the outskirts of the city and outflanked it on the east gaining several buildings in this sector. The enemy troops, charged with the mission of breaking the encirclement of Teruel, made several desperate attacks but failed to gain any ground".

The salient point of the day was the repeated efforts by the Nationalists to break the encirclement of Teruel. Franco's troops attacked in three columns, aggregating an estimated strength of some 20,000 men. Although they initially attained some advantage, they were finally stopped, on account of the fire superiority of the enemy and the heavy losses sustained, at Celada heights and in front of Concud and Campillos.

Dec. 21. "In the early afternoon, the Villaespesa village, where an isolated enemy force resisted, was taken. At the same time that the pressure on the capital was continued, our troops energetically repulsed several strong attacks of the enemy columns endeavoring to rescue the beleaguered Teruel garrison. These attacks were directed against the Celada heights and Villalba Baja. The enemy, notwithstanding his strength and display of artillery fire, failed to attain his objectives and was repulsed with heavy losses. While this fighting was going on, our artillery fired intensely upon the enemy quarters within Teruel causing great damage. The day's fighting ended with the entrance of the republican troops in Teruel".

After the new failure to break the Government lines, the Nationalist troops, evidently being convinced of their numerical inferiority, refrained for several days from launching any major attack, pending the arrival of reinforcements. Although the taking of Teruel was officially announced by the government, the Nationalists still dominated the principal buildings in the old part of the city, where a most obstinate and heroic defense was being made.

The Nationalist official communiqués and reports admitted in more or less veiled terms that during the first three days of the Government offensive, their troops, "overpowered by a Government force of some 50,000 men, supported by about 200 tanks, abundant artillery and masses of aviation, had been forced to relinquish some ground west of Teruel as a result of which the city was practically isolated". On December 22, when the Government press and radio were jubilant over the capture of Teruel, the Nationalist radio stations and official communiqués strongly denied the occupation of the city by the enemy, a fact which was not admitted as it was claimed "that the garrison was in possession of the main buildings and would continue the resistance until the approaching rescuing columns now en route to Teruel could arrive".

From a comparison of Government and Nationalist communiqués it was clear that the latter were considerably more laconic and purposely misleading with a view to prevent the public from knowing the progress made by the loyalists who had assailed Teruel from all sides and had finally entered its outskirts and the town itself at several points. This Nationalist attitude of concealing as long as possible unfavorable developments of the campaign, in the hope that their troops might later reestablish their positions, may be taken as an indication that they are not too confident of the morale of their people. This reluctance of Franco's headquarters in admitting military reverses has been observed throughout the campaign, a policy which might react most unfavorably to the Nationalist cause should they suffer a severe defeat.

The following extracts from a statement made by the Ministry of National Defense a few days after the capture of Teruel are considered of great interest and importance in connection with the Teruel offensive:

"The military operations just conducted by the East Army on the Teruel Front have attracted the attention of the military experts who are surprised at the successful developments of the offensive and the results attained.

"The planning and preparation of the offensive, which involved large masses of men and materiel, required absolute secrecy. Daring and rapidity in the execution were also essential. These requisites were completely attained. The enemy never learned of our preparations and the tactical and strategical surprise was complete from which great saving of lives for our forces resulted. The rapidity reached in the execution was remarkable. One division reached its objective, distance 12 km. from its point of departure, within 3 hours. Two columns leaving their bases 20 km. apart effected their concentration at the designated place within the time schedule issued. Thus after 12 hours of fighting the two forces charged with the main attack had broken the enemy front along a zone of 5 km. wide and advanced 12 km. in depth establishing contact on the designated line. All this was accomplished with only some 300 casualties.

"Within the large occupied zone there are four villages—Concud, San Blas, La Guea and Campillo—in addition to many isolated buildings, all well fortified. The Popular Army selected the lines of the least resistance and effected infiltrations advancing 10 kms. into enemy territory and leaving in the rearguard and flanks enemy centers of resistance which later were reduced. At Campillo 200 prisoners (among them 5 officers) were captured and at Concud and San Blas, 150 prisoners. Furthermore, 2 batteries of artillery were taken.

"Simultaneously with the encircling of Teruel another column attacked from the south, broke the enemy lines and advanced in the direction of the city.

"To cooperate in the offensive, our lines from Campillo to Cerro Gorde (Celanas sector) launched a general attack forming a fire front of 90 kms. This general attack gave us the possession of several important positions where formerly our minor surprise attacks had proven unsuccessful. Thus our victory now is a motive of pride for our forces, particularly for the veteran soldiers who had participated in prior unfortunate attacks.

"The immediate military advantages derived from the occupation of Teruel are as follows:

A new city has been incorporated in the territory of the Republic.

A more solid defensive front has been attained, having removed dangerous threats (the spearhead pointing to Valencia).

We have occupied an important communication center which shortens distances and facilitates movements of troops.

The offensive capacity of the Popular Army has been increased and its morale has greatly improved".

From December 22 to December 28th the Government forces were mainly engaged in gradually reducing the resistance of the Nationalists who had succeeded in retreating to the interior of the city where strong points—connected by tunnels—had been constructed behind the walls and in the cellars of a group of large buildings. The defense of the Nationalists in these strongholds was most obstinate and heroic taking into consideration the great superiority of the enemy in men and materiel and his determination to end as quickly as possible these centers of resistance within the city, to which end all means available were used, such as heavy artillery shelling, mortar firing, burning with gasoline, blowing of mines, etc. Some of these strongholds fell, their defenders being annihilated or taken prisoners, but others succeeded in prolonging their resistance until January 8th.

THE NATIONALIST COUNTEROFFENSIVE

After the failure of the first Nationalist desperate attacks to break the Government circle around Teruel, there was considerable speculation as to whether General Franco would sacrifice the city in order not to disrupt his preparations for his announced great offensive elsewhere, or would he throw the weight of all his armed forces in the Teruel sector to seek a decisive victory although by so doing he would relinquish the strategical initiative to the Government and battle tactically on the ground chosen by the loyalists. Judging from the latest developments and reports, if true, now coming in from many sources, it would seem for the moment that General Franco is about to follow the second course of action. If these reports turn out to be true, the Teruel battle bids fair to assume proportions never reached before during the civil war and consequently the result of the decision may be far reaching—particularly should the victory fall to the Nationalists.

The information from the Nationalist side is very meager but the indications are that the counteroffensive which Franco's troops initiated on December

29th was made with a large force of men amply supplied with tanks, artillery and aviation. As regards aviation, according to press reports published in Barcelona newspapers not less than 150 pursuit planes and 40 bombers were at times seen in the air.

During the first day of the counteroffensive the Nationalists directed their efforts against the right and left flanks of the Government forces (Celada heights and Villastar sector) apparently making some progress although the Government communiqué claimed that all attacks had been repulsed. On December 30th the attack was continued with renewed strength and the Government lines were broken. According to Nationalist communiqués "the Government forces suffered a complete defeat and were driven past the highway Campillo-Concud, leaving over 1,000 dead on the field and many prisoners and materiel in our hands". In the aerial battle, the Government was reported to have lost 8 planes. At this time it appeared that the Nationalists were in control of the air, particularly, as informed by the air officer, that the Government planes were snow bound to their fields. The Government communiqué admitted "the great force of the enemy's attack and that the loyal troops had been forced to abandon some positions".

On December 31st the Nationalists claimed that the Government forces in complete defeat had lost Concud, San Blas, the very important height of La Muela de Teruel and other positions and that they had entered the city establishing contact with the garrison. It was further claimed that the Government forces had lost thousands of casualties, many prisoners and important quantities of materiel. The Government admitted the loss of the Muela de Teruel but stated that all attempts by the enemy at infiltration into the city had been repulsed. On January 2nd the evacuation of Concud was reported by the Government but the capture of Teruel claimed by the Nationalists was strongly denied—a denial the truth of which was verified conclusively by this office.

A great snow storm and intense cold interfered with subsequent operations although fighting and great artillery activity continued for several days, the Nationalists claiming that they continued progressing and "had inflicted thousands of casualties on the enemy", while the Government made equal claims reiterating that "Teruel was in possession of loyal troops which steadily were reducing the last rebel strongholds within the city".

On January 6th, although the severe spell of bitter cold continued (temperature ranging from 10° to 16° below zero Centigrade), the Nationalists launched against the Government Teruel lines a formidable attack which however appeared to be repulsed. A synopsis of the Government communiqué for that day follows:

"The battle of Teruel continues without interruption, the fighting through-out January 6th being the most intense since the rebels initiated their counter-offensive.

"In the morning, after an intense artillery preparation by a large number of batteries which lasted two hours, and heavy aerial bombings against our lines, the enemy, supported by tanks, attacked persistently south of Cancud in the direction of Teruel. Our infantry, which had admirably resisted the terrific artillery fire and bombing repulsed all attacks. The efficacious action of our artillery frustrated two enemy attacks from the slopes of Sierra Palomera against our Petron positions, the hostile infantry retiring in disorder to Cerro Gordo and Celadas.

"In the Muela de Teruel sector our troops assumed the offensive and occu-pied positions which protect from hostile fire the highway from Villastar to Teruel.

"In the interior of Teruel, the building of the Seminario was stormed by our troops, the rebels having taken refuge in the basement. Note: The Government has announced some six times that the Seminario has been taken.

"The aerial activity was also very intense by both sides. In aerial battle our air force brought down two enemy planes".

The developments of January 7th demonstrated conclusively that, in spite of the Nationalist communiqués depicting their counteroffensive as progressing, they were effectively stopped on the very western outskirts of Teruel from which position they were helpless in their effort to relieve their besieged comrades in the battered strongholds of the city, whose capitulation was initiated on that day. The government communiqué for the 7th and 8th were exultant with the victory attained.

The Nationalist communiqués issued on January 8th admitted the surren-der of the garrison stating, "that a large group of officers and men, of those who had refused to capitulate, had succeeded in reaching the Nationalist lines while a reduced number still fought in strong points of the city." These communiqués and other Nationalist reports subsequently issued throw the blame for the capitulation on Colonel Rey d'Harcourt, the military commander of Teruel, who is charged with treason and cowardice. These announcements claimed that, "the garrison could have resisted a few days more, in view of the fact that the Nationalist van-guards were in the outskirts of the city". These communiqués stated, "that the Na-tionalists failed in liberating the garrison on account of the heavy snowfall which covered the field on the night of the 31st and the persistence of bad weather and polar cold which for several days immobilized the advancing columns and prevented the supply services from operating". These reports further stated that, "the Government troops had all the advantage since they were sheltered in the city buildings and decisive positions, a superiority that enabled them to repulse their attacks". Finally, the Nationalists claimed, "that Teruel is dominated by their fire, that the fighting has not terminated and that the capitulation of the garrison has been only a minor adverse episode, taking into consideration the transcendental consequences which will ensue from the final defeat of the enemy on this battlefield".

These non-official outbursts from rebel radios may be uncontrolled and simply an exposition of the braggadocio spirit or they may be loosened with some ulterior military purpose designed to hold the government forces to the Teruel area while Nationalist troops are being concentrated for an offensive on some other front. As this report closes the question of the hour with those watching this campaign is, "Will the Nationalists concentrate larger forces on the Teruel sector and, actuated by Spanish pride and the prestige factor, launch a great drive to recapture the city? Or, will they, now that the beleaguered garrison has surrendered, concentrate their efforts in a major offensive directed at some front other than Teruel?" The activities of the next few days should furnish evidence sufficient for a reply to these questions.

From January 9th to the date of this report the fighting around Teruel continues but not with the intensity of the past days. Both the Government and Nationalists claim having attained minor advantages, but the situation has not appreciably changed and all indicates that a relative respite is being taken by both sides, although the Government has recently massed considerable artillery to the west of the town and is pounding away almost constantly at the rebel positions on Muela de Teruel. The Government propaganda as noted in today's (January 12th) Barcelona *Vanguardia*[1] recites the following, "After having reached in two days the gates of Teruel, the enemy's counteroffensive has been stopped for eight days".

In connection with the Teruel activities, it is of interest to note that the participation on the Nationalist side of the Italian units has not been reported, in fact, officers of the Government General Staff are asking themselves the question, "Where are the Italians?" The fact that the Italian divisions in Spain have not taken any active part in the Nationalist operations since the capture of Santander is made the subject of much speculation. In this regard, there exist two current opinions, one that ascribes this Italian inactivity to some understanding between England and Nationalist Spain and the other pictures the Italians as busily engaged in training and special preparation for an offensive; the long delay of its execution being attributed to the caution to prevent any recurrence of the Guadalajara affair.

It might be of interest to note that for "his conception of the Teruel plan and for its brilliant execution" General Vicente Rojo, Chief of Staff, has been awarded the *Placa Laureada de Madrid* which has replaced the *Cruz Laureada de San Fernando* of former regimes. In today's news (Jan. 12th), General Rojo, in an open communication to the Minister of National Defense, thanking the army for its response in which he emphasizes the "bravery and sacrifices" of the troops, closes recommending: "A distinctive decoration for those who have taken part in this brilliant operation".

Comments

The Government "High Command" has utilized the Teruel victory as a propaganda agency of far reaching import both at home and abroad. The surprise reaction produced on the Nationalist side by this successful Government offensive is not surpassed by that which came over both the military and civilian communities here in Government territory and the ears of all were in a receptive and expectant mood for the news of the rebel counterattack and gains which followed. The Government has ignored that it has lost most of the ground gained in its offensive and that the city is under rebel artillery fire. In fact, it met this happening with propaganda belittling the importance of these enemy gains stressing the claim that the main objective of the Teruel offensive was to disrupt the enemy's offensive plans for other fronts and force him to commit his troops to action in a place and at a time not to his liking and which would operate to his disadvantage both strategically and tactically, and in these particulars the offensive was successful regardless of the future possessor of Teruel.

The great value of this offensive to the Government is not in the gaining of Teruel—which is not considered of great military importance—but in the fact that the Republican Army is capable of major offensive operations, although it must be noted that this campaign involved little open warfare. This thought was expressed for the Government in a recent statement by Don Juan Ignacio Mantecon, the Governor General of Aragon, who said, referring to the Teruel victory, that it demonstrated "unity and efficiency of our army. Only an army coming from the people united as is ours would be able to achieve this success under the terrible weather conditions which confronted our soldiers, who have given proofs of sacrifice and of a heroism without equal". He further added, ironically, "that our soldiers found several barrels of wine in a wine cellar in Teruel marked—To celebrate the capture of Valencia by the Nationalist army".

Regardless of future events, the taking of Teruel—the last chapter of which closed with the capitulation of the garrison—will be of tremendous importance to the Government not only in strengthening its whip hand here in Cataluña but in demonstrating by actual proof that the Republican army is capable of carrying out successfully a major offensive even under the most adverse weather conditions. Besides, it may prove sufficiently diverting to stay the great expected Franco offensive sufficiently for the Government to better cope with this long heralded rebel drive. In closing this report, it might be said that if the rebel drive against Teruel had spent itself, and Franco refrained from making any further great effort to retake the city, it is very probable that the Government will stage a second major offensive, with the forces it is now assembling for concentration against some point on the Eastern Front, estimates favoring the Huesca salient.

Barcelona   No. 6756
January 12, 1938
Subject: Air Combat Operations. Teruel Offensive

The Air Operations during the Teruel offensive can be divided into three phases:

1. December 15th–December 28th—Government supremacy.
2. December 29th–January 5th—Nationalist supremacy.
3. January 5th–to-date—Neither has air supremacy.

During the first phase the Government Air Force, probably due to the surprise factor, was able to operate with great success not only against the rebel defenses of Teruel, but also far into the rear areas. Missions of reconnaissance, bombardment, ground attack and of protection were flown in cooperation with the ground forces and as independent missions. However, it should here be stressed that these independent missions were of the most cooperative type, namely, attacking reinforcements, supplies and concentrations *before* [Author's emphasis.—Ed. Note] they actually reached the front lines.

When the Nationalists began their counter-offensive on December 29th they had already demonstrated what was to be expected from them in the air by the increased rebel air activity of December 24th, 25th and 28th. On the 30th it is reported that the Nationalists had in the air at one time 150 pursuit protecting

40 bombers. The most the Government had in any mass formation was 70. The second air phase of the Teruel offensive was crucial for the Government not only in the air but also on the ground. Government planes for a period of a few days were rarely seen whereas the rebel air force was frequently in the air.

Once again the question of Air Force of Quality vs. one of Quantity has come to the front. However this quantity factor alone did not give to the Nationalists air supremacy during this period. A more important contributing factor was the site of the respective operating airdromes. The Government used three or four emergency fields between Teruel and Segorbo as well as ones near Valencia and Requena. The rebels used fields in the vicinity of Molina, Calamocha, Daroca and Calatayud. The weather conditions were such that over night the fields near Teruel were put out of use by a heavy snow storm and *before* [Author's emphasis.—Ed. Note] the Government had the opportunity to transfer a great deal of flying equipment. These planes were forced to remain on the ground for several days. On the other hand, the Nationalists did not have the airdrome difficulty but, fortunately for the Government, during this period of "ground planes" flying conditions were such that the rebels were not able to take full advantage of the situation. When the weather had cleared the Government had replaced considerable equipment with which it had started the offensive. No official figures are available but it is estimated that during this period the Government was operating about 100 planes while the Nationalists had some 200.

The third phase of the air operations is characterized by the limited operations of both air forces from which activity it is assumed that neither has air supremacy.

It is the opinion of the undersigned that from the air operations of the Teruel offensive a summarized lesson could be learned covering all phases of air activities that have taken place since the start of the war. However, to acquire this information is possible only through personal air contacts and not through official channels. Without having the opportunity of contacting the desired air personnel it can but now be said that the outstanding air points of the Teruel offensive are these:

1. Element of surprise brought about by careful and secret preparations.
2. The importance of an Air Force of Quality being reinforced by numerical strength.
3. The value of weather information and the necessity of keeping flying equipment on usable fields.
4. The necessity of ground transportation and supply.

It is felt that the air lesson of the Teruel offensive relative to the "Most Severe Winter Flying and Operating Conditions" as well as the results of the recent Air Force reorganization would be extremely valuable to our Air Corps.

Antiaircraft

Both the Government and rebels have announced successes of their respective antiaircraft. In one instance the Government admitted the loss of two bombardment planes from ground fire but complete figures are not available. During the period December 19th–January 1st the Government antiaircraft claims to have shot down during the Teruel operations the following:

Dec. 19—One bomber between Campillo and Bezas.

Dec. 21—Two bombers between Alto de Celadas and Caudete.

Dec. 23—One bomber near Concud.

Jan. 1—Two pursuit between Concud and Alto de Celadas and another pursuit between Teruel and Sagunto.

Jan. 11—One bomber between Minas and Rubiales.

Griffiss

Barcelona   No. 6761

January 26, 1938

Subject: Further Progress of the Teruel Battle

The Teruel series of engagements constitute the most important battle in which both sides have engaged since the Brunete campaign not only on account of the employment of large masses of men, artillery and aviation but owing to its long duration and probable bearing upon the outcome of the war.

The first phase of this campaign, which was initiated on December 15th, constituted a great success for the Loyalist troops, which, through surprise and rapidity of maneuver, cut off the Teruel salient, encircled the city and forced the capitulation of the garrison. The Nationalist counterattack which followed, while gaining a great part of the ground formerly lost, was stopped some 2 kms. west of Teruel. The phase of the campaign with which this report deals covers the continuation of the Nationalist counteroffensive which was renewed on January 17th, in the sector northeast of the city, with such force that the Government troops, notwithstanding the preparations to meet it, including the massing of reserves, had to yield important key positions. This phase of the Nationalist counteroffensive is characterized by the employment of great masses of artillery and aviation with which support of the rebel infantry advance was accomplished slowly but apparently with relatively small loss of life. Rather than attempting a spectacular and rapid advance, the rebels, being evidently aware of the strength and organization of their enemy, appear to be seeking to weaken the Government forces by attrition, accomplished by constantly pounding their lines with artillery and aviation. Apparently, the Nationalist infantry does not advance until the objective of the day has been subjected to such terrific artillery shelling and aviation bombing that the enemy is left with little resistance. Nationalist radio reports have stated that in this manner several hundred Government troops who survived the artillery and bombing preparations, and thus held to their positions, were taken prisoners. All indicates that the Nationalist aviation has had numerical superiority during this rebel counteroffensive and continues to dominate the air in both this sector and the Mediterranean coastal region.

From December 21st to date the battle of Teruel has continued although, during the last two or three days, with decreasing intensity. The communiqués from both sides have been very brief and non-committal, the Nationalists claiming that they "continued progressing" and the Government stating that enemy attacks were "being repulsed". However, the Government has admitted that the enemy has made some progress south of Muleton height, and this, together with other reports indicate that the Nationalist lines are about 3 or 4 kms. north of Teruel and have reached the left bank of the Alfambra river and extend paralleling at variable distances this river up to Tortajada. Both sides continue to use large aviation masses for bombing and strafing enemy positions and rearguard concentrations, highways and cities.

Trip to Teruel

Through the courtesy of the Spanish War Department the undersigned was privileged to visit Teruel. A guide was furnished for the trip and the two of us, in the office car stocked with three days' rations, made the trip. Notes of the visit follow:

Jan. 20. Left Barcelona at 8 AM en route to Valencia. Passed through Tarragona at 10:30 AM and here noted the recent complete destruction of the CAMPSA plant—gasoline deposits and cold storage plant. The site had been bombed and fired from the air and was literally a mass of ruins. Arrived at Sagunto at 2:30 PM. When taking on gasoline for the car, three rebel planes passed over the gasoline station, seemingly from no where, so sudden was their appearance, machine gunning the main highway and open sections of the town. We were forced to quit the car and seek safety in a *refugio* with which this town is supplied with large numbers. In seeking safety we had to pass through a large shop on the roadside and it was rather surprising to note that here were being made the casings for large bombs as well as the shells for the airplane torpedo now in an experimental state. The realization that we found ourselves in an ammunition plant in an effort to seek a refuge place caused our foot movements to be correspondingly accelerated. (The "running across" accidently of these so called *aerotorpedoes* caused the undersigned, upon his return to Barcelona, to make inquiry concerning them the result of which will be embodied in another report). This town contains several munitions factories and I was told that it is an unusual day when the "Fascist bombers did not leave their visiting cards". Recently it has been bombed three or four times daily and on the day prior to our visit the gasoline station manager informed us that it had been bombed "eight times". (Since returning to Barcelona, I have heard that the civil population of the town is being evacuated to the hill villages nearby).

Passing through Castellon de la Plana we observed the destruction of large sections which had been wrought in the air raids of the day before.

On arrival at Valencia at 3:45 PM we noted the great volume of smoke which hung like a pall over the city. This we learned later was from the CAMPSA plant—gas and oil tank field located between Valencia and the Port—which had been bombed three days before and was burning toward total destruction. The magnitude of the Valencia gas and oil field may be judged from the following figures furnished by the representative of the Associated Press who personally inspected and investigated the destruction of this field.

5 tanks of 5,000,000 liters each
2 tanks of 8,000,000 liters each
3 tanks of 4,000,000 liters each
Total of tanks destroyed, 33, aggregating some 100,000,000 liters.

Stopped over night at Valencia—awakened at 4 AM (moon light night) by enemy airplane alarm and antiaircraft firing. The raiders evidently had some other nearby objective, or else were frightened away by the antiaircraft firing and search lighted skies, as no bombs were dropped in the city.

Jan. 21. Left Valencia at 7:30 AM. Before reaching the point 2 km. south of Sagunto, where the road to Teruel leaves the coastal highway, we ran into a heavy bombing raid, the nearness of the explosions forcing us to quit the car for refuge. On the road to Teruel the people in the villages were in more or less a state of panic—some had left the towns and were in the fields, many had their heads turned upward watching these "pirates of the sky" as the enemy planes are frequently called.

Aviation fields along the roadway were noted as follows:

Km. 83 (from Valencia—61 km. from Teruel) near Barracas. On the field—widely dispersed—2 bombing planes and 8 pursuits.

Km. 111 (from Valencia—33 km. from Teruel) near Sarrion. On field—widely dispersed—3 bombing planes and 9 pursuits.

Stopped at point northwest of Sarrion to note G.H.Q. (Advance Section) Teruel front located in Pullman cars in tunnel near road. G.H.Q. proper is at Mora de Rubielos (17 km. north of Sarrion) with General Hernandez Sarabia (one time Secretary of War) in command.

Arrived at Teruel at 11:00 AM. Met the Mayor of the town—a pleasant type who had just received the appointment to this unique office. He furnished me with a guide who piloted us through the narrow shell torn streets to the Plaza Carlos Castel—the center of the city.

Calls were made upon the Headquarters of the XV Brigade and the Regional Headquarters. It was impracticable to see any of the leaders owing to the military activities in which they were engaged; however, I met the Regional Commander—who was called by everyone Commandante [Juan] Modesto. He was very rough appearing, slouchy, unkempt, wearing loose fitting clothes, no headgear, hair disheveled and person dirty. He is tall, heavy set, broad shoulders, very blonde and looks very foreign—perhaps a Russian type. He was courteous offering me the freedom of the city, but apparently very busy excusing himself after about a two minute interview.

My visit to Teruel lasted four hours during which time I covered the city from east to west and back again to the east. I had opportunity to talk to officers and men of all grades and to learn something of the military situation.

Notes and impressions of visit follows:

Teruel is a mass of ruins—in the streets passed through not one building was observed undamaged. Practically all of the shops have been looted. With the exception of some thirty or forty women and old men (pitiful sights) who were being rounded up for evacuation, the civilian population has been cleared out. Water mains are out and sanitation even in a crude form does not exist. No evidence of any effort to clean up or to reorganize the town for either occupancy or defense.

The west side of the town was approached through a narrow street some twelve to fifteen feet wide which finally opened on the main Zaragoza highway which runs along the edge of the heights. From this roadway one could see the river below, the railroad tracks and the railroad station in the flats. Beyond could be noted the front line with Muela de Teruel (Tooth of Teruel) in the distance—some 2 kms. This height, held by the rebels, dominates the west side of the city and from which position the main Zaragoza and Valencia highways, as they enter and leave the town, are kept under artillery fire. Observations to the north of the city were made from the east side.

During the period of [our] visit the town was shelled from Muela de Teruel and bombed from the air. It is of interest to note that the shelling included the throwing of shrapnel bombs which exploded on time fuses just above the buildings and sprayed their bullets and fragments over the house tops and streets below. I was informed, as there was practically nothing left in the city worthy of shell fire, that these shrapnel bombs were employed almost entirely and that the firing was continuous throughout the day. Although our visit to Teruel may be classified in the category of "offensive strategy", these shrapnel shells, while in the city, compelled us to adopt "defensive tactics" which at times were quite elemental in character and, under the first primal law of nature, forced us into positions not always too dignified—yet not conspicuous as they were all doing the same.

The XV Brigade (American, English, Canadian unit) was located in the line just north of the town in the direction of Concud. The brigade had been used in the rebel counteroffensive launched to the north of the town and those with whom I talked remarked upon its fine performance and credited it with stopping the rebel advance on the main Zaragoza road to the north of Teruel.

The morale of the government troops on the Teruel front has been lowered materially since the launching of the second rebel counteroffensive on January 17th. From those with whom I talked, I drew a very decided impression that their continuance in Teruel was doubtful, in fact, that the battle then raging to the north would definitely determine the question and at the time they seemed to think the turn of the wheel was against them. There was no spirit of the braggadocio nor of any fixed mental determination manifested in the Madrid slogan *No pasaran*, in fact, the opposite attitude was apparent by the use of propaganda to the effect that Teruel had no military value.

The real value of my visit was in the obtaining of a true picture of the military situation at this front. The following comment on this situation is offered:

When the rebel counteroffensive from the direction of the Muela de Teruelo and Concud failed to reach the city and relieve the hemmed in garrison, it became evident that an offensive to the north of the city offered a better chance for successful consummation. This decision was evidently made by the rebel high command which was initiated in the launching of an offensive against the Celadas heights for left flank protection and then driving hard south east against Muleton. The taking of this dominant peak and the heights north gave the rebels the control of the Teruel-Alframba road and the valley of the Alfambra river. It now becomes the key for the attacks being launched in the direction of the Sierra Gorda heights. These heights including those which lie from 1 to 2 kms. to the south, if taken by the rebels, will cut the important road Teruel-El Pobo-Aliaga, which connects up with the Montalban-Alcaniz highway, and place them in a position to attack the Santa Barbara and Mansueto hills. As these hills dominate Teruel from the northeast and threaten the Valencia road, it is estimated that the loyal[ist] troops will retire from the city while they control these heights and not engage in battle for their future possession.

The undersigned believes that during his visit he sensed an atmosphere of preparation for this retirement eventually. As this report closes, Jan. 26th, the Government's communiqué announces an offensive from the direction of the Palomera heights—some 15 km. northwest of Alfambra—toward Singra, on the main Teruel-Zaragoza road. The announcement claims some initial success in this movement (which the Nationalists claim to have vigorously repulsed); however, the offensive seems of a diverting character.

Jan. 22. The return to Barcelona was made direct and without incident, stopping for the night at the Alberque (a government controlled tourist inn) at Benicarlo.

Comments

The military situation on the Teruel front may be briefly stated in resume as follows:

The rebel counteroffensive on the west, southwest and northwest of the city has been definitely checked—a situation which, unquestionably brought about the second rebel counteroffensive from the north and northeast directed first against the Muleton height, which has been taken, and now launched against the Sierra Gorda positions. Should these last named hills be occupied by the rebels it is estimated that the threat against Teruel will be sufficient to cause the evacuation of the city by the Government forces.

It is of interest to note that this eventuality has been foreseen in the type of propaganda now being put out by the Government. The trend of these statements issued by the high command clearly shows that the Government will not be surprised should Teruel fall to the rebels and that in any event the Teruel success will be reckoned, as stated, "our greatest military victory". Further, these statements include the following: "We have smashed Franco's winter offensive". "We have drawn Franco's reserves into the difficult Teruel area and our possession of the mountain passes east of the city will keep the rebels penned in this area and stop any advance they may attempt in the direction of the sea". Again, a high official asked a friend of the undersigned yesterday, "What if we lose Teruel? The city itself was not our main reason for our offensive, it was to attract a rebel counteroffensive in this area to our choosing. Franco bit our bait and has been set back about five or six months". Again, it was said, "We counted on Franco being too Spanish to leave Teruel to its fate. For three days, however, I admit we were in doubt whether he would do this thing or concentrate his forces on another front where he might have gained a factory of some magnitude". The opinion here in military circles is in agreement with the trend of the above thought and charges Franco with a grave error in concentrating a large force—apparently against his will and plans in the Teruel sector—while a drive on some other front (Guadalajara mentioned) would have had at this time unusual opportunity for administering a telling blow—particularly as the greater part of the Government reserves had been concentrated in the Teruel sector including the International Brigades and other shock troops.

Barcelona   No. 6770

February 12, 1938

Subject: The Military Situation

[The first several pages of this report have not been reproduced, as they were observations made of each of the major Madrid and Jarama fronts, all of which were quiet.—Ed. Note]

Teruel Front

The Teruel campaign, which has continued more or less, with both short and long periods of respite, for nearly two months, continues to be fought, by constantly increased contending forces, on a more extensive front. Since last reported (No. 6761 of January 26, 1938) there have taken place the following additional phases of these operations, now reckoned by many to be in whole or part of a campaign that will bring a definite decision in the field.

GOVERNMENT COUNTEROFFENSIVE ON THE SINGRA FRONT

After the Nationalist offensive in the sector of the Celadas heights, as the result of which the insurgents not only succeeded in gaining important key positions for future operations but inflicted heavy losses upon the enemy, the Government forces initiated (January 25) a counteroffensive in the Singra sector (some 41 km. northwest of Teruel), evidently with the purposes in view of relieving the pressure on the city and of cutting the Teruel-Zaragoza road. Had this movement succeeded, the Nationalists would have been placed in a difficult position, but well aware of the importance of this front, they evidently were prepared to meet this attack which did not, even initially, attain any appreciable advantage. According to Nationalist reports, this attack "was supported by 16 tanks and a strong mass of aviation (some 50 airplanes) but the loyalists were driven back leaving in our hands over 100 prisoners".

This Government counteroffensive was continued with more or less intensity during the 26th, 27th, 28th and 29th, however, during these days the loyal troops, from the Government communiqués, evidently failed to make any headway. The Nationalists claim that "during these engagements they captured several hundred prisoners, destroyed 8 enemy tanks and caused the enemy over 5,000 casualties". From insurgent reports it appears that most of the units used by the Government in these attacks consisted of untrained troops, poorly led, upon which the Nationalist artillery and aviation inflicted heavy losses. The Government reported that "three enemy planes were shot down by loyal antiaircraft batteries" while the Nationalists claimed to have brought down "2 enemy planes".

NATIONALIST OFFENSIVE. ALFAMBRA SECTOR

On February 5th the Nationalists launched an offensive with great force on a front of some 45 kms. extending from Celadas to a few kilometers southeast of Portalrubio (some 55 km. north of Teruel). While no accurate information is available as to the strength and composition of the Nationalist troops which effected this drive, it is known that they were organized into three strong columns supported by abundant artillery, many tanks and masses of aviation. The presence of the Italians has not been identified in this offensive. General Dávila, Franco's Minister of Defense is reported to have been in direct supreme command of the troops.

The initial phase of this offensive, which has been carried out most successfully, had evidently for its objectives: With their right flank safely pivoted on Muleton height (6 km. north of Teruel which was taken about January 17th) to gain positions which would protect their left flank southwest of Montalban and to enclose within a pocket the Government forces in the positions forming the existing salient from Celadas north to Pancrudo, including a number of important villages— thus dominating the Alfambra valley and the Rillo-Perales-Alfambra road.

Comments

The Eastern Sector is the all important front at the time of closing this report evidenced by the gravity with which the Government considers the rebel drive in the valley of the Alfambra. The French border has been closed presumably to clear the highways for the movement of great quantities of supplies now entering Spain from that direction as well as to cover to some extent this military traffic. All busses employed on the interurban routes have been taken over for troop movements to and on the eastern front and all train service has been confined solely to troop movements.

The XV Brigade (American-English units) which has been on the North Teruel front, since the rebel counterattack in that region, was being withdrawn two days ago for a long rest in a back area when their destination orders were changed to the eastern front. The undersigned talked this morning in Barcelona with Lt. Colonel Copic, the XV Brigade commander, who gave the above information. In addition, Colonel Copic stated that "the Brigade had done excellent work on the Teruel front, that the English battalion on the right of the line south west of Muleton had suffered most, and that the Americans had had some one hundred casualties in this campaign". Colonel Copic showed great disappointment that his brigade, which had been in the line for nearly a month, could not proceed to a rest area. He evidenced great anxiety over this new rebel drive and considered it one of great magnitude saying, "They (the rebels) have massed their greatest force on this front (the east, north of Teruel)". When I suggested "that this enemy movement may be his secondary attack initiated to screen his major offensive, which might follow later in the Guadalajara region", he emphatically dismissed this idea, saying in substance, "No, although it is true that there are some 60,000 Italians concentrated in the Soria area, Franco will not use them in an initial drive but only to follow the penetrations and successes attained by his other troops".

The tone of the Government propaganda for consumption abroad, since the rebel counteroffensive which took the Muleton, has been definitely changed from a "confidence of victory attitude" to the spreading of the doctrine "that the war cannot end on the battlefield as neither side is sufficiently strong to crush the other". This change of front in the field of propaganda is fortifying to the undersigned's observation that for the past four weeks the feeling has been definitely sensed in military circles that the Government forces cannot attain crushing defeat of the enemy on the battlefield.

As this report closes it is definitely clear that the Government's strategy and tactics are defensive and that the Republican forces have lost the initiative to the rebels, that their sea and air powers were inferior to the rebels' and that the measure of the strength of their land forces with the enemy at present is not to their advantage.

The war winning morale of the Catalans is definitely at a low ebb evidenced on all sides by their hostile attitude toward the central government. First, perhaps, on account of these "foreigners" being in control of "their country and beautiful city for which they have a great local pride" and, secondly, because this superimposing of the Madrid Government upon them has shorn them of many of their former independent powers which are gradually being taken over by the central government. They blamed the presence of the central government for the recent rebel bombing raids over "their city" and it was undoubtedly in deference to this thought which decided the central government to hold the recent Cortes meeting at Montserrat—out of Barcelona.[2] It is most significant that at one of the leading movie theaters—recently—with a packed house—when the taking of Teruel pictures were shown—depicting the triumphant march of the Republican Army into the city, showing Mr. Prieto there "at the front", followed with the band playing the national anthem, not one clapping sound was heard nor even any individual move at an ovation was attempted. The whole scene was received by this audience in profound silence and consequently made a deep impression upon the foreigners present registering unmistakably the unpopularity of the war in the Catalan capital.

"The Ejercito de Maniobra", commanded by Colonel Leopoldo Menendez (former regular army officer) is being organized. The headquarters are in two echelons, one in Valencia, in the hold "Headquarters of National Defense" and the other—the advance echelon—is now moving with the commanding officer from place to place throughout the area where the troops are being concentrated and trained. The "Army" is being assembled in the area not too distant from the coast line between the Ebro and the Valencia-Madrid highway. It is reported to consist of five corps of three divisions each and that it will be held in a state of readiness, with trucks spotted for troop movements, with a mission "to attack and crush—from a flank position—any rebel penetration of magnitude".

There is no reliable information possessed by the undersigned of the concentrations of the rebel forces, yet from what bits have come to him from contacts on both sides, it would seem that the Franco concentrations reported in the Avila and Soria Sections might be interpreted to mean a contemplated combined drive from the Aranjuez and Alcarria regions (centered about Cifuentes, east of Guadalajara). The spearheads of these drives might be directed at the main Madrid-Valencia road at some point, for example, between or near the crossings of the Tajuna or Tajo.

Barcelona   No. 6786
February 26, 1938
Subject: The Teruel Campaign Ends in Complete Government Defeat

The series of engagements, initiated on December 15, 1937 by the successful Government drive against the Teruel salient, and the subsequent rebel counter-offensives and loyalist reactions seem now to have been closed by a Nationalist victory in which Franco's Northern Army has clearly shown a superiority over the Republican Army of the East. This definite conclusion is evident in a study of the aftermath of the Nationalist victory, the magnitude and consequences of which cannot as yet be completely estimated. The successful rebel offensive was not the result of a surprise movement, as was the initial Government success in this sector, but the consummation of a well thought out coordinated plan, successfully executed against the Government's best trained, armed and equipped troops, organized and prepared in advance to meet their enemy on ground of their choosing.

The principal objectives of the Nationalist plan seem to have been as follows:

First: To free the Teruel-Zaragoza front from being constantly menaced by Government troops.

Second: To broaden the "Teruel salient" and the gaining of key topographical positions for future operations on this front.

Third: To engage the enemy's best field army, including its International Brigade shock troops, to force it to consume its reserves and to defeat it.

Fourth: Perhaps, for reasons of sentiment and morale to retake Teruel, thus demonstrating their slogan at home and abroad, "We lose no ground captured—while the enemy holds none that he gains".

That the Republican forces had become considerably weakened was conclusively shown after their unsuccessful offensive (January 25th) in the Singra sector, a condition which was aggravated after the subsequent Nationalist offensive of

February 5th in the Alfambra region. Here, as previously reported, the Government forces suffered a grave defeat and lost large numbers of prisoners and materiel with a considerable lowering of morale both in the army and throughout the civilian population.

On February 15th a weak Government attempt in a much heralded attack in the sector of Vival del Rio, which was easily repulsed by the Nationalists, gave additional proof that the offensive spirit of the troops had been lowered or their strength in this sector has been reduced, from all of which could be drawn the conclusion that the strategical initiative in the eastern theater had definitely reverted to the insurgent army.

The Nationalist offensive was resumed on February 17th by breaking the enemy front at three different points in the vicinity of the junction of the rivers Alfambra and Turia. On the next day, the attack was directed against the Sierra Gorda heights to the northeast of the city.

[This text is followed by many pages of Republican and Nationalist communiqués about daily events of the campaign and are omitted here.—Ed. Note]

Up to the time of closing this report, the Nationalist advance has nearly reached the old line they held before the Government offensive of December 15th, except that on the Teruel-Sagunto road the Government troops still are in possession of the Escandon Pass, a very important position barring easy access to the Valencia region.

According to Nationalist reports, since the Alfambra offensive was initiated on February 5th, the Government forces have left in the hands of the enemy 16,298 prisoners and 9,753 dead on the field. These figures are claimed to have been obtained from official sources and while they may be exaggerated to some extent, nevertheless give an idea of the blow suffered by the loyalists, the "total casualties" of which are estimated from the same sources "at 60,000".

The Government has just called to the colors the classes of 1929 and 1940, a fact which reveals not only the importance of the losses suffered in the Teruel sector but might be taken as evidence of the Government's determination to continue the war to the end.

Comments

Notwithstanding the Government's effort in its pronouncement to minimize the loss of Teruel and to exaggerate the importance of having saved Madrid from rebel attack by forcing Franco to bring his reserves to the Teruel front, the battle defeats in the Alfambra and Teruel sectors have stunned the Government and destroyed whatever was left of the Catalans' hope in the ultimate victory of the "New Republican Army". There is an undercurrent of belief among those seemingly well posted that the Government has given out of the policy, to gain support from the people, that the army will assume a defensive attitude until its materiel and equipment have increased to equal that of the enemy.

The reaction of the loss of Teruel upon "the man in the street" is pleasing for it seemingly from his viewpoint brings the war nearer to the end. A decided reaction has been noted, since the fall of Teruel, communicated directly from the workers concerned that the control committee in two of the Catalan's largest industries had advised, individually, their employees included in the last "call to the colors" to avoid service at the front as it meant only death with no hope of victory. The reaction of the Teruel disaster on the workers is further evidenced in yesterday's *Solidaridad Obrera*, the official organ of the CNT[3]—the strongest workers organization in Catalonia. The paper contained a "manifesto" and an editorial both of which used strong uncensored words directed against the Government—a follow up of the "slogans" contained in the military cable report. The "manifesto" was directed to the "Workers organizations of all classes and other antifascist organizations". The document called for direct participation in the direction of the war—for control of key positions in the Government both military and political; it stated that new demands by the Government for increased production could be accomplished through the laborer working at full capacity and with enthusiasm only by his direct participation in the Government. The manifesto stated that in view of the sad experiences in the past and failure to interest the democratic governments in "our cause", Spain can only look for assistance to the workers of the world. These bold statements against the Government are interpreted by both resident Catalans and foreigners with long backgrounds of Spanish political understanding as being ominous and far reaching.

Another reaction to the Teruel defeat was evidenced in the so-called secret session of the Cabinet, the President presiding, held in the Pedralbes barracks on the outskirts of the city—instead of the Premier's office, the usual place of meeting—when Mr. Azaña is reported to have broached the subject of an armistice—the reaction to which cannot be learned at this moment. The President is reported to have said that his suggestion was prompted by his conscience—that he could not rest quietly and see Spain destroyed. In connection with this "secret" Cabinet meeting, held on February 24th, news of which the newspaper men were forbidden to send out of Spain, it is of interest to note that the undersigned listened to an account of it broadcasted by the rebel Salamanca radio station at eleven PM that same evening.

Since the fall of Teruel several Cabinet meetings have been held of late from which reports came that consideration was being given to creating additional portfolios for the extremists but this has been denied. Also rumors were afloat that the communists were to be removed from participation in the Government and this too was denied by a Government spokesman. This latter rumor carried with it the statement that such action was based upon the effort to curry favor with the European democracies principally England and France and especially the former. This idea evidently was the result of the Anthony Eden resignation which has been interpreted in many circles here as a "selling out of Spain" by British moneyed interests to Mussolini. The press was informed that the meetings dealt with "the international situation and the intensification of war materiel production".

It is difficult at this writing to measure the full force and effect of the recent defeat of the Government forces in the Alfambra and Teruel sectors, but it is evident from what has been stated above, reinforced by the growing Catalan hostility to the prosecution of the war, that these catastrophic reverses, unless they can be overcome by some miraculous turn of the wheel of fortune, must have a direct bearing in greatly reducing the Government's military power.

As this report closes, the Nationalist advance in the Teruel sector has halted, the apex of the drive being somewhere on the Teruel-Sagunto road about at kilometer 6—the left front passing through Valdesebro and Tortajada and the right front through Castralvo and the Galician heights which lie south of Villaespesa.

8

From the Aragon Campaign to the End of the Battle of the Ebro

(March–November 1938)

"This war has produced many unexpected situations and the successful crossing of the Ebro followed by the strong Government resistance . . . must have been an outstanding event in this field of military surprises to the Nationalist command."

Col. Stephen O. Fuqua
1938

This chapter surveys events between March and roughly mid-November 1938. The central military events of the period were the offensives in Aragon and the Levante between March and July, and the great Battle of the Ebro, which occurred between July 23 and November 16.

The first campaign involved the Nationalists pushing east around Madrid toward the Mediterranean Coast, and in the process dividing the Republican zone into several pieces (April 3), while isolating Catalonia from the ongoing pressures Franco was putting on central Spain. This Aragon-Levante area of Spain became a massive battleground involving the prov-inces of Huesca, Saragossa and Teruel—a combined area east of Madrid and south of Catalonia. As the military observers point out, the Nationalists executed their military tasks far better than the Republicans, and consequently people inside and outside of Spain began wondering if the end for what had become a bloody, nasty civil war might finally be visible. Catalonia lost much of its extraterritorial support, particularly access to adequate supplies of electricity with which to run its industries, while the Republican military found it now had multiple uncoordinated military fronts and regions to manage. Aragon is a region, just as Catalonia or Castile, with its own local culture and variations in language. The same held for Levante, essentially the breadbasket, a region with productive farms growing large volumes of Spain's foodstuffs, and comprising the provinces of Valencia and Murcia. It was on the periphery of the Aragon campaign, with considerable portions still in Republican hands until the last few weeks of the war.

The American military observers were right to spend a great deal of energy understanding the Battle of the Ebro. It was one of the rare massive offensives launched by the Republicans during the war against the Nationalists' overextended lines and by the time it was over, as Raymond L. Proctor observed, it was "the ugliest, bloodiest, and longest battle of the Spanish Civil War."[1] It ended when the Nationalists were able to push the Republicans back to the west bank of the Ebro, thereby wiping out their early acquisitions of territory by the end of November 18. By the time it was over, the Republicans had probably lost around 30,000 dead and an additional 40,000 captured or wounded. The Nationalists suffered about 6,000 dead and approximately 35,000 captured, missing, or wounded; all figures are still subject to some debate. Some 200,000 soldiers from both sides in total were involved in the campaign. Significant for the immediate prosecution of the war, the organization of the Republican forces essentially disintegrated during this campaign, while the command structure of the Nationalists remained intact, crucial in making it possible for Franco to turn his attention to Catalonia and the final collapse of the remaining Republican-held territories. For most military historians, the outcome of the civil war was resolved on the west bank of the Ebro River.

The American military observers quite correctly pointed out the large swath of land involving the battle. The Segre River comes down from the north into the Ebro River (Spain's largest). The Ebro runs in a roughly north–southeast manner in upper Spain, beginning just below the corner of the Bay of Biscay and ending at the Mediterranean south of Tarragona, essentially like a necklace around Spain's northern neck. This explains to a large extent why the military lines were so long, essentially hundreds of miles, fraught with opportunities and risks for the armies involved.

With the end of this battle, the mood of the nation and the conclusion of observers inside the military and elsewhere were that the war would
soon conclude with some truce or intervention on the part of international
governments. Nothing could be further from the truth. As chapter 9 demonstrates, the fighting went on until April 1939, and if the truth is told,
isolated small groups kept fighting the Nationalists until at least the end of
the 1940s, while exiled Republicans refused to give up seeking international
intervention until the end of the 1960s.

All through 1936 and 1937, despite American military criticisms of
the way the Republican military functioned, these observers were careful
never to suggest that the war might be won by the Nationalists. However,
by the spring of 1938, one could begin to see comments in their dispatches
indicating that they saw the end coming. In addition to explicit comments
to that effect, they also began acquiring more information about the Nationalists than they had in earlier years.

Barcelona   No. 6797
March 14, 1938
Subject: Three Day Visit to the Huesca Front
[The majority of this report is not reproduced, as it is repetitive of
earlier comments regarding military preparedness.—Ed. Note]

The visit to this front was particularly interesting in view of the fact that the
Huesca salient has been a mystery problem to all military observers who have tried
to analyze why the government troops have never organized a successful attack
against the indentation in their line, the perimeter of which they had surrounded
on three sides from almost the beginning of the war. The sole answer to this apparent riddle is believed to lie in the fact that the troops fronting Huesca have always
been Catalans whose hearts have not been in this war evidenced by their total lack
of the offensive spirit. It was on this front that football teams between the two
opposing armies are reported to have engaged on "no man's land" field for games
in a spirit of friendly composition. Be this report true or not, these troops are not
offensively inclined and showed no evidence of any desire to destroy their enemy
across the narrow "no man's street", in fact, the "home team" did not seem to be
even angry with their opponents.

This comment, as registering the reaction of the undersigned, concerning the offensive spirit of the Catalans may be afforded an opportunity for a more complete test should the long heralded rebel drive to the sea cross the boundary line of Catalonia.

The undersigned desires to make of record the hospitality of Major Michael Navarro, the Division Commander, who not only showed him the courtesies mentioned in the body of this report but entertained him at a formal dinner in his honor which was attended by the members of the official families of the Division and Brigade commanders.

Barcelona   No. 6798
March 16, 1938
Subject: The Nationalist Drive on the Aragon Front

Early on the morning of March 9th the Nationalists launched, in the region of central Aragon, a formidable offensive. Up to the time of closing this report (morning of March 16), this drive has continued with marked success and ever increasing volume on a frontage of some 50 miles—from Fuentes de Ebro to a few kilometers south of Montalban. From various sources and estimates, it would seem that the Nationalists are employing in this drive about 150,000 men, organized in three attacking forces, designated in dispatches as the northern, the central and the southern columns. These columns are reported in both Nationalist and Government communiqués to include a Moroccan Corps, one or more Italian Divisions, Navarran, Castillian and Gallego Divisions. The advancing troops are being supported by "numerous tanks, and great masses of artillery and aviation".

At the time of writing this report, only piecemeal information released in the official communiqués is available; however, the magnitude of the driving power of the Nationalist forces and the remarkable maneuvering ability of their shock troops can be definitely estimated evidenced by the continuity and coordination of the advance and the rapidity and success with which the ground objectives are being taken. The republican army, while numerically strong, has shown its absolute inability to cope with the military situation now confronting it and is retiring more or less orderly but without offering determined and coordinated resistance.

[Now follows many pages of direct quotes from communiqués from both sides, omitted as not necessarily accurate.—Ed. Note]

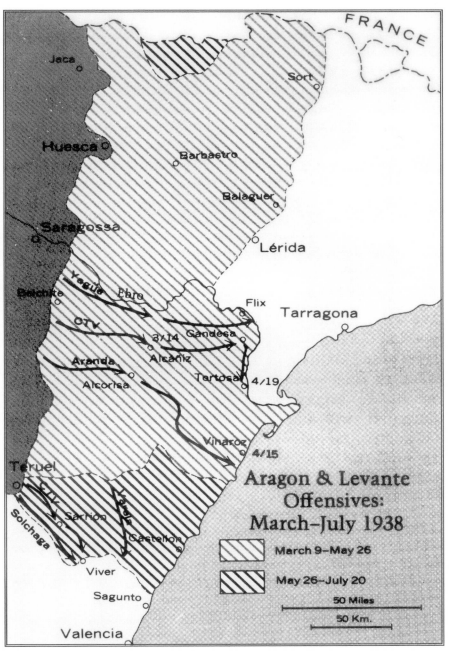

Aragon and Levante Offensives, March–July 1938. [John F. Coverdale, *Italian Intervention in the Spanish Civil War* (© 1975 by Princeton University Press), 348. Reprinted by permission of Princeton University Press.]

Comments

This Nationalist offensive on the Aragon front has given a second opportunity (for the first occasion see Report No. 6786 of February 26, 1938) to measure the relative fighting efficiency of the contending forces operating in open warfare. This drive has proven unquestionably the superiority of the rebels in both organization and command, in equipment and armament, in field maneuvers and perhaps, above all, in combat teamwork. A brief study of the rebel advance in this offensive, although based on meager information, reveals that they employed in general the following tactics: At first, the concentration of superior forces to the enemy at some three points of his front trench line. When the front had been penetrated, definite prearranged plans were executed for flanking remaining sections of the unbroken line. The enemy's rapid retirement to rear positions forced him to occupy defensive points without established lateral communication. This procedure of withdrawal, "holding attacks" fronting the occupied points, permitted the attacker opportunity to enter then to turn the defender's position by flanking maneuvers. This is briefly the method of advance employed by the Nationalists in their offensive of the last seven days.

The Government troops in falling back have, from eye witnesses, acted without central control, but have made their retirements locally and in their own way and time governed only by enemy pressure and the topographical lay of the land. Reports indicate little or no lateral communication between the elements of their command and the occupation of a most zig zag front with wide intervals between units thus inviting success of the rebel tactics employed, as noted above. Although the Government troops have been hard pressed, to date there has been no great disaster or marked disorderly route—due, however, in all probability, to lack of long determined stands in any selected positions—a course of action which undoubtedly has aided the rapidity of the rebel advance.

Reports from the front today point to considerable confusion among the Government troops caused by units being broken up in the rapid retirement during the past few days with groups straggling rearward wandering about lost from their command controls. However, the movement of reserves from other fronts caused a stiffness of the resistance and an announced determination to stop the enemy—from entering Catalonia—along the Rio Martin and which more or less parallels the north and south boundary from Fayon to Valderrobres.

Should the Nationalists continue their advance, the Catalan border would probably be crossed as follows: the northern column at Fayon, the central column on the roads Maella-Batea and Calaceite-Caseres and the south column on the

Valderrobres-Chortal road. (This is a comparatively new highway in excellent condition passed over recently by the undersigned.)

Barcelona   No. 6805
March 30, 1938
Subject: The Rebel Offensive on the East

With further reference to Report No. 6798 of March 16, 1938, the Nationalist forces operating on the Aragon front (south of the Ebro river) after taking (March 17th) the important town and communication center of Caspe and improving and consolidating their lines a few kilometers south of the Montalban-Alcaniz road, remained a few days relatively inactive in this general sector of operations.

On March 22nd the insurgents started a formidable offensive with unprecedented force, which still continues, in the extensive zone comprised between a point a few kilometers north of Huesca and the Ebro. Notwithstanding the magnitude of this effort, they continued their advance south of the Calanda-Alcaniz line having already entered the important coastal province of Castellon. As the Catalan region has also been penetrated at several places, the local military situation is becoming very grave, in fact, the Government is fast nearing the end of its power of resistance.

[The majority of this report is not reproduced, as it simply offers translations of communiqués from each side on daily events.—Ed. Note]

From March 27th to the time of closing this report, which includes the communiqués of March 29th, the Nationalist advance continued with great rapidity and driving power reaching the Cinca river from a point north east on Barbastro to the junction of this river with the Ebro at Mequinenza which town has just fallen to the insurgents. It appears that the Government forces are attempting a stand on the Cinca, Ebro and Matarrana rivers; however, the Nationalists have crossed the Cinca at Fraga and have entered Catalan territory at Masalcorreig. In the extreme southern sector of the advance the rebels have occupied Zorita in the province of Castellon.

Comments

The Nationalist advance on the Eastern front, as noted by our daily *Military Reports* prepared for the State Department has at this writing pushed to the line from north south, viz:

El Grado (12 km. N.E. of Barbastro) along both banks of the Rio Cinca to a point on Fraga-Lerida road about 20 kms. west of Lerida—through Aytona and Seros to Mequinenza and along the west bank of the Rio Matarrana to Valdeltormo (east of Alcaniz) thence south along the Morella road just within the Province of Castellon through the Sector Zorita-Palangues to Castellote, turning westward to include the region lying just south of the Alcaniz-Montalban road. It might be of interest to note here that the American Volunteer unit, now in this line, is on the banks of the Matarrana near Maella-Caspe-Gandesa road.

The spearheads of the two main drives along the center sector of this front seem to be directed toward Lerida—the key to all this western region and the second city of Cataluña—and toward Gandesa—the road juncture control to the coastal highways.

With the fall of these key points, it is difficult to see how the Republican Army could maintain any organized resistance. It is probable, if it continues as an army in being on the defensive, it will break into small units relying upon guerrilla warfare methods before final disintegration. However, such a course of action will be against the will of the Catalan people who now want peace and have no desire or inclination to prolong the war, which they now know to be lost, at the price of the destruction of their towns and country side.

The Cinca line which was heralded to be the stopping point of the rebel advance—not having any fixed fortifications—was broken almost upon contact, the insurgent forces having at this writing crossed the stream in a number of places. The line of the Rio Segre, passing through Lerida, now seems to be the *No Pasaran* front of the Government forces. It is of interest to note that in the region of the towns mentioned above in the line Aytona and Seros, are found the large hydroelectric plants, installed by the Ebro Light and Power Co., which supply the Catalan regional industries with, it is estimated, some 80 percent of their electric power. The other 20 percent is obtained from fuel generation in and around Barcelona. The cutting of the electric power from the Segre river was evidently foreseen yesterday by Mr. Prieto in his manifesto calling on the workers employed in the industries of Barcelona—through their syndicates—to be organized and prepared, should their plants close, to take their places with gun or spade in the ranks of the army.

There is a strong current of opinion in well informed circles that the [Juan] Negrin Government will soon pass over the gavel of authority to another government headed by Martinez Barrios, or some other conservative, charged with the mission of obtaining surrender terms from General Franco. This would seem to be the logical and sensible ending to this civil war.

April 20, 1938

Memorandum for the Chief of Staff:

Subject: Spain: Insurgent Offensive against Catalonia Reaches the Sea

During the period April 8 to 18, the Insurgent offensive against Catalonia made progress in three areas. In the north it advanced rapidly, with little opposition, close to the French border west of Andorra. In the center it crossed the Segre River at Balaguer and Lerida, in spite of strong resistance, thus threatening the north flank of the Loyalist position along the Ebro. In the south General [Antonio] Aranda's Corps, assisted by troops from the Corps of General [Rafael Garcia] Valino, in an operation of decisive importance forced its way 25 miles to the Mediterranean coast; diving Catalonia from the remainder of Spain and causing the retirement of Loyalist troops to the east bank of the Ebro.

This last named advance of the Insurgents along the Morella road, and through the mountainous terrain bordering it, was bitterly resisted by the Loyalists until after April 13. On that date it appears that the Insurgents succeeded in capturing after heavy fighting heights dominating San Mateo and Chortal and badly defeated the troops of some of the International Brigades. Aviation and cavalry played important parts in this action. Loyalist positions, as throughout this war of discontinuous fronts, were not mutually supporting and the familiar outflanking tactics of the Insurgents again proved effective.

On the following day General Aranda's columns found easy going down the secondary roads and valleys leading to the coast. At 5:45 PM, April 15, his 4th Navarrese Division entered Vinaros without resistance, while other troops reached Benicarlo. By the 17th the Insurgents' penetration to the coast had been widened to both north and south. In the meantime General Valino who had been held up since April 3 by Loyalist resistance north and west of Chortal, on the Ebro, sent troops to resist Aranda on the Morella road and also through the mountains to approach Tortosa from the southwest and south. The Loyalist forces west of the Ebro thus found themselves dangerously threatened, with an unfordable river at their rear and the main highway bridge at Tortosa destroyed. Evacuation to the east bank of the Ebro was effected on April 17 and 18, use being made of a footbridge and railroad bridge at Tortosa and of a pontoon bridge at Amposta. The bulk of the war materiel and most, though not all, of the troops were believed across the Ebro by the night of the 18th.

The Present Situation

The Loyalists hold the east bank of the winding Ebro-Segre River line for a length of about 100 miles. Their total forces along the rivers and in reserve are unknown. The crossings are held in considerable strength but it is likely that there is little liaison or plan for coordination of the defense among the troops guarding this line. It is also likely that reserves lack the mobility and organization to intervene rapidly against an Insurgent attempt to cross. At Lerida and Balaguer the Insurgents have strong bridgeheads across the Segre River. These have resisted Loyalist counterattacks but have themselves been stabilized by Loyalist resistance. They constitute a dangerous threat to the Loyalist defense of the river line. In the Tortosa area the Insurgents are believed superior in strength, materiel and morale and would seem able to force a crossing, though not without incurring some losses.

Comments

General Franco has achieved the major strategic objective which has been [his] goal since the culmination of the Asturian campaign in October, 1937. He should not be held up long by Loyalist resistance along the Ebro. In this connection reports, not yet confirmed, have been received that troop ships under convoy of war vessels have already brought reinforcements from Majorca (Balearic Islands) into the port of Vinaros. Based upon the situation as known today, it is believed that Franco, having isolated Catalonia from the rest of Spain, will continue to seek a military decision on his eastern front while a steadily increasing economic pressure makes itself felt upon the population and troops of Madrid and Valencia.

E.R.W. McCabe,
Col., General Staff,
Assist. Chief of Staff, G-2

Barcelona   No. 6816
April 25, 1938
Subject: Organization, Order of Battle and Strength of
the Nationalist Army—East Front

While the information in Loyal Spain concerning the organization of the Nationalist army which is conducting the present offensive on the Eastern front is very meager, it is believed that the following general data may be of some interest at this time before actual official figures can be obtained by the military historian.

This large scale offensive, which, if continued to be prosecuted successfully bids fair to bring to an end the civil war in Spain, was planned and prepared by General Franco, assisted by his foreign advisors, during the past winter months. The lesson learned from the Italian episode in March, 1937 in the Guadalajara area, evidently brought home to the Nationalist headquarters the necessity for careful planning on a large scale of an offensive designed to attain a decisive victory in the field.

It is reported that the winter months were used by General Franco and his foreign allies in carefully recruiting, organizing, training and equipping a force capable of carrying out and sustaining a prolonged major offensive while on the several fronts only local successes would be sought in particularly selected regions. This preparation must have been well screened, and conducted in back areas far removed from the front judging from the time employed by the Nationalists in launching the counter attack to recover Teruel—lost as a result of the government surprise offensive of December 15, 1937.

From piece meal information obtainable, it appears that General Franco intensified the recruiting of Moors in the Spanish Protectorate, considerable contingents of natives from the French zone being also attracted to enlist in the Nationalist army. These traditional warlike troops were intensively trained and thus was obtained a force of some 50,000 Moroccans who have attained brilliant successes in the operations on the Eastern front which were initiated on March 9, 1938. During the second stage of this offensive an Army Corps of Moroccans under General [Juan] Yague formed the spearhead of the advance in the center of the general line supported by Spanish regular divisions and motorized units. It has been reported from various sources that Moorish units also formed part of some of the army corps operating in other parts of the line.

As regards the Italians, it will be recalled that they have been absent from the front lines since the Santander offensive of August 1937 until their appearance in the present operations on the Eastern front. The Italians are apparently organized in four Divisions (23 March, *Flechas Negras*, *Flechas Azules* and Littorio). There is also a motorized column of Italian troops. The total Italian strength is estimated at some 40,000 men. From information now available, it seems the practice is to employ, at one time, only two or three Italian Divisions, the remaining force being held in reserve. The Italian forces form an Army Corps which is apparently supported by Spanish Legionnaire units under General [Francisco] Garcia Escamez and are operating south of the Ebro River. These troops took Caspe and Gandesa and have participated in the drive to the sea culminating successfully on April 15th.

On the front comprised between Huesca and the Pyrenees there has been operating an Army Corps formed by the so called Navarran Divisions which played so important a role in the subjugation of the Basque country. The province of Navarra has supplied more men to the Nationalist cause than all the others. Further, she has suffered the heaviest battle losses, as her *Requete* units have been utilized as shock troops since the very beginning of the war. At present, many Basques and men from other regions form part of these Divisions which, however, continue to be designated as *Navarran*. This Corps is under command of General [Jose] Solchaga.

South of Huesca is operating the Corps of Aragon, under General [Jose] Moscardo, the famed commander of the Alcazar de Toledo. This Corps is at present reported to occupy the front from the Tremp to the Balaguer areas which are now under constant attack by the Government forces.

The historic defender of Oviedo, General Aranda, commanding the 5th Army Corps, with his Gallego, Navarra and Phalangist Divisions, has been operating most successfully in the region south of Alcaniz centered about Morella. This Corps supported by Legionary troops, has recently succeeded in opening a corridor to the sea in the Vinaroz-Benicarlo Sector. At present, Aranda's corps, divided into two columns under Generals [Rafael] Garcia Valino and Camilo Alonso Vega is pushing forward Nationalist lines south in the province of Castellon. The Gallego Divisions did comport themselves as excellent shock troops during the Teruel campaign and perhaps this fine performance has been rewarded by the honor of operating on the "right of the line" during the present offensive on the Eastern front, and of the distinction of having been assigned the great objective— the shores of the Mediterranean.

A Cavalry Division, under General Monasterio, has participated in a most creditable way in this offensive, particularly in the Bujaraloz region. As a result of the cutting of loyal Spain into two parts, it is believed that some changes in the order of battle outlined above will be effected to meet the requirements of the next Nationalist drive, apparently at present under preparation.

It is estimated that the approximate strength of the five Nationalist Army Corps and of the auxiliary forces operating on the Eastern front is some 200,000 men.

Barcelona   No. 6817
April 27, 1938
Subject: The Nationalist Offensive on the East Front

Resume

With further reference to Report No. 6805 of March 30, 1938, the sweeping Nationalist drive on the eastern front has continued unabated to the Segre and Ebro River lines and to the Mediterranean coast. During the intervening weeks since [the] last report, the Nationalists have occupied north of the Ebro an extensive zone most valuable for future operations against Catalonia as well as an economic viewpoint. The last reported Nationalist front Graco-Fraga-Mequinenza has been pushed forward to a line resting generally on the Segre River up the Balaguer and extending along the Noguera Pallaresa to the French frontier. Furthermore, the insurgents crossed the Segre at Lerida, Balaguer and other strategic points, where bridge heads and extended protecting zones were established to defend them. The Noguera Pallaresa was crossed at various places, particularly in the Tremp sector, in order to control important electric plants from which most of the industrial zones and urban centers of Catalonia derive their light and power. The Government resistance on all fronts was comparatively weak, except in the Lerida area, where a determined stand was made to defend this important city and valley which is generally conceded to be the gateway for an invasion of Catalonia from the west. In the region extending from Huesca to the River Pallaresa and northward to the Pyrenees, the Government troops, totally demoralized, did not offer a serious defense, except here lately, in the region of the Valle de Aran. Government soldiers, variously estimated around four thousand, passed over the French border in this northern region.

Since last report, the Nationalist advance south of the Ebro, has been no less important and transcendental from all viewpoints. The provinces of Tarragona and Castellon, which had been merely touched, have been deeply penetrated and a corridor to the sea some 60 kilometers wide south of the Ebro has been gained by the Nationalists. The magnitude of the blow suffered by the Government in losing this strip of Mediterranean littoral need not be emphasized. The agricultural body of loyal Spain has been severed from its industrial head in which most of the factories of war materiel are located. The military and economic difficulties which the Government will encounter as a result of this operation, may be sufficient in itself to interfere with the continued prosecution of the war. This severance into two parts of loyal Spain, together with the fact that the Nationalists rest their line on the Ebro and Segre Rivers, will permit them the use of interior lines in furthering their drive northward and eastward to isolate Catalonia from France, in prosecuting an attack against the Valencia region or in launching an offensive on some new fronts.

While it is true that the success of the Nationalists has been greatly facilitated by their abundance of war materiel and by their control of the air, a great share of the credit is rightly due to the unity of their command, to the coordinated action of their troops and to their superiority in organization, training, discipline and morale. The Government forces, which certainly do not greatly lack war materiel and aviation, are numerically equal or superior but have again demonstrated a definite inferiority in the above military essentials.

[Omitted is a lengthy, highly tedious day-by-day account.—Ed. Note]

Comments

As pertinent comments have been made along with the events chronologically scheduled above, no further notions of the military situation will be made under this closing heading except to refer briefly to the Government's effort to maintain a spirit of confidence throughout the armed forces and among the people. The Spaniard is an ardent propagandist and few channels in this field are untouched by the present Government in the effort to have the people respond to the slogan of the hour proclaimed and posted everywhere and even made the theme for street plays—*Resister hoy para vencer mañana* (Resist today so as to conquer tomorrow). The propaganda flows river-like from the "Propaganda Department" springs of the Government, with its varied media, throughout the community into every business and trade reaching the firesides of both the high and low. The army is fed with its particular type of propaganda through the political commissars. This latter generally takes the form of preachments in effect that "France is coming to our aid," "Geneva will hear our case," "Great quantities of war materiel are arriving—

we have the men," "America is with us. Roosevelt denounces the fascists," "The United States to modify its neutrality laws," "*The London Times*—England's conservative paper—says 'Loyal Spain will win—none will be able to prevent the final result'". "The mercenaries are held on all fronts—they are stopped from Tortosa to the frontier." "More than 1,800 delegates representing 10 million people proclaim in England our irrevocable resolution to help Spain," and thus the propaganda current flows. The present Secretary of Foreign Affairs, Mr. Alvarez del Vayo, a personal friend of the undersigned, is a past master in the art of propaganda. Some three weeks ago, he told the assembled foreign newspaper men that, "the fascists will never get to the sea" and added, "Come back a month from now and have a sherry with me—you will find the lines unchanged". Recently—three days ago—he entertained at luncheon eight of the leading foreign newspaper men here in Barcelona on which occasion he made the following astounding remark, "The taking of Vinaroz and Benicarlo has been more than compensated for by the spirit and determination it has aroused in our people to defend our land to the end".

In closing this report, the final comment may be apropos at this time. Although the Nationalists are driving hard for victory, one should remember in estimating the duration of this war that things happen slowly in Spain and so it will be noted do the military movements in this war. The estimator should reckon not only with the proverbial mañana spirit of the land, but give weight to the slow plodding thoroughness and super carefulness of the rebel *Generalissimo*.

London   No. 39420
May 17, 1938
Subject: Employment of Troops in Domestic Disturbances.
The Spanish Military Situation

In accordance with letter No. G-2/2657-S-144 dated April 27, 1938, the following information on reports received by the British authorities is forwarded. It should be stated that these reports are regarded as highly confidential and were only made available with the understanding that their contents would be so classified by the American War Department.

They were perused in the presence of an officer during a limited period and the notes taken at this perusal are the basis of the following report of Wing Commander A. James, M.P., who visited the Nationalist Aragon front and furnished his observations to the War Office, as of April 1, 1938, as well as the two reports which originated with the British Military Attaché in Paris, Major C. A. de Linde. Wing Commander A. James' [report] the gist of them is as follows:

The crossing of the Ebro River at Quinto by General Yague's Algerian Corps was well done. This Corps contains Moorish, Spanish Foreign Legion and Navarrese troops. A small covering force was ferried across the river in two steel pontoons and under their protection two pontoon bridges were rapidly constructed. The preservation of secrecy with regard to this operation was excellent. The general morale of the Nationalist troops was high and the casualties sustained were comparatively few.

In the attack, the general system of infantry advance seemed to be in columns of approximately 100 men which fan out when resistance is encountered. Pack mules (presumably with machine guns and ammunition) were well up with the forward troops. Infantry organizations carried their standards which served to indicate their position to support artillery. Ground strips were employed for indicating positions to supporting aircraft.

Considerable use was made of cavalry both for shock and dismounted action. The horses are small and might be called ponies, and mounted on them, the cavalry operates successfully in the most difficult broken country.

The principal difficulty of supporting artillery is said to be locating targets at which to shoot. Their fire seems to be accurately directed but air observation is not used. This observer seemed to be struck by their fine appearance. He has been for some time with the Italians, but his only comment was to the effect that they seemed to take more and better precautions against air observation than the Spanish.

Commander James had a warm welcome from General [Mario] Berti[2] who expressed great satisfaction over Mr. [Anthony] Eden's departure from the Foreign Office and warm friendship towards Great Britain. General Berti stated that he had only 22,000 Italians and considered himself very short of troops. He had had no reinforcements for three months and said that although the Italian soldiers engaged for twelve months, they were not now returning when they went home on leave. In Commander James's opinion, the Italian troops he saw were poor in quality and lacking in enthusiasm. The Spanish openly expressed contempt for them, terming them "Non-Intervention Brigades" and "Holidays with Pay Soldiers".

The British Assistant Attaché in Paris, Major C. A. de Linde, made the following report to Sir Robert Hodgson, dated Paris, April 26, 1938, based on a visit to Franco's Army, April 14-19.[3] During this visit he and Group Captain Colyer, RAF, travelled in one of Franco's staff cars, accompanied by Colonel Maderiaga.

During his visit he neither saw nor heard anything of the Italian or German contingents and was evidently kept away from them. His welcome by Franco was cordial and he gained the impression that the Nationalist officers regarded British non-intervention as a distinct handicap to their cause, although they displayed no bitterness about it. They did, however, express great resentment towards the French. Major de Linde pointed out the singular features of a war in which the majority of the participants are entirely untrained, in which small forces face one another on vast fronts, modern weapons are used but not on a modern scale, and in which there have been more assassinations than deaths in battle. He comments also on the peculiarity of the civil war in which each side has been saved by the intervention of foreign troops. In view of these unusual features, he points out that great caution must be used in deducing general lessons, since under the circumstances it will be possible to prove almost any theory by the exercise of a little adroitness in selection or interpretation.

He was struck by the almost complete absence of warlike activities in all the three sectors visited, in spite of the fact that at least one was at the arrowhead of the present offensive. Battle appears to flare up intermittently and then only on isolated portions of the front. For 100 miles of front the enemies are out of rifle shot of one another. There is little harassing of each other's supply systems and there seems to be a mutual understanding of live and let live. Throughout his journeys the number of men in uniforms in the back areas was amazing. He was not prepared to accept the explanation that they were on leave and came to the conclusion that although the populace in Franco's territory gave every appearance of contentment, the ubiquity of Nationalist troops made it seem that General Franco has no great faith in the civilian zeal for his cause. This comment is underlined and in the margin the CIGS has written "this surprises me".[4]

Major de Linde goes on to say that although it is certain that the Nationalist forces enjoy a definite superiority in weapons, training, food supplies, transportation and foreign assistance, and that these factors undoubtedly contribute to their success, nevertheless, the essential basis of their victories has been their ability to concentrate in secrecy large masses of field and medium artillery in the sectors which they have selected for breaking through. A further important contribution has been their use of air power in the attack which has done much to lower the enemy's morale. Nevertheless, he was not able to state that the Government forces are yet beaten and thought it probable that they might make a strong stand on the Ebro and Segre Rivers.

The general impression is that the war is being conducted in an utterly haphazard way which would indicate that General Franco's organization is improvised and incomplete although the two Corps Headquarters which he visited seem to function efficiently enough. It is possible that, due to the decentralized organization and the modest scale of supply required by the Spanish soldier, a highly systematized scheme of organization and supply is unnecessary in these operations.

The organization of an Army Corps appears to be a flexible one. Its strength may vary from 3 to 6 Divisions, each Division having 12 battalions and a total strength of about 10,000 men. The fronts held are extremely variable, being from 5 to 50 miles. The names of organizations have little or no reference to their actual composition.

Tactics appear, in general, to be used on Great War principles. In the attack, great reliance is placed upon artillery preparation ensuing upon a secret concentration of guns. This is followed up by an advance by infantry and tanks under the protection of a creeping barrage and simultaneous attack on enemy ground troops from the air. This last has been highly developed and is a powerful addition to terrestrial supporting weapons. Its effect is much more than a morale one.

In conversation with a young Englishman serving as an officer in the Spanish Foreign Legion the latter told him that his battalion, with 7 others, was waiting under the shelter of a long ridge when two flights, each of 6 German planes, by mistake attacked them with bombs from 500 feet altitude. In less than 3 minutes these 12 planes had inflicted 500 casualties on a force of 4500 men. These figures were stated to be definite.

In the defense, the first thought is the construction of trenches. These are relatively rudimentary fortifications, however, and do not resemble World War trenches any more than the scanty creeping barrage resembles the World War barrage.

The greatest problem of the staff is transport. As the railroad system is relatively undeveloped and frequently runs in wrong directions, and as the secondary roads vary from bad to worse, and furthermore, as the chauffeurs and mechanics are mediocre, there has resulted an immense wastage of motor transportation.

Major de Linde found all officers of the Franco Army very reluctant to say how much longer they thought the war might last.

In sending this report to the Chief of the Imperial Staff for his perusal, the Chief of Intelligence remarked that Major de Linde's observations teach nothing new but do demonstrate the need of permanent observers with the Nationalist army if anything of technical value is to be learned.

Raymond Lee
Lt. Col., F.A.
M.A., London

June 16, 1938
Memorandum for the Chief of Staff
Subject: Situation in Spain

Ground Operations

On June 13th, two months after the Insurgent offensive in eastern Spain had cut through to the sea at Vinaroz, General Franco's troops captured Castellon de la Plana, [the] first important objective of their campaign against Valencia.

The operation involved three army corps and a total of some fifteen divisions on the front line. (The division at full strength was approximately 10,000 men and includes 12 battalions of infantry and 2 battalions of light artillery.) The action of these corps was as follows:

General Aranda's corps, southwest against the strong Loyalist line from Albocacer to the sea, made a number of local attacks during the period April 23-June 8 but failed to gain appreciably. It apparently attempted no major offensive to break through along the coast because of the losses such an effort would entail. It did succeed in taking Alcala de Chivert and in partially encircling Albocacer.

Following the break through on June 8 by the adjacent corps, which gravely threatened the Loyalist forces in the coastal sector, General Aranda's corps found less resistance, captured Albocacer and advanced rapidly down the main highways toward Castellon. On June 13 a division seized the port and moved into the city from the east.

General Valino's corps, in the center, assisted by General Vareja on its right, began a slow advance on April 23, over a wide front. Its columns, moving on poor roads in mountainous terrain, were delayed by a long spell of wet weather. Loyalist points of resistance in villages and on the heights were methodically outflanked. Aviation and mountain artillery furnished valuable assistance to the infantry.

After a month of intermittent effort, the lateral road running from Teruel to Albocacer was secured, improving communications behind the front. About May 30, the western columns were held up by the strongly fortified position of Mora de Rubielos. To the east there was no such obstacle until Lucena del Cid was encountered about June 8. Lucena, however, was quickly outflanked on the east and on June 11 advance detachments reached the outskirts of the village of Borriol, only 5 miles from Castellon. This forced the immediate withdrawal of the Loyalists on the Albocacer-Alcala de Chivert line. These troops, closely pressed by General Aranda's corps, retreated rapidly to and through Castellon making no attempt at a close-in defense of that city.

The corps of General Varela, which held the front from Teruel north to the vicinity of Montalban, attacked on April 23 to the east and south, captured Allaga on the 25th and after a month's slow progress reached the outskirts of the fortified town of Mora de Rubielos. On May 28 the right wing of this corps attacked from Teruel down the road to Sagunto, took the village of Puebla de Valverde on the third day but has since been held there. The attack of this corps seems to have been designed to keep it abreast of General Valino's corps in the center and to assist in the main effort against Castellon by diverting Loyalist reinforcements to the west flank.

The situation today is that the Loyalist main forces, after losing some thousands of men and considerable materiel in their precipitous retreat, have crossed to the south side of the Mijares River and are digging in. It is likely that a defensive position along the Mijares was already in being. The Loyalists having already learned on the Ebro the defensive value of a river line. Its strength is not known but the river at this time of year is fordable except along its lower reaches. It is also possible that a continuation of strong pressure by the Insurgents will prevent the organization of a defense along this line and that one further back will be selected.

Should Franco find it inadvisable to force an immediate crossing in the coastal sector, it is probable that General Varela's corps will be reinforced so as to strike down the river valley and Sagunto road against the Loyalist left flank.

The only other operation of importance during the period April 15-June 15 were two simultaneous Loyalist offensives against the Insurgent bridgehead over the Segre River at Balaguer and against the hydroelectric power region of Tremp.

Begun on May 22 these efforts were halted, after a few local gains, on May 31. Apparently a diversion to relieve pressure on the Castellon front, they failed to accomplish their purpose and were expensive in casualties and loss of materiel.

Air Operations

The past two months have witnessed intensive air activity on the part of the Insurgents who maintained crushing air superiority throughout the period. Aircraft continued the close support of ground forces by bombing points of resistance, rear areas, roads, and troop concentrations. The principal air effort, however, was devoted to a systematic daily attack of Loyalist ports along the Mediterranean from Castellon on the north to Alicante on the south. These attacks although causing heavy casualties to civilians seem to have been directed primarily at the docks, port facilities and shipping in the harbor. Over fifty commercial vessels were sunk or damaged. Franco has in fact constituted a blockade of the coast by aviation, lacking adequate naval strength. The effect upon the importation of war materials, oil and food into the Valencia-Madrid area has been far-reaching and may become a decisive factor in breaking the Loyalist resistance in this part of Spain.

Future Probabilities
Russia and France, unofficially, have sent and facilitated the export to Barcelona of large quantities of war materials in recent weeks. The great bulk of these are of necessity utilized in Catalonia rather than in the remaining part of Loyalist Spain. It appears, therefore, that Catalonia is determined to continue her resistance even if the Insurgents succeed in taking Valencia and eventually Madrid. The latter events would seem only a question of time. It is probable that the war will continue into the winter, or longer, unless agreement among the European nations vitally interested is brought about to force a peace between Franco and the last stronghold of the Loyalists, Catalonia.

McCabe

Barcelona   No. 6856
July 20, 1938
Subject: The Military Situation

Since last report, the Nationalist offensive on the Castellon-Teruel fronts continued for days progressing with considerable difficulty owing to the successive strongly fortified Government lines encountered and the obstinate resistance offered by the large number of Loyalist forces concentrated in this area. However, the ground gained by the Nationalists on the coast sector and mountainous districts to the west, which culminated during the first days of July in the occupation of Burriana, [unintelligible] and part of the Sierra Espadan, created a difficult situation for the Government troops defending the formidable stronghold from Sarrion to Mora de Rubielos and the pocketed area in this sector. A glance at the map shows that the lack of roads south of the Teruel-Sagunto highway would cause the situation of the loyalists in the Mora pocket to become critical should they not retreat before the insurgents reached that highway in the Segorbe sector. Taking into account that the Government had massed in the above defensive line and back areas a force estimated at some 100,000 men, it seemed that the loyal command

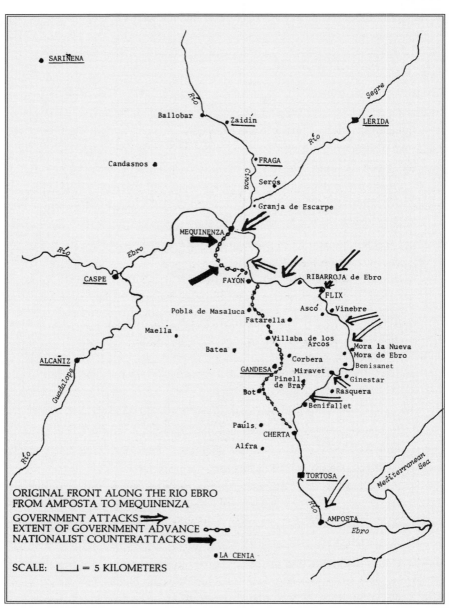

Battle of the Ebro, July 23–August 6, 1938. [Raymond L. Proctor, *Hitler's Luftwaffe in the Spanish Civil War* (© 1983 by Greenwood Press). Reprinted by permission of ABC-Clio.]

would try to avoid a disaster by withdrawing their lines before they were broken by the constantly increasing rebel pressure. Thus the fall of the Mora pocket was anticipated by this office in recent military cable reports to the State Department.

After the mopping up of the Albentosa-Rubielos pocket the Nationalist columns resumed their advance, always in the face of strong Government resistance, towards their next object, the important town of Segorbe. When this point has been attained, a large pocket formed north of the line Viver-Algimia must inevitably fall, and the closing phase of this offensive, i.e., the possession of the Teruel-Sagunto highway, will be nearing completion.

In spite of Nationalist successes, it is remarkable how the Government forces have recovered from the grave defeats encountered in the past and continue their resistance in the face of great handicaps. Even now that the southern loyalist troops are at a marked strategical disadvantage, being cut off from land communication with Catalonia, the Army of the Center is offering on the Teruel-Castellon fronts a resistance which so greatly concerned General Franco, that he felt the necessity of appearing in person in this sector.

The Negrin slogan, "Resist now, to conquer later" is being carried out most successfully and, should this stubborn resistance continue, the time honored query "What price victory" may be asked of General Franco. Of course, this continual fighting against an enemy obviously superior in strength, organization, leadership and materiel must necessarily greatly weaken the Government forces and make possible for the Nationalists in the end to attain a complete victory. The fall of the Mora de Rubielos Government stronghold and [the] following insurgent successful advance against Sagunto open great possibilities for the Nationalists in this region, and bring near the attainment of their main objective—Valencia, her port and adjacent gardens and orchards.

Irrespective of future developments, it is observed that the Army of the Center, in spite of its unfavorable comparison in equipment, organization and leadership, has up to the present succeeded in resisting a superior enemy and has adroitly escaped annihilation. It is believed that, among other reasons, this ability to resist may be found in the main in the clever use of propaganda and in the intelligent employment of field fortifications. The communist elements which seem to control at present both the Government and the Army, are successfully using propaganda in strengthening the morale of the armed forces. In the Army, this spirit of resistance is strongly enforced by the officer and commissar corps which have much to lose should Franco win.

Through the organization of a large number of fortification units, the Government is constantly building defensive lines in depth in the threatened areas along modern lines. Fortification is stressed as the best means to retard enemy advance and as reserve forces do not seem to be lacking owing to the recent call of new military classes, the Nationalists always find that, after the breaking of a front line, successive strongholds await them at short distances. Owing to the fact that the Government forces have a relative abundance of automatic weapons, considerable preparation of artillery fire and aviation bombing are required by the Nationalists before such strongholds can be taken by the infantry, and hence the slow pace of their advance.

[Here I omitted day-by-day operations reports, as these add little to the narrative.—Ed. Note]

Comments

As this report closes, the evidence is convincing—based on information obtained from both sides—that the Nationalists have assembled sufficient forces on the Levante front, notwithstanding the dogged resistance by the Government troops, to gain their present first great objective—the control of the Teruel-Sagunto highway. After the accomplishment of this task, it is generally believed, at this time, that the Franco plan contemplates a drive on Valencia from Sagunto way along the coast aided by flanking columns from the Liria region through the valley of the Turia.

The importance of the offensive power of the Government troops, as reported by this office, was never more convincingly established than in the past weeks when they have failed to launch an attack on the Catalan front, if for no other reason than to relieve, to some extent, the pressure in the Teruel-Castellon sector.

Although there has been no material change on other fronts, Government communiqués of the latter part of June claim gaining important positions in the Extremadura area around Fuenteovejuna. Both sides, however, claimed gains on the same front, which may be taken to mean that no offensive other than for local positions has occurred in this region.

The activities in the Madrid area seem to have been limited to mine blowing by Government forces (July 12th and 18th) on the University front.

The government political situation, as regards its influence on the military problem, seems unchanged. The Negrin cabinet continues to dominate the situation in furthering its policy of "Resist to conquer". However, in the speeches made on occasion of the "Second Anniversary of the War", particularly in the one delivered by Mr. Azaña, there can be found less of the "fight to the last blood drop and foot of soil attitude of the Government and more of the spirit of conciliation tempered by an unquestioned desire for peace."

Barcelona   No. 6865
August 3, 1938
Subject: The Military Situation

Resume of Military Events

Since last report the outstanding developments in the military situation have been the Government major offensive on the Ebro front, the continuous loyalist resistance in the province of Castellon, a Government minor offensive in the Sort region and the Nationalist drive in the Extremadura sector, all of which involved severe fighting and considerable losses on both sides of men and materiel, without producing any appreciable change in the general military situation.

The marked military even covered by this report is the offensive initiated by the Army of the Ebro along the river frontage from Mequinenza to Amposta, centered particularly in the region Ribarroja-Pinell, the axial line of advance being Falset-Gandesa. This offensive, with successful river crossings south of Mequinenza and in the region noted above seemingly was a surprise to the Nationalist High Command. Although the movement was sensed and reported on the Rebel radios twenty-four hours prior to its execution, it is unquestionable that the magnitude of the enterprise was not appreciated until it had become a *fait accompli*.

The movement was well known among the military observers in Barcelona [within] several days—in fact, about a week before its execution. The movement noted of a large number of guns was indicative of some operation being staged for the immediate future; however, the transfer of large numbers of fishermen boats from along the beaches north and south of Barcelona was convincing that the crossing of the Ebro was contemplated. This estimate was further fortified by the frequently stated "crying need" by many Government officials for an offensive to relieve the pressure on the Army of the Center battling in the Levante. To answer this military call for help, the most favorable theatre of operations would naturally be found in the Gandesa-Tortosa sector. Another indication was the weakness of the rebel position in this area which was well known to the Government troops along the left bank of the river, in fact, the Commander of the XV Brigade, Colonel [Vladimir] Copic, who the undersigned was visiting on the Mora la Nueva front at the time, in reply to a query "What is the enemy's strength across the river?", answered, "About a corporal's guard". Another strong point in the Government's favor was the Nationalists' underestimate of the Government's strength, staff and organizational ability to stage an offensive of any magnitude involving the crossing of the Ebro.

At this writing, observers returning from the front report that the troops in the Gandesa area are finding it difficult to maintain their river crossing communications. This situation is due to the increased resistance offered in front and to the constant action of the Rebel aviation. It will be noted that reconnoitering planes are constantly patrolling this area. These are equipped with radio apparatus, through which the waiting bombing squadrons in the airfields are informed. Thus, activities observed along the river by the reconnoitering planes, troop concentrations, truck movements, etc., can be reported and the bombers take to the air, almost simultaneously, for their targets.

On the Tortosa-Chortal sector, owing to the vital importance of this front for the security of the littoral, the Nationalists were stronger, and here, while several crossings were effected by the Loyalists, the leading troops met strong resistance and were eventually forced back to the left bank of the river suffering heavy losses. The Nationalists claim that these forces which passed the river in this sector were annihilated. The brunt of this advance fell upon the 14th International Brigades (French).

It is generally conceded here that the Government offensive on the Ebro front was a very dangerous operation, particularly in view of the Army's lack of organizational and staff training for open warfare. This may be true unless the initial penetration be extended and consolidated and a good communication system organized with the rear bases.

Irrespective of future events, the Government Ebro offensive is a new proof of the marvelous recuperative ability of the loyal Army, and although as an offensive it may result in failure, nevertheless it is believed to have attained the most important of its objectives—the delaying of the Rebel drive against Sagunto and Valencia, generally relieving the pressure in the Levante against the Army of the Center.

The details of the crossing of the river are not available at this time, but it is understood that it was accomplished by brigades and that the crossing was effected by boats (fishermen boats holding some 20 men), pontoon bridges utilizing these boats, rafts (for supplies and ammunition) and some for trestle bridges made more or less permanent for wheel transportation.

No artillery preparation was employed as none was necessary and above all the surprise factor was desired. The Rebels evidently had not fortified the river banks, but had adopted the defense plan of constructing strong points and centers of resistance well back from the river, in fact, as far back as the line Villalba-Gandesa-Prat which now holds.

The Nationalist offensive in the Levante has continued slowly, gaining some ground but always meeting stubborn resistance. At present, perhaps due to the crossing of the Ebro by the loyalists, the advance is halted. If this Nationalist movement is retarded for some other reason, it may be due to shifting troops southward from the Sagunto road toward Andilla, which is reported in their possession, with a view of placing a parallel column eventually on the Chelva-Liria-Valencia road. The reinforcing Italian Divisions in this sector have not been sufficient to break the Government resistance, although perhaps contributed in the mopping up of the Mora de Rubielos pocket.

The recent Government offensive in the Sort area, during the third week of July, directed against the town of Rialp, through the valley of the Rio Magdalena, ended in a complete disaster locally and accomplished no result whatever unless this movement, in some way, prevented rebel reinforcements in this region being shifted to the Gandesa area, an eventuality considered remote although claimed by the Seo de Urgel commander. An officer of the 133 Brigade—the main attacking unit—made to the undersigned (a personal friend) the following statement during a recent visit to the Seo de Urgel sector, "It was what you told me your General Sherman said about war. It was certainly 'Hell' and our Brigade was just about annihilated. We were in the main attack, with a brigade on each of our flanks but which never got into action. The Rebels held their fire for a long time and then opened upon us with all classes of fire: artillery, mortars, machine guns and automatics. Their artillery fire was cleverly registered pounding at first against our flanks, which had the tendency to force our troops to the center of the valley, then all of a sudden the fire rained upon us almost annihilating our brigade. We had 3,400 men and 136 officers when we started. We lost of our men 900 killed or missing and over a thousand wounded. Over half the officers were casualties, about fifty were killed."

The Rebel offensive in the Extremadura region, while important in itself owing to the extensive, rich and populated valley of the Guadiana region added to Nationalist Spain, was no doubt primarily intended to serve as a diversion movement to hold troops to this area preventing their being sent to the Castellon front.

Now remains to be seen whether this offensive is to take on some magnitude and proceed against the important quicksilver mines of Almaden or was solely a diversion movement.

[Here I omitted day-by-day accounts, as they were summarized above, covering July 20–August 2.—Ed. Note]

Comments

In resume it may be said that the front from the Pyrenees to Lerida (visited by the undersigned last week) is well fortified by the opposing forces on their respective banks of the Noguera Pallaresa and Segre rivers and that while minor actions may occur in this sector and offensives of a diverting nature initiated, no major offensives (requiring the massing of large forces) seem likely to occur for the present in this region.

The region south of Lerida to the sea, along the banks of the Ebro, holds the interest of the military observer for the moment. Should the Government maintain its foothold recently gained in the Gandesa pocket, thus threatening the Rebel occupied Castellon region, such success will have a material bearing on prolonging the war. However, should these forces meet with a disaster, or are forced to return to the left bank of the Ebro, the tide of a Government victory will fall to a low ebb, from which a peace overture may come into being. The Nationalist advance on the Levante front seems held for the moment by the Republican forces. The Government claims a minor offensive victory in the Albarracin region, which is apparently of a diverting character.

The Extremadura drive of the Nationalists is halted with the spearhead of the advance some ten kilometers east of Castuera on the railroad to Cabeza de Buey.

The successful crossing of the Ebro by the Army of Ebro, directed by General Rojo, has had a tremendous influence in bolstering the morale of the army and the people. For this reason, the aftermath of a defeat in this region would probably bring about a morale depression of great import and far reaching consequences.

While the crossing of the Ebro was a successful military enterprise, it must not be overemphasized. It must be remembered that the massing of a large body of men (reported in this case to be in all some forty thousand men) on any front assures initial success and in this particular case the crossing was greatly aided by friendly inhabitants on the enemy side of the river and accomplished without enemy opposition.

In regard to the latter phase of the question, members of the American units, here wounded in the hospital, reported that the advance gained in twenty-four hours the third day's objective and that they were not stopped by enemy fire but by lack of ability for the supply units to keep pace with the forward movement.

In closing, it might be herein noted that the food supply in Barcelona is daily growing worse and that unless some remedial measures can be found by the Government to meet this all important situation, a serious disaffection in the rearguard may be expected.

Another great factor bearing upon the morale of the Barcelona people is the electric light and power shortage—due to the necessity for conservation of electricity. In certain sections of the city the electricity current is off about half the day and the movies are about out of operation. The power for transportation, subway and surface, has been so reduced that the working groups cannot be transported during the morning and afternoon peak hours and consequently large numbers are forced to walk or stand for a "lift". Personal observation of these queues indicate a definite lowering of the people's endurance and consequent morale.

Barcelona   No. 6874
August 9, 1938
Subject: Three Days' Visit to Eastern Front

Through the courtesy of the G-2 section of the Spanish War Department, in obtaining proper authorization and the detail of Captain Jesus Prados as his guide, the undersigned visited the Eastern Front—Lerida to the Pyrenees—July 18-19-20, 1938.

Sort-Rialp Front

This was reached from the Seo de Urgel by car via main highway south to unimproved road passing through Parroquia and Pallerols to the head of the valley northwest of this town which was the dead end of this improvised military road route. At this point we mounted horses—there in readiness—and moved along the northern slopes of Tozal de Orri, gaining an elevation of over 7,000 feet, where we dismounted and entered a communication trench through which we passed to the front line and observation post overlooking the valley of the Noguera Pallaresa, with the towns of Sort and Rialp lying before us in the distance.

The rebel position is firmly entrenched some 3 to 5 kilometers to the east of the river thus protecting the main Sort-Tremp highway. At a point quite near to our observation post the trenches of the opposing forces were along the same slope—the topographical crest being in the hands of the rebels while the military crest formed the line for the government troops. While at the observation post, the ground was pointed out along the valley of the Rio de Santa Magdalena, and the approach to Rialp, over which was staged the recent disastrous Government offensive against the Sort area.

Tremp Area

This area was visited by car from Artesa de Segre, via the main Tremp highway, to a point near Benavent, 27 kilometers distant. From this point, a communication trench was followed westward to an observation post from which could be observed Tremp in the far distance and the front line passing to the north about half way between Isona and Conques and between Sant Roma and Figuerola and continuing some 6 kilometers east of the great Pantano de Tremp (Lake) to the Sort region. The little sinuous valleys of the Abella and the Conques could be seen outlined in the terrain panorama stretching beyond to the Noguera Pallaresa.

Balaguer Bridgehead-Lerida Zone

This was approached from Artesa de Segre via the road southeast to Talladell, turning off on the unimproved road to Preixens-Mongay to the front Bellmunt-Bellcaire over military roads not shown on maps. The high ground positions on this front permitted a complete observation of the bridgehead. It was noted that the Government front line passes west of Alos de Balaguer, Cubells, Mongay and Bellcaire touching the Segre just south of Vallfogona thence along the left bank of the river to Lerida.

The most impressive feature of this area was its organization for defense. The 18th Corps in the bridgehead sector and the 11th Corps to the north have each 10 battalions (650 men) [of] civilian fortification troops assigned. The force in the Balaguer sector during this period of digging in has been increased to 20 battalions, making in all in these sectors 30 battalions or a total of 20,000 men.

Observation—Notes

The Sort area, command centered at Seo de Urgel, was a difficult region to visit owing to the mountainous character of the terrain, taxing one's strength and endurance to the utmost in the long hot hours over hard going roads, trails and mountain sides.

This sector, although well defended from the entrenched positions along the ridges is believed to be vulnerable in many spots by flank approach to the occupied positions, utilizing mountain trained infantry columns in a night movement. Marches similar to these executed on many occasions by our troops in the Philippines would obtain important military successes in this region; however, such enterprises, as far as known by the undersigned, have not been employed by either side and when discussed with the Spanish officer are invariably pushed aside conversationally as "impracticable". This, fortified with many other reasons, is convincing that the Spaniard as a race—emphasized in his soldier life—is not "practical," lacks "resourcefulness" and does not understand the word "preparation," organization and "cooperation" as employed in our military vocabulary.

The undersigned was much impressed with the gradual relegation of the "Division" to the administrative category. This is particularly noted in the rise and importance of the Brigade and Corps as "combat" units. Briefly it might be said that the Corps is assigned the "task" and that the "execution" is by the distinctive combat unit—the brigade. The inspection of several "division" staffs showed their officer organization and strength as follows:

1 – Division command
2 – G-3 operations officer and assistant
  (usually have their desks in the same office)
1 – Headquarters commander
1 – G-1 Personnel
2 – G-2 Information section
1 – G-4 Map and ground information
1 – G-5 Transportation and communications.

———

9 Officers—Total.

The Corps headquarters as a rule carries the burden of supply and equipment with the upkeep depots.

One of the most striking features of this new Republican Army is the lack of proper rank of the high unit commanders. As far as known, practically all Corps are commanded by lieutenant colonels. Division commanders, in some cases are lieutenant colonels but generally are of the grade of major as are the Brigade commanders. The only generals who are known are Sarabia, actively commanding the *Ejercito de la Zona de Cataluña* and, theoretically, the *Ejercito del Ebro*, General Rojo, Chief of Staff and now actively commanding the Ebro offensive and General Miaja commanding the *Grupo de Ejercitos del Centro*. The only other generals known are leftovers from the old army, viz:

General [Carlos] Masquelet, formerly Chief of Staff and one time Secretary of War, is now in the Azaña household as *Jefe del Cuarto Militar*. General Pozas, now inactive, having been relieved from command of the Eastern Front after the rebel March offensive; General [Jose] Riquelme, quite in evidence in the early part of the war, particularly in the Guadarrama region, now commands the Barcelona local garrisons—which formerly carried a title of Captain General, General Asensio, recently released from a "state of detention" under charges of "lack of loyalty to the regime" and some "responsibility" for the "Malaga disaster" and General Cabrera, formerly Chief of Staff, under Caballero, now "detained" under charges similar to those in the case of Asensio.

The reason given the undersigned for not bestowing proper organizational rank, as noted above, was explained by an officer of high rank as follows: "The rivalry in the various political organizations in vying to have their representatives made generals would have been very adverse, if not a disrupting effect, upon the efficiency of the Army. Besides, the officers and commissars feel that this absence of high rank makes them more akin and intensifies the democracy of the service— particularly when the brotherly term of *comarada* is used as an address in all ranks".

One of the most marked impressions received by the undersigned was of the vast plan of fortifications in which the especially organized troops mentioned above were engaged in this sector. The plans for ground treatment, characterized as French, might have just as well have been taken from TR 195-5 for "principles" and 195-20 for "types".[5] The Balaguer bridgehead is being organized in "defense areas", with good depth, honeycombed with "strong points" and "centers of resistance", with sufficient "switch positions". It remains to be seen whether these ground defenses will be occupied by determined troops, efficiently trained and properly armed. The corps area commander, not having had any past experience in this particular field of the military art, informed the undersigned, "that he believed this manner of ground defense"—getting away from the old continuous trench line—was one of the great lessons of the Spanish War.

In observing the men of the "fortification battalions" at work during the noon hour under a hot July sun, the officer in charge explained that the fine spirit of the men shown by their working overtime in the heat of a noon day sun was due in great part to a system of competition and prizes which greatly stimulated the local pride of the "diggers" in their effort to outdo their neighbors.

Answers to questions propounded, concerning sickness types and health of the command, brought out the information, fortified by personal observations, that the troops are in excellent physical condition, enjoying good health and free from major disease cases in any numbers. The men were vaccinated against typhoid at the recruiting stations and the old venereal problem has been removed through the more or less isolation of the men. The outdoor camp life at this season of the year with "sun bathing" a daily pastime makes for "brown baked" bodies, physical strength and health. The sick reports showed most cases to be slight stomach troubles, occasioned in all probability by "unbalanced" food menus, surface water drinking and through raw fruit consumption.

The *retraguardia* or back area police control, particularly in the application of road discipline, is feeble and ineffective. The road guards are generally "home town" militia soldiers, who have no control over the mighty truck driver. This "road tyrant" used the highway as he wishes and speeds and parks at his will. By virtue of his own "toughness" and the mass force or "shock" value of his vehicle, he dominates the situation.

The troops in the sierra regions generally are camped in the pine groves found on the ridge slopes. The *casitas*—small huts—are built out of pine boughs constructed as follows: a ridge pole is fixed between two trees, man high, against are leaned smaller pine stripped branches forming the roofing from ground to ridge. The hut is usually completed by covering the roofing, which extends around the rear, with cut sod in bricks, about 10 in. x 10 in., fastened and held together by vine and grass ties. The front is covered and door improvised with needle boughs.

From personal observation it was noted that these huts were built throughout the woods without any attempt at minor organization grouping and with a complete disregard of any formation. This is typically Spanish, in not disturbing the "individualism" of the man or curbing his "freedom of action". The thought does not seem to arise among the leaders that this encouraged "individualism" has an adverse effect upon discipline and that at times destroys the power of the leader to lead particularly when his presence cannot be felt.

The command of an organization in the Republican Army is difficult to understand. In addition to the ever present commissar, who shares responsibility for many organizational activities, which with us are elements of command, there are generally two agencies responsible for combat, the leader on the ground and the directing staff of the higher unit in the rear with ground representation. This system is well illustrated in the recent Ebro offensive. The Eastern Front, composed of the Army of the Catalan Zone and the Army of the Ebro, is commanded by General [Hernández] Sarabia, however, the crossing of the Ebro in the recent Government offensive was done under the direction of General Rojo—the Chief of Staff of the Army—utilizing the Army of the Ebro reinforced and commanded by Lieutenant Colonel Modesto.

The "Loud Speaker" for propaganda purposes was noted in the Tremp area; however, its employment has been temporarily suspended. The Corps area commander informed the undersigned personally, that whereas the commissar believed good results accrued from the use of this novel firing line equipment, the staff thought such good was not commensurate with the losses its use entailed, adding, that whenever the plant opened for operations it drew unceasingly heavy enemy fire.

The troops are well supplied—the depots being in the towns and the dumps usually at the end of the truck roads. Corps received direct from Barcelona depots which in turn issue direct to Brigades. The supply depot of the 133 Brigade in Seo de Urgel was visited. This depot draws from the Corps depot daily, maintaining in reserve two days' rations. The brigade has three dumps at three different "road heads" from which fronts the mule pack trains "carry on" to the battalions, in which units are the kitchens. The front line troops are fed by "food bearers" working their way forward through the communicating trenches.

The commissar is much in evidence in these sectors. Corps schools are established for their instruction and training. The building and maintenance of the morale of the men is at present their great mission and seemingly every device and scheme known is employed to this end. Every piece of news destined for the troops is carefully studied and at times distorted and so colored in presentation as to give to the soldier only "good news". Even the "bad news" picture is so painted as to make it appear "good". The "stop" of an "advance" is proclaimed, "our troops, having attained their objectives, are now organizing their new positions" or, "in order to better our positions, the high command withdrew the troops to the 'x' line", or, "the invaders, exasperated by our long defense, were forced into an attacking position from which they suffered great losses", etc., etc.

As to uniforms, well, there is not such a thing. In fact, at the front there is hardly a shade yellow, blue, grey or brown or a shirt design not observed. The *mono* (overalls) of the colder season has been replaced with shorts and generally at this season no other clothing is worn. The *alpargata* (canvas sandal) is the invariable footwear of the soldier. Shaving is not encouraged, in fact, the "manly" beard is in vogue. Streams of these men passing along the trails, with their berry brown bodies, and heavy beard and long hair, dressed in shorts remind one of the typical movie ship wrecked souls on a desert island.

The word "discipline" as applied to the soldier, as we know the meaning, cannot be employed. To use this term, affirmatively or negatively, in describing this feature of the soldier's training would be misleading. As one observes this soldier of the Republican Army, he finds no outward manifestations of the various elements of what, from our point, forms the basis of true discipline. Yet, this soldier is courteous, fights and endures extreme hardships and sufferings for the *causa* and responds to leadership in mass formation. In all, he is a worthy enemy in the severest combat.

In the several headquarters visited, it was surprising to note what detailed information was possessed by the G-2 sections of the "order of battle" of the enemy. This information was shown to the undersigned in map overlays, which gave enemy distribution down to include the battalion.

Barcelona   No. 6908
October 12, 1938
Subject: The Military Situation

Resume of Military Events

Since last report (No. 6896 of September 14, 1938), no outstanding change has occurred in the general military situation. While both sides have suffered heavy losses in the Levante and Ebro campaigns, there are indications that the Nationalists are preparing a major offensive and that the Government, without departing from its general policy of resistance, will launch diversion attacks in keeping with the requirements of the moment. However, the opinion is growing among the Spanish people (outside of army circles) that during the autumn season, just entered, a settlement of the war will take place either as a result of international agreement or from internal compromise.

The rebel wedge resulting from the breaking of several Government lines in depth in the section comprised between Fatarella and Corbera, has been pushed forward deeper and now includes the heights dominating at short range the Fatarella-Venta de Camposines road, beyond which the ground generally slopes down toward the river in the Asco area. This salient involves a positive menace for the loyalists as by the gaining of this road, the Nationalists might easily cut in two the zone occupied by the Government forces west of the Ebro, a development which in all probability would force a general loyalist withdrawal to the left bank of the river.

As time passes, the opinion is reinforced that the slowness with which the Nationalists are carrying their Ebro counteroffensive is not caused by loyalist re-

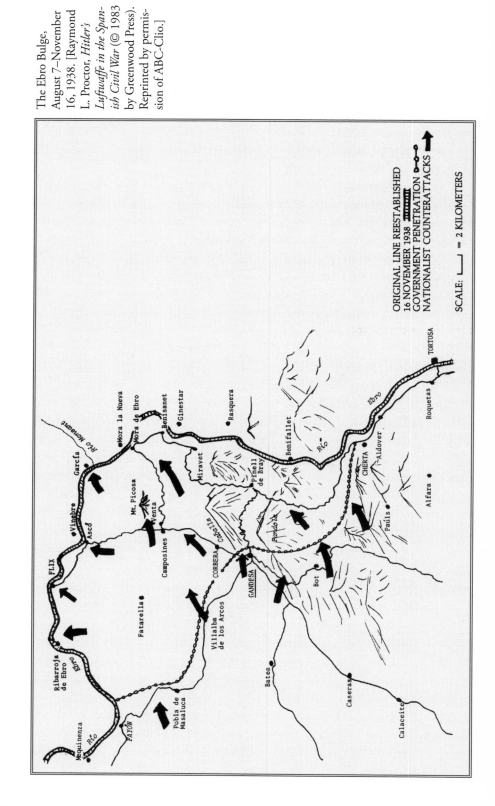

The Ebro Bulge, August 7–November 16, 1938. [Raymond L. Proctor, *Hitler's Luftwaffe in the Spanish Civil War* (© 1983 by Greenwood Press). Reprinted by permission of ABC-Clio.]

ORIGINAL LINE REESTABLISHED
16 NOVEMBER 1938
GOVERNMENT PENETRATION
NATIONALIST COUNTERATTACKS

SCALE: ⎣__⎦ = 2 KILOMETERS

sistance exclusively. It appears that the Nationalists continue their plan of gaining position improvements with the least possible number of losses, through employment of mass aviation and concentrated artillery fire, until the Government local position becomes practically untenable. There are reports that the rebels are making concentrations in the Valencia-Castellon sector preparing for a continuation of the drive against Valencia, while other sources present the Catalan front as the likely theater of operation during the Autumn. The front on which the Nationalists will next strike with a major offensive continues to be a matter of conjecture, but it appears certain that they have not as yet attacked with all their available striking force in the Ebro sector and that the past fighting for position improvement while heavy and costly to them, has not sapped their strength as much as claimed in the Government communiqués. The Italian Division appears to continue in reserve somewhere back of the Ebro front. However, the presence of Italian tank and artillery units has been reported on the Ebro front.

The recent decision of the Spanish Government to initiate a complete withdrawal of their international volunteers will considerably reduce the efficiency of the loyalist army, particularly as regards to staging offensive operations. It will be recalled that in all Government drives, the International Brigades have been used as shock troops. The total number of foreigners enlisted in the Republican Army is estimated at some 10,000. Reference to the announcement by Italy of the withdrawal of some 10,000 volunteers from Spain it may be stated here that the military efficiency of these troops is believed to be far inferior to that of the foreign volunteers serving under Republican Spain.

The offensive initiated by the Government on the Manzanera (Teruel) front on September 19th proved conclusively that the Nationalists were prepared with strong reserves in this sector as their counterattack was immediate and of crushing effect upon the loyalists. The Government forces succeeded in gaining a number of hills during the first days of their drive; however, the Nationalists counterattacked with such force that the loyalists lost in one day all the ground gained and had to retire to their original positions after suffering heavy losses in men and materiel. The Nationalist strength in this sector appears to confirm reports to the effect that they are making preparations on the Levante front for the prosecution of the Valencia offensive.

Nothing of any military importance has occurred in the remaining fronts during the period under review. The Nationalist offensive on the Extremadura front has been definitely stopped. The Government counteroffensive in this sector had evidently checked [the] Nationalist advance against the rebel coveted mercury Almaden mines.

Comments

In view of the general inactivity of the Republican forces on the Center and South fronts and the demonstrated inability of these troops to launch a major offensive, the military observer turns to the Ebro front as the true barometer in estimating the military situation of the Republican Army. It is apparent in this sector that the constant pounding by the Nationalists with their mass aviation attacks and concentrations of artillery fire is having its effect evidenced by the "giving of ground" by the loyalist forces. Although the Republican forces are fighting hard and contending for every foot of hill and valley, they have lost their main long prepared defense lines and are now slowly but surely gradually giving away on their second positions. The position of the Army of the Ebro must also be adversely affected by the food supply shortage here in Barcelona and by the present insecurity of the Negrin government—hammered as it is on all sides by the cry for peace—peace—peace.

The desire for peace felt by the civilian population is spreading to the army—although opposed at this time by the dominant military leaders who see the end of hostilities as the termination of their careers of leadership and prestige and perhaps their lives. The undersigned was informed today at a small luncheon by a high official of the air service—formerly its chief—that "the army wants peace". Upon being pressed for further information as to whether this was an individual opinion, he replied emphatically, "No, all the army except a few militia leaders want the war to end now".

It is common gossip here and is generally believed that some pressure from "the outside" will be brought to bear to end the Spanish war as soon as the relations of England and France with Italy, now in the process of adjustment, have been unified. It is difficult, from the trend of expressed opinions here in all walks of society, not to absorb the belief that the Spanish war is entering its last phase—but just how long this will last, one, knowing the peculiarity of the Spanish complex and psychology, hesitates to prophesy. This trend of thought has been fortified by Dr. Negrin's departure from Barcelona yesterday—reported to be for Paris or London.

The movement of Italian troops, in part, back to Italy, and the recall from the front of the "foreigners" of the International Brigades are read as the proverbial straws before the slow but sure wind of peace.

Barcelona   No. 6936
November 22, 1938
Subject: The Military Situation

During the period covered by this report, military activities have been re-stricted to the Eastern and Levante fronts. The fighting has been particularly heavy in the Ebro sector, where the Nationalists have carried to a successful conclusion their long and costly counteroffensive to expel the loyalists from the 600 square kilometer zone which they occupied a few days after their successful crossing of the river on July 25, 1938.

On November 3rd, the occupation by the Nationalists of the important Si-erras of Caballs and Pandols indicated a retreat to the east bank by the govern-ment forces, as these positions dominated a large area of ground generally sloping toward the river. From then on the Nationalist advance was very rapid. Rebel troops, supported by aviation, which constantly bombed the Government posi-tions, penetrated the enemy defense lines and secured the west bank of the Ebro from Chortal to Miravet. As a result of this movement, the strong defensive system which the Government troops had constructed in this area lost most of its value since it was open to attack from the flank.

The loyalists were forced to retreat rather hastily, their former tactics of strong local resistance giving away to a series of delaying actions. Considering the dif-ficulty of the undertaking, the Government troops carried out their withdrawal movement with considerable success, although at the cost of heavy losses, both in men and materiel. When the last loyalist stands along the Camposines-Mora de Ebro road and Fatarella range were made, most of the Government forces had already recrossed the river, thus avoiding a decisive defeat which the Nationalist command had hoped to inflict.

The Government offensive in the Segre sector appeared to lack sufficient strength to follow up the initial success in crossing the river, which is more readily fordable than the Ebro. It remains to be seen how long the Government will be able to retain the small area on the right bank of the river.

The diversion attacks launched by the loyalist troops on the Levante front failed to attain any important success and once more indicated the inability of the Republican Army to successfully conduct a sustained offensive.

The Nationalist aviation continued frequent bombings of the Government port and industrial areas. The blockade of loyal ports appears to be rather effective and, as a result, the Government is confronted with a shortage of materiel and ammunition and the food situation is becoming more acute. The Nationalists dominate the air on all fronts.

[Here I omitted day-to-day accounts.—Ed. Note]

The Government finally admitted the defeat on the Ebro front although considerably distorting the facts. The official communiqué stated that "following the High Command's pre-arranged plan, and after having completely attained the results sought by the wearing down tactics against the enemy, carried on since July 25th., the republican troops last night recrossed the Ebro river returning to their old positions on the left bank, this voluntary and methodical withdrawal having been effected without abandoning a single man or rifle in the hands of the enemy". The Nationalist report stated that with the occupation during the day of the villages of Flix and Ribarroja the last stage of the victorious Nationalist counteroffensive in the Ebro sector was closed, the Government troops having been forced to recross the river.

From a military point of view this operation appears to have been rather costly to the Nationalists, as no decisive advantage has been gained. The net result, aside from losses inflicted on the Government forces, has been only the occupation of a relatively unimportant area of ground, and making good Franco's often repeated statement that he will never give up ground once taken by his forces.

Comments

It is a characteristic of this struggle that an offensive is usually followed by a period of inactivity. The ability of the Loyalists to conduct a sustained offensive is very much open to doubt. It is reasonable to believe that after a period of quiet, Franco will strike again with the probabilities favoring an attack somewhere on the Catalan front.

H.B. Cheadle
Lt. Col., Infantry
Military Attaché

9

Conquest of Catalonia and End of the War

(December 1938–April 1939)

"The remnants of the Government army are no longer offering any appreciable or organized resistance, and are arriving at the French frontier in great numbers intermingled with civilian refugees, all seeking asylum in France."

Lt. Col. Henry B. Cheadle,
February 1939

In this chapter various American army officers document the end of the military campaigns in Spain. The conclusion of the fighting was so important that now the most senior officials in the U.S. War Department were receiving frequent reports on the rapid collapse of the conflict. The central military event was the conquest of Catalonia; in part, one could also call it the collapse of resistance in this northeast corner of Spain, and the occupation of Barcelona. As the dispatches make quite clear, with that event, essentially Republican resistance in various parts of Spain melted away, leading to the occupation of Madrid and various southern and central provinces at an extremely rapid rate in March. While General Franco declared the civil war over on April 1, the Americans were reporting that de facto the fighting had ended a good ten days earlier. Their reporting continued to be meticulous and, given the chaos that prevailed all over Spain from Christmas 1938 through March 1939, presented a relatively coherent reporting of events.

In dispatches written in the weeks that followed the end of the civil war, they more fully documented the mass of humanity that moved out of Spain into southern France, so one can forgive them for not making abundantly clear in the early months of 1939 how extensive that movement turned out to be. However, they continued to report quite accurately and in considerable detail the actual military events and the command thinking behind these actions.

One question we can raise at this point at the end of the civil war is why it lasted as long as it did, particularly after the second battle of the Ebro detailed in chapter 8. This final chapter documents the rapid collapse of the Republican (Loyalist) forces, beginning in December 1938 and extending through late March 1939. The reports below and in the previous chapter speak of citizens on both sides weary of war, while the same applied to Republican military forces. Yet we also read about factions within the Republican government still willing to fight on in February, after it was clear to most observers and participants that the war was over and that Franco had won. All long, drawn-out civil wars stimulate passions and bitterness that are difficult to overstate; they are personal and individual, not simply institutional or national. Often that feature of a civil war accounts for some of the reason why fighting extends longer than one would have expected in hindsight. But there are other causes hinted at in the text of this book.

It always proves difficult for a soldier, for instance, to make the personal decision to desert his unit, a group of individuals with whom he has bonded, fought with, and considers as close as family. Second, there are the practical issues of how to desert, where to go, and how to avoid the dangers of capture and possibly execution. Only at the very end of this civil war, with Republican forces near the French border, could individuals and whole units see that the way out was to walk over the Pyrenees Mountains into France because they were close enough. Indeed, that is what tens of thousands did. The bitter stubbornness displayed in this war has to be another reason for fighting long and hard—an observation made several times by various military observers of this conflict, but it is minimized by the cold, sanitary language used by these Americans to describe events. A quick glance at any illustrated military history of the civil war will make it very apparent how physically demanding and massive this war proved to be. Soldiers were tired, hungry, and often cold or hot; demoralized on the Republican side at least; and on both sides fed up. But there was also the real fear that if caught by the enemy, execution was a possible fate. In the case of the Nationalists, many military prisoners were given the opportunity to join the insurgent army, while Republican militias early in the war routinely executed their captives. In short, this was no war fought under the rules of the Geneva Convention. Political and military leaders on both sides were regularly executed, and after Franco prevailed, thousands of additional executions took place during the early 1940s.

January 4, 1939
Memorandum for the Chief of Staff
Subject: Insurgent Offensive against Catalonia

The principal points of interest in connection with the Insurgent offensive against Catalonia, which began December 23, 1938, are the following:

a) The offensive, involving about 21 divisions and with an estimated total strength of 250,000 was delivered on an initial front of some 60 miles.

b) Its immediate objective was apparently to capture, by double envelopment, the Loyalist first and second lines of defense protecting the road net to Tarragona and Barcelona; its ultimate objective to bring decisive pressure against Barcelona with a view to ending the war.

c) The Insurgents were greatly superior in aviation, artillery and tanks. The Loyalists' main reliance was placed upon machine guns and field fortifications.

d) After two days of fighting, the Insurgents had achieved an advance of some 16 miles on their south wing and of from 6 to 8 miles on their north wing and it appeared that their full strength had not yet been committed to action.

e) Prospects are that the Insurgents will push their initial successes, particularly on the north flank, with reinforcements, and will extend their area of operations further south in the direction of the important port of Tarragona.

McCabe

Enclosures:

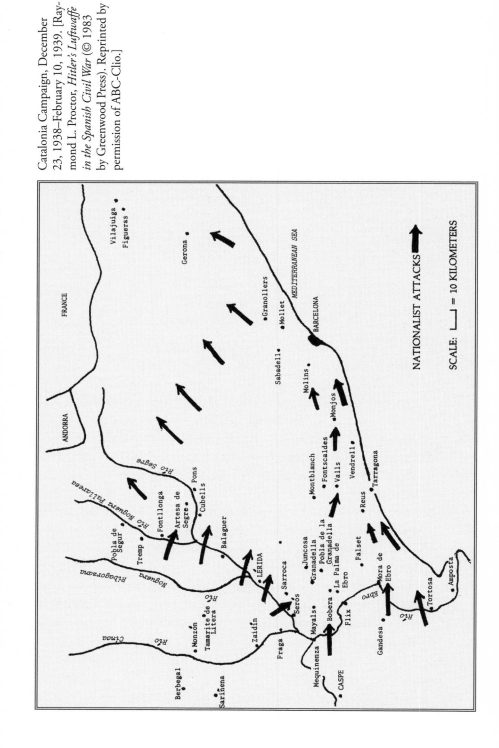

Catalonia Campaign, December 23, 1938–February 10, 1939. [Raymond L. Proctor, *Hitler's Luftwaffe in the Spanish Civil War* (© 1983 by Greenwood Press). Reprinted by permission of ABC-Clio.]

Summary of Operations to January 2, 1939

On December 23, 1938, the expected Insurgent offensive was launched to the east, against Catalonia, on a wide front of some 60 miles. The attack was from the general line of the Segre and Noguera-Pallaresa Rivers, a line which General Franco originally had reached in April 1938 and had held during the subsequent months of his uncompleted advance against Valencia. The attack, as well as its general area, had been anticipated for a period of weeks and the only elements of surprise possible were with respect to the location and timing of its principal efforts.

That this major offensive should have been started in midwinter may be explained by the following considerations: (1) The Loyalist troops had been severely punished during their withdrawal from the Ebro salient in November; it was desirable not to permit them time for reorganization and requipment. (2) The international situation, and particularly the approaching Chamberlain-Mussolini conversations, demanded a resounding Insurgent success. (3) War weariness, indications of dissatisfaction with the lack of progress since July, some dissension among the factions supporting Franco and finally, evidence that the Italian allies had outworn their welcome on Spanish soil all called for a positive and far reaching military victory to reestablish the prestige of the Insurgent generalissimo and of his armies in the field. (4) The two months [of] intensive campaign of a year ago, which culminated in the recapture of Teruel, showed that large scale winter operations in mountainous country were practicable.

Although accurate reports of the present offensive are lacking, it appears that following short and heavy artillery and air bombardments at dawn of December 23, strong infantry attacks were made at 8:00 AM at Seros on the southern wing of the zone of attack and below Tremp, on the northern wing. At the same time a feint by one battalion was made between Lerida and Balaguer. Loyalist reports indicate that 5 divisions (of which 4 were claimed to be Italian) were concentrated in the Seros area, 4 divisions in the Tremp area and 7 divisions west of the bridgehead at Balaguer. It is believed that other divisions in the area brought the total to about 21. The Insurgent forces participating in the offensive are estimated, on this basis, at 250,000. Neither the artillery or air strengths are known but they were certainly greatly superior to their opponents, whose principal defensive means were machine guns and an extensive system of field fortifications. The latter has been reported as consisting of two main lines, the forward line protecting the communication centers of Borjas Blancas and Artesa de Segre and the rear line extending along the Llena mountains on the south through Cervera to the northeast.

As revealed by its progress to date, General Franco's plan of maneuver consisted of an initial double envelopment to turn both flanks of the Loyalists' forward line of defense; Borjas Blancas to be taken from the south and Artesa by moving upon it from the north with the assistance of a strong delayed offensive from the southwest, which debouched from the Balaguer bridgehead on December 28. There may be expected, in combination with this maneuver and at a propitious moment, an extension of the front of attack southwards by means of an advance from the Ebro upon Tarragona, via routes from Mora de Ebro through Falset and along the coast. This would serve to turn the strong obstacle of the Llena mountains to the north and would enable converging pressure ultimately to be brought against Barcelona from the north, west and southwest.

Of the two principal actions of December 23, that on the south, from Seros, made greatest progress. After forcing a crossing of the Segre by pontoon bridges and fording, several divisions, in which Italian troops led, passed over the river and by the end of the first day had pushed forward some five miles. Loyalist resistance stiffened however and after 10 days of intermittent effort the Insurgents found all important objectives still unattained, their right flank having reached the Llena mountains and their left the outer defenses of Borjas Blancas. On the north wing, the initial attacks were designed to outflank the difficult Monsech mountain range, pushed south upon Artesa and cut the highway thereto from the French border. After considerable initial success, progress was slowed both by the Loyalist resistance and the nature of the terrain. On December 28, a new threat was launched against Artesa when a strong attack from Balaguer penetrated the Loyalist positions east of the bridgehead, captured Camarasa to the north and advanced upon this important town from the southwest. January 2 found Artesa in danger of being encircled, Borjas Blancas still secure and further to the south indications that the Insurgents were seeking to force a way through the Llena mountains to take the defenders of the Ebro River line in the rear.

Comment

Although Franco has gained considerable ground and claims 16,000 prisoners as a result of the first 12 days of his offensive, the Loyalist reaction has been markedly different from that which witnessed the disorganized retreat of their forces in the face of the Insurgents' Aragon offensive of March-April, 1938. They have so far fought stoutly and gave every indication of continuing to do so. In this event the reduction of their prepared defensive positions by direct attack would prove a long and costly affair. More favorable results should follow from vigorous reinforcement of the original enveloping action, on one or the other flank, provided sufficient reserves are available. The moderate extent of Franco's gains would indicate that he has not committed his full strength. It seems probable therefore that renewed effort will be made to capture the road center of Artesa on the north flank, already gravely threatened, while the possibility also exists that a surprise attack across the Ebro may be made, against depleted garrisons, with a view to a quick advance upon the important port of Tarragona.

January 17, 1939
Memorandum for the Chief of Staff
Subject: Current Situation in Spain

The following information just received from the State Department is believed of interest to the Chief of Staff:

Substance of confidential cable received at 9:45 AM, January 16, from American Embassy at Caldetas (24 miles northeast of Barcelona on the coast):

Insurgent advance appears to be progressing on all fronts and may result in the fall of Cervera, opening the direct road to Barcelona. The Government is making desperate efforts to meet situation, attempting to establish new fortified lines and assembling new reserves. There are also reports of fresh war materiel received and another diversion offensive in the south. It is probable, however, that despite these measures the insurgent offensive cannot be dominated in time to save Barcelona and that excluding the possibility of collapse the Government must soon choose between surrender and flight. Recommend early consideration of policy to be adopted with respect to Barcelona Embassy and the Consular General. My opinion is as follows: Except for reasons of personal danger we should not run the risk of losing this important consulate (as at Bilbao) by closing it. Del Vayo says if the Government yields or disorder or war operations involve the city Consulate personnel could go aboard a naval vessel until conditions improve. The Department may wish to warn resident Americans that they remain at their own risk and that no assurance can be given them of an American naval vessel evacuating them. Transportation to France is still available by highway, train and air. Evacuation of Americans such as bank personnel, telephone personnel and newsmen, held here by their work, is of course not precluded by naval vessel if necessary.

Should [the] Department regard the conquest of Catalonia by General Franco as establishing his paramountcy and desire to enter into de facto relationship the retention of this office is indicated; should it desire to maintain Embassy near the Loyalist Government as long as it exists it would be feasible for me to move to the new residence of the Government by naval vessel.

The following is the substance of the State Department's reply to the above cable, Jan. 16, 1939, 7 PM:

It is not desired that State Department officers expose themselves to danger if it can be avoided. Our first concern is the personal safety of the members of our staff.

It is considered hazardous for you and the Consular staff to return to Barcelona under present conditions. Bear in mind that it is considered safer to send one of our naval vessels to Caldetas than to Barcelona.

Whenever you consider circumstances justified the Consular General should urge American residents to leave while transportation means to France are still available.

If Barcelona should be occupied by General Franco consideration will be given to returning Consular General Flood and the Consulate staff to Barcelona on an American naval vessel.

If the Spanish Loyalist Government should move to some other place in Spain we shall probably desire you, with two clerks (by name) to follow if it is safe and practicable. Advise us of your plans prior to doing so.

Navy Department approves the dispatch of a vessel upon your request and Admiral [Henry E.] Lackey has been so informed.[1] (Note from G-2: U.S. naval detachment, consisting of one cruiser and two destroyers, is based in the vicinity of Villafranche.)

The military situation today in Catalonia, based on latest available information is as follows:

The Insurgent forces, consisting of 7 army corps (25 to 27 divisions) and totaling close to 300,000 men, are deployed on a front of almost 80 miles. Their center is on the direct road to Barcelona and approximately 40 miles distant.

Since the start of their offensive on December 23, 1938, they have advanced some 40 to 50 miles and shortened their original front by 60 miles. It is believed that all available troops have been committed but that due to the shortening of the front a number of divisions have since been withdrawn for rest and to constitute a fresh reserve.

The Insurgents are overwhelmingly superior in artillery, aviation and tanks. The majority of the Loyalist large units have suffered severely and the army as a whole has been retreating rapidly and is somewhat disorganized. In some areas the retreat has approximated a rout. The Loyalist Government is making last minute efforts to fortify two lines of defense and is sending all available troops, including police units, to the front. The present front of General Franco's forward units indicates that although natural obstacles and resistance may retard his southern wing, his center and northern wing is favorably disposed for an enveloping action upon Barcelona from the northwest and north. The fall of Barcelona may be confidently expected. Its imminence cannot be predicted in the absence of definite information as to the degree of demoralization of the Loyalist Government and high command and of the morale of the troops. It is possible that with the typical Spanish tenacity previously displayed in this war, the Loyalists may stiffen their resistance as Barcelona becomes more closely pressed and so delay the outcome for a period of weeks. On the other hand, the removal of the Government from the capital or continued Insurgent successes may so dishearten the military forces as to permit Franco a quick victory.

McCabe

January 26, 1939
Memorandum for the Chief of Staff
Subject: The Situation at Barcelona

Peaceful Occupation of Barcelona by Insurgent Forces

At noon today (Barcelona time) troops of the Moroccan Corps entered the city from the south and troops of the Navarrese Corps entered from the west. Armored car units reached the Plaza de Cataluña in the heart of the city. There was apparently but little resistance offered on the outskirts and no street fighting. The preceding night had been peaceful and without air attack. North of Barcelona additional Insurgent forces advanced rapidly eastward and appear to have cut routes of communication to France except for the coastal highway.

Retreat of Loyalist Forces

The remnants of the Loyalist Army have retreated to the northeast. The Government has announced it will continue to resist on lines to be established in the northeastern part of Catalonia and has located its Ministries in this area, most of them at the town of Figueras, 15 miles from the French border. The troops are in bad shape through exhaustion, lack of food, ammunition and equipment. Many units have disintegrated and thousands of soldiers without arms are struggling individually to the rear. It is believed the army is incapable of making a further stand unless Franco halts his advance and gives it time to recuperate and obtain supplies from outside sources. This eventuality is unlikely.

McCabe

February 6, 1939
Memorandum for the Chief of Staff
Subject: The Situation in Spain

Combat operations in Catalonia virtually ceased yesterday when General Franco's forces occupied the town of Figueras, temporary headquarters of the Loyalist Government since its flight from Barcelona on January 24. Along with this occupation, the Insurgent line was advanced generally toward the French border and is now nowhere more distant than 20 miles from it.

Latest press reports indicate that the Catalonian authorities (as distinguished from the Loyalist Government authorities) have offered to surrender. Among the Government leaders two factions have appeared, one led by President Azaña and Minister of State Giral in favor of seeking an immediate peace for all of Spain, another led by Premier Negrin and Foreign Minister del Vayo, urging continuation of the struggle in the Madrid-Valencia area.

In the meantime, the French while opening their frontier to assist Loyalist refugees and intern fleeing Loyalist troops, are also making advances to the Insurgent authorities designed to improve their position with the eventual government of the new Spain and have just sent a senator on an unannounced diplomatic mission to Burgos. A French military mission has also entered Insurgent territory to verify the fact that no fortifications or bases threatening France have been constructed in the north. The press has reported, in addition, that General Franco to placate the French has halted the all Italian Division from further advance toward the frontier.

[Miscellaneous text has been omitted, and the report continues with a description of the capture of Barcelona.—Ed. Note]

General Franco has been able to accumulate for this offensive resources of men and supplies sufficient not only to break the initial resistance of the Loyalists, but to carry on his advance without pause to its final objective. He has learned the lesson of the campaign against Madrid in the fall of 1936 when, although his advance to the outskirts had been equally successful, he had no reserves available for use against the numerically greater forces defending the city.

General Franco not only had marked superiority in aviation, artillery, tanks and mobility but he was able to use [them] to [their] fullest extent, for his offensive was launched on a broad front over an excellent road and railroad net and both his combat and supply echelons were well organized and knew their jobs after two and a half years of war.

The Loyalists on the other hand lacked trained reserves, ammunition and other supplies. They could survive a short offensive effort, even though powerful, but not a sustained one. After the fall of Artesa on January 4 and Borjas Blancas on January 5, their defense became a retreat which was not properly coordinated and had no well prepared defensive position to fall back upon.

The final disintegration of the Loyalist army may be attributed to:

(1) Material insufficiency, a result of the long imposed blockade of ports and of international restrictions. This factor, coupled with the initial Insurgent successes, broke the morale of the troops.

(2) A lack of well trained and well commanded units. There were some of these at the start of the war but they bore the brunt of the action and were exhausted by it; the remainder of the army of the Ebro was not up to its task.

(3) Having broken the Loyalist front with his initial attack, Franco pursued relentlessly, not sparing his men and making full use of his aviation, armed vehicles and motorized units. This pressure was continued without a halt beyond Barcelona and it prevented the Loyalists from reorganizing for defense of any part of Catalonia.

McCabe

RESTRICTED   Intelligence Branch
Military Intelligence Division
General Staff   January 31, 1939
Western European Section
Summary of Military Operations in Spain during Period
January 3-January 27, 1939; the Insurgent Offensive, to Include the
Capture of Barcelona.

Summary of operations dated January 4, 1939, covered the Insurgent offensive against Catalonia during the period December 23, 1938, to January 2, 1939. On January 2, the advance of General Franco's forces had reached a line in the Tremp-Balaguer area through the towns of Figueras, Benavent, Vilanova, Baldoma, Cubells, Vallfogona. The front between Balaguer and Lerida was stationary. South of Lerida, the line passed through Sudanell, Alfels, Cogull, Albages, Juncosa, Margalef, La Figuera, Flix, Vinebro. From Vinebro south along the Ebro River there has been no advance.

On this front of some 100 miles from above Tremp to Tortosa, 7 Insurgent corps were in action. From north to south there were: Catalonian (General Badia), Urgel (General Muros), Maestrazgo (General Valino), Aragon (General Moscardo), Legionnaire [Italian and Spanish mixed, General [Gastone] Gambara (Italian) or General Vega], Navarre (General Solchaga) and Moroccan (General Yague). It is believed that General Franco assumed to a large extent the direction of operations of these corps with General Dávila in nominal command. The number of divisions in line and in reserve is estimated as between 25 and 27 with a total Insurgent strength along this front of about 300,000.

While no figures are available as to the numerical strength of the Loyalists opposing the offensive, it was probably not markedly inferior at first to that of the Insurgents. Five or six corps had been identified during the Ebro fighting of which at least three had been severely punished in that action. The materiel advantage of the attackers, however, was very great. In planes, artillery and tanks they were superior in ratios estimated at from five to one up to ten to one. From three to four hundred active planes and over two hundred tanks are reported to have been employed. Concentrations of guns equaling those of the World War supported the infantry at points of main effort.

The first objective of the Insurgent offensive was the double envelopment of the Loyalist defensive position running from Artesa de Segre on the north to Borjas Blancas on the south, a distance of 28 miles. According to our military attaché, who observed them a few days before the attack, the fortifications at Artesa were well sited and consisted of numerous concrete pill boxes for machine guns, barbed wire, trenches in the intervals for automatics and riflemen and many concrete bomb proofs. While the Aragon corps in front of this position afforded flank protection with two divisions, the attack on the north flank was pressed against Valino's Maestrazgo corps from the west. On January 4 this important position was taken after a severe fight. At the same time the bulk of the Legionnaire corps (1 Italian division, 3 mixed Spanish-Italian divisions) was thrown against Borjas Blancas from the southwest. Held up for four days in the vicinity of Albagos, the Italian divisions were reinforced on the south by a division from the Navarrese corps. The Loyalist corps under General Lister, probably the best of their corps commanders, was forced out of Borjas Blancas on January 5, after having opposed a determined resistance to the Insurgent advance from the Segre for some 13 days. The Legionnaire corps in this operation was reported to have been supported by 60 tanks and large concentrations of artillery and planes. To its south, elements of General Solchaga's Navarrese corps advanced toward Vinaixa and Vimbodi on the Lerida-Tarragona highway to cut off the Loyalist retreat. Other elements of this corps below the Llena mountains pushed southeast to Vilolla Alta, Mola and Garcia gravely threatening the rear of Loyalists holding the Ebro line west of Falset.

The severe fighting resulting in the capture of Borjas Blancas and Artesa weakened considerably the powers of resistance of both Loyalist units and created a situation favorable to a rapid prosecution of the second phase of the Insurgent offensive. This was revealed as a simultaneous advance eastward along the Lerida-Barcelona highway and southeastward along the highway to Tarragona.

As this phase started, however, the Loyalists on the Estremadura front in southwestern Spain launched a sudden offensive on January 6, in an effort to threaten Franco's north-south line of communications and so to force the diversion of Insurgent troops from Catalonia to this distant front. General Miaja's attempt was an ambitious one a front of 20 miles and initially had considerable success, advancing at several places to a distance of 10 to 15 miles. Strategically sound, it was a bold effort to strike Franco at his most vulnerable point. Better troops might well have been able to continue the initial advantage gained by surprise and have achieved the purpose of the operation. As it was, the Insurgent Generals Queipo de Llano and Saliquet were able after several days to move in reserves sufficient to contain the attack and held it to nonessential gains. It appears that a number of air squadrons and possibly a few ground units were temporarily diverted from the Insurgents' main forces but without material effect upon their Barcelona offensive.

Returning to the Catalonian theater, on January 7 the Loyalists began to evacuate their lines along the Segre between Lerida and Balaguer and their whole defensive position extending from Borjas Blancas to Aresa. The Aragon corps of General Moscardo thereupon advanced to the east, establishing contact with adjacent corps on both flanks. By January, the four Insurgent corps east of the Segre had all made progress, reaching the line Pons, Agramunt, Fuliola, Mollerusa, Vimbodi, Prados. On the 11th, the very important road center of Montblanc fell after 12 hours [of] fighting to the Legionnaire corps, which enveloped it on the north. Also on January 11, the Moroccan corps (Foreign Legion, Moors and a Cavalry Division attached) under its noted leader General Yague, completed the clearing out of the Loyalist forces along the river east of Mora de Ebro and started down the main road toward Falset. This town, already threatened from the north, was entered the next day by the Moroccans who also moved south toward Tortosa. This forced the rapid evacuation by the Loyalists of the Ebro River line and the entire area included in the Tortosa pocket. In the Montblanc zone events moved with great rapidity following the capture of that town. With little resistance offered, the Navarrese corps advanced south toward Valls and took this important Loyalist aviation center on January 14. Other units of this corps moved through the Montsont Mountains towards Reus, site of the principal Loyalist ammunition factory, in conjunction with the Moroccan corps which was marching on Reus from Falset. The Loyalists had begun a general evacuation of the Valls-Reus-Tarrgona area on the 14th. On January 15, Navarrese troops from the north and Moroccans from the west entered Tarragona. Thus, three months after its start, the Insurgent offensive had gained its first great objective.

Further north, progress was slower along the Lerida-Barcelona highway. On January 15, however, the fortified town of Tarrega fell to the Maestrazgo corps of General Valino, advancing southeast from Artesa, and on the following day its road center of Cervera was taken without difficulty. It appears that at this time the Aragon corps which had moved east through Tarrega and Cervera was pinched out and its divisions either held in army reserve or attached to other corps.

During the period January 15-20, the Insurgent advance along the two main axes, the Lerida-Barcelona highway and on the coastal highway, continued rapidly. In the first named zone of action the Maestrazgo corps moved eastward from Corvera while the Legionnaire corps pushed northeast from Montblanc and the two corps effected a junction a few miles west of Igualada, next town of importance. At Igualada it was reported that severe fighting occurred on the 21st and that a Loyalist counterattack succeeded in temporarily freeing the town. On the following day, however, it was definitely captured by the Legionnaire corps. Coincident with this operation, the Maestrazgo corps was diverted northeast toward Manresa. In the southern zone of action, the Loyalists after the fall of Tarragona held the east bank of the Gaya River for three days with rear guard detachments. On January 18, however, the Moroccan corps on the coast with the Navarrese corps on its left, crossed the river at many points and thereafter found no resistance in their paths. On the 20th, the former corps occupied Vendrell and on January 21 it took Villanueva y Caltru while General Solchaga's Navarrese entered Villafranca del Panades.

It was clearly evident that the Loyalists were incapable of any organized resistance west of the Llobregat River since they had retreated steadily without attempting to hold a number of good defensive positions. The Government, however, had called every able bodied man to the front or to work on the close-in fortifications of Barcelona and showed every intention of making a last stand east of this river which, flowing into the sea five miles from the city, is a decided natural obstacle. In spite of brave words and feverish activity, the populace of Barcelona and the bulk of the military forces proved apathetic to the idea of a heroic defense of Barcelona. The intentions of the Government were of no avail when its army was defeated and knew it. On January 24, having advanced an average of 20 miles in four days, the Maestrazgo Legionnaire, Navarrese and Moroccan corps had reached the Llobregat River and the first three were across it.

The next day found the Moroccans across the river and in the southern outskirts of the city and the Navarrese corps closing in on the west and north. There was a small amount of isolated and sporadic resistance [and] it was obvious on the 25th that the Insurgents could enter at will. On the following day formal occupation of Barcelona occurred, columns marching through the streets from three sides without a shot being fired. An armored car detachment of General Solchaga's Navarrese corps was accorded the honor of arriving first at the Plaza de Cataluña, heart of the city, which it reached at 2:30 PM.

The Loyalist Government meanwhile had hastily evacuated Barcelona on the night of the 23rd and morning of the 24th and the principal ministries were established at Figueras, in the northeast corner of Catalonia, 15 miles from the French border. Although there was some destruction of gasoline and ammunition supplies, the Loyalists retreated from Barcelona without damaging the utilities of the city other than the telephone system. The retreat was unorganized and many units disintegrated. Thousands of refugees jammed the roads and towns in the rear areas. Both civil and military authorities appear to have lost complete control of the situation for several days. The Insurgents immediately pushed on beyond the city and began a vigorous pursuit, turning over the task of restoring order to a military governor, city council, police forces and relief organizations. The Loyalist Government has since announced its determination to continue the struggle on a new line of defense through Gerona and Puigcerda. It is unlikely, however, that their troops can be reorganized, reequipped and imbued with sufficient fighting spirit to impose other than temporary resistance to General Franco's victorious army.

Comment

In this notable campaign the Insurgent Commander in Chief was favored by a number of factors of which the most important were:

(1) Great materiel superiority, particularly in aviation, artillery, tanks and
     motor transportation.
(2) Attack on a broad front over terrain which, though quite mountainous
     and cut by stream lines, had an excellent road and railway net, permit-
     ting him to maneuver and to make full use of his greater mobility.
(3) An army organized and adequately supplied for this particular opera-
     tion, commanded by tested generals, willing to take necessary losses and
     inspired throughout by the feeling that it was superior to its enemy and
     that a decisive victory would end the war.

It is evident that their long resistance in the Ebro pocket and final withdrawal there from had materially weekend the Loyalist Army on this front. It
lacked trained reserves in Catalonia and could not be reinforced from other fronts,
as could Franco's troops. Its best units fought well initially but they could not continue without relief against a powerful and sustained attack. Only during the first
two weeks, from December 23 until January 5, did the Insurgents meet serious
resistance. The fall of Artesa and Borjas Blancas ended this phase and thereafter
the Loyalist defense became a retreat and the Insurgent attack an advance by maneuver rather than by fire. The maneuver involving the cooperative action of four
army corps during an advance of 75 miles from the Artesa-Borjas Blancas line to
Barcelona, was excellently coordinated by the Commander in Chief.

Subject: Military Situation

The failure of the Government troops to make a decided stand to defend Barcelona
was a strong indication that the fate of the remainder of Catalonia was sealed and
that its occupation would be effected in a short time. However, even the Nationalists could hardly have anticipated that within a fortnight they would reach the
French frontier, in view of the mountainous character of Northern Catalonia,
particularly from northwest of Barcelona to the formidable barrier of the Pyrenees. Taking advantage of this favorable defensive situation, a few determined and
properly trained divisions could have checked the Nationalist advance towards
the French frontier for some time and made the Nationalists pay dearly for the
ground gained.

It is believed that this rapid and successful culmination of this offensive is
the direct result of the greatly superior command, training, discipline, morale and
organization of the Nationalist troops as compared with that of the Government,

and not due exclusively to their superiority in aviation and materiel as claimed by Government propaganda. The great quantities of materiel captured by the Nationalists during their offensive as well as the many guns, airplanes and all varieties of modern weapons relinquished by the Loyalists upon passing the French frontier, indicates conclusively that the inferiority of the Government troops in this regard was only relative, and cannot account for the complete and sudden collapse of the Catalan Army.

Since February 1, date of the last report the Nationalist advance has been carried out in a most systematic way without risking the mechanized units in too deep penetrations, thus avoiding the possibility of a sudden Government reaction. However, no Government counterattacks have been reported during the last stage of this offensive. The Nationalist advance has averaged 10 kilometers per day, the Nationalists employing their usual tactics of driving wedges toward selected objectives and outflanking centers of resistance.

In general, the Government troops, containing many middle aged conscripts with very little military training, and with apparently no desire to fight in spite of the constant propaganda of the political commissars, retreated or surrendered upon the approach of the enemy. Isolated cases of stubborn of resistance by some shock units have been reported. The general poor quality of the troops, the apparent lack of coordination in the defense plan, the existing confusion and inefficiency in command functioning are among the causes which have contributed to the Government defeat.

The three Nationalist drives which were initiated after the fall of Barcelona, along the coast, toward Vich and on [to] Ripoll, have been carried out with a regularity of a field maneuver. The important key towns and road centers of Vich and Barga fell on February 1 and 2, respectively. On February 3 the occupation of Santa Coloma, [an] important objective of the drive on Gerona was reported. February 4, the provincial capital of Gerona and the stronghold of Seo de Urgel, key place for the subsequent advance to the Andorra border and Puigcerda, had fallen. With the occupation on February 7 of the important road centers of Olot and Ripoll, possession of most of the frontier had been gained.

North of Gerona, along the River Ter, the Government resistance succeeded in delaying for a little time the Nationalist advance on Figueras. Here the Lister division assisted by other shock troops, protected the retreat of the main body of troops and movement of materiel toward the French frontier. After breaking this resistance, the Nationalists advanced by forced marches, reached the Perthus port in two days and by February 10 the whole border from Andorra to Portbou on the sea coast was completely occupied, thus bringing to a successful completion the offensive which was initiated on December 23, 1938.

[The day-by-day account of the Catalan campaign was omitted here.—Ed. Note]

Comments

The Nationalists have brought their Catalan campaign to a successful conclusion during the first ten days of February. Such Loyalist resistance as has existed has been overcome swiftly and surely. Military activity in Catalonia, except for cleaning out the frontier in the mountains, is at an end.

In spite of the speed of the Nationalist advance, and in the absence of any prearranged plans, some 400,000 men, women and children, together with huge amounts of household and personal effects, thousands of animals and trucks, and large quantities of arms, ammunition, tanks, armored cars, field pieces and other equipment crossed into France in a very few days.

The administration of General Franco is at present confronted with an undertaking which it is believed will put its strength and soundness to [the] test. This problem is the reorganization of the administrative, political and economic life of the Catalan region and the feeding of its large population (over 3,000,000 inhabitants). As all activities in Catalonia have been controlled by the syndicates during two and a half years and most leaders and public officials have taken refuge into France, the resources of Nationalist Spain will be greatly taxed in order to effect a reorganization of life along entirely new principles. Furthermore, economic resources in Catalonia are nearly exhausted and this condition has been aggravated by the systematic destruction of property and havoc caused by the Government troops during their withdrawal movement into France.

In the meantime, reports of early recognition of the Franco Government by France and England, and the possibility of an arranged peace, continued to circulate. On the other hand, the so called Madrid Government, which is headed by Dr. Negrin, Sr. del Vayo and General Miaja, continues to assert that it will fight to the end.

Should this resistance continue, it is possible that the effort required to restore Cataluña to normal conditions, and the undesirability, at present, of adding more millions to be organized and fed, may delay for some time the initiation of a campaign against the southern portion of Spain not yet taken by the Nationalists.

Cheadle

Spain   No. 6997
February 28, 1939
Subject: The Military Situation

Since the last report (No. 6990 of February 13, 1939), as far as ground operations are concerned, the Government troops and civilian refugees, numbering 20,000, who had been resisting the Nationalist advance in the sector of Camprodon (south of Prats de Mollo) finally passed with most of their materiel and equipment into France. The Nationalists reached and took possession of the Spanish side of the frontier port of Col d'Ares by noon of February 13th. As this was the last center of Government resistance along the Pyrenees, the military operations proper in Catalonia were at an end.

Absolute calm has prevailed throughout the Central and Southern fronts. The loyalist troops have given no signs of activity. According to Government reports, the military authorities are mobilizing and training all men comprised in the recent calls (including men up to 45 years of age) with which they claim the army will expand to 500,000 men. In this connection it is believed that the calling of middle aged men to the colors, who lack military training, will reduce the efficiency of the army, as the Catalan experience has conclusively proved. Furthermore, materiel and equipment is lacking as well as sufficient commissioned and non-commissioned officers, which will have to be improvised.

The Nationalists are believed to be actively concentrating their forces for operations against Central and Southern Republican Spain, while they are tightening the blockade of the Government territory both by sea and air. The port areas of Valencia, Gandia, Alicante, Almeria and the Naval Base of Cartagena have been bombed almost daily during the period covered by this report. The Nationalists claim that at the last named port, several warships have been damaged. A number of victims and great material damage have resulted from these persistent bombings, which in addition to making extremely difficult the supply of the government territory, must have a telling effect upon the morale of the people, which is taken by the loss of Catalonia and the subsequent recognition of the Government of General Franco by many European and American nations.

The city of Madrid, particularly since the Negrin cabinet returned to the capital, has been subjected to frequent shellings by the Nationalist artillery, which are reported to have caused a high number of victims and important material damages. It is further stated in the press that the food shortage in Madrid is extremely acute.

While reports from Government sources present Dr. Negrin and his cabinet as decided to resist to the end, and to be making preparations to meet a Nationalist offensive, the impression is almost general in the French and British press that the end of the war will be forthcoming soon. The President of the Republic, Sr. Azaña, has resigned, and a number of politicians and military leaders who are in France, in view of the hopeless situation, favor surrendering to the Nationalists in order to avoid further bloodshed and economic damage to the country.

General Rojo, who was the Chief of Staff of the Republican Army, and most of the officers forming the high command of the defeated Catalan divisions, refuse to return to Spain as they deem that the war is lost. The only noted exceptions to this general attitude, have been Colonels Lister, Galan and Modesto, who have returned to organize resistance in Central and Southern loyalist Spain. General Miaja, General in Chief of the Republican Army, is reported to have been removed from his command on account of his defeatist attitude and to have been replaced by General Casado, a protégé of Dr. Negrin.

Comments

Although the Negrin Government has stated time and again that it will resist to the end, it is quite possible that in view of the political confusion, the lack of aviation and war materiel, the great shortage of food, and the war weariness of the people, that a capitulation will soon be arranged.

Should this not eventuate, it is believed that a Franco offensive against southern Spain will be completely successful within a short period of time.

Cheadle

Spain   No. 7001
March 15, 1939
Subject: Military Situation

As regards ground operations, the absolute calm prevailing since the occupation of Catalonia has continued until the closing date of this report. In fact, a sort of military truce seems to have been observed by the contending forces on all fronts. The Nationalist air activity against the littoral towns of Loyalist Spain has continued, [and] the port areas of Sagunto, Valencia, Gandia, Alicante, Cartagena and Almeria have been occasionally bombed although not with the frequency and intensity of other times.

The maritime blockade appears to have been intensified by the Nationalists who on March 9th issued a notice declaring the entire Government coast from Sagunto (Valencia) to Adra (Almeria) closed to navigation and announcing that any ship entering the jurisdictional waters without due authorization was liable to be captured or sunk. It is believed that the escape of the Republican fleet from Cartagena will greatly facilitate the Nationalist blockade.

In contrast with the military inactivity, important political events have taken place on the Republican side during the period under review. On March 5th, Colonel Casado, Chief of the Army of the Center, ousted the Negrin Government from power and formed a National Defense Council under General Miaja with the avowed purpose of securing "honorable peace terms" from the Nationalists. The members of the Negrin Party fled to France. This Government was confronted from the beginning with great hostility by the communist elements which supported Dr. Negrin in his policy of resisting to the end and denounced the National Defense Council summarily for its defeatist attitude.

The opposition culminated in an uprising on March 6th. The dispatches concerning this uprising published in the press have been most confused and contradictory. However, it appears that the movement was initiated in Madrid with considerable strength, and soon spread to Guadalajara, Cuenca, Ciudad Real, Murcia and other places, where it was reported part of the armed forces sided with the communists. Particularly in Madrid heavy street fighting ensued, which continued throughout the 7th, with many casualties on both sides. A number of communist leaders, including Colonels Lister and Modesto, who were in southern Spain, escaped by plane into France prior to the uprising.

[Here I omitted what the writer called vague and unsubstantiated accounts of further political and fighting activities in Madrid and elsewhere.—Ed. Note]

Cheadle

March 28, 1939
Memorandum for the Chief of Staff[2]
Subject: The Surrender of Madrid, March 28, 1939

After a siege starting in November 1936, the National Defense Council today unconditionally surrendered Madrid to the Nationalist forces under General Franco. The latter's troops then entered the city without fighting, and no disorder has since taken place. This brought to a close the unsuccessful peace efforts which the Council had been making since March 5, 1939, when it was formed in Madrid, after the overthrow of the Negrin Government. Its conditions for peace, including no reprisals and the elimination from Spain of foreign influence once peace had been signed, had been continuously met by General Franco's demand for unconditional surrender and a promise that only those guilty of crime would be punished.

On March 26, Franco, apparently considering that sufficient time had been given the National Defense Council, launched two offensives, in the Cordoba and Toledo Sectors, to force an immediate surrender. The first offensive rapidly broke through the Republican defenses and captured the rich Almaden mercury mines, encountering little opposition. The second offensive, likewise successful, has reached a point southeast of Madrid, threatening the main highways joining that city with Alicante and Cartagena.

While Madrid was of strategic importance prior to the loss of Catalonia, such value was lost when the latter fell in January of this year, and it constituted a continued drain on the remaining supplies of the Republican Government. The surrender of Madrid, together with the food shortage and war weariness of the population, the reported lack of resistance to Franco's latest offensives and General Miaja's efforts in Valencia to arrange the surrender of the rest of Spain, warrant the conclusion that the remainder of Republican Spain will shortly surrender.

Spain   No. 7007
April 3, 1939
Subject: The Closing Chapter of the Spanish Civil War

During the period covered by the last report (No. 7001 of March 15, 1939) and March 26th, absolute calm prevailed on all fronts. The military inactivity was due to the fact that negotiations for a peace were being conducted between the National Council of Defense under General Miaja and the Nationalist Government. While the latter observed great reserve concerning the loyalist overture for peace, the National Council of Defense repeatedly announced that the Republican Army would surrender provided an "honorable peace", including a generous amnesty, could be granted. The peace negotiations finally failed as a result of the flat refusal by General Franco to consider anything short of unconditional surrender. On March 26th the Nationalist headquarters issued an ultimatum by radio to the Republican Army stating that a crushing offensive had been initiated, that the war was hopelessly lost by the Government and urging the enemy troops to surrender in order to spare further bloodshed, promising that no reprisals would be made except against those responsible for crimes and other excesses who would be subjected to trial.

The Nationalist offensive was initiated on March 26th with great force on the Cordoba front. The Republican troops, which in some places offered slight resistance, in others surrendered in mass, as shown by the fact that over 10,000 prisoners were captured by the Nationalists, who during the day occupied some 2,000 square kilometers, including ten important villages and the Hinojosa-Pozoblanco road. On the 27th the Nationalists continued their advance vigorously, taking a number of villages, among them Villanueva, Venta de Cardena and Almaden with its valuable mercury mines.

On March 27th the Nationalists broke the enemy lines south and southeast of Toledo on a front of 90 kilometers advancing along the road to Navahermosa and the various highways leading to Ciudad Real, occupied an extensive zone, and pushed their lines forward to include Mora, Ajofrin, Pulgar and Galvez. This new offensive, carried out with great force, had for its objective the cutting of the communications between Madrid and the southeast, thus completing the investment of the city. This threat, together with the critical shortage of food and ammunition, brought about the capitulation of the capital on March 28th, shortly after the flight of the National Council and other leaders to Valencia and other littoral towns. According to statements of the Nationalist Minister of the Interior, some 300,000 men, including the four Italian Divisions under General [Gastone] Gambara, participated in the operations against Madrid.

After the fall of Madrid, a complete collapse of Republican forces followed. Franco sympathizers assumed control of all important towns, and the loyalist troops surrendered in mass upon the arrival of the Nationalist troops, or fled towards the coast with the hope of escaping by sea. However, the close blockade maintained by the Nationalist fleet prevented their escape, as it has been reported that only a few hundred political and military leaders succeeded in leaving Spain on board of British and French vessels and by air.

On March 29th the Nationalist troops entered the cities of Alcala, Cuenca, Guadalajara, Ciudad Real, Jaen and Albacete. Valencia and Alicante were occupied on the 30th and Murcia, Almeria and Cartagena fell on the 31st. By April 1st the Nationalist Army was in control everywhere and the Spanish Civil War was over.

[Here I omitted the day-by-day account summarized above, except for what happened on April 1.—Ed. Note]

April 1. The Nationalist communiqué laconically stated: "The red army having been captured and disarmed and the last military objective attained, THE WAR IS OVER."

Comment

The occupation of Madrid and the remaining territory under the jurisdiction of the National Council of Defense by Nationalist forces terminated the war in Spain. There have been an estimated total of over one and one half million casualties, including nearly a million dead.[3] Materiel damage including physical destruction and loss of revenue is believed to exceed the equivalent of twenty billion dollars. Casualties among the civilian population have been high due to aerial attacks and mass murders. This war, which lasted for 989 days, has been one of the longest, bloodiest, and most brutal internecine struggles of modern history.

Cheadle

NOTES

Preface

1. For a brief description of this collection of papers, see National Archives Trust Fund Board, *Correspondence of the Military Intelligence Division Relating to General, Political, Economic, and Military Conditions in Spain, 1918–1941* (Washington, D.C.: National Archives and Records Administration, 1987).
2. H. Edward Knoblaugh, *Correspondent in Spain* (London: Sheed & Ward, 1937), 232.
3. Ibid.
4. Ibid., 233.

Selected Chronology of Military Events of the Spanish Civil War, 1936–39

1. For a highly detailed chronology that covers all aspects of the conflict, including political, military, economic, and social events, see Douglas W. Foard, "A Chronology of the Spanish Civil War, 1930–1939," in *Historical Dictionary of the Spanish Civil War, 1936–1939*, James W. Cortada, ed. (Westport, CT: Greenwood Press, 1982), 483–514.

Chapter 1: Start of the Rebellion (July–September 1936)

1. U.S. Army colonel Lincoln was at the time attached to the General Army Staff and specifically to its intelligence gathering arm (G-2). He reported periodically on Spanish affairs while in Europe and his dispatches are intermingled in the files with those written by Fuqua.
2. Claude G. Bowers, U.S. ambassador to the Second Republic during the civil war, wrote in his memoir of that tour of duty about Fuqua: "The professional habit of years had made him a slave of the map, and out it would come with every change of scenery, and along with it, from some mysterious hiding place, would appear a book with full information about every village we touched." *My Mission to Spain: Watching the Rehearsal for World War II* (New York: Simon & Schuster, 1954), 123.

3. In the 1990s, as all major Spanish cities expanded, construction of new apartment buildings, offices, and factories on the edge of these communities resulted in the discovery of many such anonymous graves all over Spain, leading to a major national discussion about the violence of the civil war, to the renewal of many passions and memoirs, and to a renewed interest in all aspects of this conflict by the press, citizens, scholars, and book publishers.

4. Fuqua visited Toledo on September 18, 1936, and personally saw the Alcazar, the siege of which was already emerging as a historic event.

5. Gen. Jose Asensio Torrado was commanding Republican troops defending areas around Madrid in the fall of 1936 as commander of the central theater of operations. He ran into considerable difficulties with his large pool of poorly trained and disciplined militia forces. This career army officer was in the process of imposing military discipline on these forces when Fuqua visited his headquarters. Within a month the militia was able to get the Republican government to take General Asensio out of his field command.

Chapter 2: Battle of Madrid and Other Campaigns (October 1936–February 1937)

1. Valencia, No. 6453, January 8, 1937.

2. Lt. Col. O. S. Wood (General Staff executive officer, G-2) to Colonel Fuqua, January 28, 1937.

3. PCs is military slang for "posts of command," a phrase widely used before World War II by American Army personnel meaning the physical place where a commander and/or a group of soldiers was stationed.

4. At that time he held the combined Republican cabinet portfolios of prime minister and minister of war.

5. References to forty acres and reconstruction mean the granting of land to nineteenth-century pioneers in the United States and the period 1865–77, the period of economic and social rebuilding in the South following the American Civil War.

6. A description of airplanes was written separately in Report No. 6429, October 30, 1936.

7. This refers to the Battle of Amiens in which Canadians, supported by Australian troops, pushed back the German army some seven miles, relying extensively on tanks, thereby discrediting the use of trench warfare as military strategy. The battle is normally viewed by historians as the turning point that led to the defeat of the Germans in World War I.

Chapter 3: Campaigns in Central Spain, Fall of Malaga, and Battle of Guadalajara (January–April 1937)

1. Comment by Lt. Col. Hayes A. Kroner, Infantry, acting military attaché, March 9, 1937, "Subject: Eyewitness Information on Spanish War," London, No. 38607. The officer was expressing his own conclusions at the end of his dispatch, which was focused largely on the observations of Elmer Peterson, an Associated Press correspondent who was with Franco's Nationalist forces from July 1936 to the end of January 1937.

2. I could not validate the spelling or location of Torroledonee, so obviously there is a problem with the author's spelling. However, maps of the 1930s do indicate the existence of secondary u-named roads branching off Coruña Road in this region.

3. Knoblough worked for the Associated Press in Spain from February 1933 through May 1939. He published an account of his experiences in the Spanish Civil War, *Correspondent in Spain* (London: Sheed and Ward, 1939).

4. The use of the pejorative term "Spicks," refers obviously to Italian troops in Spain, and since it does not appear in any other dispatch written by an American officer, one can conclude this document may have been prepared by a third party, such as an American reporter, businessman, pilot, or other visitor to Spain.

5. This class of machine gun was one of the most widely used weapons of the twentieth century. During World War I it was standard issue for both the British and French armies, and by World War II variants were in wide use by armies and air forces all over the world. It came in different caliber sizes and could be used on the ground or affixed to aircraft. In the early years of the twenty-first century, this highly reliable and practical machine gun was still in use by some armies.

6. HE means high explosive.

7. AA means antiaircraft guns.

8. The spelling is suspect; I could not find the town on various maps or in atlases. Nonetheless, military action occurred west of Malaga.

9. Indeed, the Second Republic presented considerable evidence of Italian intervention to various international diplomatic bodies and published a widely circulated "White Book" with over 300 pages of photocopies of captured Italian documents, personal letters of Italian troops, and so forth. Spanish Government, *The Italian Invasion of Spain: Official Documents and Papers Seized from Italian Units in Action at Guadalajara Presented by the Spanish Government to the League of Nations* (Washington, D.C.: Spanish Embassy, 1937).

10. Fuqua attached the list to his original report.

11. Many appendices with organizational charts, photographs, and so on that were included with this dispatch are not reproduced in this book.

Chapter 4: Daily Routine of War and the Fall of Bilbao (April–July 1937)

1. "Political Issues and Problems," Paris, no. 23, 392-W, April 29, 1937.

2. Erwin Rommel, *Neunzehn Gefechts-Aufgaben für Zug und Kompanie, ein Handbuch für den Offizierunterricht* (Berlin: E. S. Mittler, 1935), and just as important, his second, far more-detailed monograph, *Infanterie greift an, erlebnis und erfahrung* (Potsdam: L. Voggenreiter, 1941).

3. Today called Thailand.

4. Radio transmitters.

5. The American ambassador was Claude G. Bowers, who later published his memoir of his mission during the Spanish Civil War, *My Mission to Spain*, most of which was spent, as stated by Fuqua, parked in a little town on the French side of the Franco-Spanish border.

6. Sometimes called the Invergordon Mutiny in Scotland, it was a mutiny by British sailors of the Royal Navy that occurred on September 15 and 16, 1931. It was triggered by the decision of the British Government to reduce salaries of sailors as part of a government-wide austerity initiative taken during the Great Depression. It was resolved when some of the pay cuts were rescinded and a number of sailors were either jailed or discharged. See Alan Ereira, *The Invergordon Mutiny* (London: Routledge, 1981).

Chapter 5: Intensification of the War in the North (July–November 1937)

1. Dispatch No. 6711, November 1, 1937.
2. Quoted in Cortada, *Historical Dictionary of the Spanish Civil War*, 94.
3. Komsomols were Russian youth organizations.
4. Armored fighting vehicle, such as a tank.
5. Various definitions, normally military transport.
6. Olive drab, a color of uniforms that began to be used by various armies in the late nineteenth century and by the U.S. Army during the Spanish-American War (1898) and subsequently in the Philippines in the years prior to World War I.

Chapter 6: Lessons from the Spanish Civil War (November–December 1937)

1. Refers to the village of Appomattox, Virginia, where in the spring of 1865 the majority of the American Civil War ended with the surrender of the Confederate Army to the Union Army.
2. Italian career army officer Guilio Douhet argued in a highly influential book on air power, *Command of the Air* (1921), that quick military victory could be achieved by launching early air attacks in a battle on an enemy's vital centers, while using ground forces to contain the enemy. This theory stood in sharp contrast to those of other theorists who advocated using airpower to bomb civilians. Both approaches were used in the Spanish Civil War. The American lecturer in all probability would have known about this theory by word of mouth within the military community, as an English translation was not published until 1942.
3. Portre means a truck that carries a gun, such as a machine gun on the truck bed.
4. A battle fought between October 14 and November 9, 1917, on the Austro-Italian front, in which Austro-Hungarian and German forces broke the Italian line, routing the force. It was a major defeat for the Italians, including some 11,000 Italians killed, 20,000 wounded, 275,000 prisoners taken, and massive amounts of matériel and weapons seized. Hemingway described this battle in his novel *A Farewell to Arms*, published in 1929, just a few years before the Spanish Civil War, and thus probably was on his mind when he was in Spain.
5. In fact, this Basque town was bombed on April 27, 1937, by German and Italian aviators on Franco's side, causing considerable damage and deaths of civilians. For a recent account of this highly controversial event see Ian Patterson, *Guernica and Total War* (Cambridge, MA: Harvard University Press, 2007).

Chapter 7: The Teruel Campaign (December 1937–February 1938)

1. *La Vanguardia* was—and still is—Barcelona's leading daily newspaper, and in the 1930s it was a major Republican and Catalan voice.
2. Montserrat is the ancient Benedictine monastery in the Pyrenees Mountains that has long served as a historic center of Catalan regionalism and culture.
3. Confederación Nacional del Trabajo, the largest anarchosyndicalist party in Spain.

Chapter 8: From the Aragon Campaign to the End
of the Battle of the Ebro (March–November 1938)

1. Raymond L. Proctor, "The Battle of the Ebro," in Cortada, *Historical Dictionary of the Spanish Civil War*, 176.
2. Italian commander of Corpo di Truppe Voluntarie in Spain during the Aragon offensive.
3. British diplomatic agent assigned to the Nationalists. He subsequently published his memoir, *Spain Resurgent* (London: Hutchinson, 1953).
4. CIGS stood for chief of the Imperial General Staff.
5. Refers to U.S. Army training manuals.

Chapter 9: Conquest of Catalonia and End of the War
(December 1938–April 1939)

1. Commanded U.S. naval forces in the Mediterranean during the Spanish Civil War.
2. This report included a short discussion of recent Italian reinforcements to Nationalist Spain that was irrelevant to the outcome of the fighting and hence was omitted from the text reproduced in this book.
3. By the 1990s historians had concluded that a more accurate number of the dead would be closer to 700,000, with the figure having dropped incrementally all through the 1960s, 1970s, and 1980s. No final, definite reckoning has yet been reached. The discovery of mass graves in the 1990s and early 2000s, as cities expanded to build apartments and factories, reopened the discussion and analysis.

INDEX

329

ABOUT THE AUTHOR

D r. James W. Cortada holds a PhD in modern European history and is the author of nearly a dozen books on modern Spain. His publications include *Spain and the American Civil War*; *Two Nations Over Time*; *Historical Dictionary of the Spanish Civil War, 1936–1939*; *A City in War: American Views on Barcelona and the Spanish Civil War, 1936–39*; *Spain in the Nineteenth-Century World*; and *Spain in the Twentieth-Century World*. He is also the author of numerous articles on modern Spanish history. Dr. Cortada works at IBM, where he is responsible for conducting research on public administration and helping governments improve their work.